THE ESSENTIALS OF SPORTS REPORTING AND WRITING

This text covers the full experience of sports writing. Authors Scott Reinardy and Wayne Wanta approach the topic using their own professional experience as sports writers and editors to give students a realistic view of the sports writing profession. After the overview and introduction to sports journalism, the authors move into the stages of article writing, organized around article beginnings, middles, and endings. The text also covers other types of sports stories, such as columns, profiles, and news, and addresses style and ethics issues. It provides students with a full understanding of how to produce quality content for sports stories, as well as offering insights as to what to expect in the sports reporter position.

Scott Reinardy is an Assistant Professor of Journalism at the University of Kansas. His research interests include news reporting and writing, sports journalism, and newspaper management. He has more than 14 years experience as a professional journalist, working as a sports writer, editor, and columnist on numerous local and regional newspapers.

Wayne Wanta is a Professor in the School of Journalism at the University of Missouri, Columbia and was 2006–2007 President of AEJMC. He has been an active researcher in political communication and media effects, particularly in the area of the agenda-setting function of the news media—how news coverage of issues influences the public's perceptions of those issues. Wanta has also conducted research in visual communication, sports journalism, Internet use and effects, and negative political advertising. Before entering the academic field, Wanta worked for eight years at newspapers, and has experience as a copy editor, page designer, and feature writer.

THE ESSENTIALS OF SPORTS REPORTING AND WRITING

Scott Reinardy and Wayne Wanta

Routledge
Taylor & Francis Group

NEW YORK AND LONDON

First published 2009
by Routledge
270 Madison Ave, New York NY 10016

Simultaneously published in the UK
by Routledge
2 Park Square, Milton Park, Abingdon, Oxon, OX14 4RN

*Routledge is an imprint of the Taylor & Francis Group, an
informa business*

Transferred to Digital Printing 2011

© 2009 Taylor & Francis

Typeset in Sabon by GreenGate Publishing Services, Tonbridge, Kent

Library of Congress Cataloging in Publication Data

Reinardy, Scott.
The Essentials of Sports Reporting / by Scott Reinardy and
Wayne Wanta.
p. cm.
1. Sports journalism. 2. Sports journalism–Authorship.
I. Wanta, Wayne. II. Title.
PN4784.S6R45 2008
070.4'49796–dc22
2008007513

ISBN10: 0-8058-6447-4 (hbk)
ISBN10: 0-8058-6448-2 (pbk)
ISBN10: 1-4106-1876-5 (ebk)

ISBN13: 978-0-8058-6447-2 (hbk)
ISBN13: 978-0-8058-6448-9 (pbk)
ISBN13: 978-1-4106-1876-4 (ebk)

FOR CINDY AND TRENT,
WHO MAKE ALL THINGS POSSIBLE

FOR CAROL AND CAITLIN

CONTENTS

PREFACE

Sports are a microcosm of life, and the sports section is the official historical record of the daily occurrences. The other sections of the paper are parsed out to specifically identify hero from villain, wealthy from poor, living from dead. Sports includes all that and more, but the lines become blurred compared to the courtroom, financial world or cemetery. It offers an escape from the mundane 40-plus-hour work week. It allows us to live vicariously through our favorite teams or players. Sports scratch at our ancestral being of association and achievement. When our teams win, we win. There is no greater reward for the investment.

But escapism is not the only allure of sports. Athletic contests provide a level playing field for all. Retribution for a foul act is swift and (usually) fair. The playing surface has well-defined boundaries, and the rules are clear and concise. On the field, court, pitch, or rink, social status is measured in ability, not money, property ownership or lineage.

And the sports journalist has a front-row seat.

Sports journalism is rapidly changing. Traditional newspaper sports writers are facing a new host of issues. They have to figure out how to effectively use the newspaper's Web page, whether to partake in local radio and television sports shows, compete with bloggers and other online media, write stories in a fashion that is interesting to the readers ten hours after the event ended, and contend with reduced staffing and budgets. Additionally, the readers have changed. They have become more proactive. Readers are participants: writing blogs, posting videos, and pontificating on sports talk shows.

Athletes have changed as well. They are surrounded by "posses" or "people" who protect their interests. Coaches, athletes and teams are insulated by layers of public relations personnel and handlers, many of whom believe sports writers should be shills for the athletes and teams. And then there are the relentless fans whose insatiable appetite for information is never fulfilled.

The best way to learn sports writing is to do sports writing. But before you jump into your new career, you might need some guidance.

The Essentials of Sports Reporting and Writing is designed to provide that guidance. It is a nuts-and-bolts handbook for those starting out in sports journalism. As with all journalism books, what is presented here is not gospel, but merely our perspectives drawn from years of experience as sports journalists and as journalism professors. We believe *Essentials* offers a different perspective than other sports writing books, one that is fresh and entertaining.

Essentials is divided into several easily digestible bites. Chapters 1 and 2 provide a sports journalism background and an explanation of story types. Chapter 3 discusses preparation in writing sports stories; chapters 4, 5 and 6 discuss the beginnings of writing the story, including different types of lead writing. Chapters 7, 8, 9 and 10 examine the middle of stories, which focuses on story structure, interviewing, using quotes and handling play-by-play in game stories. Chapters 11 and 12 discuss effective conclusions to stories.

Chapters 13 through 17 provide guidelines in writing specific types of stories: sidebars, advances and follows, columns, features and profiles, and sports news. Chapters 18 and 19 provide some final points, including stylistic issues and sports journalism ethics. Finally, Chapter 20 discusses writing sports for online outlets.

We cannot guarantee you'll become a great sports writer by reading *The Essentials of Sports Reporting and Writing*, but we can guarantee you won't get any worse.

1

INTRODUCTION

The Field of Sports Writing

Sports journalism is more pervasive today than ever. We now have several sports cable networks, 24-hour sports talk radio stations and, of course, the Internet, where googling "Green Bay Packers" will produce 7,140,000 hits (as of September 3, 2008).

Not only is sports reporting permeating society, sports figures are the subject of news stories in an unprecedented manner. A steroid suspension for Rafael Palmeiro, for instance, warrants front-page coverage in newspapers such as the *Kansas City Star*.

The Super Bowl used to be that once-a-year sporting event everyone watched but now several events become societal spectacles to specific audiences. *Monday Night Football* was quaint but now it's "All my rowdy friends are coming over tonight." It's entertainment as much as sports.

Sports is news. News is sports.

Differences Between Sports and News

While sports stories have many similarities to news stories, there are many differences as well. Some differences include:

- Leads. News stories tend to be straightforward and factual. Sports stories tend to be more creative and unusual.
- The Five Ws. News stories try to answer the basic questions of Who, What, When, Where, Why, and How. Sports stories concentrate on Why and How.
- People and places. News stories focus on buildings: the courthouse, the police station, etc. Sports stories concentrate on people.
- Objectivity. News stories try to provide balanced information without opinionated statements. Sports stories often include evaluations of players and teams.

- Sources. News reporters typically keep their distance from people they use as sources. Sports reporters often travel with teams and thus have close relationships with some of their sources.
- Events. Sports reporters usually know when and where an event will take place and therefore can write advances. News reporters most times do not know when an event will take place and therefore must react to news events.

Similarities Between Sports and News

News and sports stories, on the other hand, share many similarities.

- Emphasis on accuracy. Nothing is more important to preserving the credibility of a reporter than accuracy.
- Ethical standards. Sports reporters usually follow the same ethical standards as news reporters.
- Fairness and objectivity.
- News gathering routines. Both sports and news reporters gather information in similar ways. Both tend to be highly reliant on sources for quotes and information. Both use news judgment in determining what is and isn't news.
- Vividness in writing. Both sports and news reporters try to make events understandable for readers. As Walter Lippmann wrote in his 1922 book *Public Opinion*, reporters try to take the world outside and produce pictures in our heads.

History of Sports Journalism

When and where sports news first appeared is unclear; sports journalism nonetheless has a long tradition in American newspapers. Sports stories appeared in newspapers as far back as the 1700s. In 1733, the *Boston Gazette*, for instance, ran a story on a boxing match between John Faulcomer and Bob Russel (Beck and Bosshart, 2003). In 1832, the *New York Herald* published a story about a boxer who died after losing a 120-round bout.

In the early 1800s, industrialization on the East Coast led to many changes in society. One of those changes was an increased interest in spectator sports. In 1829, the nation's first sports newspaper—the *American Turf Register*—was published. The horse-racing publication lasted 15 years (Harper, 1999). Another sports publication—*Spirit of the Times*—was published from 1831 to 1901 (Mott, 1962).

Not surprisingly, many of the early sports writing innovations appeared in New York newspapers, where competition was especially fierce. The *New York Sunday Mercury* in 1853 is generally credited with running the first newspaper story of a baseball game (Wolseley and Campbell, 1949). Most of the early sports writers were general assignment news reporters, with the exception being reporters trained specifically to cover horse racing (Garrison, 1985).

The *New York Herald* became the world's largest daily paper in 1860 with a circulation of 77,000. Two years later, the *Herald*'s Henry Chadwick became what is commonly considered the country's first baseball writer (Emery, 1972). This was more than a decade before the National League was officially formed in 1876.

Also about this time, Joseph Pulitzer took over the *New York World*. Hoping to compete in an already saturated New York newspaper market, Pulitzer, in one of his first acts with the *World*, organized a separate sports department (Cozens and Stumpf, 1953).

The New York Times was equally innovative during this time. As early as 1896, when visuals in newspapers consisted mostly of woodcuts, the *Times* introduced a special Sunday picture section that included sports photographs from the previous week.

The biggest innovation, however, came from the *New York Journal*. In 1895, the *Journal* became the first newspaper in the United States to print an entire section devoted only to sports. Thus was formed the sports section, now a staple of daily newspapers.

Newspapers in other cities were slow to jump on the sports section bandwagon, however. The *Chicago Tribune* in 1899 introduced a Sunday sports section but did not publish a daily sports section until 1905. Newspapers in Boston, Philadelphia, and Washington started sports sections even later.

Sports journalism also made significant inroads in magazines. *Egan's Life* was published in London and *Sporting Guide* in Great Britain in 1824 (Nugent, 1929). After it was renamed *Bell's Life* in London, it reached a circulation of 75,000 in the mid-1800s. In the United States, sports coverage helped the *National Police Gazette* amass a national circulation of 150,000 (Betts, 1974).

Between 1880 and 1900, technology exponentially expanded the landscape of American sport. Electricity provided the means for night events, results of the events were instantaneously transmitted via telegraph and the print media expanded its coverage, elevating the sports page (Gems, 1996). Consequently, more newspaper column space was devoted to sports and entire staffs were hired to report and write about the less important, but more enjoyable, aspects of life.

By the 1920s, sports coverage was firmly entrenched in the nation's newsrooms. Several legendary sports figures—Babe Ruth, Red Grange, to name two—emerged in this decade. Radio station KDKA in Pittsburgh began providing baseball scores in 1921 (Garrison, 1985).

The 1920s also was a period of flowery language in sports writing. One of the most famous sports stories of the era was written by Grantland Rice after the Notre Dame–Army game in 1924:

> Outlined against a blue, gray October sky the Four Horsemen rode again. In dramatic lore they are known as Famine, Pestilence, Destruction, and Death. These are only aliases. Their real names are: Stuhldreher, Miller, Crowley, and Layden. They formed the crest of the South Bend cyclone before which another fighting Army team was swept over the precipice at the Polo Grounds this afternoon as 55,000 spectators peered down upon the bewildering panorama spread out upon the green plain below.

Sports writing has indeed come a long way.

Newspapers, meanwhile, battled for scoops about athletes and teams, creating serious concerns about ethical standards of sports reporting. These ethical concerns led to the formation of a committee appointed by the American Society of Newspaper Editors that in 1927 recommended several changes for sports reporting (Carvalho, 1998). This committee recommended increasing coverage of amateur athletics and ending free publicity for upcoming sporting events.

Ethical concerns, of course, persist today. Some newspapers are so concerned with ethical behavior by their staffs that they refuse to allow their sports reporters to attend events without paying to enter the sports venue. Some newsroom workers also are concerned about sports journalists who become friends with athletes and thus do not keep professional distances from sources.

During the ensuing decades, sports sections and staffs expanded as the "toy department" provided a multitude of forums in which to tell its stories. Sports was packaged and delivered in a similar way to the other sections of the newspaper, constantly growing in readership if not respectability. Sports magazines, radio, television, cable television, and the Internet revolutionized how Americans received their sports information, and it provided the opportunity for sports writers to become multimedia celebrities in their own right. And, similar to the late 1800s, technology and opportunity would once again allow athletes to play the role of journalists.

The modern era of sports reporting was ushered in with the advent of television. Televised sporting events made instant celebrities of some sports journalists. Howard Cosell became a household name because of his work with *Monday Night Football* and professional boxing. More recently, sports writers have expanded into other media. Tony Kornheiser, a longtime reporter for the *Washington Post*, not only has his own television program on ESPN (*Pardon the Interruption*), but he also was hired to provide color commentary on *Monday Night Football*.

Perhaps the biggest innovation in sports journalism was the creation of ESPN, the 24-hour cable sports network. ESPN is to sports fans what MTV is (or was) to music enthusiasts and CNN is to news junkies. All three networks debuted and evolved during the same period of time when cable television was growing into a significant player in the television industry during the early 1980s.

With ESPN, sports fans no longer had to wait for the morning paper or stay up to watch the late news to receive scores and highlights. Sports fans are no longer just detached viewers. ESPN has made everyone an expert, to some degree. If you watch enough ESPN you will be able to coach the motion offense, explain a nickel package and demonstrate the proper grip in throwing a circle change. With a nation of know-it-all sports fans, there's far more scrutiny on coaches and players. Sure, fans have always had a propensity to scream advice from the stands. What's different now is their advice might actually be good advice—and they know it.

With the expanded fan scrutiny comes more media scrutiny. We live in a "win-at-all-costs" society. Nice guys not only finish last but they are unemployed. With sports talk radio, 24-hour TV sports coverage, and Web sites and blogs, there is no escape for a struggling coach, player, or team. The expectation for a team's success has been exacerbated by the exposure. More exposure means more pressure to win.

ESPN has placed an enormous lens on the athletes. Through competition, ESPN has encouraged other media, primarily newspapers, to be more diligent in their coverage. No medium wants to be beaten on a story. ESPN scares newspapers.

Consequently, that coverage has amplified the profiles of athletes. Athletes know they've made it when they are highlighted on ESPN. They enjoy being invited to be on the (insert sponsor) Hot Seat or are discussed on *Pardon the Interruption*. To some degree, ESPN can make and break athletes because many media follow ESPN's lead. If it reports that a player is a jerk, the player has to be concerned about how that will play in other media. That's particularly true for middling athletes who do not have superstar allure.

Along these same lines, just as media evolved so did sport. Unprecedented wealth and opportunity arose for owners and players of sport, which led to a drastic alteration of the relationship between the sports writer and the athlete. Press agents, sports agents, and athletic entourages attempt to insulate athletes from the vulturous throngs of media and fans. A team no longer courts a sports editor for coverage in the morning print edition. Radio, television, cable television, and, to some extent, the Internet have become the desired media.

5

The final development in sports journalism was the introduction of the Internet. This had two profound influences on the sports field. First, the Internet has allowed any individual to become a sports writer. Fans have blogs, many of which are highly read. Web sites have become important sources for sports writers. Rivals.com, for example, is often quoted in newspaper stories because this Web site has become an authority on college recruiting around the country. Indeed, it is increasingly difficult to distinguish who exactly is a sports journalist.

Second, the Internet has allowed fans to follow sporting events from anywhere in the world. Soccer games involving English Premiere League teams such as Chelsea, Arsenal, and Manchester United are gamecasted on the Internet. Fans can even keep up-to-date on how the Sydney Swans or the Adelaide Crows are doing in the Aussie Rules Football League. Not only are fans around the world able to follow sports worldwide through the Internet, but this global sports coverage has demonstrated to US fans that passion for sports is not unique to America.

Today, more than ever, sports news is everywhere. Radio stations are devoted to sports talk 24 hours a day. Internet sites sing the praises of athletes or call for the firing of coaches. Anonymous bloggers give opinions about athletes' strengths and weaknesses.

Current Trends in Sports Reporting

Several other current issues are worth noting. First is the increased coverage of women's sports, a trend that began in the 1980s but one that has certainly picked up speed in more recent years. The women's basketball teams in some communities get better coverage than the men's basketball teams. Women's volleyball, gymnastics, and softball teams also receive much greater coverage than at anytime in the past. Along with the increased amount of coverage, women's sports are also receiving greater quality in their coverage. Gone are the days when a female athlete might be referred to as "the perky blonde."

Along with increased coverage of women in sports are increased opportunities for female sports writers. Female sports writers have also moved beyond covering only women's sports. Women now have top beats at many newspapers. The *Kansas City Star*, for example, has both an editor (Holly Lawton) and an NFL beat writer (Elizabeth Merrill) on its sports staff.

Long gone are the days of sports writers acting as cheerleaders for local teams, but sports writers today tend to be more critical of athletes than in the past. This may be in response to major national scandals involving steroids, drugs, and domestic violence cases. It also may be in response to increased scrutiny by sports forums on the Internet or by sports talk radio programs.

The current media environment has also created other problems for sports writers. Not only do sports writers have to compete with bloggers, but they also are often forced to spend hours tracking down false leads from rumors that appeared on the Internet.

Sports has also become big business, with sports writers often played as pawns by sports organizations. Every team now has sports media specialists controlling the flow of information, trying to spin the story or create a protective wall of deception. Even the "good" stories are controlled and manipulated. How can a sports writer achieve good journalism in that environment? But with the billions of dollars at stake, teams are going to protect their investments. The *SportsBusiness Journal* publishers had a reason to believe their magazine would draw a crowd. In February 2006, the *Journal* reported that the sports business industry was one of the largest and fastest growing at $213 billion per year—twice the size of the US automotive industry. In 1989, the sports business industry was a $50 to $60 billion industry (Shaw, 1989; Rambo, 1989).

Sports writers also have increasingly become celebrities. Besides Tony Kornheiser appearing on *Monday Night Football*, sports writers routinely appear on cable sports channels—for instance, the "Sports Reporters" on ESPN. Sports writers also have their own popular blogs. Fans can have their own blogs as well, but sports writers have much more credibility.

Against this negative backdrop, the overall quality of sports writing remarkably has managed to improve. The occasional cliché still appears in print, but sports writers demonstrate a greater degree of professionalism.

2

TYPES OF SPORTS STORIES
The Basics

As with news stories, sports stories are written with three broad purposes in mind: to inform, to entertain, and to persuade. Within these three categories are several specific types of stories.

Writing to Inform

The most basic informative sports story is the game report. Game reports are stories that are timely—appearing the day after an event takes place—and are typically written in a more hard-news style. They will concentrate on the who, when, where, why, and how of a sporting event. Because these stories are so timely, sports reporters often face difficult deadlines. A night baseball game on the West Coast may end after 1:00 a.m. on the East Coast. If a newspaper has a 1:30 a.m. copy deadline, reporters will need to write a complete story with only game details and write a sub with quotes to replace the original story for later press runs.

Beyond game reports, sports writers commonly write both pre-event stories—advances—and post-event stories—follows. Advances concentrate on the most important aspects of a future sporting event and include reactions of coaches and players. Follows wrap up a previously held event and concentrate on putting the result of the event in perspective. Follows concentrate heavily on reactions of players and coaches, while including very little play-by-play.

Writing to Entertain

Because sports events essentially are entertainment, many sports stories, above all else, strive to entertain. But, unlike reports that concentrate on sporting events, stories in this category are written with a more creative writing style where the time element is of secondary importance.

One type of entertainment story is written in conjunction with game reports: sidebars. Sidebars are stories that examine some aspect of a sporting event, but the writer takes a less hard-news approach. Sidebars often are run alongside game reports (thus, the term "side" bar). Sometimes, sidebars are written because they don't quite fit in with the flow of the game report. Other times, a reporter will write a sidebar because he/she noticed an unusual topic for a story that deserves to stand alone as its own story.

Two other broad categories of entertainment stories are human interest features and personality profiles. Human interest features concentrate on unusual aspects of sports or sports figures and tend to be less timely. Personality profiles give insights into athletes—what makes them who they are.

Writing to Persuade

The final category of sports writing involves those stories that attempt to persuade. This includes editorials and columns.

Sports journalists write editorials to share their opinions about some aspect of sports: the reasons for a losing streak and the ways to get back on track, for instance. Since the opinions are those of the individual sports writer, editorials are often written in the first person.

Columns are similar to editorials in that they allow the reporter to share his or her opinion. They tend to be less about an individual writer's opinion, though, and more about a point the writer wants to make: that a team may be in the middle of a losing streak, but there is hope for the future.

3

PREPARATION

Tools for Successful Sports Reporting and Writing

"Failure to prepare is preparing to fail."
(John Wooden, former UCLA basketball coach
who won 10 NCAA championships)

"Luck is what happens when preparation meets opportunity."
(Darrell Royal, College Football Hall of Fame coach
from the University of Texas)

Some sports writers would argue that they've spent a lifetime preparing for their profession. The unofficial qualifications for becoming a sports writer include collecting and trading baseball cards, combing through newspaper boxscores, playing Little League baseball, midget football and/or youth basketball, watching and listening to ESPN, and most importantly, arguing with childhood friends about crucial issues such as the legitimacy of bowling as a sport, the athleticism of auto racers and whether soccer will ever catch on in the United States. The truth is, it takes more than that to be a sports writer.

As a journalist covering sports, you will be asked to perform a multitude of duties that cannot be perfected during sports camps and adolescence. What you have to realize is that everyone working in the sports department has experienced a similar sports childhood. They too have scrapbooks filled with articles written about their favorite team, have bantered with the neighbor kid about the athleticism of NASCAR drivers, and watched enough SportsCenter to leave them stupefied with athletic superlatives and clichés. So, when you enter the realm of organized sports writing at a newspaper, you are anything but unique. In fact, your uniqueness lies in your newness, which makes you a rookie. And we all know what happens to rookies.

"Hey, kid," the sports editor growls. "Got an assignment for you."

The blood rushes to your head and you begin to salivate profusely.

10

"It's time to show these old dogs how the young hounds run," you think.

"What is it?" You try to act cool but it's lost on the sports editor.

"The Westside field hockey team is playing St. Mathias on Thursday. I want you to cover it."

"Field hockey?" you think. "Isn't that like polo without horses?"

"But I don't know anything about field hockey," you blurt.

"Well, you'd better learn," the sports editor says.

Translation: "There's the creek, here's the boat, but we'll keep the paddles. Good luck, rook. And don't screw it up."

Preparing for the Gamer

In an instant, all that playing, collecting, cutting and pasting, and memorization of inane statistics are of little use. Field hockey to you is like the metric system to American school children. You understand that girls run around a large field, swing sticks, and chase a white ball toward a goal. It's golf on steroids without the mulligans, gimme three-foot putts and the 19th hole. Self-education now becomes essential. You have only a short time to learn a game you know little or nothing about.

Usually the initial stop is the newspaper archives, but because your field hockey knowledge is rather limited, you will first want to research the sport. An Internet search for "field hockey" yields about a bazillion hits so you probably want to narrow your scope. Try "USA field hockey". That directs you to the "official" site for field hockey in the United States, which includes history, rules, and an abundance of information. Although the local high school league might have slightly different rules, you can learn the gist of the sport through this Web site.

After learning that a "bully" isn't your seventh-grade nemesis and a "flick" isn't what he used to do to your ears, you can begin researching the local teams. In your newspaper's archives, you should find previous articles that can provide some general knowledge of the teams, such as records, name of the goalkeeper, scorers, etc. Of course, because you can assume the previous reporter covering field hockey knew as little as you do about the sport, you will want to confirm the information with the coach.

That brings us to the next step. After sorting through the basic elements of the game, contact one or both of the schools you will be covering and ask when and where the field hockey team is practicing. Then, attend practice. This will give you a feel for the game and how it works. And here's a great tip for learning the game—swallow your sports-writer pride and admit you are a field hockey moron. Sure, it's not easy to admit you don't know everything about *all* sports, but the fact is, you

11

don't. No one does. Asking for assistance from the coach or a team manager or someone on the sidelines is part of your education. They can walk you through the nuances of the game. Ask how scoring works and discuss strategy. You'll discover there are similarities between field hockey and other sports, which will allow you to use your knowledge from those sports and apply it to field hockey. It also does one more thing: it allows you to build a rapport with the coach or the team manager. They will be more tolerant of your "dumb" questions and take the time to explain things to you.

Think of it in these terms: if someone asked you to explain sports writing, how would you feel? You would probably ramble on as if you were on ESPN's "Sports Reporters". People enjoy telling others about their lives. They also enjoy educating others. Asking questions is part of your job. There's no shame in learning and there's no disgrace in admitting you do not know everything. But, proceed with caution. Admitting ignorance can open you up to criticism. If something you write rubs the coach the wrong way, he or she might use your pleas of ignorance as leverage to complain to your boss (as in, "Why did you send a field hockey moron to cover our game?"). Also, do not allow the source (the coach) to dictate the story. You are still the reporter and it is still your story. Remember to maintain control of your learning experience. One way to do that is to show the coach that you are not as ignorant as you might have originally claimed. You can do that by throwing information back at the coach. For instance, if the coach is discussing the previous game's overtime loss, you could ask how the coach determines which seven players to play during overtime. Because you've done your research you understand that although the game is played with eleven players, during overtime, high school federation play dictates that the teams play seven-on-seven. Then you can ask how the coach decides which players to use during the five-player penalty stroke competition because you know that if the game is tied after overtime it can be decided by penalty strokes (think hockey shootout). Suddenly, it's a conversation about field hockey strategy and not a "Field Hockey for Dummies" instructional clinic.

When you arrive for the game armed with your newfound knowledge, immediately locate the scorer's table. As with every sport, get the starting lineups. Take notes during the game and record goals, assists, saves, and other pertinent statistics. At half-time—yes, there is a half-time in field hockey, but usually no marching band—check with the scorer's table to confirm goals, assists, shots on goal, etc. You'll also want to check at the end of the game. Once again, if you don't understand something, ask. Parents, team managers, benchwarmers, and fans are usually willing to assist you. It's better to be privately embarrassed and correct than to be publicly humiliated and wrong in the next day's newspaper. Newspaper corrections are a part of being a journalist but they should not occur because of self-inflicted ignorance, pride, or sloppy reporting.

If you are covering a more traditional sport, one that you are familiar with, the same steps apply. Although you probably will not be required to research the intricacies of football, basketball, baseball, soccer, or hockey, checking the archives for previous articles and attending practice are always good ideas. But in this case, the real work is not learning the sport but learning the teams or individuals participating in the sport. Take notes during practice with the intention of using the information in the future. Recognizing that last week's starting quarterback is not suited up for Wednesday's practice can become a key component to your Friday night story. But if you don't attend practice you won't know the quarterback is injured, suspended or demoted until you arrive for the game. "News" remains the primary goal of newspapers, even in the sports section.

After practice, even if you're not writing an advance or preview story, talk with the coaches and players. Once again, establishing rapport is essential and casual conversation is a gateway to pertinent information. On gameday, you should not be a stranger to the coach. If you are, then you have not properly prepared to do your job.

Preparing for the Feature Story

Now that you've become a field hockey "expert," the grizzled sports editor wants to tap into your genius.

"Hey, kid. How 'bout doin' a feature story about that Westside goalie, what's her name?"

"Jaime McFarlene."

"Yeah, that's her. Give me a 600-word feature and we'll run it before the play-offs begin next week."

Not realizing that 600 words is only about a 14-inch story, you begin to mentally visualize the possibilities. "First, the Jaime McFarlene piece and then *Sports Illustrated*." Sure. Just like the sports writer who was working at a 20,000-circulation daily newspaper in the Midwest. One night, the wife of the sports writer called and excitedly said, "*Sports Illustrated* called and wants you to call right away." The sports writer had always dreamed of writing for SI and had assumed they were finally going to offer him a job.

"Yes, Mr. Miller," the woman's voice said. "We were wondering if you wanted to renew your subscription?"

Although the anecdote provides a good point about assumption, it also tells us to never stop dreaming. A 14-inch story about a field hockey player might not directly lead to a job at a major national sports magazine, but it's the first step. Everything you write should build on what you have previously written. But, first things first. The trick to writing any good story is doing the research.

Research for the McFarlene feature includes the following:

- Read previous school and local newspaper stories about her and the team. Pay particular attention to her quotes, quotes about her and particular performances, such as shutouts and blowouts. Losses can tell as much about a person as wins.
- Conduct an online search for her name. Perhaps she has an online account such as Facebook or MySpace that will provide details about her.
- Check the school yearbook to see what has been written about her.
- If McFarlene were a college athlete, check the biography provided in the media guide. Look at quirky information sometimes provided in those biographies, such as favorite foods, favorite movie, and hobbies.
- Check your notes from previous game stories. You might have some nuggets of information about McFarlene that you hadn't used in the previous story.
- Interview family and friends. Although we'll discuss interviewing in another chapter, interviews can be an important element of preparation. Family members and friends will provide information that gives you leverage going into an interview. For example, if McFarlene's father tells you she started playing goalie because she hates to run, that can be a significant element in the story.
- Talk with others in the sports department who might have information regarding the subject of your story. Sports writers and editors, particularly those with long tenures and institutional knowledge, are invaluable resources of information. Old sports journalists are like elephants—they don't forget anything.
- Look beyond the usual suspects. Interview coaches, school secretaries, janitors, and anyone else who has had contact with your subject. For instance, after a small college star athlete died in a car accident, it was discovered that she was a good friend to one of the college's maintenance men. He had been sick and when he returned to work he found a homemade get-well card the athlete had sent to him. He didn't see the card until two days after her death. The maintenance man was a wonderful source who was able to provide another perspective of the young lady's life that had nothing to do with her athleticism.

These information-gathering techniques can be used when writing any kind of feature story. In gathering all this information, the idea is to "wow" your subject. The more you know, the more you can discuss a variety of subjects with the source. It also builds trust and confidence that you are competent enough to write an accurate story. The source will appreciate your hard work and be thrilled you showed great interest. The worst interviews that result in the worst stories are those in which the writer is ill-prepared to conduct a conversation with the source. People generally view themselves as boring. If you cannot tap into the interesting aspects of their lives, boring is what you'll get. See beyond the goalie equipment and start to develop an idea of who McFarlene is prior to talking with her. When you conduct the interview, together you'll develop a more complete picture.

Preparing for the "Big" Announcement

It always starts with a press release, phone call or e-mail. The message will say something like, "Press conference at 3 p.m. tomorrow to make an important announcement." The good reporter starts digging into what the "important" announcement will be, while the bad reporter waits for the "unveiling" of a new coach or some other declaration. The magnitude of the announcement might in fact be as "important" as indicated but it could just as easily be that the university's basketball team is modeling new uniforms or the minor league baseball team has a new mascot. While you are somewhat obligated to cover the event you are not obligated to wait for the news. Your job as a journalist is to provide news when it happens and not wait for others to determine the time, date, and place. So when you arrive at the press conference, you should not be surprised by the announcement. Because you have already reported the news in that day's newspaper, the press conference should be a time for you to collect additional details to be used in a follow-up story.

But how do you get the story before the scheduled announcement, particularly when athletic organizations love to "spring" news on eager fans? Some sports teams, particularly universities, guard these secrets as if they were classified CIA documents. There is no surefire way to get the story, but you certainly can play the role of press conference spoiler. And here's how:

First, contact everyone in the organization that is making the announcement. This is a good time to talk with the secretary, janitor, team manager, waterboy, or anyone with whom you've established a relationship. If possible, talk with these people in person and not via the telephone. They are more likely to talk face-to-face. Many times, this will be a dead end for fear of reprisals—people don't like being fired for talking with reporters. But at this stage, you are not conducting interviews or even using the information for the record. It's usually off-the-record information and the source will never be named in the newspaper. It's simply background information that can be confirmed by other sources. For example, you can say, "Mr. Athletic Director, I understand Joe Jock will be your new football coach. How did he compare with the other candidates who applied for the job?" If he comments, then he has confirmed that Joe Jock is the new football coach. If he says, "I can't comment on that," you can backtrack and ask the athletic director if Jock is the new coach. If the AD continues to play cat-and-mouse, move on to another source.

Second, contact everyone in the league/conference/division and ask if they know what the announcement might be. Sports information directors talk with other sports information directors. Several people know the big secret so it's just a matter of talking with one who is willing to speak up. Once again, the source will not necessarily be cited in the newspaper but the information can be a foothold to asking others the questions you need answered.

Third, if the announcement involves a coach or athletic director, and you know the short list of candidates, contact the current employer of those candidates and ask if they are making a big announcement tomorrow. Generally speaking, before someone begins a new job he or she quits the old job. If you have a list of candidates, start checking who has recently submitted a resignation. You can also contact the local newspaper of a potential candidate. Sharing information with the sports writer in another city can be extremely beneficial to you and that sports writer.

Fourth, contact alumni, boosters or fan club members. These people are oftentimes closely connected to the team. They hear and see things that others do not. If you were smart, you would have established a rapport with some fan club members or alumni. This is the time to tap into that rapport. And again, the information would be background information only and not for attributing in a story.

Fifth, use old-fashioned honesty. If you do discover the information, contact the sports media relations director and ask, "Look, I understand Joe Jock is going to be the new football coach. I also know you cannot tell me until tomorrow. But if I were to print that, would I be wrong? I don't want to be wrong and I don't think you want me to be wrong." You are not asking for an official word, you are simply asking for confirmation. Sports information personnel worth their salt will not allow you to walk down an incorrect path. Besides, they will still receive ample coverage at the press conference. It isn't as if you will not attend the big announcement.

Sixth, check the online chat rooms. Fans love to speculate, and although it could provide a multitude of false leads, some might be correct. The chat-room buzz usually has some inclination of truth. And if you've followed the chat rooms in the past and are familiar with the characters, you'll know who's legitimate and who's blowing smoke.

The idea isn't to rain on the team's parade but if the information is out there then you are obligated to provide it to your readers. You are a journalist. Informing and educating the public is your journalistic responsibility. Generally, news is not something hand delivered. It is extracted from sources and presented to readers. Waiting for it to happen, or worse yet, allowing a source to set the time and place, rubs contrary to your purpose. Be one step ahead of the game and be creative.

Once, a university in the Midwest was interviewing candidates for a new football coach. Instead of bringing the candidates to town, the athletic director was flying around the country to interview the prospects in their home cities. The beat writer for a local paper realized that the AD was using a booster's private plane to fly to these locations. The sports writer tracked down the wing number of the plane. Each day he would contact the airport, and by using the wing number, ask where the plane was going. As you know, planes have to file a flight plan. A few hours later, the reporter would contact the airport where the plane was flying to and again use the wing number to track its next location. Because the reporter had a short list of candidates, he could piece together who was being interviewed on what days. Eventually, he was able to figure out the AD had visited one coach twice in Ohio and that the Ohio coach would be the new football coach. Afterward, the AD asked the sports writer, "How did you figure out who I was interviewing?" When the sports writer explained it, the AD was thoroughly impressed.

There's always a way to get information. You just have to be dogged enough and creative enough to find it. Most people cannot keep a secret. And, quite honestly, one of the best parts of sports is being able to tell someone something they did not already know. How else can you explain the popularity of sports trivia?

Of course, not all events are "big announcements." College and professional athletes routinely tour smaller communities during their offseason to promote the team and create goodwill with the fans. Whether it's a journeyman for the Chicago Cubs or LeBron James, memorize statistics, read autobiographies, and learn what you can about the subject before he or she arrives. Observe and take notes when the star interacts with fans, particularly children. Is the athlete wearing a suit or dressed casually? Is he or she wearing championship rings or excessive jewelry? Former dual-sport athlete Deion Sanders was recognized for his gold chains. Does he still play the role of "Neon Deion" or has he changed? Those details humanize athletes.

You have to remember that athletes, even the greatest ones, are simply human beings who happen to have an extraordinary physical gift. When you strip away that gift, they are the same eating, sleeping, slobbering mammals as the rest of us. So when you meet these athletes, treat them as people and not as gods. While you should be respectful, be sure that they know they should respect you as well. Being prepared is one way to gain that respect.

Observation

Preparation does not end when you arrive at the event. It is a continuous process. Using all your senses to soak in the atmosphere will enhance the story. What does the ballpark sound like? How does it smell? What makes it interesting or unique? What can be seen on the field? As a trained observer, you are expected to provide richness to the experience for those who are not there. You are the readers' eyes, ears, nose, mouth, and skin. Does the damp night air create a chill, and if so, what kind of chill? Is it the kind of chill that requires a sweater or a raging fire to keep warm? Does the ballpark smell like popcorn or fresh, hot popcorn with extra butter? Specifics are always better than generalities.

Prior to the event, watch the players. Check for routines. Who's joking around and who is deadly serious? Are the players enthusiastic or listless? Pre-game activities can be indicators of what is to come.

At events, check the crowd. Who is attending? How many? What is the set-up? What is the body language of the speakers? The visual cues are as telling as the verbal ones. How does a source react when you ask a touchy question? Does she stammer with the words or squirm in her seat? Be careful not to misinterpret the reaction, but you certainly need to be aware of it. If in doubt, ask, "Does that question make you uncomfortable?"

Although you are a trained observer, sometimes interpreting what you're observing can be difficult. The action happens quickly. Do not expect always to know exactly what is occurring on the field. Who got the rebound or assist isn't always clear. Don't solely depend upon what you think you saw to interpret the play. When in doubt, sports writers will sometimes consult each other and attempt to come to a consensus. That's not exactly the best-case scenario. Who says those clods sitting next to you in the pressbox know exactly what happened? Confirming the events with the players or coach afterward will assist in getting it right. Their vantage point from the field or court is much better than yours.

One final note about observing events—don't ever fictionalize. Making up a piece of information does not make it true. If you are unsure of the events that occurred, write what you know even if it is a bit vague. It's better to be vague than attempt to fill in the blanks and be wrong. If you're uncertain, ask yourself, "What do I know and what do I think I know?" Stick with what you know. It's a much safer path than that of make believe.

Tools of the Trade

When the Buffalo Bills played the Washington Redskins in Super Bowl XXVI, 1991 NFL Player of the Year Thurman Thomas missed the first few plays because he could not find his helmet. Thomas, a five-time pro bowl running for Buffalo, rushed 10 times for 13 yards as Washington won the game, 37–24.

Being prepared is more than just knowing what to do. Having the correct tools is part of your preparation as well. So here are a few tips:

- Carry a pen and pencil with you at all times. A pen works great unless it runs out of ink or you encounter inclement weather, such as rain, cold, snow, sleet, hail, hurricane, or plague of locusts. During these times, a pencil is mighty handy. A pen is handy when the pencil lead breaks or becomes too dull to write. Of course, a second pen and pencil stashed in your vehicle is always a good idea.
- Recording devices are great except when they stop working. Be certain the batteries and tape are fresh. If you have a digital recorder, that's all the better. Do a check to make sure the recorder is working before starting the interview.
- Even if you are recording, take notes. Mechanical devices go on the fritz so taking notes is essential to documenting information. No reporter or source enjoys conducting an interview twice. Using a notebook also allows you to write down "reminder" questions while conducting the interview. These are questions you think of while the source is speaking, and writing them down reminds you to backtrack and ask.
- Use a recorder with a counter. When a source gives you a particularly good quote or piece of information, jot down the counter number in your notebook. That allows you to quickly extract information from the recorder without wasting valuable time, particularly on deadline.
- Set up an allotted time and place to meet. Also, designate a specific amount of time needed to conduct the interview. If you only need a few minutes, say so. And stick to the time allotment. People are busy and if you take more time than requested the source might not be as accommodating next time.

Being prepared is the essence of journalism. Without proper preparation, you will be ill-equipped to interview a source, report on an event or write a story. And ignorance is one of the quickest ways to lose credibility with sources and readers. If you can provide your own paddle to get that boat up the creek, then bigger and better assignments await. Who knows? Maybe someday *Sports Illustrated* will call asking you to renew your subscription...or offer you a job.

New Orleans Times-Picayune
June 16, 2006 Friday

HEADLINE: "To ensure your city's future, you have to have a program for your youth. If you want a viable city, you have to get an insurance policy called a recreation department. But you can't buy it, you have to build it";

Staggering financially beforehand, NORD took a severe blow from Katrina and—with a major assist from volunteers—now must reinvent itself.

(By Benjamin Hochman, Staff writer)

Hurricane Katrina demolished Ronnie North's home, but, for a moment, his biggest concern was avoiding a line drive headed straight for his noggin, courtesy of a seven year old and his aluminum bat.

Three Saturdays ago was opening day at Lakeview Playground, a New Orleans Recreational Department facility laid waste by Hurricane Katrina. Surrounded by gutted homes with fading watermarks, kids bounced around the six glorious fields, tidy uniforms succumbing to dirt and dust. In the stands, parents beamed and old friends hugged. And North, wearing the same red shirt as his son's team, pitched to the players, basking in the purity.

"You couldn't tell the hurricane came if you look at the playground," said North.

One Saturday later, Nancy Broadhurst went for a drive. In the half-decade before the storm, Broadhurst headed the group Friends of NORD, raising millions of dollars to revitalize the department's facilities. That Saturday, she visited numerous playgrounds and fields, many that she once helped improve.

Now neglect was omnipresent. These facilities, some even before the storm, became wastelands without maintenance from the city or involved parental groups such as the Lakeview boosters.

"Noticing anything missing at all these playgrounds?" Broadhurst said. "The kids."

NORD's presence, too, was conspicuously absent.

NORD, which struggled with organization and financing before Katrina, was nearly dealt a knockout blow by the hurricane. The department lost numerous employees and money because of budget cuts. Some of its facilities—be it parks, pools or gymnasiums—are unused or ruined. But others are trying to make a comeback, thanks to parents and a handful of loyal NORD employees who didn't lose their jobs or passion.

"NORD, like everything else in New Orleans, is in recovery mode," said Cynthia Sylvain-Lear, deputy chief administrative officer for the city. "We are doing everything we can in our partnerships to make sure this is a successful program."

"I really believe that the recreation department lacks some continuity and consistency, but I look at problems as opportunities," Broadhurst said. "We believe NORD is sitting on a gold mine, we really do...But government can only do so much."

Such is the quandary the city faces with its once-thriving recreational department.

The goal is to serve as many children as possible with opportunities, from sports teams to swimming pools to summer camps. But of the 13 NORD centers, only Cut-Off in Algiers wasn't heavily damaged by the storm. None of the 18 swimming pools is open, though four should open by the end of June, Sylvain-Lear said. And a majority of the 105 play spots were either affected by the storm or were already in poor condition.

NORD's budget in previous years hovered around $8 million, according to Sylvain-Lear. Post-Katrina, it's about $800,000.

In 2004, there were 145 NORD employees, though Sylvain-Lear pointed out that many were only involved in summer programs. Now NORD has 18 employees.

And since 1999, NORD has replaced its director six times. The job is vacant, as Sylvain-Lear and other city officials sift through résumés. After Katrina, Charlene Braud resigned as director, and she now has a similar position in Atlanta. Lora Johnson served as an interim director, but she, too, has left. Whereas decades ago NORD fielded athletic teams for numerous sports, the official teams have essentially been expunged. The teams that do play on NORD facilities, such as those in Lakeview, are organized by parental booster clubs, not NORD.

In the coming months, NORD will offer a fraction of its previous summertime smorgasbord. Thanks to partnerships with groups such as Young Audiences, Operation Blessing, and Operation Reach, there will be summer camps for hundreds of kids. And gyms such as Cut-Off and Norman in the West Bank are open for informal activities, such as basketball and volleyball. And there's talk of organizing a NORD fall football league, but basic issues—such as where to play and who will coach—linger.

The sobering fact is many kids don't have a place to play.

"That's the unfortunate reality of Katrina," Sylvain-Lear said. "That's the issue."

A Summer Lost

Archie Manning was the Saints' quarterback when Carlette Washington began working with NORD. She has seen kids heave jump shots, and then *their* kids heave jump shots. At Cut-Off, her job description was "to supervise, coach, transport, whatever needs to be done with the children." After 29 years, she finally felt her work was done. But the storm came before her retirement, and she decided to stay at Cut-Off, fighting to keep youth recreation alive in New Orleans.

"I know there's more going on than just recreation," Washington said. "People are trying to get their homes back together. I was ready to retire, but when I look at the big picture, our kids need this. They need us. I'm here for the long haul."

The faces aren't as familiar in pickup games on the Cut-Off courts. With some NORD facilities vacant, kids from Gentilly, eastern New Orleans and the Lower 9th Ward have arrived in Algiers wearing hightops. But, Washington said, sighing, "Some of the kids come here, but not all of them can get here...The only way we can get NORD back running is find out where the kids are, get them in one central location and, from there, make teams."

Many of the kids stuck in their neighborhoods can't play on the playgrounds—because they're living on the playgrounds.

Said former NORD athlete and coach Alden Hagardorn, "Where I used to play ball, at Lyons and Laurel, the only way they're going to play is if first base is this FEMA trailer, second base is that FEMA trailer and so on."

Some of NORD's most popular athletic facilities have been converted to trailer parks—Harrell, Leeman, Wisner. A summer lost.

"We tried to encourage FEMA to approve sites that were vacant property and not necessarily parks and playgrounds," Sylvain-Lear said. "We gave them several lists. But FEMA has a selection process, and some of the properties we had given them, they found not to be suitable.

"In some sections of the cities, people didn't have space to put a trailer in their driveways. So you couldn't say, 'Absolutely no trailers in the parks,' because then some people wouldn't have a place to live. We're trying to do a balance. What do we have, where can kids play, we have partnerships for summer programs."

Jude Luke's three children played ball at Kenilworth in eastern New Orleans. Like the playground, the Kenilworth league also received a tremendous hit from the storm.

"And there were kids playing at Goretti in New Orleans East," Luke said of that desolate park. "With some parents not having transportation, they can't play until that park gets up and running."

Luke's kids now play in the Lakeview league run by the parents. Entering the spring, there were opportunities for displaced kids to play ball—there are booster-club leagues such as Carrollton, Lakeview and the Babe Ruth League at Algiers (and the recreation department leagues in Jefferson Parish). But lack of transportation and awareness kept other kids on the sideline.

On Its Own Terms

The families who joined the booster leagues found themselves in a haven of recreation. The booster organizations, with little coordination with NORD, pieced together leagues on their own terms.

In Lakeview, Katrina ripped apart the playground. The wind knocked down trees, which knocked down scoreboards and fences. Dugout roofs fell onto the benches, and batting cages fell to the ground.

"We cried," said Darryl Fricke, the head of the booster club. "But we knew we could do this."

Parents whose homes were gone, who were tight on money, donated time and funds to the playground. In the early months of 2006, parents such as Brad Murret were armed with chain saws and rakes, their mission to renovate the six fields.

"I think the parents had a sense of 'hey, this is something we really need to get back to some normalcy,'" said Murret, a Lakeview coach. "We've heard that term so much after the hurricane, but it's really true. You look for something to be back to normal, to get back together with family and friends.

"When it was brought up that the fields could possibly be used as a FEMA trailer park, parents called in and made an uproar: 'What's more important, 50 trailers that can possibly be put somewhere else? Or giving 1,000 kids a place to play?' Especially when they're not even living any more in Lakeview because they can't. Let's give them, at least, the playground that they used to play at. Some of these kids this summer had not seen their friends since last summer. Psychologically, they need that. And parents, too. It goes beyond just playing baseball."

Registration fees for baseball or softball ran at $75 per child, which was used for uniform costs and maintenance. Concession stand sales would help keep money flowing. And the booster club accepted sponsorships and, more simply, donations of any kind—from equipment to cases of bottled water to office chairs. By late May, 730 kids had registered, down from 1,186 the previous summer.

And on May 27, the league held its kickoff jamboree.

"This field is an oasis, so to speak, in the middle of the devastation," Murret said.

That morning, Fricke cried again.

"I've had tears in my eyes all day," Fricke said. "I've had parents come up to us and say, 'I can't believe you guys pulled this off.'"

A Vicious Cycle

Across town at Warren Easton Playground in Mid-City, only an abandoned car was on the baseball field. At Comiskey Playground in Mid-City, even the sign was not welcoming, tattered, and covered in graffiti. Numerous parks were only mildly hit by the storm—and didn't have FEMA trailers—yet they remained unused for organized sports.

NORD struggles to maintain these facilities, much less organize teams for competition. In other communities, NORD relies on parents to run the leagues. But in these communities, there is no booster club—and thus no sports.

But as Broadhurst asked the day she toured the playgrounds, why should these residents be penalized, just because they don't have the organization or funding of a Lakeview?

Especially in post-Katrina New Orleans, why should families have to pay the bill for recreation?

NORD has sparked a vicious cycle—there is a lack of organization, lack of money, lack of maintenance, and a lack of kids targeted to play. And so NORD relies on parents and volunteers where, in some neighborhoods, there is a lack of organization, lack of money, lack of maintenance, and a lack of kids targeted to play.

"We all want better programs for our children," Broadhurst said. "And if you keep running it the same way, like it has been, nothing gets accomplished."

Before the Hurricane

It's unequivocal that Katrina stripped NORD of much of its strength. But you can't blame Katrina for everything, said Hagardorn, who unsuccessfully ran for a seat on the City Council this spring. One of his key campaign issues was to refurbish NORD as well as its facilities.

"If you say, should NORD be like they were before the hurricane, I'd say, 'Yeah—before Hurricane Camille,'" he said. That storm struck in 1969.

Hagardorn remembers generations ago when NORD was fervent. Since its inception in 1947, NORD became the model program for urban recreation, running numerous sports programs and churning out youth national champions. But in the past quarter-century, the organization faced numerous setbacks, notably with funding and leadership.

As an example of failed management, Hagardorn pointed to the role of the park supervisors—some of them his friends—who were paid by the city to watch over parks, but not required to organize teams or maintain the fields.

And while private teams and booster clubs sprouted—and NORD had its leadership flux—teams dwindled.

In 2001, for instance, Hagardorn decided to return to coaching because his daughter was old enough to play softball. He contacted NORD about assembling a team to play other NORD teams in the Uptown district. Soon he was informed that his was the only Uptown team. And so his team was the champion and would then play champions from other districts. Yet his roster wasn't even filled.

"To win the city championship, that used to be quite an honor," Hagardorn said. "Now here's NORD, with people on the payroll, and the team that goes to the city championship hasn't even had a practice...

"If you're going to build a NORD program, do it from the roots up. Identify the neighborhood and parks that don't need a lot of repair and try to start it with a couple of teams. And go from there. But you can't just say, all the playgrounds are open, and everyone start. But, it's got to be appealing."

Because of the Love

This summer, NORD will try to appeal to children in numerous facets.

In the halls of Cut-Off, girls in ballet outfits pirouette past boys in basketball jerseys. Pools such as Stalling Center in Gentilly and Fisher in Algiers are expected to open by month's end. And programs such as Operation Reach's "Gulf South Summer Youth Action Corps" will serve about 300 children in a six-week academic and recreational camp. Thanks to a $25,000 grant from the PBSJ Foundation—and the $125,000 Operation Reach raised—Operation Reach and NORD united for this camp effort, similar to other collaborations this summer.

"Because of the love for NORD and the children and the city, the partners have stepped up to the plate so much," Sylvain-Lear said. "This is the natural thing to do."

"I'm positive that there is a light at the end of the tunnel," said Kyshun Webster, director of Operation Reach. "This will provide a positive option for [kids] to connect with."

But the coming months are crucial for NORD, while it rediscovers itself—and re-evaluates its mission.

Said Rich Jackson, who has worked on and off with NORD since 1959, "We don't let the devastation serve as a deterrent."

Friends of NORD will continue to raise money for the rebuilding of NORD facilities. Broadhurst said her organization has already raised $800,000 post-Katrina. And numerous organizations have called to partner up, Broadhurst said. The U.S. Tennis Association is in talks to donate $100,000 to revitalize NORD tennis centers. The television channel Nickelodeon plans to build a skate park on one of the NORD properties. Walltown Children Theatre has offered to run a workshop in the fall called

"Children Of The Storm." Samaritan Purse has offered to pay for the renewal of five NORD playgrounds. And Indianapolis Colts quarterback Peyton Manning, Archie's son, donated $10,000 to help the playgrounds.

But NORD has taken financial hits through budget cuts and the loss of a bond issue that, before the storm, could have pumped $10 million into the playgrounds, Broadhurst and Sylvain-Lear said. The bond issue, $260 million overall, was overwhelmingly approved by voters on Nov. 2, 2004. It provided funding for recreation and for equipment. Now there isn't bonding capacity, and NORD suffers.

And volunteers "are the backbone of recreation," said Washington of the Cut-Off center. With reduced staffs at NORD facilities, NORD continues to seek coaches, game officials, camp counselors, and basically anyone with time on his or her hands. In one conversation alone, Washington brought up the need for volunteers five times.

Broadhurst spoke of two key characteristics for a post-Katrina NORD: "continuity and accountability." The hiring of a director is first on NORD's agenda—someone who will build the former, while sticking around long enough to build the latter.

"But," Broadhurst said, "you could get a Harvard graduate in there—and you need a support system, too...

"Quite frankly, the city does need all the help it can get. In [Mayor Ray] Nagin's inaugural speech, he was telling us all to get off our duffs and to play a part. You can't believe that just one man, the mayor, can do it all. It is time for us to get off our duffs."

"It's not going to be easy," Washington said. "But guess what— we're not going to lose NORD. It's too important to all of the community—to every boy and girl living in New Orleans."

Hagardorn is well aware of NORD's importance. As a player, NORD instilled in him discipline and values. As a coach, he did his part to pass that along to a younger generation.

"I've had more than one former player tell me, 'If it wasn't for you and if I didn't have that playground, I'd have been in jail, I wouldn't have a job, I'd been in a gang,'" Hagardorn said. "To ensure your city's future, you have to have a program for your youth. If you want a viable city, you have to get an insurance policy called a recreation department.

"But you can't buy it. You have to build it."

Figure 3.1 Benjamin Hochman.

Professional Perspective
By Benjamin Hochman
The Denver Post

Things didn't get off to a smooth start.

Editor: "Benjamin, I want you to write the definitive story about NORD."

Benjamin (to self): "What's NORD?"

I covered the NBA for the *Times-Picayune* in New Orleans, so I began to sift through my mental rolodex of players—but there was nothing between Andres Nocioni and Dirk Nowitzki.

I then read previous stories from the *Times-Picayune* about this mysterious NORD, and I was soon introduced to the New Orleans Recreation Department—the organization that runs youth athletic programs in the city.

Apparently, NORD had disintegrated after Hurricane Katrina. So nine months after the storm, my job was to uncover what happened to NORD. And, more poignantly, answer the question: are kids getting a chance to play?

My obstacles were innumerable. Phone numbers to NORD facilities were disconnected. E-mails were lost in cyberspace. And the folks at City Hall provided little cooperation; they didn't seem thrilled to talk about the demise of a once-prospering department.

I remembered the fantastically cheesy saying by Lao Tzu, a favorite of my high school soccer coach while we ran up hills in August: "A journey of a thousand miles begins with a single step." Translation: I need to start talking to people who may know someone who heard something and—hopefully by deadline—I'll have a dynamic story.

First, I searched for nuggets in previous stories written about NORD. I tried to find out who was in charge of NORD, but City Hall was evasive, and the past names in the stories showed up in Google and Lexis Nexis in different cities (later, I would find out the NORD didn't have a director).

There was one story about Carlette Washington, a steadfast, proud woman who ran one of the NORD centers. I drove to her center, which, wouldn't you know, was one of the few centers functioning after Katrina. She gave me some background information and more names.

I went into my database of previous sources—always keep names and phone numbers because you never know when you'll need them. I called a bunch of people around town to see if they knew anyone involved with NORD. I also e-mailed every writer at the *Times-Picayune*, and some of my co-workers pointed me toward possible sources.

One writer lived in the Lakeview neighborhood, which was ravaged by the storm. Her son still played in the baseball league out there. I began to contact parents and coaches, and discoverd that with NORD on the fritz, parents in neighborhoods ran booster clubs, basically putting on their own recreation leagues.

On opening day, I was in the stands, capturing the scene and interviewing parents who lost their homes but still wanted their kids playing ball. I did a dozen interviews that day—only three made the paper, but the other nine gave me background information and, more importantly, helped me capture the vibe. (Don't just do the interviews you think will suffice for the story. Always ask that extra question or prod that extra source. It can only improve your story.)

In the coming weeks, I continued to conduct interviews— lunches with politicians, after-dinner phone conversations with coaches. Each interview helped clear up my foggy understanding of NORD.

One woman I found in previous stories was Nancy Broadhurst, who worked for the non-profit organization "Friends of NORD." She was connected to City Hall and had a fascinating outlook about NORD. She spent a day with me, driving me around town to the different NORD facilities.

Finally, I had some specific questions about money and employees and facilities that I could throw at City Hall. Cynthia Sylvain-Lear was helpful in getting me answers to a complex matter.

And, sure enough, I had traveled my thousand miles.

Now all I had to do was write the darn thing.

(Benjamin Hochman is a former sports writer for the *New Orleans Times-Picayune*. He is now a sports writer for *The Denver Post*.)

4

BEGINNINGS I

Basic Lead Writing

Based on a (mostly) true story. A novice reporter was assigned to cover the South High vs. North High baseball game. Understanding it was a heated rivalry, he did the necessary pre-reporting and memorization of each team's statistics. The reporter arrived a half-hour before the game, established himself in the bleachers behind home plate and intently watched as the players warmed up. With the three-inch, No. 2 pencil he lifted from the golf course during last week's tournament, he tallied every ball, strike, hit, out, and error in his spiral-bound Rawlings scorebook. As the game droned on and South began to dominate, the reporter's enthusiasm waned. This year's rivalry was a dud.

Afterward, the reporter spoke with Joe Sizemore, a senior who hit a two-run double in the fourth, and South's coach, Steve Turner. He also interviewed North coach, Bob Jackson, who was a bit surly after the loss and had little to say. (Note: all names have been changed to protect the guilty.)

When the reporter returned to the office, he approached the sports editor.

"Well, how was the game?" the sports editor inquired. The sports editor required his reporters, particularly the young ones, to tell him the story before they wrote a word. He knew if reporters "talked their stories out," their writing would be more focused. It helped reporters organize their thoughts.

"It was a blowout," the deflated reporter said. "South won, 8–0, scoring four runs in the fourth to break it open."

"Write it up," the sports editor said.

And so the reporter did.

Joe Sizemore's two-run double in a four-run fourth inning led the South High Rebels to an 8–0 victory against the North High Warriors on Friday afternoon at Schaffer Stadium.

South managed a 2–0 lead going into the fourth, but two walks, a hit batsman, and two hits accounted for the four runs.

"We were able to take advantage of a few mistakes and Joe really stepped up," South coach Steve Turner said. "We also got the pitching when we needed it."

The reporter tacked on an additional 12 paragraphs, carefully recapping the scoring and top performances. He wrote about the diving catch by South outfield Rob Caplan in the third, and the inning-ending double play in the fifth. The reporter supplemented the descriptions with standard quotes from the coaches.

Then, in the 15th paragraph, the reporter wrote, "South's starting pitcher Mike Turner did not allow a hit and only walked one batter."

Confident he had written a solid game story, the reporter took a few minutes to reead his work before sending it to the sports editor. The sports editor scrolled down, thinking it wasn't a bad effort. A blowout story is rather routine unless something extraordinary happens, and his young reporter seemed to capture the essence of what had occurred. That was until the editor read the final paragraph. "WHAT? ARE YOU TELLING ME THIS TURNER KID THREW A NO-HITTER AND YOU BURIED IT IN THE FINAL PARA-GRAPH?"

The reporter shrunk in his chair. In his diligence, he had overlooked Turner's no-hitter. While it was an impressive feat, the game was nonetheless a blowout, the reporter thought.

"Did you interview the kid?" the sports editor inquired.

"Uh, no. It didn't seem that important."

Of course, you're thinking, "How could the reporter be so stupid?" Sometimes, the story that should be written isn't the one being reported. And sometimes, the story is so obvious we fail to see it. The lead is the window into the story. Providing a clean, clear window allows the reader to see the rest of the story.

In this chapter, we'll discuss what to lead with and how you should approach that lead. While these tips specifically target game stories, they can be used in any type of story.

Identifying the Lead

Sometimes leads simply happen. Other times you have to search for the lead. If a reserve basketball player scores eight points in the final quarter to lead a 54–52 victory, she would be your lead. But what if six players scored eight points in the same victory, and none of them did anything spectacular in the final quarter? The lead would not be so clear-cut.

There are a number of ways to identify a story's lead. Try writing a simple headline that sums up the story. Be a bit more creative than, "South beats North." That says little and will not help with lead development.

What can be said about the game in a few words? "Turner tosses no-hitter in Rebel victory." It's not Hemingway, but it cuts to the heart of the story.

Sometimes leads can be found by writing a summary paragraph. What is the story about? Summarizing the story in 10 to 20 words will provide focus and help extract the lead. Leads can also be found by jotting down key words. What words seem to comprise the story? "No hits." "South win." "Sizemore double." Key words help sort through the minutia of information and identify the true story.

Talking with someone about the story can help formulate the lead as well. When sports fans discuss games, they generally do not start at the beginning. "Hey, Jim, you should have seen the Red Sox–Yankees game. In the first inning..." Unless the news happened in the first inning, fans usually begin with the drama. "Hey, Jim, Derek Jeter's two-run homer in the ninth beat the Sox, 4–3."

The story's lead is the foundation. On that foundation, the story can be constructed. While carpenters use studs, crossbeams, and rafters to frame the house, a good writer frames the story with facts, quotes, and statistics. Good writers, like good carpenters, realize the foundation sets the tone. They also know not to use a hammer when a screwdriver will do. In other words, do not write a lead that cannot be supported. If you write, "The two basketball teams slugged it out like a pair of heavyweight boxers," you'd better be able to support that statement. Although it might sound good, if the writer fails to follow through in comparing the game to a heavyweight fight, then the lead fails.

The Score Lead

The game story is the most basic type of sports story. The common belief is that you attend a sporting event, record the details, interview participants, and intertwine those elements into a story that provides the who, what, where, why, when, and how. To a large degree, that is the core of the gamer. But ascribing to the belief that the game story is comprised of statistics and play-by-play is an enormous and misguided presumption, particularly in the Internet age when game details can be made available instantaneously. A next day's newspaper game story that rehashes the game's basic elements (score, top scorer, team statistics, etc.) is not news. It's history. The story has little or no news value for the reader or the publication.

Nonetheless, there are sports editors who routinely scream, "Get the score in the lead, dammit!" And although readers expect to find the score early in a story, cluttering the lead with the score is self-defeating. It can be argued that anyone moderately interested in the event already knows the score after attending the game, watching television highlights, hearing it on the radio, viewing the sports scroll during the nightly newscast, or reading about the game on the Web. Newspaper reporters determined to write interesting stories must embrace the idea that the score is of no surprise to the readers. For a sports editor who makes such demands, convince him or her to post a summary story with the score in the lead on the newspaper's Web page. This way you can save the limited newspaper space to tell interesting stories that are not restricted by old news, such as the score.

Generally speaking, if the score does not appear until the third or fourth paragraph, and is preceded by a good anecdote, readers won't complain. Moving the score down in the story, and writing about some other element of the game, provides a surprise for the readers. Granted, sometimes the score is the news. If a football team is beaten by 70 points or a basketball team wins by 100, the score would be the headliner. That does not mean you forego good writing. For example:

> Eighteen first downs.
> Four-hundred sixty-two rushing yards.
> Seventy-six to 6.
> The 70-point North High victory was the most lopsided
> game in the history of North-South football rivalry.

There are plenty of places in journalism to bore readers. The sports section is not one of them. If one football team drops 76 points on another, finding something other than the score to report should be rather easy. A more interesting approach would be to put the game into historical context or lead with the running back that scored six touchdowns. Or better yet, write about the third-string quarterback who led an insignificant scoring drive in the final quarter. Although the game lacked excitement, it's the greatest game of all time for the third stringers. It might be the only time the benchwarmers get to play all season. And everyone likes the benchwarmer story.

Sometimes it's not the placement of the score but the lack of score that gets reporters in trouble. On occasion, a sports writer will simply forget to include the score. That is as egregious as leading with the score. This would be similar to a football player forgetting his protective cup. If you're playing full-contact sports, wear your cup. If you're writing game stories, remember to include the score.

The Turning Point Lead

Another possible lead, and probably the most common, is the turning point lead. If struggling for a lead, ask yourself, "What was the turning point?" Or better yet, ask the coach or the players. Sometimes what you might consider the turning point is different from what the coach thinks.

Close games typically have several turning points where momentum shifts between teams. In those cases, the final turning point will be the story's focus. Sometimes the game will come down to the final shot, possession, or at bat. If nothing of interest happens in those cases, work backward in determining the outcome. What the bejesus does that mean? Well, if Homer University beats Visitor College in women's volleyball three games to one, and the scores are 30–26, 26–30, 30–27 and 30–22, the turning point game appears to be Game 3. Homer won by three points, and a loss would have changed the momentum of the match. Other than closing the match with a victory, Game 4 was rather insignificant. With apologies to Matthew 19:30 in the New Testament, the last shall not always be first.

Or for instance, if a basketball player misses the final shot at the buzzer, and her team loses 47–46, the missed shot isn't as important as the 47th point. The importance lies in the final points.

The turning point could be one play or it could be a large segment of a game. Often turning points occur after half-time when teams are able to make adjustments. Identifying those adjustments can be crucial in identifying your lead. If you are unable to identify the adjustments but recognize a shift in momentum, ask the coach or players what adjustments were made.

The Assessment Lead

Attempting to get inside the heads of players is no easy task. Athletes, particularly exceptional athletes, react to situations without over-thinking them. Some call it instinct, and perhaps to some degree it is, but much of it is routine established through practice. At an early age, coaches ask players to assess their own performance. It's an attempt to get athletes to recognize and repeat good routines so when the situation arises in a game, the athlete will be prepared to react. A good sports editor will do the same with sports reporters in an effort to instill good routines.

So with that line of thinking, as a reporter you can ask a player to assess his or her performance: "How would you assess your performance tonight?" Don't make assumptions about what is good or bad. If you approach an athlete and say, "You seemed to lose your shooting touch in the second half. Why?" You have made the assumption that the basketball player lost his or her shooting touch and that there was a specific cause. The athlete might become defensive or offended, and your intent isn't to create a hostile situation. Allow the athlete to explain before drawing conclusions. That does not rule out asking tough questions. Just be certain the tough questions are not laden with assumption. Another way to ask that question would be, "How would you assess your shooting in the second half?" It puts the ball in his or her court, so to speak, and allows for an open dialogue between reporter and athlete.

One question to absolutely avoid is the "how do you feel?" question. To help eliminate the temptation to ask that question, we'll answer it for you: winning feels great and losing sucks. Asking an athlete to remember how it "felt" to score the winning touchdown is akin to asking you how it felt to write a lead that worked. Beyond, "It felt good," what more can be said? Attempt to be more thought-provoking than that.

Another approach to the assessment lead is comparing this game to the previous game. If a player had significantly different performances in each, inquire about it. "What was different in this game? Did you have a different routine before this game and if so what was it?" Build additional questions off the answers. Whether you label them superstitious or routines, most athletes have them. They eat certain foods on certain days, get dressed a certain way, wear certain clothes under their uniforms (Michael Jordan wore a pair of University of North Carolina shorts under his Chicago Bulls shorts), and the list goes on. Learning about those superstitions/routines and how an athlete changed them before a certain performance can certainly provide an interesting lead.

The Context Lead

Often, individual games have a larger meaning for a team. For the readers, you can put the game into context in terms of the season, the league or even team history. What does the game mean on the whole? There are certain games in a season that determine which course the team will take. Even during a 162-game baseball season, specific games alter a team's direction. What does a 16-inning victory do for a team? How about a loss to a rival in the bottom of the ninth? The larger context tells a more complete story.

Also, is it a rivalry game or a revenge game? Tread lightly on both accounts. Sometimes rivalry games can be real dogs (see the North High/South High baseball example) and sometimes the rivalry is between fans and not players, particularly long-running rivalries. People who no longer play, particularly among high schools, seem to have stronger feelings of rivalry than those who are actually playing. The "good old days" for the fans might be the Stone Age for the players.

Writing about revenge also requires a word of caution. Does one team actually take "revenge" upon another? Although there might be a deep-seated desire to beat a team it lost to previously, revenge is a bit strong. Revenge indicates vengeance or inflicting harm upon someone or something. Is that what is really happening?

An overall approach to what the game means in terms of the season can also be effective. How did the team standings change with the win or loss? Could the win or loss be a turning point in the season, particularly when examining the upcoming schedule? How does the win or loss change the momentum for the season? The coaches and players can and should provide context of one game in the larger sense of the season.

The History Lead

The history lead combines a few of the previous elements. The score could be a historical milestone, the turning point could be similar to previous games and the context could be compared to past seasons. In fact, you could probably find some historical component of almost any sporting event. But could does not mean should.

The problem with the history lead is it typically requires several paragraphs to explain past history before discussing present activity. In the process of linking the two, your readers might move on to something less taxing, such as cleaning the garage. For example:

> When the North High baseball team played South High last year, North's starting pitcher, Kyle Roberts, led the Warriors' 10–0 victory by tossing a two-hitter. Roberts again pitched against South in the District 5 tournament where he allowed three Rebel hits in the Warriors' 11-1 win.
>
> During the past eight meetings between the two teams, North has posted a 6–2 record, including a four-game win streak that included three double-digit victories.
>
> If Friday's game is any indication, maybe North's dominance over South has ended. South's starting pitcher, Mike Turner, threw a no-hitter as South beat North, 8–0.

Chapter 1 of *War and Peace* is shorter. It takes far too long to get to the point. Instead, the author could have written:

> During the past eight meetings, the North High baseball team has dominated South High by winning six of those games, including four straight.
>
> The Rebels were able to end that dominance Friday when South's starting pitcher, Mike Turner, threw a no-hitter in the Rebels' 8–0 victory.

More details about the previous eight games can be included later in the story but for the lead, it is best to keep it short and concise.

When using a historical approach, remember there is short-term history and long-term. Short term usually requires less explanation because people reading your story probably have some recollection of recent past events. Long term would require more explanation because the older the history the less recall and awareness there is of past events.

The best time to use a history lead is when the history is of major consequence to the present story. It can be far too easy to rely upon history to bail you out when you are struggling with a lead, so use it sparingly.

The Quote Lead

When discussing quote leads, long-time *Florida Sun-Sentinel* sports writer and copy editor Ray Murray says, "The only quote lead you should use is, 'I'm back,' Jesus said."

Murray, now an assistant professor at Oklahoma State University, clearly emphasizes the rarity of using a quote lead. His point is certainly one to consider. The quote needs to be unique in the greatest sense of the word. As you well know, "unique" means one of a kind.

In sports, unique quotes are hard to come by. Sportspeak dominates the language of coaches and athletes. But even unique phrases used as leads fail most of the time. Without context, the quote is lost on the readers. For instance this quote from long-time Florida State University football coach Bobby Bowden, "They're getting the bonnets on the right people." It might be interesting, but what does it mean? Do not leave your readers guessing. Yogi Berra has provided a multitude of interesting and entertaining quotes (see http://rinkworks.com/said/yogiberra.shtml) but his comments usually create confusion. For instance, Berra's, "If you come to a fork in the road, take it," quote will lead readers down the wrong path—or at least a confusing one.

So the general rule with quote leads is avoid them. Naked quotes without context create far more problems than they solve. But, as with all journalism rules, there are exceptions. The trick is identifying the exceptions. In 1995, after quitting professional baseball, Michael Jordan made a two-word statement announcing his return to the NBA. It said, "I'm back." Although Jordan isn't Jesus, the magnitude of his return meant salvation for the Chicago Bulls and their fans. So, in that case several sports writers used the quote lead.

Additional Tips for Leads

There are a few other leads you probably should avoid because, quite honestly, they do not provide good stories. They include the weather lead, the "Senior Night" lead and the homecoming lead. These are regular events that happen each year. Attempting to construct an interesting story around the weather or "Senior Night" detracts from the real story. Both teams play in the same weather so how does weather really play a factor in the outcome? Of course, sometimes one team does benefit from the weather but emphasizing the weather can detract from the real context of the game. Most times if the weather is the lead (a hurricane, tornado, blizzard, earthquake, etc.), the story is a weather story and not a game story. Just ask the writers covering Game 3 of the 1989 Oakland Athletics–San Francisco Giants World Series.

The "Senior Night" lead has been used so often that it could be considered a cliché. If you are so desperate as to resort to the "Senior Night" lead then you are not working hard enough to find the real story. These leads usually take on one of two tones: "The seniors stepped up on Senior Night" or "On a night designated to honor the seniors, it was the underclassmen who stole the show." Yawn. Do not fall into this trap. It's a disservice to sports journalism, the teams, the fans, the seniors, and your parents.

With a 162-game schedule, Major League Baseball beat writers have the daunting task of writing dozens of leads each season. They utilize several different approaches in writing their leads. Some work and some don't, but writers are always testing creative techniques to lure readers into their stories. The beat writers are also writing to an audience that might have watched or listened to the game. If they can discover interesting ways to write compelling leads, then you can as well.

Professional Perspective
By Jessica Hopp
The Tennessean

So, you have a quote list ripe with more winners than a vegetable garden primed for the county fair.

You have an array of scene setters so colorful they make the lights of the Vegas Strip look like the dying bulbs of a corner bar.

And you are sure that buried within your stacks of facts and files of figures you have the makings of a Pulitzer.

There's just one problem...you don't know where to begin.

Don't worry. You are not alone.

Writing a strong lead is one of the most essential—and therefore one of the most stressful—things a journalist does. Because it helps readers determine whether they want to continue to read a story the first several sentences are critical—they have to scream for Terrell Owens-like attention (and do it without the aid of pompons or a Sharpie).

But how do you craft that calling sign in both a creative and concise way? First, you must determine the information that is most compelling.

Figure 4.1 Jessica Hopp.

I know, easier said than done, but here's a secret: what's most interesting to you will also likely be most interesting to your mom, your best friend, and your reader. So try this. After an interview seek out someone who will listen as you recount your latest interview and start telling him or her the story.

What did you start with? The surprise? The emotion? Character, setting, conflict? Whatever it was, it was likely the strongest element of your story and a perfect lead. (Or at least a good starting point.)

Of course, there are other things to consider after the subject matter bubbles to the surface. So here are some other quick suggestions:

1   Don't stare at a blank screen. If the perfect words aren't there, write something simple and come back to it later. That will keep you from wasting time and perhaps allow the creative juices to meld into a tasteful concoction.
2   Don't stray from the point. Anecdotal and scene-setting leads can be compelling, but it's good to at least allude to the news element early.

3 Keep in mind the basics. The who, what, why, when, where, and how are always good reference points to keeping to the story's purpose.

4 Beware of starting from the beginning. Most of the time there isn't the space nor is there enough captivating information to tell an entire chronological story. Best to start at a critical moment.

5 Don't fret. Although, as writers, we would like to (and should strive to) write a knock-out lead every time, sometimes we only get a Tyson-like bite of perfection. The good news is there's always another round.

(Jessica Hopp is a sports writer for
The Tennessean.)

Professional Perspective
By Kyle Nagel
Dayton Daily News

It took me 20 minutes to come up with this lead.

I sat here, pondering the question of what makes a good lead. I stared. I shifted in my chair. I got up and walked around. Sometimes, that's how it goes. Or sometimes you just sit down and start writing, almost unconsciously.

In sports writing, the lead can be even more critical, because readers expect some of the best writing in the paper to be on the sports page.

A few thoughts:

• Anecdotes. You are, after all, telling a story. Particularly with athletes, who don't often show their personal lives to a mass audience, people want to know how they dress, what their houses look like, what you see, what you smell. In an age when television has allowed people the ability to see the whole world with their eyes, give them a chance to experience what you went through to get the story. That's why you're there. You have access they can't get.

• Details. Instead of writing, "Maurice Clarett allegedly committed a robbery at a place you wouldn't expect," try this:

Figure 4.2 Kyle Nagel.

"The robbery allegedly took place directly across the inter-section from the Franklin County Government Center, the heart of the judicial services here and home to the county prosecutor's office, and the courtroom where Maurice Clarett was arraigned.

"The law enforcement theme extends through the neighbor-hood. Two bail bonds businesses are nearby and, around the corner, there's the Jury Room, a bar with OSU-painted windows that asks passers-by to treat themselves to a 'Hung Jury.'"

- Play on words. One sign of intelligent writing is creativity. Instead of, "Eric Steinbach came to the Bengals when fans weren't as excited about the team," try:

   "Eric Steinbach came to Cincinnati at a time when things were more Boo Dem than Who Dey."

- Personification. A useful literary tool for making a point is giving an inanimate object human qualities and emotions. For instance:

   "At least during this one lunch, Martin Nance is a talker. He's usually a laugher. A smiler. Not so much a talker. But

45 minutes into a conversation in a Miami University dining hall, Nance's pasta is getting lonely."
(Kyle Nagel is a sports enterprise reporter for the *Dayton Daily News*.)

5

BEGINNINGS II

Advanced Lead Writing

Regarding sports journalism, legendary college basketball coach Bobby Knight once said, "All of us learn to write in the second grade. Most of us go on to greater things." While some sports writers have argued that most adult men named Robert no longer answer to "Bobby" after second grade, Knight makes an interesting point.

Writing, all writing, is a work in progress. Producing good journalism is the constant motivation of good writers, or at least it should be. Writers are in search of the perfect word, phrase, sentence, paragraph, and story. For those who are fortunate to capture that literary lightning, there's still a nagging voice that says, "OK big shot, what do you have for tomorrow's paper?" Sports editors never let up.

Chapter 4 outlined a few devices in establishing a story's lead. Although those techniques are most useful with game stories, they can be used in other stories as well, such as previews, follow-ups, sidebars, analysis, columns, and features. Nonetheless, there are other lead options as well. Good storytelling begins with the first word and ends with the last. It's the process of stringing together interesting, related pieces of information and building one word, sentence, and paragraph off the other.

But before writing a story, two questions need to be answered:

1   Why is the story being written?
2   For whom is it being written?

If the answer to those questions are "because my sports editor said so" and "my sports editor," the story is destined to fail. Not all stories will be candidates for the "Best American Sports Writing" series, but that should not diminish your effort. Each assignment provides the opportunity to write something interesting. A few years ago, a sports writer was assigned to cover a Catholic League eighth-grade basketball championship. The sports editor did not want a game story but a feature about the top player in the league. After watching three quarters of unimpressive basketball, the writer returned to the office. "There's really no story there," he told the editor. So the story died. A few years later, the player was a freshman starter on an NCAA Division I championship team and eventually played professionally. Although hindsight is 20/20, foresight has far greater value. Looking beyond the surface of the story will resonate in good story telling.

This chapter will assist in further lead development for all types of stories and provide tips in digging beneath the surface to find the story's roots.

Avoiding "Crop Dust" Journalism

A common mistake among sports writers is the act of crop dusting the top of stories and missing the deeper elements. The mistake is somewhat understandable. A sports writer is told to write a feature. He or she interviews the source, the coach, and teammates. After writing a lead, adding some statistics and quotes, abracadabra, a feature magically appears. Well, it's not so much a story as an article or maybe just a few paragraphs of disconnected information. Think of SportsCenter without the video highlights.

Crop dusting is common for several reasons. Time constraints are usually first on the list, followed by the lack of story identification. When a sports writer went to interview a high school all-star basketball player, she said, "Why are you doing a story about me? We're all all-stars." Good point, one the writer hadn't considered.

Sometimes athletes are uncooperative, and there are different types of uncooperation. At the high school level, an athlete might deflect every question about him or her and only talk in terms of the team. The quotes usually sound as if they came directly from the Boy Scout oath: "If not for my teammates...," "It was a team effort," "I'm only as good as my teammates." Although the humility can be appreciated, it makes for lame storytelling. Preparing for the story (see Chapter 3) can assist in breaking this pattern. Sometimes, asking a totally bizarre question can break the athlete of the "team" spell: "If you were a tree, what kind of tree would you be?" If the response is, "If it weren't for the other trees in the forest, I would just be an ordinary tree," you'll have to try a different tact.

At the college level, lack of cooperation comes in different packages. Sports information personnel can be obstacles to digging beneath the surface. Restrictions about when and where to interview an athlete can limit the information gathering process. Some college coaches close practices to the media. Others limit media access. Sports writers have been banned from college football practices after writing a story that displeased the coach. Coaches will routinely remind writers, "You are guests at my practices." Translation: do not write about trick plays, player injuries, offensive or defensive formations, position changes or fights between players. Coaches are concerned that reporters will provide the opposing team with "classified" information. A reporter's job is to report the news. Keeping secrets contradicts that premise. The question you need to answer is, "What is news?" Is it really important to report that two starting players fought in practice? Probably not, unless during the fight one player tears a hamstring and is out for the season. And those decisions should not be made alone. Consult your sports editor early and often.

College athletes generally are not allowed to speak with the media without prior approval from the athletic department. And sometimes, the university requires that interviews be conducted in the presence of a sports information director. Conducting an interview in that setting is similar to trying to kiss your prom date in front of her parents. That's particularly true when the sports information director is interrupting and censoring which questions you can ask. So, if possible, avoid these scenarios. Build rapport and trust with the sports information director's office so interviews can truly be one-on-one. If that fails, interview people of knowledge who are not restricted by the athletic department. Parents, friends, siblings, and relatives are free of athletic department censorship. And besides, good reporters would be interviewing these people regardless of accessibility of the athlete.

At the professional level, the saturation of media coverage restricts original reporting. Saturation also causes media fatigue with some athletes. They become weary of answering reporters' questions and resort to "canned" answers. Also, with millions of dollars in endorsement deals on the line, professional athletes provide "safe" answers. Safe answers are usually boring, redundant, and provide no insight. Handlers, such as agents, attorneys, and financial consultants, prefer safe answers. Soft-drink companies and fast-food restaurants prefer to have athletes with good, clean images. The belief is, "The comments might be boring but at least they are not offensive." An outspoken athlete receives fewer endorsements but is far more quotable. Usually for a professional athlete, money trumps good quotes.

In the movie *Bull Durham*, catcher Crash Davis (Kevin Costner) coaches pitching phenom "Nuke" LaLoosh (Tim Robbins) on how to conduct interviews. LaLoosh was a loose cannon so Davis provided him with some safe quotes.

Davis: It's time to work on your interviews.
LaLoosh: My interviews? What do I gotta do?
Davis: You're going to have to learn your clichés. You're going to have to study them. You're going to have to know them. They're your friends. Write this down. "We gotta play them one day at a time."

LaLoosh: It's pretty boring.

Davis: Of course it's boring. That's the point. Write it down. "I'm just happy to be here. I hope I can help the ball club. I just want to give it my best shot, and the good Lord willing, things will work out."

No one ever said journalism was easy. Avoiding crop dust journalism takes work. The payoff will be a memorable story with interesting details instead of an article of loosely connected paragraphs. But, first, we need to develop the lead.

Straight Leads

Straight leads are similar to utility infielders—they're not flashy but they get the job done. Most straight leads are written on deadline or when newspaper space is minimal. Straight leads also primarily apply to game stories. If a sports editor assigns you to write a feature or enterprise story, he or she will usually make space for it, so a straight lead isn't necessary.

Generally, straight leads should be less than 25 words. Often they will include the basic elements of the game: Teams. Where? When? Score. Top performers. In fact, straight leads are so routine that it could be a fill-in-the-blank exercise:

_____ scored _____ points to lead _____

to a _____ victory against _____ on _____

night in _____.

The Associated Press is well known for its straight leads on game stories. Because the AP distributes stories to thousands of media sources, timeliness is an issue. AP writers usually follow the straight lead story with a write-through that uses one of the other lead techniques. Straight leads are also a staple of online writing.

Although sports writers do not necessarily enjoy writing the straight lead, it allows the reader to receive the information quickly. It's also the most non-biased of lead writing. A fill-in-the-blank lead leaves no room for showing favoritism toward one team or another.

Anecdotal Leads

An anecdote is a short story. In journalism, anecdotes are included in larger stories. Telling an interesting anecdote provides a glimpse into a

47

person's life. It's like a supermarket sampler: it gives you a taste without spoiling your dinner. The anecdote is a slice describing a person's character without revealing the entire story.

Anecdotes propel stories forward and keep the reader engaged. They allow readers to build relationships with the story's subject and create understanding. It's a good way to "show" and not just "tell" the story. For instance, saying a player is a team leader says little. Writing how the player leads is far more effective:

> Three weeks before fall practice officially began, Shawn O'Neal organized non-mandatory captain's practices. He directed drills, coached offensive and defensive formations, and even issued punishment when players messed up. And the practices were non-mandatory in the same sense that registering for military service is "non-mandatory" when turning 18.

The anecdote tells us that O'Neal is demanding, disciplined and has great knowledge of the game. Those are understandable leadership skills far more telling than, "Shawn O'Neal is a team leader."

While mid-story anecdotes keep the story moving, anecdotes as leads get the story rolling. They immediately grab the readers' interest. Consider the following example from the *Kansas City Star*:

> FLUSHING MEADOWS, N.Y. – A man burst into the National Tennis Center locker room, looking harried. He had $1.1 million burning a hole in his pocket.
> "Have you seen Roger?" he asked.
> "Uh, he's over there."
> "Do you know if he wants the prize money tonight?"
> Winning Grand Slams has become that familiar for Roger Federer.

It's short, concise, and develops a mental picture of the event, which in this case is the U.S. Open. Also, consider the language: "burst," "harried," "burning a hole in his pocket." Those are common words or phrases we've all heard before. It creates an association between the anecdote and the reader. "Burning a hole in his pocket" creates the image of a person who cannot rid himself of money quick enough. Of course, who honestly wants to be quickly relieved of $1.1 million? The anecdote works because it's saying, "Federer wins so often that a million bucks appears to be chump change." Or at least that's the public perception. It's relatively safe to say Federer accepted his prize money.

Other anecdotes take more time to develop. The trick is to use strong words and descriptive language to keep the reader interested, such as this example from the *Dayton Daily News*:

OXFORD, Ohio – Josh Betts stood in a parking lot on a lazy night several years ago when something whizzed past him. Something thrown as a joke, probably inspired by boredom. He looked up to see a group of kids hop into a car and speed into the darkness.

Betts and a friend slipped into his car to follow. They blazed across Vandalia streets, easily hitting 90 mph. Then Betts saw brake lights. The road was ending.

He smashed his own brakes and swerved to the left but missed turning onto the crossroad. The car left the street, slid down a grassy drop-off, spun full circle and came to a rest.

Shaken, Betts got out and surveyed the scene.

"To the right, where we went left, there were huge trees," said Betts, adjusting his red Miami University ballcap in a quiet restaurant booth recently. "If I would've gone in there, I would've been dead. If I would've turned right..."

Betts thinks about that night a lot. Then he thinks about opportunities, and the one he has in front of him. Saturday, Betts, a junior Vandalia Butler graduate, will become Miami's starting quarterback when the RedHawks host Indiana State.

Anecdotes work well as long as the anecdote relates to the larger story. Writing about a soccer player's hobby to refurbish classic cars is meaningless unless it can be related to his soccer. There must be a direct connection between the anecdote and the story. If not, the anecdote will be lost on the readers and only create confusion.

Descriptive Leads

Descriptive leads or scene setters allow the reader to be a part of the action. It gives the reader a front-row seat in the story. Good descriptive leads can make the reader feel as if he or she were watching a movie unfold before them. Obviously descriptive leads are flush with details and information, similar to this lead from the (Nashville) Tennessean:

Andrew Bumbalough was strolling around Target picking up a few things yesterday afternoon.

One of the things he was on the prowl for was a USA Today. A Mom just loves to see her son's name in print.

Bumbalough, a Brentwood Academy graduate and Georgetown signee, was one of 50 male athletes to be named to the All-USA High School Track and Field Team.

It's easy to visualize this high school athlete "strolling" the aisles of Target, unwilling to ask for assistance but certain of what he's searching for. Again, notice the strong language: "strolling," "prowl," "loves to see." It personifies characteristics of the larger story while making implications about the young man, such as his thoughtfulness for his mother or his mother's pride. Bumbalough's actions are not without thought and consideration, and neither are the writer's.

Not all descriptive leads have deeper meaning. Some are simply meant to recreate an atmosphere. For instance this lead from the *Toledo Blade*:

> To stand in the outfield seats during the home run derby practically requires bringing a glove. Except if you're Hens' fan Brent Thober. During batting practice for the Promedica Health System Home Run Derby, Thober and his wife Stephanie stood behind the right field fence among the throng of kids trying to claim the home run balls.

Some of the descriptions in this lead are left to the imagination; kids excitedly running around chasing baseballs; a pair of grown-ups towering over the kids; baseballs zipping above the open baseball field of grass and dirt and landing beyond the outfield wall. Some details can be left to the imagination, allowing readers to fill in the blanks, but the basic structure must be provided. In the above example, the writer does not need to construct the sound the bat makes when colliding with the ball. Writing "thwack!" is not essential unless there is a greater purpose:

> As soon as the ash baseball bat cracks the white baseball, the kids are startled into action. "Thwack!" Instantly, the glove-wearing children looked skyward waiting for the sphere to clear the 12-foot outfield wall. When it did, a chaotic scrambled ensued. The owner of the home run derby ball held it high, allowing others to marvel at his souvenir.

The "thwack!" is the ignition to the action. It's the starting gun of the race to capture the elusive home run balls. The next sentence could read, "During Monday's home run derby, nobody provided more scrambling than the thwack of the Texas Rangers, Josh Hamilton." It ties the descriptive elements together and moves the story forward.

Descriptive leads are not restricted to current events. Describing past events or even abstract ideas or concepts can be just as effective as the physical present. For example, this lead from the *Scranton Times-Tribune*:

The champ knew brutality. He felt it in the ring, he saw it in the war, and when he had a chance to escape it, he tucked himself deep in the Poconos, where the snow falls gently and the water ripples with grace.

Out on Lake Wallenpaupack, the champ settled into a life with no need for a clinched fist, in a place far from the savage world that allowed his early retirement.

It wasn't always his home, but he made it as such. It wasn't always his life, but it's the life he chose.

It's the life he fought for.

Setting the scene is a relatively easy way to get the readers involved in the story. Just be certain the descriptive lead complements the greater story.

Foreshadowing

A foreshadowing lead is one that indicates something more will happen. It alludes to the bigger story by teasing the reader. It provides limited details, yet is interesting enough to prevent frustration. The foreshadowing lead can be as simple as:

For Jackson High School, the scoring started early and ended late.

It creates intrigue and encourages the reader to think, "I wonder what that means?" Foreshadowing is like a neon billboard that says, "Interesting story ahead." A sports writer at the *Arizona Daily Star* used foreshadowing to invite readers into this story:

David Young was seeking balance.

Two weeks ago Friday, he received the key to it. Two days after that, he tested it himself, curious whether he would feel the way he used to when he was on a bicycle.

The writer begins discussing balance and leads the reader to the bicycle. But there's more. Similar to how music in horror movies creates heart-pumping tempo, the writer foreshadows to a larger issue. What's the big deal about a guy and his bike? So, the writer continues:

Young walked outside his home in Kenosha, Wis., pulling his bicycle behind him. He climbed onto the seat and swung his legs around the frame. He reached one arm out and leaned on his black Jeep Cherokee, afraid he might fall.

After a few moments, he pulled his arm back in and placed it on his handlebars. The balance was still there, after a lifetime's worth of trauma crammed into the past six months.

"It was," Young said, "like riding a bicycle."

The description paints a picture of this man carefully climbing onto his bicycle. Again, the reader is being enticed by words that spark the imagination. The tempo of information, similar to horror movie music, lures the reader down an intriguing path. "There must be more to the story." And it continues:

> In April, Young had finished first in El Tour de Phoenix, a race put on by El Tour de Tucson founder Richard DeBernardis. After finishing second a year earlier, Young, 22, had stayed at DeBernardis' home during the winter to train for the race. His racing future, though clouded by a promise to his mother to return to college, was bright.

The paragraph breaks away from the description and foreshadowing to provide context. It says, "This story is important and if you keep reading, you'll learn why." It also says that an experienced cyclist should not have difficulty finding balance on a new bicycle. So, why does Young? The author provides the payoff:

> Young will ride in the 35-mile event of today's El Tour de Tucson. It will be a far different experience from his past races. He will ride without his left leg.

He will ride without his left leg. It's the payoff. It clarifies why the previous paragraphs were written. And although it brings resolution to the lead, it also opens a new path of intrigue. How does a one-legged cyclist cycle?

Foreshadowing establishes an unwritten contract between the reader and the writer. The reader agrees to read on if the writer agrees to payoff.

Multiple-Element Lead

Multiple-element leads include more than one idea in the lead. Game stories will oftentimes contain multiple elements. Those elements can include information about the team and a player or coach, the current game and the larger context (how it affected league standings) or a multitude of other elements. Although there is more than one element in the lead, the elements must be connected to avoid confusing the reader:

The Jefferson Bluejackets not only won Friday's game but earned a piece of the Southern League title as well.

The lead introduces two aspects of Friday's game: 1, The Bluejackets win; 2, Jefferson will at least be league co-champions this year. The writer would need to determine which is more important. Jefferson does not earn a share of the championship without Friday's win. But, Friday's win is just one game in a season. So the next paragraph could continue the multiple-element aspect of the story.

Jefferson improved to 10–1 on the season with its 42–17 victory against Central and can win the league championship outright next week against Highland. Highland is also 10–1 after beating Jackson on Friday.

The next few paragraphs can discuss Jefferson's win against Central in detail. Later in the story, details of the upcoming matchup with Highland would be prudent. The story would include both elements—the news and the larger context.

Similar to many of the leads discussed earlier, the multiple-element lead can mix with other types of leads, such as the foreshadowing in this *Toledo Blade* story:

The scouts wanted to start their sleepover, and the Mud Hens were nearly out of pitchers.

Josh Phelps heard the cries.

In the longest game innings-wise in the history of Fifth Third Field, Phelps hit a two-run home run to left in the bottom of the 16th inning to lift Toledo to a 2–0 win over Syracuse.

"It was a plea from both benches, both sides," Phelps said. "We were looking for lightning to strike, and fortunately it happened for us."

Lance Davis, who began the year in the Hens' starting rotation, pitched the final four innings for his first win of the season. Rodney Ormond took the loss for Syracuse.

"Our guys pitched very well tonight for a long time," Hens manager Larry Parrish said. "And then at the end, Lance just kept going out there and getting them out."

Many of the sold-out crowd of 10,300 stuck around for the 4-hour, 27-minute contest. Planned afterward were a high school home run derby, fireworks, and a scout sleepover on the field.

The story begins with a multiple-element lead but also some foreshadowing. The subsequent paragraphs fill in the details of the elements and then includes the payoff sentence: *Planned afterward were a high school home run derby, fireworks, and a scout sleepover on the field.*

Multiple-element leads should be used with caution. A common mistake is including too much information in the lead and losing the readers.

Leads make or break stories. The only bad stories are the ones that are poorly reported and written. Sometimes a good story is buried beneath the lead but the readers never get that far. And what was a good lead once might not be a good lead today. In October 1924, Grantland Rice wrote one of the most well-known sports leads ever. After the Notre Dame football team beat Army 13–7, Rice wrote:

> Outlined against a blue, gray October sky the Four Horsemen rode again.
>
> In dramatic lore they are known as Famine, Pestilence, Destruction, and Death. These are only aliases. Their real names are: Stuhldreher, Miller, Crowley, and Layden. They formed the crest of the South Bend cyclone before which another fighting Army team was swept over the precipice at the Polo Grounds this afternoon as 55,000 spectators peered down upon the bewildering panorama spread out upon the green plain below.

Although lauded as one of the great sports leads of all time, Mr. Rice might have had difficulty today finding a sports editor so accepting of his prose. Consequently, the lead would be edited:

> Outlined against a blue, gray October sky the Four Horsemen rode again. *(What are you talking about? Don't give me a weather lead? "Four Horsemen rode again" is a cliché.)*
>
> In dramatic lore *(Who says?)* they are known as Famine, Pestilence, Destruction, and Death *(What is the focus of your story?)*. These are only aliases. Their real names are: Stuhldreher, Miller, Crowley, and Layden *(Where are the first names? Do not assume everyone knows these players.)* They formed the crest of the South Bend cyclone *(Cyclone? What cyclone? There was a cyclone at the football game? That sounds like the lead.)* before which another fighting Army team was swept over the precipice *(Really? Did any get killed?)* at the Polo Grounds this afternoon as 55,000 spectators peered *(Who says?)* down upon the bewildering panorama *(What is this? I thought this was a football game.)* spread out upon the green plain below. *(Do you mean the field?)*

Although the editing is a bit dramatic, the point is obvious. Overwriting a lead will lose readers. In 1924, Rice had an attentive audience. Radio was in its infancy, the first televised football game would not happen for another 15 years and the information superhighway wasn't even a cow path. Readers spent more time reading the newspaper when Rice wrote his lead. The Readership Institute reports that the average reader spends 27 minutes with the newspaper per day. Would today's readers truly want to spend time deciphering Rice's lead?

Sometimes writers fall into the trap of writing beyond their reporting. There have been times with anecdotal or descriptive leads when a writer has taken some liberties with the facts. Some would call these exaggerations. Others would say they are lies. Whatever the label, it's not factual writing but fictional. It might make for a more interesting lead but straying from the truth is always a dangerous proposition in journalism. So stick to what you know and do not rely upon what you think you know. Providing accurate details speaks to your credibility. And besides, sometimes fact is stranger than fiction.

Before moving forward with the story, there are two final questions that need to be asked:

1   How successfully does the lead represent the essence of the story?
2   How well does it encourage the reader to read on?

Answering those questions can save time when developing the remainder of the story. It'll also keep the copy editors off your back. Because they can be a surly, unpleasant bunch, copy editors are the litmus test for good leads. If a copy editor likes the lead, you can be sure the readers probably will as well.

6

BEGINNINGS III

Overused Leads

Perhaps the most important thing to keep in mind when writing sports stories is that there is a fine line between clever and cute. One reason that a clever idea crosses the boundary to cute is that it has been done before (maybe hundreds of times) and therefore has been transformed into a cliché.

Clichés can enter into stories anywhere, but they are especially a problem in the lead. Overused leads can make stories appear dull and trite. Readers may stop reading stories if they think that a lead is stale. If a writer doesn't take the time to come up with a fresh angle to a story, why should a reader take the time to read the story?

Here are some types of leads to avoid.

The Quick Trip to the Almanac

This lead shows how long it's been since something has happened:

> The last time the Chicago Cubs won the World Series, World War I hadn't happened, Theodore Roosevelt was president, and Russia was still ruled by Czars.

The purpose of this type of lead is to get the reader to think, "Wow, that's a mighty long time ago..." The problem is that, usually, the list of historical events has nothing to do with the topic of the story (unless President Roosevelt put a hex on the Cubs). The lead therefore takes too long to get to the main point by emphasizing irrelevant facts. Readers also often know the point you're trying to make. (All Cubs fans know it had been a long time since they had won a World Series. They don't need reminding.) And since Americans—especially young Americans—are relatively poor at understanding historical events, some readers won't understand the point.

This lead, of course, can be ridiculous in some cases, especially if the tone of the article does not work well with the main topic, as in:

Disco music ruled the air waves, Watergate was an obscure hotel, Spiro Agnew was vice president and the Washington Senators had just moved to Texas. The year was 1973—the last time more than a dozen teenagers died from sports-related injuries.

Don't bury the lead by introducing unrelated information in an attempt to make a point that could be made much more simply.

The One-Word Lead

One of the first rules beginning journalism students learn is that leads— for news and features alike—need to be short. Beginning reporting textbooks usually argue that leads should be no longer than 35 words, with some exceptions. Sometimes, writers take this rule to an extreme by using a single word as their lead. The idea is that the one word will tease the reader into reading further into a story. However, seldom do we find one word that completely summarizes a story. And often, readers will be so confused by the word that they will stop reading entirely. For example:

Ugly.
That's the only way to describe the Chicago Bears' 3–0 victory over Dallas on Sunday.

Again, these leads can be ridiculous in some cases, such as:

Dead.
That's what former Yankee great George Wilhelm was after suffering a heart attack Monday night.

Or:

Pizza.
That's what Tim Duncan wanted to eat after he scored 45 points leading the San Antonio Spurs to a 110–108 victory over New Jersey Tuesday night.

Teaser-type leads can be dangerous because some readers will not take the bait. Instead of being lured into a story, some readers will simply stop reading.

The "It" Lead

This is another type of teaser lead, meant to lure a reader into reading a story by describing some unnamed person or object. The reader is forced to guess what the "clues" refer to, as in:

> It's orange, it's round and it's coming to Kemper Arena Friday night.
> It's a basketball, and it'll be bouncing through the Kemper basketball hoops when the NCAA Midwest Regional begins with three games.

Or:

> It's green, it smells awful, and it glows in the dark.
> It's toxic waste, and a bunch of it was found near the Meadowlands Stadium Tuesday night.

Don't play games with readers. Reporters are supposed to provide information to readers, not make them guess what they're writing about.

The "That's The Word" Lead

This type of lead concentrates on information from a source but delays the identification of the source until the second sentence. It is meant to get the most important information in the first sentence, but teases the reader into going further into the story to get important, significant details. For instance:

> The knee is finally healed. That's the word from running back Priest Holmes, who returned to the Kansas City starting lineup Sunday and scored the winning touchdown in a 24–20 victory over Oakland.

The lead, though, harkens back to nursery rhymes:

> The sky is falling. That's the word from Chicken Little, claiming a piece of the sky hit her on the head Monday.

The "Leaning Back in the Chair" Lead

This type of lead tries to bring the reader into a story by painting a picture of a post-game moment. The lead, however, concentrates on aspects that are totally outside the reason behind a victory or loss. An example:

> Coach Steve Spurrier leaned back in his chair and smiled after being asked to explain his decision to try a 67-yard field goal with five seconds left in South Carolina's 67–0 victory over Kentucky Sunday.

Obviously, the fact that a coach leaned back in his chair had nothing to do with the game. In addition, readers don't really care about what happened when a reporter asked a question. They want to know what happened in the game. Why did South Carolina beat Kentucky? Chair leaning didn't play a role.
  Or:

> Coach Bill Broyles leaned back in his chair and smiled after being asked to explain why he murdered three city employees in a fit of rage after Sunday's loss to Miami.

Leading with someone leaning back in his chair makes the more important information (like three murders) of secondary importance.

The Question Lead

Readers don't want to be involved in stories. They read stories for information. They do not want to be asked for information they do not have. Writers using questions in their stories also run the risk of having readers stop reading because they don't care about the answer. Question leads are thus usually ineffective. For example:

> Why would a coach kick a field goal with a 67–0 lead? (Answer: How should I know? You tell me.)

> Want to know why the Tampa Bay Rays defeated Kansas City Sunday? (Answer: Well, um, not really.)

> Where are the best hot dogs in the National League? (Answer: Shouldn't you tell me?)

Often, the question lead can be eliminated by concentrating on the answer to the question. For example:

> Why would a coach kick a field goal with a 67–0 lead? South Carolina's Steve Spurrier said he did it to send a message to the Kentucky Wildcats that his team now firmly controls this rivalry.

This lead could be changed to:

> South Carolina coach Steve Spurrier wanted to send a message to the Kentucky Wildcats that his team now firmly controls this rivalry. So with five seconds left and South Carolina ahead, 67–0, Spurrier had his team kick a field goal...

Notice how the second lead gives information that the first lead asks the reader to provide. The two leads make the same point. The second lead, though, concentrates on the "why" of the story immediately.

The Uncommonly Common Lead

This lead tries to emphasize conflict where, in reality, little conflict exists. It tries to show how a person, team, or object is different from similar people, teams, and objects. Since no two entities are exactly the same, the contrasts can often be meaningless:

> Priest Holmes isn't like your typical running back. While most running backs drive sports cars and talk as fast as they run, Holmes drives a sports car and talks slowly.

Other times, the contrasts can be absurd:

> Sleaze Dollarsigns isn't like your typical college football coach. While most coaches try to follow NCAA rules, Dollarsigns prefers to pay players and bribe officials.

This type of lead again is slow in developing. Is the point of the story that someone is "different" from other people? That should be obvious. What is the point of the story?

The Unusual Usual Lead

The opposite of the uncommonly common lead, this lead concentrates on how people, teams, and objects are extremely similar to other people, teams, and objects. The lead is followed by the reason the entity is somehow different, as in:

> At first glance, Steve Spurrier looks like your typical football coach. He has ulcers and a nasty temper and drives a huge, gas-guzzling car.

But he's anything but normal when it comes to coaching football.

Or:

At first glance, Charles Manson looks like your typical mass-murderer. He's scary...

Since this lead concentrates on similarities, it fails to provide a strong news peg. Someone looks like everyone else? Where's the news in that? While contrast is introduced in the second paragraph, the first sentence sounds like we've read this before. Give readers a fresher lead that they haven't seen before.

The "Not Alone" Lead

A subset of the uncommonly common lead, this lead begins with a description of something that sounds unusual, but is followed by a sentence that shows that it's very common. For example:

David Ortiz thought that the New York Yankees' pitchers were purposely trying to hit him every time he stepped to the plate.
He's not alone.

Closely related to the "not alone" lead is the "no exception" lead. Again, the writer tries to show contrast when there really isn't any:

Most home run hitters lift tons of weights and drink gallons of vitamin supplements. Tim Johnson is no exception.

The Common Thread Lead

This is another teaser-type lead, giving a list of seemingly unrelated objects and forcing the reader to guess how they are related. Often phrased in the form of a question, this type of lead again involves the reader in the story, running the risk that the reader will be uninterested and stop reading. And often, there could be an infinite number of commonalities between elements in the list. For example:

What do Tony Gwynn, Ted Williams, and Garry Templeton have in common? (The answer could be that they are all former professional baseball players, or that they all at one time lived in San Diego, or they all have never been to the moon.)

Or:

What do Steve Spurrier, Charles Manson, and George W. Bush have in common?

The Rodney Dangerfield Lead

This lead plays on the famous line used by comedian Rodney Danger-field: "I tell you, I don't get no respect..." Since respect is so subjective (Aretha Franklin just wanted a little of it), it could be argued that everyone and everything, from the President to bothersome insects, aren't respected. This is especially true in sports, such as:

Offensive linemen don't get no respect.

This type of lead has been used so often that a writer could just replace "offensive linemen" with any sports group or individual: "Three-time NFL MVP Brett Favre doesn't get no respect;" "The New York Yankees don't get no respect;" "Tiger Woods doesn't get no respect," etc., etc.
How about:

Members of the media don't get no respect.

The "English 101" Lead

One of the surest ways to cross the line from clever to cute is to try to force a famous literary work onto a sports story. Writers may think they will impress readers with their knowledge of literature. Many readers will think the lead is corny. Some examples:

For the Green Bay Packers, Sunday's game with Chicago was the best of times, and the worst of times.

It was a dark and stormy night Monday, when the Buffalo Bills beat Miami.

"English 101" leads again lack imagination. Readers will recognize these leads as being a weak way for writers to begin their stories.
Of course, this type of stale lead can also come from "modern liter-ature"—from commercials, political campaigns, television programs, etc. If it's well known from other areas, it'll be a cliché if used in sports. Some examples are: "Where's the beef" from Wendy's commercials; "Don't have a cow, man" from *The Simpsons*; "Oops, I did it again" from Britney Spears. Equally as bad is if the "modern literature" is not

well known by most people, like the time a writer tried to lead with a pun on "Walking in LA" from the rock group Missing Persons. Readers under 25 years old at the time might have known the lyrics sung by Dale Bozzio, but most readers would have been confused.

The Holiday Lead

Sporting events happen year round. Often, the date has little to do with an event's outcome. That doesn't stop some writers from writing leads, such as:

> Christmas came early for the Cleveland Cavaliers in their 110–99 victory over Detroit Tuesday night.

> It was like Christmas in July for the Detroit Tigers Tuesday night.

Of course, Christmas isn't the only holiday that gets abused in sports writing.

> The Chicago Bears had lots to be thankful for in their Thanksgiving Day victory over Dallas Thursday.

> The Texas Rangers provided fireworks after the game, but Sammy Sosa provided the fireworks during the game in the Baltimore Orioles' 8–4 Fourth of July victory Tuesday night.

> The Milwaukee Brewer bats took Labor Day off in a 3–0 loss to Philadelphia Monday.

> The Easter Bunny didn't have to look far to find goose eggs Sunday, when the Milwaukee Brewers shut out Chicago 1–0.

> It was a Memorial Day to remember...

> The Philadelphia defense looked as pale as a ghost, and the Cleveland Browns bewitched the Eagles 27–20 in a haunting Halloween game Thursday night.

The Imagine Lead

Imagine a world where sports writers avoided using leads that had been written a thousand times. The "imagine" lead (like the previous sentence) is another type of direct address lead, in which the writer directly talks to the reader. As mentioned earlier, most readers are passively looking for information and do not want to be brought into stories.

Here, the reader is asked to think of a hypothetical situation that may be beyond their comprehension. For example:

> Imagine being a millionaire at the age of 18 before playing your first NBA game.

Another problem with this type of lead is that it expects too much from the reader. Here, the reader not only has to read this story, but also process information in the story and place themselves in a totally foreign frame of mind. Most readers will be unwilling to invest this much energy.

The Dictionary Lead

One of the easiest ways that writers can form a lead is to use materials readily available on their desks. For example, writers could use their dictionary to come up with a lead, such as:

> Webster's dictionary defines "leadership" as...
> Webster's dictionary defines "rivalry" as...
> Webster's dictionary defines "boring" as this type of lead.

Most readers don't need a dictionary to understand the definition of terms such as "leadership","rivalry," etc. It seems odd, then, that a writer would use a dictionary to define these concepts for their readers.

The Good News/Bad News Lead

Another attempt to show contrast happens when writers try to show that not all events are all good or all bad. Many teams and athletes have good and bad things happen together. It would very, very strange if every possible break in a sporting event went to one side. An example:

> The good news is that the New York Yankees defeated Detroit 38–0 Tuesday night. The bad news is that it was the Yankees' last game against Detroit this season.

Notice how the above lead gives the appearance that both the good news and bad news are equally important. This is rarely the case. Certainly, a team winning 38–0 should have little bad news.

Puns

All writers want to be entertaining, but some get carried away and revert to making inappropriate jokes by playing on words. This is especially a problem when the puns involve athletes' names. No one likes to have his or her name turned into a joke. (Certainly, with a name like Wanta, one of the authors of this book has heard more than his share of name jokes).

Avoid referring to anyone named Mack as a truck. Cruz is the last name of several major leaguers, past and present. It is not a verb, such as in "Mariners Cruz to victory." And never force a person's name into an inappropriate and illogical use, as in the headline "Rod Isn't Lavering in Australian Open."

Team names also can lead to bad puns, such as:

> Stephon Marbury scored 28 points as the Phoenix Suns set the San Antonio Spurs Tuesday night.

And of course, Native American nicknames can cause all sorts of trouble. Never use verbs such as "scalped" or "tomahawked."

Along with puns, writers need to pay special attention to double entendres: double meanings that can often have comical—and embarrassing—consequences. Some examples are classic, such as the time former Virginia coach Terry Holland took a trip to Mexico and someone wrote the headline "Holland visits Mexico." And you can only imagine the headlines that were written when track star Craig Virgin was finally healthy after recovering from an injury and so was "ready for the Foreign Legion" track meet.

The "Welcome To" Lead

This type of lead begins with a description of someone's everyday life, followed by a sentence welcoming the reader to this person's world. This lead is less of a cliché as most of the other leads in this chapter, but it has been used so often that, as with many leads above, it demonstrates a lack of creativity on the part of the writer. For example:

> Each out is cheered by a standing ovation. Each home run is greeted by chants of "Check for cork. Check for cork."
> Welcome to another road trip with Sammy Sosa.

A close relative is the "Meet" lead. The first paragraph could be identical, but instead of following it by welcoming the reader to someone's world, the writer invites the reader to "meet" the subject. In the above example, for instance, the writer might follow the first paragraph with "Meet Sammy Sosa, a known corked-bat user."

The Obvious Fact Lead

Here, the writer begins the story with a fact that only stupid people wouldn't know. The story often begins with an awkward construction, such as:

> It's common knowledge that James Posey is the best remaining free agent in the NBA.

This construction causes two problems among readers. Either (a) the reader already knows the fact because it is common knowledge; or (b) the reader doesn't know the fact and feels stupid. In the case of (a), readers may stop reading because they feel the whole story will contain only old information. In the case of (b), readers may stop reading because they feel insulted.

This type of lead can also begin, "It is often said/thought/believed..." or "There is a well-known saying among..."

Some journalism instructors call this type of lead a "TEK" lead: This Everybody Knows. It's also sometimes referred to as an "NS" lead; the "N" stands for "No."

7

MIDDLES I

Story Structures

Once you determine the most effective type of lead for your story, the next decision is what type of overall structure to use for the body of the story. Basically, there are as many structures available as types of leads. Overall, though, there are a handful of story structures that are especially useful for sports writers.

Inverted Pyramid

The most basic story structure is the inverted pyramid. This structure has been used in news writing since before the Civil War. Because reporters often had to worry about telegraph wires being cut by saboteurs, reporters resorted to putting the most important information at the top of their stories, followed by less important information, followed by other information in descending order of importance. Thus, the least significant information appeared at the end of stories. If a telegraph message was interrupted, a newspaper could use whatever information they had received before the interruption and be confident that readers would get the most significant news.

This type of story format lends itself especially well for hard-news leads. If a game ends near a newspaper's deadline, or if a feature-type lead is deemed inappropriate or not effective, an inverted pyramid structure might work best.

By Dan Gelston, AP Sports Writer
The Associated Press
August 17, 2006

Jon Lieber pitched his first shutout in more than five years, Chris Coste hit a two-run homer and the Philadelphia Phillies won their third straight over the New York Mets, 3–0 Wednesday night.

Seemingly out of the playoff picture on July 30 after trading Bobby Abreu as part of a roster overhaul, the Phillies began the day only 2½ games behind Cincinnati in the NL wild-card race and showed some life against the best team in the league.

Philadelphia lost two of three to the Reds last weekend, but took the first three games of this four-game set with sharp pitching and big hits. The Phillies thumped the Mets by a combined 24–4 score in the first two games of the series—hardly indicative of a team that trails NL East-leading New York by 12 games.

Lieber (5–9) was terrific, putting together his third straight solid start since an awful outing against Florida on the day of the trade deadline. He scattered five hits, walked none, and struck out four for his second complete game this season and first shutout since May 24, 2001, with the Chicago Cubs. He went 20–6 that season.

Lieber threw 72 of his 101 pitches for strikes Wednesday in a game that took just 2 hours, 3 minutes.

Hours after the Mets put ace Pedro Martinez on the disabled list with a strained right calf, Tom Glavine (12–6) gave the sagging rotation and tired bullpen a boost with an effective seven-inning stint.

Martinez went only one inning in the first game of the series and Orlando Hernandez was roughed up for 11 runs in four innings on Tuesday. Martinez was placed on the 15-day disabled list Wednesday with a minor strain in his right calf, a move manager Willie Randolph called a "precaution."

After the Phillies scored a combined 10 runs in the first inning of the last two games, Glavine retired the side in order to start this one. The offensive damage was only delayed an inning.

Glavine hit Ryan Howard with a pitch to open the second and, three batters later, Coste hit his fifth homer into the second row of the left-field seats. Coste also doubled and singled.

Glavine allowed six hits, three runs, and lost his second straight start.

Lieber cruised with the early run support. Only once did he allow a baserunner to reach second, and that was in the fourth inning.

Two starts ago in a losing effort, Lieber tossed a complete game against the Mets. He blew the game in that one when his fielding error helped turn a two-run lead into a one-run loss.

Light-hitting Abraham Nunez added a sacrifice fly off Glavine in the sixth, helping the Phillies improve to 19–13 since the All-Star break.

Diamond Structure

The diamond story structure is closely related to the inverted pyramid. Indeed, the diamond structure uses a similar ranking scale for the information in the story: the least important information is at the end of the story. But instead of the most important information appearing in the first paragraph, the "nut graph"—the paragraph with the heart of the story—appears just below the lead. Thus, the lead concentrates on something slightly less important than the nut graph; an anecdote about the winning play, for example. The lead then moves into the most important aspect of the story, and the remainder of the story is written the same as an inverted pyramid lead.

Associated Press often uses a similar writing style, taking a typical inverted pyramid story and topping it with an element of an event that makes a point about the most important aspect of the story.

In the following story, note how the writer begins with a somewhat insignificant event (a hit batter) that makes a larger point about the game. The heart of the story (who won and how) appears in paragraph 3. Also note how the story progresses, concentrating on important aspects of the game until finishing with relatively minor points.

By Roch Kubatko
Baltimore Sun Staff
August 12, 2003

ST. PETERSBURG, Fla. – As a pitch from Tampa Bay starter Joe Kennedy hit Tony Batista in the foot last night, forcing in a run in the first inning, the Orioles weren't sure what kind of break they just received.

Should they be grateful for the early lead, or prepared for another health crisis? It's been that kind of season for the Orioles. They keep moving toward .500, but with a noticeable limp.

Fielding a lineup that reflected their mounting injuries and roster limitations, the Orioles lost to the Devil Rays, 4–3, at Tropicana Field when pinch hitter Jared Sandberg doubled off BJ Ryan with two outs in the ninth inning to score Julio Lugo.

Travis Lee hit a two-run homer off reliever Eric DuBose with two outs in the eighth inning, tying the game, and denying Pat Hentgen a win. Lugo began the ninth with a single off Hector Carrasco, and Sandberg's double rolled to the fence in left-center field.

"Being ahead like that," said Larry Bigbie, "it's always a game you want to finish off."

The Orioles were four outs away from getting within a game of .500 for the first time since June 4, and doing it without Jeff Conine, who was found by team physician Dr. Charles Silberstein yesterday to have bursitis in his right biceps area. Manager Mike Hargrove would have gone to closer Jorge Julio if DuBose, who hadn't allowed a run in five relief appearances, recorded the last out in the eighth.

DuBose threw 97 pitches during Friday's start, so last night's outing was the equivalent of a side session. He retired the first five batters before Rocco Baldelli singled and Lee hit his 13th homer.

"You never feel comfortable here," Hargrove said, "but the way DuBose was pitching and the way their lineup was coming up, we felt good about getting to Julio."

It's much worse to lose Conine. He remained in Baltimore yesterday, again removing a hitter from the middle of the lineup.

Conine missed his third straight game, and he could be out much longer. The Orioles will know more after 72 hours when some of the swelling goes down.

"It's not serious, but how much time he'll be down is still open to question," Hargrove said.

"I think it's a relief," vice president Mike Flanagan said, "that there's not a tear or anything major."

Manwhile, the bullpen is growing more fatigued, and with only one day off until Sept. 1, the Orioles recalled Rick Bauer from Triple-A Ottawa after the game and sent down infielder Carlos Mendez, giving them 13 pitchers for the first time this season.

While the Orioles waited to determine the severity of Conine's injury, they kept BJ Surhoff and David Segui on the disabled list and patched another hole. Hargrove clutches his lineup card in one hand and a jar of spackle in the other.

Segui's sore left wrist doesn't prevent him from batting left-handed, but he still experiences pain while hitting from the other side. Surhoff was eligible to return Saturday from a strained left quadriceps muscle.

Factor in Melvin Mora's sore right hand, which has kept him from swinging a bat, and the Orioles are challenged long before taking the field each night.

"In the meantime," Flanagan joked, "we'll just do without our three, four, and five hitters...and our two."

More personnel moves should come today, with reliever Travis Driskill a candidate to be optioned after allowing runs in 12 of his past 16 appearances.

Down to two healthy reserves after Mendez's demotion, the Orioles could activate Surhoff or Segui.

Only three starters remained from the Opening Day lineup, and none of them batted in the same spot. Deivi Cruz, usually eighth in the order, has hit second in four straight games.

With Conine's flight scheduled to leave Baltimore this morning, Hargrove's bench consisted of only three players. One of them (Robert Machado) wasn't in the organization when the season began, and another (Jack Cust) was at Triple-A Ottawa. Rule 5 shortstop Jose Morban would be in the minors if the Orioles didn't have to expose him to waivers.

But who's complaining? "Anything I say comes out sounding like I'm whining and I'm not going to do that," Hargrove said. "The people we have, we like. Do we wish we had Conine, Segui, Surhoff, and Mora? Sure we do, but I don't think you'll find any of us trying to apologize for the people we're playing. They're good people."

With the Devil Rays starting Kennedy, a left-hander, Hargrove had to become even more creative. Besides having Cruz follow leadoff hitter Brian Roberts, he moved up catcher Brook Fordyce to sixth—the first time the catcher has hit that high since April 8, 2001. Jose Leon started at first base and Mendez served as the designated hitter.

Fordyce hit his second homer in three nights, a bases-empty shot in the sixth inning that increased the Orioles' lead to 3–1. He also had a run-scoring single in the first after Batista was nailed in the foot with the bases loaded.

His trade value increasing as teams prepare to set their playoff rosters, Hentgen nearly won for the fourth time in five starts. The only run off him came on Carl Crawford's leadoff homer in the third, but he needed 108 pitches to get through six innings.

"Pat had to battle tonight. He wasn't on top of his game," Hargrove said.

"But he threw well enough to give us a chance to win."

Inverted Chronological Order

This type of story structure concentrates on the timeline of an event. It starts with the end of a game—the winning basket, for example. It then goes backwards in time to explain how the basket came to be the winning play. The story may talk about the last two minutes, then the beginning of the fourth quarter, followed by details of the third quarter, the second quarter, and the beginning of the game.

The inverted chronological order structure is especially effective for stories involving closely contested games when certain ebbs and flows can be described. Since the winning basket is the most important aspect of the story, and the opening basket is one of the least important aspects, this type of structure is very similar to a story written in an inverted pyramid style.

By Maureen Fulton
The (Toledo) Blade Sports Writer
July 2, 2006

For the first six innings of last night's game, Indianapolis starter Oliver Perez made the Mud Hens batters look silly.

With one swing of the bat, Ryan Ludwick made none of that matter.

Ludwick's two-run home run in the seventh lifted Toledo to its fourth straight win and seventh in its past eight games, 2–1 over the Indians at Fifth Third Field.

With the win the Mud Hens took the lead in the International League West division. They are a half-game ahead of Louisville, which lost last night.

After spending most of the first half of the season with a losing record, the Hens (45–37) are now eight games above the .500 mark.

"Lee Gardner was hurt, and we lost four games on the first road trip with walk-off home runs," Hens manager Larry Parrish said. "We had some things that abnormally went against us at the beginning of the season, and now we've played through it."

Perez, recently optioned from the Indians' big-league club, Pittsburgh, allowed the Hens little. Perez tied a Fifth Third Field record with 13 strikeouts in his seven innings pitched.

But Ludwick broke through with a home run for the second straight night, this one landing out of the ballpark on Monroe Street. His blast scored Jack Hannahan.

"He was throwing very well," Parrish said of Perez. "Even Ludwick was baffled in his first two at-bats, and all of a sudden, bam. I don't know what he did."

Reliever Lance Davis (2–2) got the win. Toledo's starter, Corey Hamman, did not factor in the decision but had another strong outing for the Mud Hens since joining the rotation out of the bullpen.

In the fifth inning, Hamman allowed runners on first and second with nobody out, but he struck out two batters and got Rajai Davis to fly out to center.

"You give them credit, too, but I think our guys are not producing in RBI situations the way we should be," Indianapolis manager Trent Jewett said.

In front of the crowd of 10,300, the scoring started in the third when Indians second baseman Craig Stansberry led off the inning with a home run to left field, his first home run since being called up from Double-A Altoona last week.

Hourglass Structure

The hourglass type of story structure is a difficult style of writing that is part inverted pyramid and part normal pyramid. It starts out with the most important aspect of the story, like the inverted pyramid. However, the second-most important aspect appears at the end of the story to give some punch to the story's conclusion. In the middle, the story is written mainly in an inverted pyramid style, but the latter part of the story builds to a climax in which the story ends with a punch.

This story structure is often effective when a writer can assume a reader will read the entire story—for a major sporting event, for example. The worry, though, is that a reader will stop reading a story before reaching the conclusion, thus missing the second-most important aspect of a story.

The sports news story below includes a concluding paragraph that summarizes many of the details that a normal inverted pyramid story would have much higher. Including these details at the end avoids any interruptions in the flow of the story.

By Amy Donaldson and Jennifer Toomer-Cook
Deseret Morning News
August 19, 2006

Former Mountain View High School coach Dave Houle will face a new fight this fall—but it won't be on a basketball court or a cross-country course.

The Utah Hall of Fame coach, who owns 11 state championships in girls' basketball and dozens of others in cross country and track, faces a two-day hearing before the Utah Professional Practices Advisory Commission, which recommends teacher licensing actions to the State Board of Education.

The investigation was initiated March 10, an action spurred by news reports and information from the Alpine School District, according to Jean Hill, commission investigator and attorney at the State Office of Education. Earlier this month, the commission met and scheduled a hearing for Nov. 15 and 16.

Houle said Friday he didn't know the hearing had been scheduled. He said he's not teaching and isn't sure if he'll contest the allegations.

Before the hearing was scheduled, Houle was nonchalant about the investigation because he said he is moving in a totally different direction. Houle, a few weeks after leaving Mountain View, was hired as an assistant principal and girls' basketball coach at American Leadership Academy, a charter school in Spanish Fork that will compete at the 2A level.

"For me, it's over with," he said, referring comments about the specific allegations and upcoming hearing to his attorney. "I care, but I want to move on. I'm having more fun here trying to get programs started than I have in a while...It's a fun atmosphere here because it's our first year with sports. For some of these kids, it's the first time they'll be playing basketball or football."

Christine Watkins, the director of Bonneville UniServ, which mediates these types of actions on behalf of teachers for the Utah Education Association, represents Houle in the action. She said Houle can either accept whatever happens at the hearing or he can contest it. While any teacher can be investigated, a hearing is held only when investigators feel there is enough evidence that they may need to take licensing action against a teacher.

Hill said that most hearings are finished in a day, but they anticipate a lot of witnesses in Houle's case.

The investigation includes allegations Houle violated state law and state board policies and rules, Hill said. She confirmed they included praying with students and "a history of being inappropriate with the girls—nothing sexual but crossing professional boundaries," Hill said.

"The commission thinks there's enough evidence to proceed with some licensing action," Hill said.

The commission has forwarded its complaint to Houle, and he has responded, Hill said.

Houle left Mountain View after teaching and coaching there for 18 years. He officially retired but he did so amid controversy.

The controversy was about whether or not he should have had two players sleep in his room while he stayed in a living room area of a hotel suite. The team was in Arizona participating in the Nike Tournament of Champions.

After about a week of meetings with school administrators and district officials, Houle opted to retire rather than continue fighting. A few weeks later, he took the job at American Leadership Academy.

Kalin Hall, assistant director of the academy, said he had been notified of the investigation and it would likely not affect Houle's job security or description.

"I can only base my opinion from the time I've spent with him," said Hall. "He has been nothing but professional and helpful as we try to get our athletic programs up and running. He's really helped out everywhere...He's been nothing but positive for us."

The Utah Professional Practices Advisory Commission investigates allegations of teacher misconduct. It sends complaints to the accused when evidence is strong enough to hold a hearing regarding the person's licensure. The commission holds hearings and recommends action to the State Board of Education. Potential actions in this case, like any other, include a letter of warning, a letter of reprimand, suspending or revoking a license, or probation.

Building Bridges

Regardless of the type of structure that you use, you need transitions to move between the various points in your story. The most important transition is the link between your lead and the body of your story, sometimes called a bridge.

Though a bridge between the lead and the body of the story is not always necessary, it often is an effective writing tool. A bridge can include facts that would unnecessarily slow the progression of the story if placed in the lead.

The bridge allows the writer to answer the question: "Why am I writing this story?"

Beyond the bridge, other transitions can also be attained in several other ways. It is important to remember why transitions are used: to move from one section of a story to another. Reporters use transitions to show what important information is coming up in the next section, while keeping in mind what the main point of the story is.

By David Climer, Senior Writer,
Tennessean
September 3, 2006

ANN ARBOR, Mich. – Unlikely as it might have seemed, Vanderbilt jogged onto the field after intermission trailing Michigan just 13–7 and preparing to receive the second-half kick.

Three plays later, the Commodores arrived at a crossroads.

Facing third-and-one at the Vanderbilt 39, Cassen Jackson-Garrison was stuffed for a 3-yard loss.

For a team in need of a quick second-half start, it was a big step backward.

"They did a good job of stuffing us," said Vanderbilt Coach Bobby Johnson. "We just weren't very physical right there—not physical enough...

"You get third-and-one, you've got to convert it just to stay alive, just to keep your defense off the field. Our defense played a lot—too much."

[Note the transition here]

That was the first of consecutive three-and-outs by the Vanderbilt offense in the second half. The latter was followed by a 10-play, 41-yard touchdown drive by Michigan that ended with a 14-yard pass from Chad Henne to Tyler Ecker.

Vanderbilt's offensive struggles left the Commodores defense twisting in the Midwest breeze. Michigan snapped the ball 73 times compared to Vanderbilt's 52, leaving the Commodores holding on for dear life.

"You see the defensive linemen huffing and puffing," said Michigan senior offensive tackle Rueben Riley. "That's when the killer instinct needs to come into play. You need to put your foot on their necks, to be blunt.

"As long as you can continue to control the ball and make sure you keep the extra hits off the quarterback and off the running back, that's how you want to play the game."

Despite the disparity in plays, Vanderbilt's defense actually held up reasonably well. The Commodores gave up 236 yards in the first half—including 81 on Michigan's first possession—and 145 after intermission.

"Most of the time, we answered the bell on defense," Johnson said.

But even though Vanderbilt's offense managed only nine first downs and just one touchdown, linebacker Jonathan Goff said there were no hard feelings.

"It's our job to stop them," said Goff, who was credited with 12 tackles and two assists. "You've always got to be ready to go because you don't know what's going to happen during the course of the game.

"You can never point fingers... There are too many opportunities for everybody to make a game-changing play."

Vanderbilt was gashed for 246 rushing yards, including 146 by Michigan junior Mike Hart, who benefited from some dominating blocking by the offensive line.

"As far as run blocking, they couldn't have blocked any better, including the receivers," Hart said.

Only on two series did Michigan fail to get at least one first down. One of those was at the end of the first half.

"We've got to get three-and-outs," said defensive tackle Theo Horrocks. "We've got to get the ball back to our offense and give them a chance to score."

The Three Ts: Taste, Touch, and Timing

Experienced sports writers have a well-developed writing style. Through years of covering sporting events, writers find a writing style that feels comfortable to them. Three elements come into play: taste, touch, and timing.

Taste

Taste involves a writer's choice of words. Some writers use complicated words that are difficult to understand outside the context of a story. Other writers use simple language that is easily understood by all readers.

When deciding on the words to include in a story, writers should keep in mind several simple rules:

- Avoid the old fashioned. Avoid worn out phrases. Take fresh approaches in your writing. Use variety in your writing.
- Avoid the verbose. The first rule of writing should always be: write to express, not to impress. Prefer simple words, rather than complex. Use familiar words.
- Appeal to the senses. As Walter Lippmann wrote back in 1922, we in the news media take the world outside and try to create pictures in people's heads. Tie in with readers' experiences. Use terms that your readers can picture.
- Appeal to emotions. Put action in your verbs.

In the following column by John Eisenberg of the *Baltimore Sun*, notice how his choice of words—taste—lead to an entertaining article.

By John Eisenberg
Baltimore Sun
September 9, 2006

After stumbling to a 6–10 record a season ago, the Ravens took a sizable risk: Instead of tearing up their losing team, they kept it together.

There was a chance Brian Billick wouldn't be back, but he's still the head coach.

Jamal Lewis was a free agent, but he elected to stay and run here.

Ray Lewis was upset enough about some perceived slight that his agent obtained permission to look around for a better contract, but all that seems forgotten now; Ray is back and amped up for tomorrow's season opener against the Buccaneers in Tampa, Fla.

The acquisition of quarterback Steve McNair gives the impression that a new era is beginning, but don't be fooled. Eighteen starters are back. For better or worse, these are the Ravens you know.

But they won't be if they stumble again. Another disappointing season would almost surely lead to sweeping changes.

A new head coach? Very likely. A new cast of characters? Bank on it. A whole new aura? Don't be surprised.

Again, that's only if the team implodes as it did a year ago. It might not.

But the point is that a lot—make that a whole lot—is on the line.

Ravens president Dick Cass insinuated that this core might not have that much more time when he said earlier this year that the team's salary cap situation could get "tight" relatively soon, though "not in the near future."

But the organization could speed up the timetable if owner Steve Bisciotti decided he had been throwing good money after bad and called for a makeover.

Bisciotti, like many owners, is accustomed to rousing success, but the Ravens are 15–17 and haven't made the playoffs since he assumed sole ownership. He might be low-key and patient, but everyone has his limit, and it seemed he was approaching his when he asked the voluble Billick to tone it down this year.

My guess is another losing season would push Bisciotti beyond what he can tolerate.

He would have to swallow only the last year of Billick's contract to make a coaching change, and while some players have long-term deals that would necessitate their return in 2007, there's always room to maneuver in a league without guaranteed contracts. With more starters over age 30 than any other AFC North team, the Ravens could easily be reconfigured.

Kind of casts tomorrow's game in a different light, doesn't it?

As road underdogs against a 2005 playoff team, the Ravens shouldn't be expected to win, especially since they're notoriously slow starters who haven't won a season opener since 2001. But if they're going to be a surprise team, they had better start surprising—and the Buccaneers, with still-developing Chris Simms at quarterback, are a good fit for them as playoff-caliber opponents go.

It's a prime opportunity to make something happen.

At the same time, the arc of the Ravens' season depends mostly on how much (if at all) the offense improves, and with a new quarterback in charge, the unit is liable to be more cohesive and productive at midseason than it is now. It is bound to experience some "getting to know you" pains.

Those pains can't last long if the team wants to avoid another losing season and what that might bring.

It is widely believed an improved passing game, led by McNair, will dictate any offensive turnaround. That's obviously true to some extent, given how poorly the passing game has fared.

But really, it's the running game that holds the key. The Ravens' per-game rushing average has dropped precipitously in the past few years, from 167.1 yards in 2003 to 128.9 yards in 2004 to 100.3 yards in 2005. Last year's average was the second lowest in team history.

Quite simply, the running game has to improve drastically for McNair to have time to throw. Will it? A lot of factors are involved, and typically, the preseason offered mixed signals. The line had some good and bad blocking moments. Jamal Lewis didn't run much before being sidelined with a hip injury, but there were moments when it seemed he had his devastating burst back. The return of that burst is the single element that, more than any other, could put the Ravens back over .500 and into the playoffs for the first time since 2003. A healthy Lewis is a Pro Bowl runner, capable of dominating a game.

But can he stay healthy?

The Ravens gambled when they brought him back this year along with most of a losing team. Their conviction is admirable. They believe in what they've put together, regardless of their 2005 record.

Now, their very future here depends on whether they're right.

Touch

Touch is the use of comparisons and figures of speech. Writers often like to use colorful analogies to describe players and action. Oftentimes, however, the comparisons are stale from overuse. A basketball player with quick moves shouldn't be described as a bellydancer. A football player scoring a touchdown shouldn't be hitting paydirt.

Analogies most of all should be accurate. Don't try to reach for an analogy that isn't there. A writer once wrote that a certain game was like a pizza. Most games don't have cheese and pepperoni.

The writer below makes an excellent comparison to show how unimportant preseason football games are by comparing them to a current news topic.

Joe Posnanski
The Kansas City Star
August 17, 2006

EAST RUTHERFORD, N.J. – The Chiefs lost their eighth consecutive preseason game on Thursday night, which means...well, I have absolutely no idea what that means. Really, outside of the discussions revolving around what Katie Couric is going to wear for her first news broadcast, is there anything more meaningless than preseason football?

Timing

Timing involves the rhythm of an article. The best sports stories include variations in rhythm—both in length of paragraphs, sentences, and words. Writers need to change the rhythm throughout their stories so that the content does not seem monotonous, droning on and on at a constant pace.

To avoid monotony, writers can vary several aspects of sentences: length, structure, and voice. Note how in the following story, the short, choppy lead seems so unusual that it draws the reader into the story.

By Tom Jones, Staff Writer
St. Petersburg Times
July 31, 2003

TORONTO – Shipped off. Cast out. Sent down.

The Devil Rays' Victor Zambrano and Jeff Liefer each hit a spot this season when he needed to get out of the major leagues and back on track. Their careers were in serious need of a makeover, and the only address to iron out the kinks was the minor leagues, not the majors.

So out they went, discharged to Triple-A Durham. But they're back in the majors now and both played key roles in the Rays'

5–3 victory Wednesday over the Toronto Blue Jays before 21,068 at SkyDome.

Liefer, called up from Triple-A Durham just hours before Wednesday's game, delivered a two-run homer that put the Rays ahead to stay, and Zambrano pitched 62/3 innings for his team-leading eighth victory as the Rays made a little history.

Note in the following story, the short sentence in paragraph two follows two longer sentences in the lead. The short sentence becomes more powerful because of the variation in length.

By Tom Clark Spencer
St. Louis Herald
August 9, 2003

ST. LOUIS – All the proper ingredients were in place for the Marlins to walk out of Busch Stadium with a sweep and tied with Philadelphia atop the wild-card leaderboard. The Phillies had lost by the time the Marlins took the field Thursday night, and Brett Tomko—who had never won a game in his home park—was on the mound for the St. Louis Cardinals.

So much for that.

Tomko, on his 17th try at Busch, finally won. And the Marlins headed off to Milwaukee with neither a sweep nor a share of the top wild-card position. The Cardinals won 3–0.

Sentence structures, while a bit trickier, can also be varied. For instance, instead of writing in the typical noun-verb-noun structure, a sentence such as "He had never encountered such filth" could be written as "Never had he encountered such filth." Notice how the "never" becomes NEVER—emphasized—by moving the word to the beginning of the sentence.

While it is always a good idea to write grammatically correct sentences, breaking a rule now and then can both change the rhythm of a sentence and emphasize certain words. For example, a sentence such as "Brett Favre's magic may have run out after all this time" could be written as "Brett Favre's magic may have, after all this time, run out." Again, this structure emphasizes "after all this time"—making it seem like it's been a really, really long time. However, this structure also splits the verb (may have run out), which will drive some copy editors crazy.

Overall

When working on the body of a story, underwrite rather than over-write. Let the action and dialogue carry the story.

Keep the story moving. This requires a plan of the best way to enter the story, to proceed through the middle, and to come to a logical ending.

Use transitional devices to move smoothly from one section to another.

Let people talk. Show people doing things.

Don't get bogged down in details.

8

MIDDLES II

Effective Interviewing

As an ambitious University of Missouri journalism student, Wright Thompson was eager to bolster his resume. So each month Thompson would contact the *New York Times* sports editor to pitch story ideas. And each month Thompson was politely told, "Thanks, but no thanks."

But in February 2001 Thompson finally pitched a story the *Times* could not refuse. Southwest Missouri State basketball player Jackie Stiles was about to become the all-time leading scorer in NCAA basketball history. She had already surpassed the women's scoring record and was quickly closing in on the men's.

After reading every article he could find about Stiles, Thompson was determined to make his story unique. He realized this wasn't only a story about a scoring record but emblematic of Stiles' grit and determination. Thompson wanted to discover the motivating force behind that determination. So, he called Stiles' father, Pat. "Mr. Stiles," the conversation began, "my name is Wright Thompson and I'm writing a story for the *New York Times* regarding Jackie. Do you have a few minutes?" Through Thompson's research he learned that Jackie was raised on a family farm near Claflin, Kan., (population 688) where hard work was a way of life. When she left for college Stiles took that work ethic with her. Each day after practice she would shoot until she made at least 100 baskets, unusual for any basketball player, particularly an All-American.

While Stiles was honing her basketball skills, Thompson was honing his as a journalist. He learned how to properly research stories, conduct interviews, ask tough questions, and encourage ordinary sources to provide extraordinary information. By the time Thompson had telephoned Pat Stiles, he had outlined the story and established a theme. He wanted to know how a country girl from the Kansas Plains becomes college basketball's most prolific story.

"I hope I didn't interrupt your supper," Thompson continued. "What'd ya'll have for supper this evening?"

For the next 20 minutes, Thompson and Pat Stiles shared a common interest—cooking. Thompson did not take notes or fire questions at Mr. Stiles. They spoke as if they were old friends trying to catch up on lost years. At this point, the interview wasn't an interview at all. It was a casual, comfortable conversation. Thompson understood that the key to a good interview is trust. And although he—a college student from Mississippi—and Mr. Stiles had little to nothing in common, they could talk cooking.

Interviewing Anxiety

Your sports editor approaches your desk and says, "Give Northside High's football coach a call and write a preview for Friday night's game."

"Sure, boss. I'll get right on it."

After a quick trip to the newspaper's archives to research Northside, you prepare a few questions for the coach. You pick up the phone and begin to dial. A knot climbs up your throat and settles behind your thick, dry tongue. A cool sweat dampens the back of your neck as the coach answers the phone. Suddenly, for you, English is a second language.

"Yeath, coauch. Diz iz Blob Smithe froum da Thimes. Dou yaaaaa halfff aw ffew minnuts?"

For some reason, interviewing creates a physiological transformation that alters perfectly normal human beings into blubbering idiots. Firing questions at strangers can be incredibly unnerving and one of the most difficult obstacles for young journalists. Unfortunately for those young journalists, there is no silver-bullet solution to overcoming interview jitters. But there are ways to reduce the anxiety:

1 Thoroughly research your topic. Read everything you can find about the subject before conducting the interview. Become an expert on the subject so much so that you will surprise your source with your knowledge and your questions.

2 Understand the topic. For example, in auto racing, know what a restrictor plate is and its purpose; in football, understand the 5-2 defense; in basketball, be able to identify the motion offense; in baseball, know when the infield fly rule is in effect, and so on.

3 Understand the language of the game. A Major League Baseball manager is "Skip," calling a hockey goalie a "sieve" is disparaging, and being waived is not the same as being drafted. To fully comprehend the story you must be able to talk the talk.

4 Practice, practice, practice. How do you practice interviewing? While standing in line at Jocko's Convenience Store, initiate a

conversation with the guy next to you. If he's carrying a box of shotgun shells and a case of beer, ask him where he hunts or what he likes to hunt. If the woman at the grocery store loads 16 gallons of bleach into her shopping cart, ask her how long she's being doing tie-dye. The world is full of interesting (and unusual) people. Find some and talk with them. If your assumption about the bleach is wrong, so what? No harm in starting a conversation with a stranger. Although these tips can assist you in overcoming the interview jitters, the best way to get better at interviewing is to interview. The more interviews you conduct, the better you'll be.

But getting comfortable is only the beginning. Interviewing is an art. The best interviewers are able to extract the best information in order to write the best stories. Without good information there are no good stories.

What is an Interview?

In journalism, conversations spurred on by questions are sterilized and formalized and labeled "interviews." An interview establishes the official boundary between the source, who has the information, and the reporter, who is attempting to extract it. The interview is different from a "chat" with friends or a "talk" with parents. Unlike newspaper interviews, what's said among friends probably won't be read by thousands of readers unless it's posted on someone's blog or Facebook.

But while some of the best journalism interviews are, in essence, conversations, the term "interview" carries the formal stigma of job interview, police interview or airport security interview ("did you pack your own luggage?") Nonetheless, all interviews have a similar purpose of extracting information. And information is a form of currency for a journalist. A source with accurate, trustworthy information is more valuable than a source that is inaccurate and not trustworthy. The same can be said for a journalist. A fair, accurate, diligent reporter who asks intelligent and informed questions during an interview is more valuable than one with lesser qualities.

Of course, the supply and demand metaphor should not be taken literally. Paying money for information violates journalistic ethics and principles. If a source requests payment for information, find another source. An exchange of money would actually diminish the information because people will say almost anything for money. And journalists who pay for information reduce their own value as a nonpartisan journalist. Bad sources—those who provide inaccurate information—lose their value just as bad reporters—those who are not fair or accurate—lose their credibility; another commodity that will be discussed in a later chapter.

The commodity aspect is the stumbling block that makes an interview an interview and reduces the possibility of having an informed conversation with a source. Somewhere during the information collection process, reporters have to find the middle ground between the interrogation approach ("Where were you on the night of Friday, June 13?") and the passive drive-thru window approach ("Would you like fries with that?"). In essence, a journalistic interview is a conversation on steroids, or at the very least, human growth hormones. A good interview is as comfortable as a casual conversation with a friend but has the informational value of a priceless piece of art.

Compiling Questions

After researching the subject (see Chapter 3), compile a list of questions you want to ask the source. Or better yet, compile a list of key words that will spark a question. If you are interviewing a high school football coach about field position, write, "FP" in your notebook. Of course, be certain you can decode your own code. Here are a few more tips:

- Do not feel compelled to ask the questions in order. The questions, or key words, are simply a guide.
- Be curious about the subject of the story. Ask questions that interest you.
- Talk about the story with an editor, fellow reporter or friend. Talking about the story allows you to broaden your perspective. Others might think of questions or story angles you have not.
- The best interviews are structured conversations. Do not force questions that do not flow with the conversation. Let's say you ask the football coach, "What do you think your team will need to do to beat Championship Central this week?" He says, "Our starting quarterback broke his leg in practice today. I'm not sure what we're going to do." Your next question should not be the "field position" question. The obvious follow-up question should involve the quarterback situation and the injury.
- Listen, listen, and listen. What your source is saying is far more important than what you have to say. Show interest when someone is speaking and ask follow-up questions that pertain to the subject of the story.
- To some degree allow the interview, or discussion, to flow naturally without losing focus of what the story is about. But sometimes the story changes. You have to be rigid enough to keep the source on topic and flexible enough to alter the questioning when the story changes. In the quarterback example, what the coach says about

Championship Central is far less important than the starting quarterback situation but the topics are certainly intertwined.

- Do not be restricted by your list of key words or your own biases. Remain receptive to what the source is saying.

Setting the Scene

There is no substitute for face-to-face interviews. Sometimes because of time constraints and availability, telephone interviews are a necessity. In a pinch, a telephone exchange can provide essential information for writing your story, but to capture the true essence of the individual you must conduct interviews in person. Hearing the words through a receiver and not witnessing facial expressions or body language limits your information gathering.

Although conducting interviews via e-mail might be convenient for the source, it carries unwanted baggage. First, there's no guarantee that your source was the person answering the questions. Instead of a coach or player, a media relations person might be writing the answers. Second, there's no spontaneity with an e-mail interview. Writing is a deliberate, intentional act where the authors write and rewrite in an attempt to craft the perfect sentence. So instead of receiving a sincere reaction to a question, an e-mail answer is oftentimes sterilized and provides little original information. Third, it's difficult to ask follow-up questions and receive a timely response through e-mail. Fourth, e-mail interviews are impersonal. Black letters on a white screen provide minimal insight into a person's character. Fifth, an e-mail response can be misinterpreted. Without tone of voice and expression, sarcastic words might read like anger. Sixth, you give up some control of your story. If restricted to e-mail answers, there's no give-and-take dialogue between the reporter and the source. It's really no different than receiving a press release with canned quotes. And seventh, there's no assurance that the comments you are receiving haven't been distributed to another reporter. Wouldn't it be incredibly convenient for a source to create a Word document of canned answers? Interviews would be reduced to a menu of comments from which to choose, or worse yet, comments chosen for you.

Although e-mail interviews might be less time-consuming and greatly reduce interview anxiety, the downside isn't worth it. Good reporters and writers make every effort to provide the best information possible. E-mails can interfere with that effort. That doesn't mean you never conduct e-mail interviews. On rare occasions, it might be the only alternative, such as an interview with an athlete located at the Olympic Village in China. So, keep your options open but remember that a face-to-face interview is the best scenario and a telephone conversation is a good alternative.

For face-to-face interviews, when contacting the source to set up the interview, request a specific amount of time, usually 15 to 30 minutes. If your interview is an hour long, it's probably too long and should be divided into two interviews. Other tips include:

- Interview the source in a place where he or she will be comfortable and willing to talk. The source's office or home usually provides the best setting. The sidelines of a football field, basketball court, baseball diamond, arena corridor or locker room will usually be your office. Coaches or managers usually have rules about when the media can and cannot conduct interviews. Be sure you know the rules before starting the interview.

- Be aware of your surroundings. Sports interviews are often conducted in noisy environments. Coaches, players, and fans can be disruptive, as can bouncing basketballs, public address systems, and roaring car engines. If you are tape-recording your interview, be sure to back up the recorder with written notes otherwise your interview with a basketball player before a game might sound like this: "I understand," thump, thump, thump, thump, "named," thump, thump, "player," thump, thump, "week." Don't let the pre-game shoot-around interfere with the information. Taking notes provides insurance that will not happen.

- Greet a source you do not know by introducing yourself with a firm handshake.

- If you are conducting a telephone interview, be polite and professional. Professionalism has little to do with being paid. Mike Tyson earned millions of dollars as a heavyweight boxer but what kind of professionalism did he display when he bit off part of Evander Holyfield's ear? Professionalism involves respect, courtesy, and consideration. One simple rule to remember is when you conduct an interview you represent not only yourself but also your parents, your editor, your colleagues and all of journalism. If a source has one bad experience with a reporter, you can be sure there will not be a second. Many times the source will not grant another interview.

- Unless the subject is a teenager, using courtesy titles such as "Mr." or "Mrs." or "Miss" is appropriate. If the subject is a medical doctor, use "Dr." "Skip" for a baseball manager, or "Coach" for a coach is also acceptable. You might overhear athletes refer to the coach by a nickname. To play it safe, call the source by his title (coach, for instance) until he or she gives you permission to use the nickname. For example, legendary University of Alabama football coach Paul Bryant was wellknown as "Bear," but at your first meeting you wouldn't want to say, "Hey, Bear. How's the team look this year?" Of course, if you meet Coach Bryant these days you probably have larger issues to deal with than writing about Alabama football. Bryant died in 1983.

- Make eye contact with the source and be attentive and interested in what is being said. Remember, the source has taken time from his or her busy schedule to talk with you.

Interview the Environment

When you arrive for the interview, look around the home, office or athletic venue and interview the environment. What pictures are on the desk? Is there artwork on the walls? What kind of furniture? What is the source wearing? Jewelry? Shoes? Does the source have calluses on his or her hands? Calluses are indicative of someone who works with their hands. If so, what kind of work? Does a coach garden as a hobby or roof houses in the summer? You do not just interview the source; you interview the source's life. That does not mean making assumptions; it's simply a way to spark conversation and learn more about the subject. Use all your senses when reporting. What does it smell like? What do you hear, see, and feel? You are a trained observer so be certain to observe.

Interviewing the environment also provides an opportunity to find common ground with the source. If he collects baseball cards, you can chat about baseball card collecting. Perhaps you have a similar hobby or interest. Common ground creates a connection between source and reporter, but tread lightly. If you are doing a story about a high school baseball player who collapsed and died, telling the story about how your cat died does not create common ground. In fact, it might have the opposite effect. Comparing someone's dead son to your cat could be seen as insulting. At that point, the source might end the interview.

One word of caution: do not attempt to play psychiatrist with a source. Sometimes reporters have a tendency to put sources "on the couch," and attempt to extract deeper meaning from comments, reaction or environmental conditions. What does it mean if a source has a messy house? It could mean the person is disorganized or perhaps it represents a life of clutter. Or it could mean the person has been too busy to clean. In any case, do not assume. Be reluctant to assign deep meaning to something that could have a simple explanation. Just because a player is the first to take the field doesn't mean he or she is demonstrating leadership. Perhaps the player needs more time to stretch. Instead of generating your own meaning, ask the source. Let him or her provide the context. It could save you some embarrassment later when the source asks, "What do you mean my messy house represents the clutter in my life? Did you ever think that maybe the maid is on vacation this week?"

Getting Comfortable

If you are writing a feature story, start the interview with casual conversation. There might be a piece of artwork in the room you can discuss, or the college class ring the person is wearing. Keep it light and friendly. After a couple minutes of chitchat, you'll be ready to start the interview.

If you are writing a game story, ditch the chitchat and get to the point. Because you have a deadline and the player or coach wants to celebrate or sulk, your interview time will be limited. Have your questions ready and fire away.

When writing a feature story, the line of questioning might go something like this:

- First question, "Could you spell your name for me?" Do not assume the previous stories had his or her name spelled correctly.
- Ask "softball" questions—easy questions that the source can hit out of the ballpark. It allows them to get loose to handle the other questions.
- The conversation will usually direct the remainder of the interview. Although it is a conversation, keep in mind your original list of questions. You do not want to make this a simple question-and-answer session but keeping the source on track is important.
- Allow the source to talk. Do not interrupt or complete sentences for the source.
- If the interview stalls, allow for some silence. If the source gives you a short answer, don't immediately fire off another question. Look the source in the eye and say nothing for a few seconds. Sometimes lulls in conversation spark answers to questions. Silence makes people uneasy, so they'll keep talking to avoid dead air. Sometimes that's when the source provides the most interesting and pertinent information.
- Do not overlook information. If a player says, "I'm looking to have a great season. I just hope my chemotherapy doesn't slow me down," your next questions should not involve last year's all-conference performance.
- Save the tough questions for last. Get all the information you need to write the story before asking a question that could end the interview. At least that way you have a story, even if it probably will not address the difficult issues. For example, "Coach, I understand your starting point guard was arrested for shoplifting earlier this season. How did that affect the team's play?" If the coach curses and stomps off, it's OK because you already have the story you need. You can chase the story you want later through alternative sources.

The Interview's On/Off Switch

When a reporter approaches a source and requests an interview, there are few unspoken parameters. Once the interview begins, everything is *on the record* unless otherwise stated. What does that mean exactly? Is there some mysterious, invisible galactic recorder keeping us honest? Will lightning strike from above or the earth split open from below if a source or reporter fail to honor "the record?" As near as anyone can tell that hasn't happened.

Although it is not a legally binding statement, "on the record" is a professional agreement between a source and a journalist that allows a journalist to publish information provided by the source. If a source says it, and a reporter writes it in a notebook or tapes it with a recorder, it signifies that a record of statement has been documented. The on-the-record recording of that statement allows the journalist to publish the information in good faith because the source has granted permission. Although there is no signed affidavit, secret handshake or Hippocratic-type oath, the "lady's and gentleman's" agreement establishes the ground rules. And even though a referee is not available to ensure fair play, violators of the unwritten rules are bound by their value as a source or their credibility as a journalist.

You might wonder, then, how somebody can suddenly go "off the record." Sometimes the interview ventures into uncomfortable territory for a source. It might be sensitive personal information or legally contentious information that nudges the source into a journalist's no-man's land. The exchange usually goes something like this:

Source: This is off the record, but...
Reporter: Wait! Off the record? Why?
Source: I can't tell you. That's off the record too.
Reporter: Do I really want to hear this?
Source: Absolutely. I think you need to hear this.
Reporter: Then why can't it be on the record?
Source: Because it's too sensitive to tell anyone.

For anyone to go off the record, source and reporter have to come to some agreement. Sometimes "off-the-record" information can be incredibly useful and other times it has little news value. A savvy reporter will utilize the off-the-record information to get the information on the record from another source. For instance, if a high school football coach says, "You didn't hear it from me but the basketball coach is going to be fired. That's off the record." A reporter can telephone the athletic director and say, "According to a reliable source, the basketball coach is going to be fired. What is the job status of the basketball coach?"

Of course you do not want to jeopardize your relationship with the football coach, so you do not reveal your source. Additionally, you do not want to lie to the athletic director because it'll damage your credibility. Take extreme caution when using this tactic. Be honest to both on- and off-the-record sources.

Sometimes it's difficult to determine when the "record switch" is on or off. A basketball coach might say, "Our center really sucks. He can't shoot, rebound or even set a pick. But that's off the record."

According to the unwritten, non-binding, interview agreement, the statement is on the record. An "off the record" disclaimer after the fact does not erase the statement from your notebook or tape recorder. The source does not receive a retroactive waiver. But instead of saying, "Tough luck, coach, that's on the record," you'll want to negotiate an agreement. "Coach, you cannot say something like that and claim it's 'off the record.' Would you like to rephrase it?" Giving the coach an opportunity to soften the statement does a couple things: 1) It allows him to save face and not destroy the confidence of his center; and 2) It allows you to build trust with the coach.

Some sports journalism purists might disagree with negotiating with the coach, saying what is said on the record is on the record. That's an excellent point, but when you have the opportunity to gain goodwill with a source without truly damaging the story, the trade-off can reap huge rewards. It's acceptable to compromise as long as the compromise does not interfere with the news. If the same coach is asking you to keep his public drunkenness charge out of the paper, there is no room for compromise.

Establishing goodwill with a source regarding on- and off-the-record information does not make you a leashed Chihuahua being dragged by his owner. The interview is a mutual agreement. And if a source wants to tell you something off the record, you have the option to refuse. It might not be the ideal situation, but at least the source knows where you stand. And if a source goes off the record be certain to establish when he or she returns to the record. Gray areas in reporting can only lead to trouble, so when in doubt, ask, "Are we back on the record?" If you're going to play the game, you have to know the rules.

Wrapping up the Interview

When your time has expired (15 to 30 minutes), say, "I think our time is up." If the source wants to continue the interview, you can continue.

Your final question of the interview should be, "If I have further questions, may I contact you?" Politely ask for a phone number. Shake the source's hand, and thank the source for his or her time.

Immediately after the interview organize your notes and transcribe your tape if you used a tape recorder. Be certain to check facts, statistics, dates, quotes, and name spellings. To be accurate you might have to talk with a source several times. There is no shame in repeatedly contacting a source to check and double check information. You can explain, "I want to be certain to get the story right." You will discover the source wants that as well.

Final Tips

Do not be a stenographer and publish everything you are told. Leave something in the notebook. There will be information that does not fit the story's theme. Sometimes it's the best quote of the interview. Although it's tempting to include the quote, if it does not belong, leave it out. For instance, if while interviewing for the Northside High football preview the coach says, "I once chugged down 36 hot dogs at the county fair and never even broke a sweat," it's interesting but has nothing to do with Friday night's game. Of course, you might want to include the coach's penchant for sausage consumption in a notebook or a sidebar concerning oddities in coaching.

Also, remember to be a thorough reporter. As the old saying goes, "If your mother tells you she loves you, check it out." A reporter investigates what he or she is told in an effort to determine what is fact and what is fiction. Providing an open microphone to a source to speak freely without confirmation or accountability is irresponsible journalism. If the football coach says, "We rushed for 5,000 yards last season," take time to check it out. Check the newspaper's archive or ask the coach for a copy of the team statistics. Many times sources do not accurately quote statistics. Help them out by checking it out. It's also a good idea to do an accuracy check; reading quotes and information back to a source to confirm its accuracy. The accuracy check is *not* an invitation for a source to change quotes. It's only a method for checking the facts. If a source wants to change a quote, talk with your editor. If there is a disagreement, the first question you should ask a source is, "Is the quote accurate?" If the response is, "Yes, but..." you are under no obligation to alter the quote. Nonetheless, consult with your editor. When doing an accuracy check, read the paragraph before the quote and the paragraph after the quote. That way the source will know that the quote was used in the proper context.

Probably the most important aspect to remember when interviewing is to be fair to the sources and be accurate with the information. As one University of Missouri professor says, "Journalism is not rocket science; it's much more difficult. Provable commodities, such as the laws of physics, guide rocket scientists. Journalists do not have such provable commodities." Trust, respect, and accuracy are characteristics of journalism that come with hard work and concerted effort. Nonetheless, there is no proven formula for those characteristics in journalism. But hopefully, these tips will assist you in becoming the most responsible journalist possible.

By Wright Thompson
ESPN.com

It's no surprise that the best writers are great reporters. People like *Sports Illustrated*'s Gary Smith and *Esquire's* Chris Jones are amazing storytellers because they uncover amazing stories to tell. Good reporting comes in all different shapes and sizes.

There is the basic work you'll do covering news stories. Checklist reporting. Make sure you're prepared so you don't sit down to write and realize you've forgotten something. Daily journalism doesn't afford do-overs. You're not gonna get Bill Belichick on the phone to ask that thing you forgot. So if you're covering a press conference or a practice or a post-game locker room, take a minute to think before you go in there. Make a simple checklist on the cover of your notebook. Make sure not to forget anything. Ask follow-ups. They were listening to music? What singer? iPod? Car stereo? What song? What verse? Details, details, details.

Next, there are the document-based reporting techniques that help you gather in raw facts. A good rule of thumb is this: if public dollars paid for it, odds are you can get it. Learn how to file Freedom of Information Act requests. Don't be intimidated by the courthouse. If you cover a college football team, it's not a bad idea to periodically run the starters through the police station computer. You'll often be stunned by what you find. Also, don't be scared to be creative. Covering a coaching search? Figure out what private airplane the athletic director is taking and then use one of the myriad Web sites devoted to plane tracking. See where he's going, which will put you three steps ahead of the competition. A good way of reporting is to always ask yourself this question: who knows what I need to know? Trying to find someone in a neighborhood? The postman will know where they live. You get the idea.

When you're writing about people, that's a totally different kind of reporting. You've got to be able to walk comfortably through trash strewn alleys and corporate hallways. Sometimes, you need to wear a suit to an interview. Other times you need to wear ripped jeans and a Ramones T-shirt. Know the difference.

Always be prepared. Don't waste people's time with stupid questions. Read everything that's been written. If there are books to read, hop on Amazon. Do your homework. Then, before you interview the main subject, if you can, use the circle method. Start on the outside and work your way in. But remember: the second you hang up with your subject's friends/family, their first call is to the subject. If there are a few unpleasant questions to ask, you might want to wait until you no longer need time from the subject.

Getting access is also a challenge, especially with high profile college athletes and professionals. Sometimes, you'll get none and have to manufacture it. Covering the Masters the year Phil Mickelson won his first major, I knew he wasn't going to let me hang out with him. So, I figured out all the public areas he'd be in and made it my business to always be a few feet away. I ended up with enough intimate moments to tell a story that readers couldn't get anywhere else. Sure, it's like eating crab sometimes: lots of work for a few seconds of real moments. But those moments make the story and set you apart. So work for them.

Other times, you can talk your way into someone's inner circle. The most important part of a successful profile is often in the way you sell it. Take your time. Show the subject other things you've written. Make them understand how it can be good for them. It sounds silly, but be cool. People will open up to people they feel comfortable around.

(Wright Thompson is a senior writer for ESPN.com and a contributing writer for *ESPN The Magazine*.)

9

MIDDLES III

Use of Quotes

Quotes are an extremely important part of any sports story. Quotes provide perspectives from key individuals and break up the monotony of narrative descriptions of events.

Basically, there are three broad reasons for using quotes:

1   When someone says something unusual: "Growing old is mandatory. Growing up is optional." Tom Wargo of the Senior PGA tour.
2   When someone says something in an unusual way: "It was well worth it—like a mid-town Manhattan ATM surcharge."
3   When someone important says something: Typically, a quote from a third-string quarterback is not very important. But a game story without a few quotes from the head coach is an incomplete story. The perspective of the coach is one of the most important elements of a game report. The coach can explain why he decided to run a fake punt with a 30-point lead, or why he didn't replace a pitcher who walked five straight batters.

Other instances where you would want to use direct quotations:

* The quotation clusters words together in an unusual way: "Today was like a mango on a tree I thought would never bear fruit. It's a fine gem, sparkling in an otherwise dim existence."
* The quotation emphasizes a point: "It's like licking the underbelly of a snake."
* The quotation reveals someone's character in a way the writer cannot: He was called "Mousey" by everyone except his wife ("I call him 'Honey' because I knew him before he was a mouse.")...
* The quotation displays authoritative expertise or opinion: "We're in the middle of a shakedown," personnel director Pete Jones said. "I expect more wholesale changes."

The quotation identifies or denies blame for a serious accusation: "His agent acknowledged that his client admits to 'serious lapses in judgment' in his use of steroids."

- The quotation demonstrates the speaker's characteristic rhythm of language: "Can't nobody stop me when I'm in the zone. Nobody comes near. I get the touch going, I make grown men cry. They cry 'cause they can't stop me. They cry 'cause they know I'm in the zone."

When Not to Use Quotes

However, as with leads, overused phrases can detract from a story. Would the following quotes add anything to a story?

"It was like a war out there."
"Well, it ain't over till the fat lady sings."
"The game was closer than the score indicated."

In addition to bad quotes, there are several other reasons to use paraphrasing instead of direct quotations:

- When you can make a statement or clarify a thought better than your interviewee. Remember, people don't talk so good. When they don't talk good, paraphrase.
- When you can verify information from several sources. Don't quote statistical or factual information. They make for dull quotes. Quote opinions and clarifying statements. Put statistical information in your own words.
- When the speaker talks about generally known information in common language. You don't need a quote from a coach saying, "We played well" if his team won by 50 points.
- When you have only "orphans" to use because you do not have an entire sentence that is quotable. Don't write a sentence such as, "LaRussa said that the Cardinals 'struggled offensively' despite Albert Pujols 'playing his heart out' with three hits, including a 'moon shot' that came on a 'nasty slider.'" Such a sentence makes LaRussa appear to be unable to string a complete sentence together. It would be better to paraphrase the partial quotes.
- When the person you are quoting is authoritative but unintelligible. Paraphrase instead of using a quote such as, "We be goin' bowlin', you know, 'cause, you know, um, we be playin', you know, friggin' good." A quote like this should never be used.

Basic Rules on Handling Quotes

Several basic rules are used by almost every news organization when including quotes in stories:

- If a direct quote is more than one sentence long, place the attribution at the end of the first sentence, as in: "That's one of the greatest adrenaline rushes you can have as a baseball player," Johnson said. "I'm not talking just about me because I hit the home run. Anytime your team wins like that, it's awesome."
- The first time you attribute a direct or indirect quote, identify the speaker with full name and title or other identification.
- Don't attribute direct quotes to more than one person, as in "We wanted to win this for Coach," members of the offensive line said.
- Use the past tense. And try to limit verbs. "Said" is an excellent verb to use. It does not call attention to itself (people rarely even notice the word), and it does not have an added connotation, such as "stated," which implies the person said something for the record, or "enthused," which implies the person was absolutely giddy about his or her quote. Other verbs can be even worse: "deadpanned," "exclaimed," "cooed," etc., but even "remarked" and "claimed" have connotations that may add unwanted hidden meanings to a quote.
- Ordinarily, place the noun or pronoun before the verb: "Tony LaRussa said." The exception to this rule is when the identification is so long that it would create an awkward sentence with two commas. Instead of: "Vice president of player personnel Joe Smith said," or "Joe Smith, vice president of player personnel, said," use: "said Joe Smith, vice president of player personnel." Otherwise, put the name before the verb, since who said the quote is more important than the fact that someone "said" something.

Modifying Quotes

A general rule of thumb is: don't modify quotes. Be as accurate as you can. However, because people don't talk so good, there are instances when modifying a quote slightly is the only option. You do not want one of your main sources to look stupid because he or she said something that was embarrassing.

One option to modifying quotes is to use partial quotes. Instead of a grammatically incorrect quote, you could write, "Art Shell expressed his 'complete and unwavering support' to the 'much maligned' Randy Moss, saying he 'has complete faith' in his 'misunderstood' star." This, of course, would create confusion for the reader—where does the quote begin and end—while creating a series of "orphans" (see explanation in this chapter) so limiting partial quotes to one in a sentence would be wise.

Another question of whether to modify a quote arises when a source stutters or uses inappropriate language, such as: "Like, you know, man, I just, you know, do the best @#$! I can." Using this quote verbatim would be inappropriate. A writer might want to clean the quote up and just write, "I just do the best I can." Note that this does not change the meaning of the quote. It still uses the source's exact words. It merely eliminates garbage that would make the source look less credible.

Finally, quotes at times need explanatory information. For instance, a quote from a coach might say, "Ralph has served our team well for the past 20 years." If Ralph had not been identified previously, he would need his last name inserted into the quote: "Ralph [Greenberg] has served our team well for the past 20 years." In such cases, however, it would be preferable to identify Ralph before the quote so the information in parentheses would not need to be added. You might write: Coach Sherm Tucker praised equipment manager Ralph Greenberg. "Ralph has served our team well for the past 20 years," Tucker said. Here, the identification is not only taken out of the quote, but it acts as a transitional device, making the quote come into the story more smoothly.

Getting Good Quotes From Athletes

Interview questions are obviously the key to getting good quotes. Ask a stupid question, you'll get a stupid answer. There are several questions strategies, however, that can help elicit good quotes:

- Focus on "how" and "why" questions. They ask for an opinion that will allow the interviewee to give his or her point of view and can lead to more sources of information. If you ask a yes/no question ("Did you think you had a chance to win?"), you might get a yes/no answer ("Yes.") and nothing more.
- Consider the interviewee's point of view. How do you anticipate he or she will answer your question? Attorney F. Lee Bailey once said that he never asked a question in court that he didn't know the answer to. If you think about potential answers ahead of time, you may get usable quotes more easily from your sources.
- Ask only questions the interviewee is qualified to answer. Don't ask a coach what a player was thinking. Ask the player.
- Separate yourself from criticisms of the interviewee. You can begin tough questions with "Some critics say..."

Follow-Up Questions

Of course, sports figures do not always answer questions completely, so be ready for follow-up questions. Several follow-up strategies can encourage sources to give better quotes: "Why do you say that?" "Can you give an example?" "And then what happened?"

- Sometimes, displaying ignorance can get a source to explain issues in simple language. For example, you could start a question with: "I'm not a mechanic, so I'm not clear on how this new technology is being used."
- Restate the answer: "Are you staying that..." Sources will typically appreciate your effort to clarify answers. And if you've misunderstood a quote, it's better to find out during an interview than after a story appears.
- Clarify generalizations. Make sure the source produces evidence to back up vague claims. If a source says, "I always pitch well against the Yankees," get his lifetime record and other stats.
- If a source is unable to answer a question, ask: "Who would you ask if you wanted to know the answer?" This will show the interviewee that you are being persistent and are interested enough to want to track down information from key sources.
- When all else fails, use five seconds of silence. This offers your source time to consider his or her answer. They often will volunteer more information. If an interview moves nonstop, the source has little opportunity to reconsider an answer or to expand on a point. A pause often helps sources gather their thoughts. Don't pause too long, though, or the source will assume the interview is over.

Bad Interview Questions

Bad questions lead to bad responses. Here are some types of questions that should be avoided.

- Two-part questions. Don't ask: "Did you consider pinch-hitting for the starting pitcher in the fifth inning, and is the injury to your third baseman serious?" These questions often confuse a source because they are forced to focus on two completely different areas. Sources then will often answer one part adequately, but not the other.
- Whether or not questions. What can you determine when you ask: "Can you tell me whether or not you'll return next year?" and the source says, "No"?
- Questions longer than two sentences. Three or more sentences is not a question. It's a speech. The interviewee will lose interest and will likely forget what you said in your early sentences.
- Unfocused questions and non-questions. Don't ask: "Can you tell me a funny story?" And don't ask: "That was a great game you had there." Actually, this isn't even a question.
- Cliché questions: "How did you feel when you scored the winning touchdown?"
- Leading questions: "Don't you just hate the Kansas Jayhawks?"

Incorporating Quotes into Stories with Transition

One of the most noticeable differences between a good story and a great story is how quotes are used. A good story uses quotes to emphasize key points made in the narrative. A great story uses transition to set up the quotes, which makes the story flow much better. For example, a reporter might write:

> The loss dropped Atlanta a half-game behind Florida.
> "It takes a lot to get me down," Atlanta manager Bobby Cox said. "This is as disappointing a loss as we've had this year. But we can't cry about it. We just have to go out and get the job done tomorrow."

The above two paragraphs are fine grammatically. However, note how the quote comes in abruptly. The reader is not prepared for the quote, and does not know the origin of the quote until the attribution. A better way to incorporate the quote into the story would be to paraphrase part of it and use that as a transitional device leading into the direct quote, such as:

> The loss, which dropped Atlanta a half-game behind Florida, was the one of the most disappointing of the season, Atlanta manager Bobby Cox said.
> "It takes a lot to get me down," Cox said. "But we can't cry about it. We just have to go out and get the job done tomorrow."

Transitions before quotes also allow a writer an opportunity to clear up potential confusion from an awkward quote. For example, take a look at the following awkward quote:

> "Favre had another incredible game, but it was [Jevon] Walker's 12 catches [actually he had 11] that were the key to the game," Packer Coach Mike Sherman said of his star wide receiver. "Walker has completely changed the entire chemistry of the team..."

Instead, a writer could explain several aspects of the quote in the transition, such as:

> Packer Coach Mike Sherman said that wide receiver Jevon Walker, who had 11 receptions, was the key to the game. "Walker has completely changed the entire chemistry of the team..."

The transition here not only provided an opportunity for the writer to correct the statistical mistake made in the quote, but it also allowed the writer to use the player's first name on first reference without awkwardly including it in parentheses within the quote. The transition also fully identifies the player, unlike in the original where the identification is part of the quote's attribution.

One danger in using a paraphrase as a transitional device is that sometimes, the paraphrases parrot the quote too closely. This creates an awkward redundancy. For example, you wouldn't want to write:

> Packer Coach Mike Sherman said that wide receiver Javon Walker was the key to the game. "Walker was the key to the game," Sherman said.

Other Quote Transitions

Transition also can be attained in several other ways:

- Linking thoughts. Often, all that is needed to create a smooth transition leading into a quote is a simple word or phrase, such as "also." For example, instead of following one quote with another, a transitional sentence might read: "In addition to praising Walker, Sherman also praised running back Ahmad Green. 'Green...'"
- Showing sequence of time. Sports stories are almost never written chronologically. What happens late in the game is usually much more important than the start. Therefore, time transitions can be used to go from one time period to another, as in: "Earlier in the game, Favre had three passes intercepted before settling down in the second half. 'One of the worst halves of football I've ever played,' Favre said."
- Contrasting ideas. Sporting events are full of contrasts. Comparing one bit of information with another often allows a story to progress smoothly. For instance: "While Favre was struggling in the first half, Green was enjoying great success. 'Without Green, we would have been buried in the first half,' Favre said." Other contrasting phrases include: "for instance," "for example," "as a result," and "on the other hand."
- Repetition of a word or phrase. A natural mental link is formed between a narrative sentence and an ensuing quote if a word or phrase is common in both. For example: "Sanders' interception gave the Ravens excellent field position. 'Sanders' interception got us out of a deep hole,' Raven Coach Brian Billick said."

10

MIDDLES IV

Play-By-Play

Televised sporting events usually have two announcers. One provides play-by-play while the other adds color commentary. The "straight" announcer sticks closely to the events at hand while his or her sidekick can go astray and even resort to buffoonery to entertain the audience (John Madden being one example).

In sports journalism, the writer functions as both the straight and color person. It's a one-person show where the story includes the event's structure covered in anecdotes and analysis. It requires the writer to gather statistics, quotes, and other information, and then meld them into one cohesive story.

The sports writer covering an event is sitting in for the readers who are not attending the game. He or she is expected to provide a complete and accurate picture of events. Of course, what is complete and accurate? How does a reporter strike a balance between writing too much and too little play-by-play? In this chapter, we'll discuss the utility of recording statistics during a game and the importance of play-by-play.

Overall Responsibilities

When a journalist types his or her byline atop a story, it's a statement that says, "I'm responsible for everything that follows." Although sports editors and copy editors might tinker with the story, the story has but one byline. And that byline carries incredible responsibility. It also creates anxiety. All the story's blemishes are now yours. The typos: your fault. The incorrect information: your fault. The misplaced modifiers: your fault. The weak verbs, poor transitions, and incorrect grammar: your fault, your fault, your fault. Even if the copy editor makes the mistakes, you are to blame—or at least the readers think so.

But that's only the half of it. The alluring lead, the insightful quote and the snappy transitions are yours as well. For journalists, there are few better feelings than opening the newspaper, seeing their byline and realizing they have produced a good story. It's that emotional rush that entices journalists to write story after story.

As a sports writer, you will cover hundreds and possibly thousands of games. For instance, a Major League Baseball beat writer might cover as many as 200 games during the three seasons: preseason, regular season, and postseason. And each game has its individual importance. Grandma wants to know how little Jimmy did in his basketball game and the diehard Oakland Raiders fan wants to know if the skull mask is appropriate to wear to work Monday.

The sports journalist's responsibility to be fair and accurate goes beyond the current interests of the readers. In time, the newspaper account of an event is a historical document. Hundreds of years from now someone can read your account of what transpired. Providing a clear picture of the events carries not only current responsibilities but generational as well.

The Heart of the Game Story

There are several techniques to write games stories. Some sports journalists start with the lead and write vertically, top to bottom. Some build the story around good quotes. Others identify the key elements of the game and build around those elements. Still others write the play-by-play and work outward, incorporating key elements and quotes. The story radiates from the nucleus, which in this case is the play-by-play or action.

Although the play-by-play might not be the most important element of the story, it is the story's core. Good stories are buried within the action on the playing field. Sports journalists need not only to record the action but also put it into context. They also need to identify when the play-by-play is necessary and when it is not. So taking thorough notes during a game is essential to informing the readers and identifying the larger story.

Recording Play-by-Play

Every sports journalist covering a game develops his or her own technique in recording play-by-play. Some will use official scorebooks. Others will write in a reporter's notebook or legal pad. The process of recording the information is not nearly as important as the information. Substance definitely trumps style. Here are a few tips in covering different sports.

Baseball

Keeping the scorebook is always a good idea. Recording every at bat, pitch, hit, out, error, RBI, walk, strikeout, and runners left on base will provide great statistical data. Filling in the blanks for attendance, umpires, and time of game can prove valuable as well. But keeping the book is not enough. A baseball scoresheet does not show how an error with the bases loaded allowed two runs to score in the fourth inning. So along with keeping the scorebook, taking notes in a separate notepad is wise. The scorebook provides the raw data while the notes provide the context.

For those who do not know how to keep score, many scorebooks have instructions. Even if you've kept the book in the past, the instructions can provide useful tips. Learning to keep the book is part of the pre-reporting process discussed in Chapter 3.

During the game, write a re-cap of each inning. You can record it in your notebook or laptop. There will be some innings where nothing happens: three up; three down. Some innings will include scoring, others will feature runners in scoring position who fail to score. That will be useful information if the game ends 4–3 and the losing team had loaded the bases in the second inning but failed to score. The detailed play-by-play assists in determining turning points of games.

The amount of play-by-play used in a game story is determined by the game's outcome. Close games will include more play-by-play than blowouts. For instance, in a 4–3 game the reporter will probably include all the scoring. It's only seven total runs and each run is important. As mentioned in Chapter 4, working backward from the last score to the first is best. The final run is the most interesting and the first run is the least. Here's an example of the notes from a game between Northside and Southside:

> **First inning:** Southside: Smith singles; thrown out trying to steal second; strikeout; strikeout.
>
> Northside: flyout; groundout; groundout.
>
> **Second inning:** Southside: one out; Jackson doubles to LC (left-center); moves to third on Jefferson's groundout; 2 outs; Jackson scores on Murphy's single between third and short; strikeout ends inning: **Northside 0, Southside 1.**
>
> Northside: Three consecutive singles, Handley, Dean, Sanders, load the bases; Francis doubles, scoring three runs. Relief pitcher Jackson: groundout, flyout, strikeout. **Northside 3, Southside 1.**
>
> **Third inning:** Southside: Truman walks; Smith sacrifice bunt moves Truman to second; strikeout; Jacobson singles to center (groundball) to score Truman; flyout. **Northside 3, Southside 2.**
>
> Northside: flyout, groundout, groundout.
>
> **Fourth inning:** Southside: Jackson hits to shortstop Sanders, reaches on throwing error, advancing to second; groundout;

flyout; Noonan singles through right side of infield, scoring Jackson; flyout. **Northside 3, Southside 3.**

Northside: groundout; groundout; groundout.

Fifth inning: Southside: groundout; Reese singles to center; Jacobson hits into double play.

Northside: Logan singles, steals second; (first hit off Jackson); strikeout; passed ball moves Logan to third; Irving hits sacrifice fly to left; Logan slides under tag; groundout. **Northside 4, Southside 3.**

Sixth inning: Southside; strikeout; Jackson doubles; Jackson moves to third on wild pitch; groundout; Murphy hits ball to deep center, but it's caught by Logan to end the inning.

Northside: flyout; flyout; strikeout.

Seventh inning: Southside: groundout; groundout; flyout.

Northside: Did not bat.

Final: Northside 4, Southside 3.

The scorebook will fill in the details such as outs, hits, and other statistics but your notes provide the meat of the story. And bolding the inning and score makes it easy to identify the highlights. If using a notebook, circling or underlining the inning and score is just as effective. The play-by-play for this story could read:

Northside manufactured the winning run after Lewis Logan led off with a single and stole second. With one out, Logan moved to third on a passed ball, and scored on Paul Irving's sacrifice fly to left, sliding under the tag of catcher Brandon Jefferson.

The winning run was explained in two sentences. From there, the play-by-play can be built outward. For instance:

After Jeff Jackson doubled in the second and scored on Caleb Murphy's single to give Southside a 1–0 lead, Northside rallied for three runs on four hits in the bottom of the inning. Jim Francis' three-run double with no outs gave Northside a 3–1 lead.

Southside chipped away with solo runs in each the third and fourth innings. In the third, Pat Truman walked, moved to second on Todd Smith's sacrifice bunt, and with two outs, scored on Tom Jacobson's groundball single to center.

Jackson tied the game at 3 in the fourth inning when he reached second on a throwing error by Northside shortstop Chip Sanders. With two outs, Brian Noonan singled through the right side of the infield to score Jackson.

In four paragraphs and 167 words, the game's entire play-by-play was written. Additional statistics, extracted from the scorebook (i.e., Jackson 5 innings pitched, 1 hit; also scored twice), still need to be included, but the core of the game's action is complete. Granted, there's no great storytelling in the play-by-play but it's quick, clean, and concise.

Football

Covering a football game can be overwhelming. While baseball moves at a slow, leisurely pace, football is dispersed in violent five-second intervals. A collection of consecutive intervals account for scoring drives, which become the core of the story. The reporter's job is to record every interval: those that result in scores and those that do not. When writing the story, failure in football can be equally important as success. Some teams play to win games and others play not to lose. A team that plays not to lose is one attempting to prevent as many mistakes as possible, but doing little to advance the football toward the goal line. Reporting that lack of forward progress just might be the highlight of the game.

Sports journalists develop their own style for keeping football statistics. It generally involves writing down the events of every play. Here's an example of the notes from a game between Northside and Southside:

> Southside kickoff 56 yards to the Northside 9, Rogers return 48 yards to the Southside 43.
>
> N 1-10 S43 Logan pass to Daniels, 3 yards
> N 2-7 S40 Charles rush, no gain: 13:42
> N 3-7 S40 Logan pass to Sanders, 13 yards to S27
>   1ST DOWN
> N 1-10 S27 Dean rush, 27 yards TD; 12:59
>   1ST DOWN
>
> X-TRA Pt.: Logan kick, good
> Northside 7, Southside 0

There are a couple items to note in this scenario: 1-10 is first down and 10 yards to go before another first down. S43 means the ball is on Southside's 43 yardline. Also, be sure to record a first down whenever a touchdown is longer than 10 yards. Frequently marking the time assists in determining how long the scoring drive takes. This scoring drive was four plays, 43 yards in 2:01. The play-by-play could read:

> Northside scored just 2:01 into the game when Howard Dean's 27-yard touchdown run capped a four-play, 43-yard drive. The

drive was sparked by a 13-yard completion from Lewis Logan to Ted Sanders on third-and-7. The next play, Dean ran off tackle, sidestepped the middle linebacker and outraced the strong safety to score.

The details of Dean's run would have to be recorded in your notebook as well. Similar to keeping the baseball scorebook, tallying statistics is not enough.

Football warrants careful bookkeeping. Readers not only want rushing and passing yardage, but also gritty details such as penalty yards, punt return yardage and time of possession. Those stats probably will be included in newspaper boxscores but sometimes they are necessary in the game story. "Our penalties killed us tonight." If that becomes a pivotal quote from a coach, it's essential to have the number of penalties and the yardage. It would also be important to write about a penalty that stalled a scoring drive or negated a touchdown.

Keeping tabs of all the statistics certainly can impede watching the game. Sometimes you'll be writing down the information from the last play when the next play begins. But in the process, do not get so involved in the bookkeeping that you miss the larger picture. Not only watch the game, but also see what is happening. Be sure to identify a change in quarterback or the adjustments a defense makes at half-time. Remember, the storytelling isn't in the statistics but in what the statistics mean.

Also, half-time for everyone else does not mean a break for you. During the intermission, calculate the rushing attempts and yardage for players on both teams. Do the same with passing and receiving yardage. Carrying a pocket calculator is always a good idea. If you add the statistics at half-time, you'll only have to add the second half statistics after the game. That can save precious time, particularly on deadline. Here's another shortcut: instead of writing the names of the players involved in the action, just write their numbers. Because you have a roster, you can decode the statistics later, transforming the numbers into names. For instance, instead of writing, "Logan pass to Daniels, 3 yards," it could read, "10 pass to 81, 3 yards." Or better yet, "10 ps 81, 3 yds."

Over time you'll develop your own shorthand and shortcuts. As with any sport, when writing football game stories, focus on the most significant scoring drives. Less play-by-play will be used in blowouts than in close games.

Basketball

Covering basketball is as simple or complicated as the sports editor wants it to be. Some newspapers only report shots made, free throws made and attempted, and total points of each player. Others will include those statistics along with shots attempted, rebounds, steals, assists, turnovers, blocks, and personal fouls. With one ball among 10 players, that's some serious stat keeping.

Besides the leading scorers and rebounders, team scoring runs, shooting slumps, and free-throw trends are particularly important. If a team misses its first six shots, that could influence the game's outcome. If after missing six straight the coach calls timeout or substitutes players, it could be the game's turning point. For good reason, many coaches believe turnovers determine the outcome of games. Pay particular attention to the number of turnovers and who is committing them.

Probably more than any other sport, basketball games include "in-the-zone" players. Those are the players who cannot miss a shot. The defense cannot seem to stop them and everything they chuck up goes in. Basketball also has its share of "out-of-the-zone" players. Those players cannot hit the ocean with their shot but continue to shoot. Identifying both is essential to every game story.

Basketball stat keeping is similar to football. Keeping track of every play is ideal. Divide an 8 ½ by 11-inch legal pad with a line that separates the home team and visitors. Table 10.1 shows an example of a few minutes of a high school game.

After 3 minutes, 51 seconds, Northside was winning 7–6. During that time, the sports writer was busy recording every statistical occurrence. What the stats tell us is that after making its first shot, Southside missed five straight, including two 3-pointers. Also, Northside had three turnovers, two of which resulted in Southside baskets. Individually for Southside, Combs leads the scoring with four points and Black has been involved in the action (a steal, a basket, a missed 3-pointer and an assist). For Northside, Johnson has five points and Turner has had an active 3:51 (two rebounds, three turnovers, a foul, a missed shot and an assist). Play-by-play for the first half of the first quarter could read:

> After Shawn Black gave Southside a 2–0 lead, the Rebels missed their next five shots, allowing Northside to build a 7–6 lead midway through the first quarter. Erin Johnson's 3-pointer gave Northside a 7–4 lead but Jennifer Combs hit a jumper to cut Southside's deficit to 1.

As discussed earlier, a sports journalist would not necessarily provide the play-by-play of the first four minutes of the game in the game story. If the sequence of events has no real bearing on the overall game, leave it out.

Table 10.1 Basketball scoring play-by-play

		1st quarter		
Home: Southside Rebels	Time	Score		Visitors: Northside Warriors
	7:46			MISSED JUMPER by Parker
	7:46			REBOUND (OFF) by Smith
	7:39			MISSED JUMPER by Parker
	7:39			REBOUND (OFF) by Turner
	7:34			TURNOVER by Turner
STEAL by Black	7:33			
LAYUP by Black	7:31	2–0		
	7:09	2–2		JUMPER by Johnson
MISSED 3 PTR by Black	6:29			
REBOUND (OFF) by (TEAM)	6:29			
MISSED 3 PTR by Booth	6:21			
	6:21			REBOUND (DEF) by Turner
FOUL by Hastings	6:13			
	6:07			FOUL by Turner
	6:07			TURNOVER by Turner
MISSED JUMPER by Combs	5:47			
REBOUND (OFF) by Demo	5:47			
MISSED JUMPER by Demo	5:44			
	5:44			REBOUND (DEF) by Parker
	5:33	2–4		JUMPER by Parker
	5:33			ASSIST by Smith
MISSED JUMPER by Hastings	5:11			
	5:11			REBOUND (DEF) by Smith
	5:03			TURNOVER by Turner
STEAL by Gee	5:03			
LAYUP by Combs	4:57	4–4		
ASSIST by Black	4:57			
	4:34	4–7		3 PTR by Johnson
	4:34			ASSIST by Turner
JUMPER by Combs	4:09	6–7		
ASSIST by Hastings	4:09			

Obviously, the notes of an entire game can be rather extensive. But using player numbers and abbreviations can minimize the work as shown in Table 10.2.

Of course, remembering how to decode the material is essential, so be sure the abbreviations make sense. Including the distance of the shots might be worth recording as well. A 6-foot jumper at the buzzer is very different from a 34-foot jumper. Specifics are always much better than general information. Knowing the difference between 6 and 34 feet is easy but estimating a jumpshot between 14 feet and 19 can be difficult.

Table 10.2 Basketball scoring play-by-play using abbreviations

	1st quarter		
Home: Southside Rebels	*Time*	*Score*	*Visitors: Northside Warriors*
	7:46		MS JPR/10
	7:46		REB (O)/13
	7:39		MS JPR/10
	7:39		REB (O)/22
	7:34		TO/22
STL/18	7:33		
LYUP/18	7:31	2–0	
	7:09	2–2	JPR/6
MS 3/18	6:29		
REB (O)/Team	6:29		
MS 3/23	6:21		
	6:21		REB (D)/22
FL/14	6:13		
	6:07		FL/22
	6:07		TO/22

Because you will not be allowed to rush out to the court with a tape measure, estimating the distance is acceptable. Use the dimensions of the court to determine distance. In basketball, the free-throw line is 15 feet from the rim. In high school, the 3-point arc is 19 feet, 9 inches. Starting the 2008–09 season, a 3-pointer for college basketball will be 20 feet, 9 inches. And the key for high school and college is 12-feet wide. With those dimensions in mind, estimations between a 14-foot jumper and a 19-footer should be relatively easy. So a 34-footer in high school would be nearly 14 feet behind the 3-point arc and 8 feet from center court.

Relatively speaking, basketball is an easy sport to follow. Whereas baseball and football have difficult nuances (i.e., infield fly rule or the free kick after a safety), basketball is simple: put the ball in the cylinder. Depending on the circumstances, a basket is worth 1, 2 or 3 points. It's a simple game with simple math. Keeping track of the math is where the difficulty lies.

Other Sports

Most newspaper sports journalists cover a variety of sports. Some sports are so similar that they can be discussed in general terms.

"Ball and net" games have certain similarities. The objective of soccer, hockey, field hockey, and lacrosse is to put the ball (or puck) into the net. Recording who scored, assisted in scoring the goal, and the time and circumstances of the score are the primary statistics. The important stats for the entire game include shots or shots on goal, saves by the goalkeeper and penalty situations (i.e., penalty minutes for hockey; yellow/red cards in soccer; penalty corners or corner kicks, etc.). Because the statistics and play-by-play are minimal compared to other sports, ball and net games allow for a great deal of storytelling.

Other types of sports include team sports with individual elements such as wrestling, swimming, track and field, gymnastics, and tennis. Although teams accumulate points, athletes perform as individuals to get those points. In wrestling, for instance, the team winner might not be determined until the final match between heavyweights. In that case, winning 8 of 14 matches might not be nearly as important as the heavyweight match.

In other sports where individuals compete in several events in one meet (swimming, gymnastics, track and field), individual performances trump team performance. Athletes in these sports can win championships as individuals and as team members. Those who perform well in two or more sports provide the heart of the play-by-play.

Tennis players and golfers also can win individual and team championships. But unlike swimming, gymnastics, and track and field, tennis players do not compete in more than two events (singles and doubles). Golfers, of course, compete in just one event.

Volleyball is the one sport that is neither a ball and net nor team with individual elements. Sure, there is a ball and net, but the object isn't to put the ball in the net. And, there are individual performances but not in the same sense as the previously mentioned sports. In volleyball, individual statistics include kills, sets, digs, blocks, and service points. Similar to basketball, hot and cold streaks in volleyball should be recorded.

Then there are sports where statistics are not important to the final result. Boxing is a good example. One guy can beat the ugly off another and still lose with a knockout. The play-by-play might include an exchange of punches in certain rounds or a knockdown early in the fight. It's actually more descriptive writing than play-by-play, although for some professional fights sports journalists can track down official punch totals (i.e., CompuBox stats). Before the fight, ask the fight promoter or coordinator where to get those statistics.

When in doubt about scoring or statistics, check with the scorer's table or home team. The home team is designated the official scorer of the event. If you are unsure if a batted ball is a hit or an error, consult the home team's scorer. In fact, all statistics should be double-checked with the official scorer after the game. Verifying statistics with the scorer ensures accuracy. Football would be the exception. Coaches usually do not record official statistics until after viewing the videotape. Because the sports writer is on deadline, the statistics recorded during the game are the ones published. Of course, at college and professional events, statistics are provided. But even at college and professional games, keeping your own play-by-play helps identify key plays.

Providing play-by-play in stories is essential to storytelling. The best play-by-play is short and concise. Get to the point and then get to the storytelling. Good game stories do just that. The statistics and details are only vehicles that carry the story.

Play-by-Play: Past

Those who read sports stories have a working knowledge of sports terminology. They understand what a shortstop is and who snaps the ball to the quarterback. But in the 1800s, many readers did not understand the terminology. Games stories were a combination of explanation and information. First, the writer had to explain the game, and second, he had to explain what happened.

In the mid-1840s, baseball was developed in the image of the British game "rounders." The *New York Morning News* published a story and agate of a game between the New York Ball Club and a team from Brooklyn. The October 22, 1845 story included the following play-by-play:

> The match was for the first twenty-one aces – three out, all out. Hunt made a single ace, but before another was added to the score, three of the New Yorkers went out in rapid succession, and the bats were yielded to Brooklyn. Many of the Brooklyn players were eminent cricketers, but the severe tactics of the NY Club proved too effective, and they soon resigned their innings to their opponents, not scoring one.
>
> New York now took her second chance, and the score began slowly to tell. During this inning, four aces were made off a single hit, but by the arbitrary nature of the game, a single mistake sometimes proving fatally irretrievable, they were soon driven to the field again. The second innings of the Brooklyn players proved alike disastrous, and the close of the third still left them, all their tickets blank. On the fourth innings the New York Club made up their score to twenty-four aces. The Brooklyn players then took their fourth, against hopeless odds, but with undiminished spirits. They were, however, forced to yield with a score of four only, and the New Yorkers were declared winners with a spare three and a flush of twenty. The fielding

Table 10.3 In case you missed it, New York beat Brooklyn, 24–4. The boxscore read:

Runs	Hands out	Runs	Hands out
New York Ball Club.			
Davis 5		Case. 2	2
Tucker 2	3	Vail 3	1
Miller 4	1	Kline 2	3
Winslow 4	2		
Murphy 2		—	—
		12	
Brooklyn Players.			
Hunt	2	Sharp	1
Gilmore 1	2	Whaley 1	1
Hardy 1	2	Ayres	
Forman 1	2		
Hine	1	—	—
		12	

of the Brooklyn players was, for the most part, beautiful, but they were evidently not so well practiced in the game as their opponents.

Baseball aficionados can piece together the occurrences of the New York–Brooklyn game, but clearly the language of the day creates confusion. In rounders, common terms included "innings," "outs," and "bases." But while a score in rounders was called a "rounder," baseball adapted "runs" and used bases instead of wooden posts to mark the four locations around the field or pitch. The trick for early baseball writers was to keep the language simple enough for readers to understand but provide enough detail to accurately tell the story.

We can learn a lesson from the early baseball writers. In an era of fantasy teams and instant message scores, statistics can overwhelm a reader. Including the VORP (Value Over Replacement Player) or OPS (On-base percentage + Slugging percentage) in a story without extensive explanation would only add confusion.

Early football writers had similar problems. Football evolved from rugby, soccer, and a variety of other kicking games. Through the 1860s and 1870s, teams would agree to a set of rules prior to playing. Some preferred soccer rules and others preferred rugby. That changed in 1880 when the Intercollegiate Football Association initiated a new set of rules. When Yale played Princeton in November 1880, the new rules were applied. Part of the *New York Daily Tribune* included this play-by-play:

> At 2:30 o'clock the ball was placed in the centre of the field, and Camp, of Yale, kicked it off. The ball was quickly recovered by Morgan, of Princeton, who lifted it high over Yale's rushers. Lamb muffed the ball, and in a twinkling the Princeton rushers were upon him. They captured the ball directly in front of Yale's goal. In the scrimmage that followed, Peace sent the ball over Yale's line, counselling her to touch down for safety, amid the cheers of Princeton, and the waving of orange ribbons.

Football play-by-play obviously relied upon generalities and lacked specific details seen in today's game stories. Because few statistics were incorporated in the stories it was difficult to determine field position or good performances. While the play-by-play lacked statistics, it included colorful details. One part of the Yale–Princeton story read:

> There was a rush in which yellow, black, and white flashed before the eye like the colors of a kaleidoscope—then the ball was forced out of bounds. Just at this point had been heaped a large pile of snow. A Princeton rusher tripped and went into it head foremost. Three others met the same fate while the snow flew in clouds, almost concealing them from sight. But Princeton emerged, half smothered, with the ball.

Although the snow incident has little affect on the game's outcome, it provides colorful details entertaining to the reader. The Yale–Princeton game was for the "College Foot-ball Championship" but the game story never provides a final score. The story reports: "There was much disgust expressed that the game ended in a draw, and also that Princeton peremptorily refused Yale's challenge to another game." By limiting the statistics, the writer can focus on the drama of the event. Numbers can sometimes be a hindrance to readers and the story. Sure, it can be argued that readers want stats, and that's a valid argument, but readers want good stories too. Besides, the game statistics can be placed on the agate page. Minimizing statistics frees up space to write about other aspects of the game.

Basketball did not become popular until the 1890s. As discussed earlier in this chapter, the game's concept is rather simple. A December 27, 1896 article from the *Brooklyn Eagle* reads:

> The basketball team representing the Central YMCA. journeyed to New Britain, Conn., on Christmas day and played the New Britain YMCA. team an exciting game [*sic*]. The contest

was close and a feature was the absence of fouls. The final score was 9 points to 7 in favor of the Connecticut boys. For Central three goals were thrown from the field by Leeds, Keown, and Cameron respectively and one from the foul line by Leeds. For New Britain four goals were thrown from the field, two of which were by Kron and one each by Lehman and Clark. Kron also threw one from the foul line.

The play-by-play of this game is not dramatically different from what a reader might see today. The information is easily understood. Unlike early baseball and football games, basketball established statistics that could easily be incorporated into a newspaper report.

Play-by-Play: Present and Future

With the emergence of the Internet and 24-hour sports networks, game coverage and analysis has grown tremendously. Game information can be received instantly via cell phones and retrieved just as quickly on the Internet. While the package for presenting information has changed, the significance of the information has not. Perhaps more than ever readers want to know the play-by-play; they just want it quicker than ever before.

Some argue that play-by-play and even game stories in newspapers are unnecessary. To some degree that's true. Compared to the Internet, television, and radio, newspapers lag behind in timeliness. For many readers, what happened at 10 p.m. is no longer news at 6 a.m. But newspapers provide detail and analysis that other media do not. Boxscores and "how they scored" summaries are elements typically not present in other media. Those items can also minimize the amount of play-by-play included in the game story.

Being obsolete is the downfall of newspapers, as it is the downfall of your game stories. By quickly providing the play-by-play, and then adding context, game stories can be interesting and significant for the readers.

Instead of neglecting Internet readers, post a summarized game story on the newspaper's Web page shortly after the game. It will mostly be constructed of play-by-play, but it's a nice service for the readers. Because you will be writing an analysis of the game for the newspaper version, even Web readers will read the paper.

Another thing to remember is that most high school and small college events are not covered by radio or television. The newspaper is the medium of record, and readers will want the information. Providing information to readers online or in the newspaper is still your primary purpose.

Play-by-play does not have to be a speedbump in a good story. If properly presented, play-by-play can be the mechanism that allows for you to include good storytelling.

Using Slang

Englishman Pierce Egan is considered by many to be the father of newspaper sports slang. Mingling with vagabonds, jailbirds, bartenders, soldiers, and actors, Egan incorporated their language into his articles for sporting magazines in the early-1800s. Many of the words Egan used were excluded from Samuel Johnson's dictionary after he labeled them as "impure" and "not legitimate English." In 1823, Egan produced the *Francis Grose's Dictionary of the Vulgar Tongue as Revised and Corrected by Pierce Egan*. Egan's dictionary included items such as a "racket" or "rig" defined as a "particular kind of fraud or robbery;" money was "dust," "iron," "pony" or "darby;" "even Stephen" was even money; and to "post the pony" or "pony up" meant to "put up the coin." In his boxing stories, Egan would call the head "a knowledge box," "tea canister," "can," "block," "nob," "pimple" or "dome." The nose was a "conk," "snuffer-tray," "beak," "snorer," "bugle" or "smeller." The mouth was a "gob," "mug" or "potato trap." The eyes were "peepers," "squinters," "shutters," "blinkers" or "lamps." For instance, a black eye was "a touch of the blue bag under the peeper."

Although ESPN—particularly SportsCenter—has elevated the use of slang in sports commentary, colorful language and subjective words need to be monitored. What works for Stewart Scott on SportsCenter does not necessarily read well. "Boo-jah!" might sound good on TV but in print it reads like a sexually-transmitted disease.

Phrases such as "walk-off home run," "takes it to the house," "cleans the glass" might sound good but do they truly describe the action? Sports editors and readers prefer simple language. And not everyone understands ESPNisms. If the phrase alienates some of the audience, then they'll stop reading.

Subjective language should also be avoided. Allowing opinions to seep into your stories can alienate readers. The sentence, "Doug Brand made a one-handed, spectacular diving catch in the back of the end zone to score the winning touchdown" includes subjective language. While the writer can verify that Brand made a "one-handed, diving catch" he or she cannot verify "spectacular." What is spectacular to one person might not be so for another. As a sports journalist, sticking close to the actual provable events adds credence and credibility to the story. Besides, avoiding slang will make your sports editor happy. As a case in point, here is a memo *San Antonio Express-News* Deputy Sports Editor Al Carter sent to his staff:

We Do Not Write the Way ESPN Talks

One of our goals in writing is originality in style. Hence, we are not keen on clichés—and ESPN (citing that as the most notorious example) has become a Chernobyl of clichés. That may be what you hear day-in and day-out. That may be the way you talk to your buddy. But that isn't the way you should write.

We don't need to gimmick-up the simplest words and descriptions of sports reporting. We gain nothing by substituting "hoops" for basketball or "pick" for interception or "win" (the slang noun form) when "victory" always has been and always will be perfectly descriptive and far more proper. (The noun "win" is fine for headlines. But not everything that's fine for headlines is fine for a story.) "Walk-off homer" became a cliché the instant it jumped out of Dan Patrick's mouth. "Walk-off homer," in your story, could easily evolve into "walk-off strikeout" in my story, or maybe a "walk-off ground ball to the shortstop" in someone else's. Here's where we draw the line. Believe it or not, we had words to describe those things before SportsCenter came along. That's their style. If you copy it, you have no style. You're just borrowing theirs.

This, from another Carter memo, Followed a week later:

Clichés and Verbal Contrivances

Our lone appeal for "walk-off homer" was denied. Questions were presented about what constitutes a cliché. Well, it's kind of like a strike in baseball. It's hard to define—but you know it when you see it. Clichés are basically contrived words or phrases that may have been original in their youth but have since moved way past their prime. Some wear out more quickly than others. Some are so contrived, they should never have been uttered in the first place. Like "walk-off homer." I've never seen a person who has just hit a home run walk. The other team may be walking off—but that's not the active party in what we're describing. It's cute for TV, but not for us. Cliché police, keep your pistols loaded. Burt brought up "vertical passing game." That's coach-speak. And since you're writing, and not coaching, skip it. "Athleticism" is another one to dump. What does it mean? I would assume that an athlete has athleticism. Let's get specific.

In an e-mail, Carter, who has been working in newspapers for more than 30 years, added: "Getting our younger writers converted back to the English language—and to the use of good grammar—has been no easy task, but we're getting there. It's shocking how many candidates for entry level jobs think that all they have to do is transcribe what they hear on TV and—wham!—they're a sports writer! Wrong."

Writing and reading good writing can help improve your storytelling. Simple language that correctly conveys information is preferred. And while this chapter outlined some rules for game coverage, each sports editor and department will have his or her own guidelines.

Suggested Reading

Anderson, Douglas A. *Contemporary Sports Reporting*. Chicago: Nelson-Hall Publishers, 1994. It includes extensive detail on game coverage and statistical note-keeping.

11

ENDINGS I

Story Endings

The lead is the most important part of a sports story. Without an effective lead, readers won't become interested in the content of the story. Transitions and the body of stories are important because readers may lose interest and stop reading if the middles of stories are not effective.

How to end a story is also important. Writers need to bring closure to stories, not just end the story when they run out of things to write. Writers can spend hours laboring over their leads, yet not think twice about the best way to end their story.

Often, the best endings refer back to the opening paragraphs, returning to points made in the lead. This brings the story full circle, demonstrating a strong plan on the part of the writer. For example, note how the following story talks about struggles by the Milwaukee Brewers in PNC Park in Pittsburgh. The ending links back to the lead, bringing a sense of closure to the story.

By Tom Haudricourt
Pittsburgh Journal-Sentinal
August 15, 2006

PITTSBURGH – Some of the newcomers on the Milwaukee Brewers' roster who contributed Tuesday night to a badly needed 6–3 victory over Pittsburgh haven't been around long enough to know they aren't supposed to win at PNC Park.

Left-hander Doug Davis, on the other hand, was well aware of the sordid past.

"I felt I had something to prove," Davis said. "This team has given us so much trouble. I wanted to break the streak they've got going. That was in the back of my mind."

With Davis turning in seven strong innings and the offense breaking through for four late runs against a Pittsburgh bullpen that was impervious the previous evening, the Brewers finally won at PNC for the first time in six tries this season. They've got a ways to go to dent their all-time record of 16–35 in this ballpark but you have to start somewhere.

The Ending

Acquired in a trade with Kansas City on July 25, (Tony) Graffanino was blissfully unaware of the Brewers' string of failures at PNC Park. But he did understand that a team that fell eight games below .500 the previous evening was in dire need of a positive outcome.

"We needed a win and we got one," he said. "We've got to go out and try to play each game to win."

Which has been easier said than done for the Brewers in this scenic park on the banks of the Allegheny River. Though Davis indicated otherwise, Yost has insisted all along that the six years of torment for the Brewers at PNC has not gotten into his players' heads.

"You guys put too much stock in that," Yost told reporters. "If you play good and score some runs, you'll win anywhere."

Even here.

Several types of endings are commonly used. Many of these types of endings are the same as lead types.

Quote

Probably the most common ending sports writers utilize is a quote. Essentially, this type of ending allows the writer to put the conclusion in the hands of a source. Coaches or players very often can summarize the main points of a sporting event in their quotes.

Notice how the ending quote summarizes an important point about the report.

By Carter Gaddis
The Tampa Tribune
August 16, 2006

ST. PETERSBURG – The game was there for the taking Tuesday, as it has been so often this season for the Devil Rays. And, as also has happened so often—especially since the All-Star break—the Rays didn't take it.

On a night when Toronto ace Roy Halladay was closer to mortal than usual and Tampa Bay right-hander Jae Seo continued his second-half resurgence, the Blue Jays still prevailed, 4–3, in front of 9,217 fans at Tropicana Field.

Rays manager Joe Maddon didn't get the hoped-for boost of playing at home after a winless, six-game road trip to Seattle and Oakland.

"It's the same old story," Maddon said, meaning that, in his opinion, the "effort, preparation and intent" were there on the part of his team, but that certain something that leads to victory still was missing as Tampa Bay equaled its season-worst losing streak (seven).

"I feel like it's the first year of the existence of this franchise this year," Maddon said. "I'm looking at it as a first year. I'm not thinking they've been here for several years. It's the first year, and all the growing pains attached.

"Understand, these games are no fun. It's no fun to go home after this game. It's no fun to wake up in the morning and ask myself, 'What did we do last night?' 'Oh, we lost.' That's a bad thing. But I like what we're doing. I really like what we're doing, and I think it's going to continue to get better."

Maddon chose, as always, to focus on the little moments of success. And there were a few, even as Halladay (15–3) became the first 15-game winner in the majors and the Rays blew a lead for an American League-leading 65th time.

Third baseman BJ Upton robbed Vernon Wells of extra bases with a diving stop and pinpoint throw to end the top of the ninth. Rocco Baldelli singled home Upton in the eighth to cut the lead to a run.

Catcher Dioner Navarro threw out John McDonald trying to steal second to end the eighth. Rookie shortstop Ben

Zobrist battled Blue Jays closer BJ Ryan in a tough ninth-inning at-bat, forcing a full count before striking out to end the game.

And Seo received his third consecutive no-decision, despite his third consecutive respectable outing: seven innings, two runs.

The game was tied at 2 until the Jays scored a pair of runs off part-time Rays closer Brian Meadows in the eighth, which came on singles by Alex Rios and McDonald.

Tampa Bay took a 2–0 lead against Halladay in the first, when Carl Crawford singled and Greg Norton hit his 10th home run. Seo gave up runs in the fourth and fifth, but managed to limit the damage despite allowing seven hits over the course of those two innings.

Although conscious that a major-league worst, 8–22 record since the All-Star break made his words of optimism seem contradictory ("I'm really not trying to be a salesman here," he said), Maddon remained unwavering during a post-game delivery that evolved into a succinct discussion of the state of the franchise.

Not surprising, considering the Rays are on pace for 98 losses.

"It just takes time," Maddon said. "It takes time, and you have to be patient. As long as you're doing the right things, and as long as that [locker] room is good and people are sticking together, it's going to come around. And that's what I'm seeing. The moment I waver, they'll waver."

Question

Question leads are usually not effective because it would be better to answer questions than ask them. So, too, question endings are, typically, not effective. Sometimes, question endings directly address the reader. Sometimes, they ask rhetorical questions that can't be answered.

The ending below takes a creative approach by informally concluding the story with a conversational-style question.

By Dave Hyde, Sports Columnist
South Florida Sun-Sentinel
February 11, 2008
Marion's elation to join Heat begs question: Why?

Now that some time has passed, and the raw relief of Shaquille O'Neal's exit is gone, let's ask the question that should nag at Heat fans just a bit:

Why is Shawn Marion so darned happy to be here?

He turned lemonade to lemons. He went from a contending team in Phoenix to the worst team in the Heat. He went from a franchise that gave him a four-time All-Star platform to one where he'll play out the season in gloomy anonymity.

He didn't get promised more millions. He didn't get promised a bigger role. He was told, even before arriving, this was Heat guard Dwyane Wade's team.

By any rational measure, shouldn't Marion be a bit cranky about being put on a team whose season is a "disaster," as coach Pat Riley called it Sunday? Or couldn't Marion be lukewarm about the deal? Or anything on the dial below "delighted," as he put it.

"Sometimes change is good," Marion said.

How is this one of those times?

He shrugs. "It just is," he says. "Everybody gets used to doing the same thing over and over. Sometimes it's good to change it up."

If by change, it would mean the Heat is winning, that would be one thing. But the only change you saw in Sunday's loss was from the style of losing. The Heat ran a lot more in a 104–94 loss to the Lakers—"good energy," Riley called it.

Marion had 15 points and 14 rebounds, which is good, I suppose. You can make the numbers mean whatever you want this Heat season. Mark Blount led the Heat with 22 points Sunday. Is that good?

But there was Marion at his new locker after the game, saying, "I think this is a great situation for me."

Not something hopeful like: "I'd like for this to work out." Or upbeat like: "My personality is always to make the best of a situation."

Instead, his words were, "I really want to be here."

This is the mini-mystery of the mega-trade. The big mystery, the doozy, the one David Caruso can't crack, is why Phoenix was interested in the 2008 vintage O'Neal. Everyone knows that. But the local one that's off the national radar now is Marion.

Who is he? What is he? And does it say anything good that a skipper of the Good Ship Lollipop is delighted to be on the Titanic?

You can run through a list of possible reasons he'd like this trade, if you want. Maybe he didn't feel like being the third wheel in Phoenix behind Steve Nash and Amare Stoudemire. (He shot that down.)

Maybe he didn't think Phoenix's do-run-run system was conducive to his game. (Makes no sense considering it defines his career.)

Maybe he thinks people here don't know that the tattoo in Japanese script on his leg that he wanted to mean "Matrix" actually translates into "demon bird moth balls," as deadspin.com reported. (Oops, that one's out now.)

Riley tried to explain Marion's happiness by relating it to his own nine years of coaching the Los Angeles Lakers. He won four titles there. But he was happy to change, he said. He wanted to move on, he said. Of course, then he added under his breath. "Not really."

Marion bought a house in Miami four years ago. By some fit of construction delays, he didn't actually close on it until Tuesday. But he thought enough of the city, or the income-tax relief, or maybe just South Beach, to make it his offseason home.

And as Riley said, "Life will take you home. Maybe this is where he is supposed to be."

We'll see when it comes time to redo his deal. He supposedly was asking Phoenix for a new contract in the three-year, $60 million range. That's Wade money. That's the kind of deal this franchise was delighted to dump with O'Neal.

If he's happy because he thinks the Heat will feed him that money, we might see a Sybil-like personality change at some point.

If he's happy because he'll get more shots on a bad team, what does that say?

Maybe he's just an upbeat person. Maybe, considering it took him four years to build his home here, he really does like rebuilding jobs. But the underlying question to this trade, considering Phoenix wins at the same rate the Heat loses, is just this about Marion:

Why is this man smiling?

Summary

This type of ending attempts to wrap up the report of an event by looking at the big picture, summarizing the game, or in the case below, a trend.

By Paul Hoynes
Plain Dealer Reporter,
August 4, 2003

ARLINGTON, TEXAS – This trip ended just in time. Manager Eric Wedge's traveling baby-sitting service needed to replenish its supply of pacifiers, formula, and ice.

The ice can be used to ease the bruised psyche of a pitching staff that used to be the best part of this rebuilding process. Yes, it happened again to Wedge and his 13 rookies.

Texas hit three more homers last night to complete a three-game sweep of the Indians with an 8–5 victory at The Ballpark in Arlington.

The Rangers hit 13 homers in the series. The long balls went like this: seven Friday, three Saturday and three last night. The seven homers Friday tied team records for the most allowed by the Indians and the most hit by the Rangers.

Alex Rodriguez and Rafael Palmeiro were particularly sad to see the Tribe go. They accounted for six of the 13 homers with three each. Rodriguez has homered in four straight games, one shy of a Rangers' record. Palmeiro has hit six homers in his last 11 games.

The loss marked the second straight night a Tribe starter has failed to hold an early lead.

The Tribe gave Brian Anderson (8–9, 4.23 ERA) a 3–0 lead in the first, but he went through it faster than a gray-haired old lady goes through a bucket of quarters at a Las Vegas slot machine. Jason Davis blew leads of 1–0, 5–1, 6–3 and 7–6 in Saturday's loss.

Errors by shortstop Jhonny Peralta and catcher Tim Laker added to Anderson's problems.

Anderson lasted just three innings.

"I'm not real happy right now," said Anderson. "I laid a big egg."

The Indians' rocky defense, one of the worst in the American League, hasn't been Anderson's best friend. He's allowed 83 runs this season, but 29 percent of them (24) have been unearned.

Last night, five of the seven runs he allowed were unearned.

"When you give a team like that extra opportunities, you put yourself in a position to get hurt," said Wedge, referring to the errors.

The Rangers, who lead the big leagues with 170 homers, have hit 103 at The Ballpark in Arlington. No other team in baseball has that kind of home-field advantage. Milton Bradley hit a two-run triple off reliever-turned-starter RA Dickey and scored on Ryan Ludwick's grounder for the Tribe's early 3–0 lead. Bradley, 5-for-13 in the series, could be suspended this week for his run-in with umpire Bruce Froemming in Oakland at the start of this trip.

Rodriguez and Palmeiro brought the Rangers right back with consecutive two-out homers in the first to make it 3–2. Rodriguez has hit 28 and Palmeiro 27 for the season. Texas moved in front, 4–3, in the second on two unearned runs after Peralta double-clutched on Ramon Nivar's grounder with one out. Einar Diaz and Michael Young followed with singles to tie the score, 3–3. Then Rodriguez hit a two-out single to score Diaz for a 4–3 lead.

Ludwick momentarily stopped Texas' momentum. He pulled the Indians into a 4–4 tie with a one-out homer in the third off Dickey (5–5, 4.98 ERA). It was his third home run as an Indian.

Texas put the game away on Diaz's three-run homer in the third. All three runs were unearned.

After Marcus Thames hit a two-out single to center, Nivar bunted in front of the plate. Laker tried to barehand the ball, dropped it and then slipped.

"That error hurt us big-time," said Laker.

Diaz, the former Indians catcher, followed Laker's error with a long homer over the left-field wall for a 7–4 lead.

"I've had a lot of weird stuff happen to me this year," said Anderson, "but you've got to discipline yourself. Human beings make errors. It's my job to make quality pitches after errors and I didn't do it."

After the Rangers made it 8–4 on Nivar's triple in the seventh, Casey Blake homered in the eighth to put the Tribe back in the game at 8–5. It was Blake's 12th homer. Victor Martinez singled and Jody Gerut reached on an error in the ninth, but Francisco Cordero struck out Coco Crisp and Blake for his fifth save.

The Indians went 1–5 on this trip. Texas hit 10 of the 13 homers against lefties Billy Traber, Terry Mulholland, and Anderson.

Anecdote

Some writers will end their story with a colorful anecdote that makes a point about the sporting event, or shows the character of a player or team. The ending below paints a picture for the reader of something that happened well after the game was already concluded.

By Jason Williams
Pioneer Press
August 19, 2006

(Boof) Bonser struck out (Jermaine) Dye swinging on a curveball in the sixth. That was an indication of how much he has matured since his first two tries in the rotation. He attacked the strike zone and mixed up his pitches.

"I went at them tonight," Bonser said.

As Bonser jogged off the field after turning the ball over to the bullpen, he received a standing ovation, and a drawn-out Boooooofffff echoed throughout the Dome.

The Twins can only hope to hear more of that.

Editorial

Editorial endings allow writers to insert his or her opinions without having their bias dominate the story. It is a subtle way of including a personal point in a low-key way.

For example, in the following story, note how the writer introduces a point in such a way that it seems to naturally follow from the body of the story. The point seems like an obvious extension of the information in the previous paragraphs.

By Ann Killion
Mercury News
August 17, 2006

What more can the A's do for attention? Sign Terrell Owens to roam center field? Have one of their players photographed leaving Paris Hilton's house? Bring reptiles to games and rename themselves Snakes on a Diamond?

The A's are the hottest team in baseball since the All-Star break, going 23–9. They've opened up their biggest lead in the division in

14 years—since back when they were a superpower. They leave for a 10-game trip having won 12 of 13.

Yet nobody seems to notice.

Check that: the Seattle Mariners have noticed, and, after losing the past 15 games they've played with the A's, should be receiving a bouquet when the A's clinch the division. But not many others have the A's on their radar.

"That doesn't bother me," Manager Ken Macha said. "We'd rather have it that way."

But the A's have noticed that no one's noticed.

"We were just talking about that today," third baseman Eric Chavez said. "No one talks about us."

Not so much locally, where the obsession is still a past-his-prime slugger across the Bay and where fans continue to show up in modest numbers (though Wednesday's game was a sellout thanks to those $2 tickets).

There's even less interest nationally, where the Detroit Tigers are the surprise darlings and a host of other teams get more publicity. An ESPN columnist picked six other teams as having better chances of winning the World Series, including the Los Angeles Angels, who are now 6½ games behind Oakland. The A's were described as "whatever."

But maybe "whatever" suits this team better than being picked World Series favorites by spring pundits (including this one).

"It's better to be the underdog," Chavez said. "We're in a good position. We've got a good team."

The A's have a good team. Not a great team. Not a Wow! team. But a good team, with solid pitching and defense and a knack for winning one-run games.

The big whatever with them is the postseason.

Yes, yes! It's too early! Far too early to discuss the postseason!

But that's when the A's could gain some serious buzz. We've already seen them be the little team that could for most of the past seven seasons. We've already seen them win in August and September.

We've already seen the genius trading of Billy Beane, the ability to succeed on a shoestring. Besides, neither of those story lines applies this year, since the A's spent money in the off-season and were quiet at the trade deadline.

So what remains in terms of novelty is the postseason. And that goes for the fans too, who have become sort of Atlanta West without the annoying chant. For the past 11 years, Braves fans have yawned at division titles. They can't be bothered to show up for first-round playoff series. It's deep into the postseason or nothing (which appears to be this year's alternative).

The A's run smack into that first-round wall as hard—though not as often—as the Braves. If the season ended today, they'd get the Tigers in the first round. Oh joy!

These A's may be more confident than they have been in other years, with the veteran additions of Milton Bradley and Frank Thomas. Shortstop Bobby Crosby should be activated this weekend from the disabled list. Right-hander Rich Harden remains the A's biggest question and at the top of their get-well-soon list.

"With Rich there's no doubt we're a team that would threaten," Chavez said. The A's still have 42 games to play, taking on every team in the American League except the New York Yankees and Detroit. They still have seven games left with the Angels. The upshot is life could change dramatically in the next six weeks. "We've got an extremely difficult schedule," Macha said.

Then again, the hottest team in baseball could remain the hottest, quietest team.

"We're better equipped to finish it out this year," Chavez said.

It looks that way in August. But October is where the A's will get noticed.

First- or Second-Person

It is relatively rare when a first-person or second-person writing style is effective. Normally, readers prefer to be told information, not introduced into the story (through second-person writing). And reporters appear to be egotistical if they include themselves in stories (through first-person writing).

The story below from the PGA tournament included a question for the readers that follows from the main point made in the lead: there were lots of people bunched atop the leaderboard, though television coverage was concentrating more on Tiger Woods. The writer returns to this point in the concluding paragraph.

By Mike Kern
Philadelphia Daily News
Phillynews.com
August 19, 2006

MEDINAH, Ill. – So what's the more relevant storyline at the midway point of the 88th PGA Championship: that Sweden's Henrik Stenson, England's Luke Donald, Rhode Island's Billy Andrade and a guy nicknamed "Lumpy" (Tim Herron) share the top spot on a rather congested leaderboard, or that Tiger Woods is a single shot back?

Thought so. The folks at CBS certainly value your support.

The foursome at 138 includes 2001 champ David Toms, 50-year-old Fred Funk and Billy Mayfair, who had testicular-cancer surgery 2 weeks ago. Among the six at 139 is 2003 champ Shaun Micheel, 2003 Masters winner Mike Weir and Sergio Garcia, who nearly won the 1999 PGA here.

West Chester's Sean O'Hair started out with five straight threes, which left him 5-under for the day and the tournament. He finished at 2-under.

A lot of guys could win, many who have the proper credentials. Only one can. So, whom do you like?

Future

A last possible ending is merely to point to details pertaining to the next game, such as:

The Brewers return to action Tuesday night, when they travel to St. Louis for the opening game of a three-game series. The scheduled startng pitchers are...

This type of ending is relatively standard. Some newspapers require writers to include details of upcoming games in their stories at some point.

Final Point

When writing a story, don't miss an opportunity to do something useful and effective with the ending. Remember the points you made in your lead. The ending might be a good place to re-emphasize your most important point.

12

ENDINGS II

What Needs to be Included in Sports Stories

Editors have certain expectations of what reporters need to include in their sports stories. Here is a checklist of information that always should be included.

The Score

This may seem obvious: of course, the score is one of the most important aspects of a game story. Maybe reporters are too concerned with coming up with creative leads. Maybe they don't want to interrupt the flow of their story early on. Whatever the reason, in rare cases, reporters have been known to forget to include the final score.

More common, though, are complaints from sports editors that the score appears too late in a story. A general rule of thumb: the score should be stated in the first three paragraphs. That should give reporters enough poetic license to use a creative lead without being too restricted.

The Atmosphere

Along with the final score, some editors require crowd attendance to be reported in the first three paragraphs. Crowd size says something about how well a franchise or program is doing. If a university routinely draws 17,000 fans to its home basketball games but 5,000 fans attend a certain game, that's significant. If a stadium seats 68,000 and the announced attendance is 68,200, that's important. Of course, if a university has 270 consecutive sellouts, the attendance is of limited importance.

Often, reporters will describe those in attendance along with the crowd size—"before 17,211 raucous fans" or "in front of 65,881 sun-drenched fans."

Records

Obviously, a team's record after just the first game of the season is meaningless. However, late in the season, when teams are jockeying for position for postseason play (or for finalizing the draft order), records are important.

Fans also are interested in how other key teams are doing, so it is common to mention results from other teams in the league: "The Cardinals improved to 8–6, while Oakland fell to 5–9. Arizona trails the Seattle Seahawks, who are 9–5 after their 38–7 victory over Dallas."

History

Sports are full of history. Lafayette and Lehigh have played each other 142 times between 1884 and 2006. A game report between these two rivals would need to at least mention the rich history of the series.

Trends in a series also should be noted. When the Kansas football team defeated Nebraska in 2005, it broke a streak of 36 consecutive victories by the Cornhuskers. This would be difficult to ignore.

Not all historical facts are created equal, however. If a team wins for the first time in two years, this is a relatively meaningless trend. A three-game winning streak in baseball likewise is insignificant. If a reader sees a trend in your story and wouldn't necessarily think "Gosh, has it been that long?" then the trend probably isn't worth mentioning.

Injuries

Fans want to know when a player is injured, even if it is a slight injury that won't affect the player's availability for a game. Terrell Owens' hamstring injury in the Cowboys' 2006 training camp, for example, made headlines around the country.

Whether a player is injured during a game, or whether they were limited during a game because of an injury, sports stories should inform readers about possible health issues facing players.

Statistics

All sports stories are full of statistics: leading scorers, leading hitters, slumping stars. Many of these statistics are important to readers.

Readers want to know a player's batting average with runners in scoring position—especially if he struck out with the bases loaded in the ninth inning. Other statistics that could affect the outcome of a game—yards per carry for a running back, three-point shooting percentage for a point guard—should be included in all sports stories.

Team statistics are as important as individual statistics. Football reporters often include in their stories time of possession, first downs, total yards and total offensive plays. Baseball writers include runners left on base and the earned run average of a bullpen. Basketball reporters include field goal percentage, team fouls, and team rebounds. Of course, what statistics are reported varies based on how important the information is to the outcome of the event.

Quotes

Opposing coaches are the key sources in game reports. Their quotes can put statistical material into perspective, so their quotes should be used often. Qotes from star players likewise add much to game reports.

Qotes also break up the monotony of   play-by-play. Good quotes are a key to good sports writing.

Play-by-Play

Fans will expect to see why and how a team won. Scoring trends in basketball, scoring drives in football, and scoring rallies in baseball should be detailed.

How much play-by-play to include in a story varies. If the final score of a football game is 65–52, you wouldn't want to detail every play in every scoring drive. However, in a 3–0 game, you should point out the key plays leading up to the game-winning field goal.

13

OTHER TYPES OF STORIES I

Sidebars

The Chuckleheads, the local minor league baseball team, is having a decent season. They lead the Nowhere League with a 20–14 record, led by slugger Jack M. Farr and pitcher Noah Hidder.

Now that you've mastered the game story, the sports editor thinks it is time you expand your horizons.

"Hey, kid."

The words grate like sandpaper across your forehead.

"Why don't you go with Chuckleheads' beat writer Wright Welle to tonight's game? You can write a sidebar."

"A sidebar?" As soon as the words hit the air you cringe. The boss hates repetition.

"REPEATING MY WORDS DON'T CHANGE 'EM. Yes, a sidebar."

Until now you thought the sidebar was a table of desserts next to the buffet bar at Ike's Chicken Shack. Although dessert and buffets are important, they are not associated with journalism sidebars.

Sidebars are stories that complement the main story. The sidebar sometimes examines a slice of the main story and sometimes it examines a unique aspect that is loosely related to the main. Sidebars provide additional perspective about a game or event. It takes the reader beyond the sidelines. This chapter discusses where to find sidebars and how to write them.

Finding the Sidebar

Nebraska quarterback Eric Crouch was awarded the Heisman Trophy as college football's top player in 2001. Although he did not receive the award until December, it can be argued he won it September 29. In a mostly routine 36–3 thrashing of Missouri, Crouch zigzagged 95 yards through the Tigers' defense to score a touchdown. He dropped back to pass from Nebraska's end zone, and Crouch didn't stop running until he reached Missouri's end zone. It was considered one of the top plays in the nation that season.

The *Columbia Missourian* sent three reporters to cover the Nebraska–Missouri game that day. One was assigned to write the game story, another was to write a notebook and the third a sidebar. Obviously, Crouch's run would be a sidebar story but what would be the angle? There were several possibilities. The story could be from Crouch's perspective, what it meant for Nebraska's season, what it meant in terms of the game (the score was 16–3 at the time), how it affected Missouri, etc. Instead of picking the obvious sidebars, the writer chose to dissect Crouch's run from Missouri's perspective.

The game story included just three paragraphs about the run:

> It took the longest run in Nebraska's 111-year history to deflate the Missouri Tigers on Saturday.
>
> With 2:40 left in the third quarter and Nebraska leading 16–3, MU's defense had the Huskers backed to their goal line. On third-and-8 with Nebraska on its 5, quarterback Eric Crouch scrambled into the end zone ahead of the grasping arms of MU defensive end Nick Tarpoff. Crouch broke away and navigated his way for a 95-yard touchdown.
>
> "It was a big back-breaker," MU defensive end Antwaun Bynum said. "I mean 95 yards and you got hands on him in the end zone. It's a big turnaround; we get two points, get our offense the ball, we score and get some momentum."
>
> Behind Crouch, the No. 4 Huskers beat MU for the 23rd straight time, a 36–3 defeat at Memorial Stadium in the Tigers' Big 12 Conference opener.

The sidebar story focused on Missouri's defense and the specifics of what went wrong during Crouch's 95-yard run. It read:

> At least six months of planning and a chance for national recognition slipped through the Tigers', and defensive end Nick Tarpoff's, arms with 2:21 remaining in the third quarter.
>
> Faced with a third-and-8 from the Cornhuskers' 5-yard line, Nebraska quarterback Eric Crouch dropped back to pass and was rushed from the left side by Tarpoff, a redshirt freshman. Tarpoff had his arms around Crouch 2 yards deep in the end zone before the Cornhusker quarterback broke loose for a 95-yard touchdown run to put Nebraska ahead 22–3.
>
> A Tarpoff safety would have cut MU's deficit to 16–5 with the Tigers' offense receiving the ball after the Nebraska free kick.
>
> Before the snap, Tarpoff replaced starting defensive end Antwaun Bynum, who left the game with a leg cramp.

Bynum said Tarpoff wasn't the only Tiger to miss a tackle on the play. Crouch juked at least three Tigers during the run.

"I was on the field and caught a cramp and had to run off for a minute," Bynum said. "All of a sudden I get off to the sideline and he goes for 95 yards. I think Tarpoff had a couple hands on him in the end zone…a couple other guys had a couple hands on him."

Tarpoff, in tears, said he took full blame for missing the tackle.

"I just didn't wrap good enough," he said. "I got him around the hips and I just slid off. That's totally my fault.

"We had a good blitz and it was set up perfect. We just missed it."

The sidebar continued for another dozen paragraphs, mostly focusing on Crouch's performance (17 carries, 191 yards) and Missouri's poor defensive performance against Nebraska's running game. But the lead of the sidebar takes the perspective of one significant play—and player—and magnifies it.

Truly good sidebars are a slice of the main story that adds context to the larger event. Generally, sports writers are given little instruction when sent to write a sidebar. The sports editor expects the writer to "find" a story. That can be easier said than done.

While each event has many subplots, selecting the appropriate one takes a keen eye for detail, knowledge of the subject and a little luck. Sidebars don't miraculously fall from the sky but sometimes they do materialize. Some of the more obvious sidebars include:

- The Stars. It's so obvious it's almost a cliché but readers do not get bored reading about the top performers. The key is to find a different story, particularly among athletes who always seem to be the stars. What made this performance different? Did the star struggle early and then perform well? What were the influences that made this performance special? A sidebar can also feature a star when he or she performs poorly. Why did things go wrong? How will it affect the athlete in future performances? The stars are the obvious choice, but remember the star will be featured in the main story as well.
- The Goats. There are usually better stories in the losing locker room than the winning locker room. And few reporters delve into the losing locker room stories, so it's open season. Featuring the player who was a key figure in a loss makes for good storytelling. The idea is not to exploit the goat but to tell his or her story. These stories have a great deal of emotion and readers appreciate that. Athletes at all levels have, at some point, made mistakes that cost

his or her team a win. It's the story of the common person who tried, and failed, but will try again next time.

- The Benchwarmer. The seldom-used player finally gets his or her chance and succeeds. And it does not have to be game-winning success. Success comes in all kinds of packages: the benchwarmer's first tackle, basket, save, dig, ace, etc. Benchwarmers are not usually involved in game-altering plays. They play during blowouts or in exceptional circumstances. Thus the benchwarmer sidebar is more about the individual performance and not a slice of the larger event. Also, in rare occasions, the story can be about the benchwarmer's failure.

- The Incident. A sidebar does not have to feature a person. It can be a single play or series of plays. It can be the turning point of a game. Dissecting exactly what happened, why it happened, and how it happened provides a unique peek into the inner workings of a game. It can be similar to a coach's chalk-talk session where the experts explain what occurred. And it can be written from either one team's perspective or both teams. Each turning point has at least two sides: those who succeeded and those who failed. Writing about the struggle between the two makes for an interesting sidebar.

- The Incident II. Incidents can be the ugliness that occurs between teams or players, such as fights or vulgarity. A middle-finger salute or spitting incident can trigger cause for a sidebar. Its impact on the overall game can be monumental or minuscule. The reporter does not want to make more of the incident than it really is but asking about it certainly can lead to a quality sidebar story.

- The Milestone. Writing about a basketball coach's 500th win or a soccer player's record-setting goal makes for a good story. There are inevitable milestones as well. Milestones of longevity are not as interesting as milestones of success or futility. Some milestones are unenviable. In the movie *Bull Durham*, catcher Crash Davis broke the minor league home-run record. Having a record is generally good but in the minor leagues it can be a badge of disgrace. No player wants to be in the minor leagues so long that he has a record. Also, stories can focus on career, season or game milestones. If a player is closing in on a career or season mark, be aware that it could happen during this particular game.

- The Last Hurrah. The final games for athletes come in different packages. Some athletes choose to retire or quit. Others complete their eligibility. And others just do not have the talent to play any longer. Most athletes leave reluctantly, but regardless of the exit there's a good story to be told. Tracking an athlete through his or his final moments can make for compelling copy. Did the athlete leave with grace or achievement, or did he stumble to the finish line of his career? Also observe how an athlete acts following the final event. Does she hang around the court a few extra minutes or rush off to the locker room? The journey to the end is just as important as the end itself.

- The Player Injury. If a star is injured and leaves the game, writing about the impact on the game is significant. What impact did it have on the game? How well did the replacement play? What does the injury mean for the season? The injury also might provide an opportunity for a benchwarmer to succeed, which, as we know, makes a great sidebar. Another story could be how the injury impacted the opposing team. If a 7-foot, All-Everything center blows a knee in the first half, it's sure to boost the opposing team's confidence. Another sidebar could be if a player is injured and returns to the game. He or she would have to do something other than just return but the possibilities are there.

- The Head-to-Head Matchup. When star players meet head-to-head there's a sidebar in the making. Pitcher vs. hitter, running back vs. linebacker, guard vs. guard, goalie vs. scorer. This is the epitome of sports—mano a mano. Recreating the confrontation for the readers can be a great sidebar. Who was the better player on that day? How did one outdo the other? Will they meet again, and if so, what will be different?

Sidebars come in a variety of packages and there are stumbling blocks along the way. Sometimes athletes and coaches do not want to discuss an injury, the goat or the head-to-head matchup. That should not prevent you from writing the sidebar. Gather information from other players, an assistant coach or another source willing to provide details. There are other complications with sidebars as well.

Getting the Sidebar

One of the biggest mistakes sports journalists make with sidebars is indecisiveness. The sports writer will have several ideas but can't decide which to pursue. Waiting until the last minute to decide what sidebar to write is never a good idea. The time wasted in deciding is time that could be spent reporting. So decide on a story angle and run with it. Sure, it might change, but at least you have a start on a story and you won't be caught scrambling on deadline.

Sidebar stories do not always jump out. Sometimes they have to be found. Having a backup sidebar is always a good idea. Before the game begins, have a sidebar in mind. The beat writer can usually make suggestions. It might not be the best story idea but in a pinch it would work. Or, something might happen during the game that makes the backup the starter. Planning to write a sidebar about a major league pitcher working a rehabilitation assignment in the minor leagues is fine, but what happens if the pitcher walks three and allows five earned runs, including a grand slam? Now that's a sidebar.

Identifying the sidebar is only half the battle. The other half is making sure it does not impinge on the main story too much. Clearly there will be some overlap between the game story and the sidebar. The objective is to minimize the overlap. Talking with the game-story writer is imperative. Discussing the story with him or her will provide some guidelines about how to approach the story. The beat writer has intimate knowledge of the team and can offer tips on how to approach an athlete or coach. Knowing that an athlete is sensitive about his minor league home-run record is useful information when writing a sidebar about the record.

In a way, the sidebar writer is considered the guest of the beat writer. To some degree, the beat writer has first crack at information, but that can be negotiated. Unless the beat writer is incredibly territorial—and all beat writers are territorial—the sidebar ventures into terrain the game story cannot. In microscopic fashion, it enlarges an aspect of the story that only accounts for a few sentences in the main story. Therefore, the beat writer should not be an impediment to writing the sidebar.

At the second round of the 2005 Jamie Farr Owens Corning Classic LPGA Tournament, Beth Daniels took sole possession of first place. Of course, the *Toledo Blade*'s event story focused on Daniels' performance. In the 15th paragraph, the reporter mentions that Dorothy Delasin was tied for fourth with five other golfers. The *Toledo Blade* sports writer, Maureen Fulton, examined Delasin's performance. She wrote this sidebar under the headline, "Delasin is back in the swing of things."

> In the past year, Dorothy Delasin has taken on a demanding task for a pro—changing her swing. But the tougher thing, she has discovered, is keeping her patience.
>
> A former LPGA rookie of the year, Delasin has traveled a long road back after making a major overhaul in her game in 2004. Yesterday at the Jamie Farr Owens Corning Classic, she experienced a tiny bit of redemption. Delasin shot a 4-under par 67 to finish at 5-under after two rounds. She is tied for fourth with five other players.
>
> Delasin hit just eight of 14 fairways and 11 of 18 greens in regulation, but relied on her putter to move her closer to the top.
>
> "I'm in a really good position for the weekend," Delasin said. "It's going to be exciting. Hopefully my putter will stay hot."

Delasin, 24, turned pro just after she graduated from high school in 2000. She won the Giant Eagle Classic in Warren, Ohio that year, two tournaments in 2001, and one in 2003.

But Delasin's desire to be one of the top players in the world, to win majors and be in the Hall of Fame, led her to leave behind her trusty swing of 15 years for a tighter, more stable one on the recommendation of her swing coach.

"When you change your swing, you ask, why fix something that's not broken?" Delasin said. "But it's something I had to do to be a top player week in and week out and not just have streaks."

The change made the second half of last season a trying time for Delasin. She finished tied for 49th on the money list last year—she had never finished lower than 31st—and missed the cut in three of the four majors.

Thirteen months later, Delasin feels her swing is close to being "just there" rather than something she has to worry about. She has three top-10 finishes this season. Her goal is to have the swing feel normal by the Solheim Cup in September.

"It's slowly but surely coming around. I'm starting to see the results," Delasin said. "It's still not quite there yet. It's something I've got to keep working on."

Last season, Delasin finished tied for 13th in the Farr Classic, her best finish since her rookie year, when she tied for 11th. Yesterday she was tied for second until play resumed after the two-hour weather delay, when she bogeyed the seventh hole (her 16th). It was her only bogey of the day.

Sports editors assign sidebars because they think the event warrants more than just one story. Oftentimes readers will bypass the main story and only read the sidebar. For those readers, include at least one paragraph with the score and some statistics pertinent to your sidebar. If the sidebar features the star player, include the star player's stats or big play. Do not assume all readers attended the event or read the main story. Although it's called a "sidebar," the story should stand on its own without forcing readers to venture elsewhere to fill in the blanks.

Sometimes the sidebar has little to do with the event. At a district track meet, John Dessoye broke the district record in the 100 meters. Dessoye's accomplishment was the focus of the main story. Instead of Dessoye, the sidebar reporter, Scott Reinardy, wrote about the starter, "Two-Gun" Dinny Noonan. The sidebar in the *Scranton Times-Tribune* read:

At just about any of the larger area track meets you can find him.

With a gun clenched in each hand, "Two Gun" Dinny Noonan is like the marshal of any dusty, two-bit town west of the Pecos. And at each track meet, he meets his High Noon several times over.

This day was no different.

The bright spring sun sat high in the sky, dodging large puffy-white clouds against an ocean-blue backdrop. With his starting pistols pointed skyward, Noonan would try to punch holes in those clouds as almost every high school athlete in the area competed for a top finish at the District 6 Track Championships on Tuesday.

The day started fast for Noonan and just as fast for John Dessoye. Noonan galloped past the scorers' table repeating, "I predicted he'd do 10.6 and he did it. And he'll do it the finals, too."

It's true. Dessoye had already cracked the District 6 record with his preliminary run of 10.6 in the 100-meter dash. And, just as Noonan had projected, Dessoye bettered that with a 10.4 in the finals.

Who is This Guy?

Decked out in his snow-white pants and fluorescent orange shirt, the 80-year-old Noonan points his pistols skyward, gunning down the Black Barts of the world. Of course, white puffs of smoke and not hot lead flowed from his starter's pistol.

"It's 43 years today and I'm still good," Noonan said. "I love it. It's in my bones. I like people. I like athletes. The main thing of it is I want to do it honestly and let the kids get what's coming to them. Don't cheat the kids."

Noonan rattles off his resume like a college senior at a job fair, emphasizing certain facts in his unique style.

"This will be my 23rd straight year at states, and I've worked the Philadelphia Junior Olympics 35 straight years. I'll be 81 years old in three weeks. Whoa!" he screeched. "You like that kid?"

The Challenge

Although Noonan was enjoying himself probably a bit more than a starter should, when it came to race time, he was all business.

"The 100 meters is my challenge," he said. "That is the best that I can do. I have to be good. I have to be fair. I have to be honest to the kids and make sure everybody gets a fair start.

And I do. They'll get it. I think the guy up above is in my corner.

"And I'm old. The numbers are there but the numbers don't bother me. Look what I'm doing."

With that, Noonan scampers away. It was time to start the girls' 3200-meter run.

"Let's go gang," he said to the crowd of over-anxious young runners. "Let's do it nice and easy.

"On your mark. Nice and easy now.

"Bang!"

Noonan guns down another.

In less than 500 words, the writer provided a slice of an event that can be overwhelming. District track meets can include a dozen or more teams and hundreds of athletes. Instead of featuring an athlete, the writer selected an individual who represents one aspect of the event. The sidebar uses descriptive language and colorful quotes that personify Noonan's energy and excitement. Although sidebars can be a slice of the main story they also can capture the essence of an event. Going off the beaten path to find the sidebar is one way to do that.

Writing sidebar stories are a way to break from the game story rut. Sometimes beat writers are asked to write the main story and the sidebar. Although it is additional work, it can be an enjoyable respite from the daily grind.

For non-beat writers, sidebars allow sports reporters to attend events without the obligations of gathering statistics or producing game information. Sidebars are a chance to expand your journalistic horizons. It's also an opportunity to write stories that otherwise would not be available to the readers.

Professional Perspective
By Maureen Fulton
The (Toledo) Blade **Sports Writer**

You know the score, you know the hero, you know what the coaches said. But did you know the winning pitcher forgot to wear his lucky underwear? Or that the guy with the two interceptions was playing in front of 30 friends and family? Welcome to the wonderful, if sometimes quirky and challenging, world of sidebars.

The sidebar contains the stuff not important enough for game stories but too important to let interested fans go without. It

Figure 13.1 Maureen Fulton.

should provide additional facts, perspective, and insight. A sidebar should be a quick read, with information that can be easily digested.

Sidebar possibilities include feature angles on a player, a trend within the team, or within the contest. Look for a detail or nugget that adds color. If it is a technical sidebar, like breaking down a big play, get as many details as possible. Historical angles, such as a team or player setting records, can lead to a sidebar, so make sure you have available as much of that information as possible.

There's likely not enough space to quote more than three or so sources in a sidebar, but still feel free to interview as many sources as time allows. Sidebars are all about the details. Try to get sources that might not be quoted in the game story. Give your readers an "insider" feel.

It's important to communicate with the game-story writer to make sure your stories don't overlap. Using a few of the same details is OK, but any more than that and instead of something that furthers the coverage, you'll end up with a second game story.

As with any story, the more preparation you can do beforehand the better. If you know what's happened to the player or team in the past month or last season, it will make your assignment easier, and you'll be able to identify the angle that's most relevant to the event.

Maureen Fulton is a sports writer for
The (Toledo) Blade.

14

OTHER TYPES OF STORIES II
Advances and Follows

The sports calendar dictates the life of a sports journalist. Whenever sports are being played, sports journalists are there to cover the action. Crime, fire, and death are breaking news, while sports are not happenstance. Sports schedules are set months and possibly years in advance. Beat writers can locate the date of next year's season opener before this season is finished.

Expanded leagues and schedules allow sports to bleed into several seasons. For instance, Major League pitchers report for training camp in mid-February. The World Series finishes in late October. Baseball is now a three-season sport. The same can be said of the NFL, NBA, NHL, NASCAR, PGA, LPGA, Major League Soccer and almost any professional sport. The beat for a sports writer is 12 months, 365 days a year.

During the 12/365 cycle, a beat writer has specific obligations, which include not only covering the team's games. Athletic organizations build stadiums and arenas, negotiate television and radio contracts, hire and fire personnel, and have an economic impact on a city or region. Athletes get into legal trouble, quarrel with teammates, and wipe out on their motorcycles. And the beat writer is expected to write it all.

But the essence of sports coverage is the game. Actually, it's the game's three stages: before, during, and after. The advance or preview, the game story, and the follow-up story consume a large portion of the beat writer's time. Readers want to know what is about to happen, what happens, and what it means after it happens. This chapter discusses advances and follows.

The Advance

Mark Twain once said, "The poetry is all in the anticipation, for there is none in reality." Twain certainly wasn't speaking of the Super Bowl, but he could have been. Two weeks of Super Bowl anticipation and media overkill is the advance story on steroids. Beat writers scramble to

147

fill pages with stories that include everything from injury reports to possible wardrobe malfunctions.

The standard advance story provides perspective of an event. Fueled by fans' anticipation, the advance speculates as to what can be expected from the game. The advance has two functions. First, it is to inform the readers of the essentials: time, place, date, and teams involved. Second, the advance attempts to capture the game's potential meaning without predicting the outcome. Unless you are a bona fide psychic, leave prognostication to those who do not cover the game. Let coaches and players provide the information that is expected to influence the outcome. Besides, predicting a winner compromises your credibility. If you pick against a team, the coaches and players from that team might not grant you an interview after the game.

The advance can assume several forms, including:

- Key matchups. The story can emphasize the matchups between top players or offense vs. defense. It can also feature coaching matchups or even strategies (the run-and-gun offense vs. the 3–4 defense). Head-to-head contests in wrestling, golf, tennis, or track for example, can also top the advance. Sometimes the individual matchups have more drama and interest than the team matchup.
- Injuries. Injuries to starting players invariably influence the outcome of an event. Writing about who will replace the player or players and how it will affect the game is of interest to the readers. Sometimes, coaches and players will not discuss injuries, particularly if the player intends to play. The fear is the other team will exploit that injury. For instance, if a running back has an injured knee, the opposing team's linebacker might go after that knee. So it's understandable if a coach does not want to discuss the knee injury. But if the starting shortstop has a broken thumb, that's worth writing about.
- Star reaction. If a top player was awful in the previous game, the advance might focus on his or her return. How players react to diverse situations can make the difference between winning and losing. Readers generally know when a top player is off his or her game. The advance can explore the player's mental condition going into the next game.
- Team trends. Teams generally go through winning and losing streaks. The next game can either end or continue the streak. A team's fortune can change with one game. The writer can put the streak into perspective with the advance.
- Redemption games. Some would call these revenge games, but as discussed in Chapter 4, revenge is inflicting harm. Redemption indicates that one team beat another earlier in the season (or the

previous season) and the losing team is determined to win the upcoming matchup. These advances are filled with emotion and "let's go get them" type of quotes. But before writing the redemption angle, be certain the coaches and players support it. Do not assume because a team lost to another that the losing team is looking for redemption. It might have bigger problems, such as a losing streak or injured player.

- Rivalry games. When long-time rivals meet it's often the talk of both schools and towns. This is probably the most overdone of the advance stories. The problem with the rivalry advance is that coaches and players give stale, boring quotes. "Sure there's a rivalry, but we'll treat it as if it were any other game." Coaches and players do not want to be distracted by the fans' notion of rivalry. It's better to focus on something other than the rivalry in an advance. Besides, if a team plays twice a season the rivalry angle can be redundant.

- Team reaction. Losing a big game or winning on a last-second play affects teams differently. The next game becomes a test for that team. It can be a make or break game that determines the season's outcome. The advance can provide some perspective as to how the team will react. Also, reaction after controversy can be the emphasis of the advance. How will a team play when a top player is dismissed from the team or arrested? These are questions readers ask.

- Season changers. Some games will alter the course of a season. Identifying those games can sometimes be difficult. Playing weak teams during a losing streak can change the season's course. Sometimes teams and players just need some confidence. It can also go the other way. A weak team can surprise a top team. It's hard to anticipate upsets, but the advance certainly can explore that option.

- Unique games. A historical meeting (an inaugural season opener or two teams playing for the first time) can be the focus of the advance. There's an air of uncertainty when two teams meet for the first time. Exploring that story is of great interest to the readers.

- Milestones. Readers often are not aware of coaching or playing milestones. The advance can be a feature on the coach or player about to reach the milestone. Included in the feature are the significant details of the game (time, date, place, etc.).

- The end is near. Advances can emphasis the season-ending game for a team or career-ending game for a player. The story can discuss the playoff implications of the final regular-season game or how it will be the final home game of the season. It could also be a recap of the season as the team plays its final game. It is suggested you avoid writing about special events, such as "Senior Night." Those events have little influence on the game. And once the coaches or players say, "We really want to win the final game for the seniors," what more is there to say?

- Championships. If a team can win the league, conference or division championship, that should be the emphasis of the advance. Although the emphasis is winning the title, the advance can include several elements, such as a season recap, the turning point game or results from the previous meeting between the teams. You can also provide context as to what a win would do in terms of playoffs.
- The underdog. If a team consistently beats another, emphasizing the underdog aspect of the losing team could make for an interesting advance. It can be written from the perspective of, "This time the team will win," or, "For the 100th consecutive time the team will lose." Of course, that perspective has to be provided by the coaches and players. As stated earlier, predicting an outcome is not a good idea. The advance can also be written from the point of the view of how the players and coaches mentally prepare themselves for another thrashing or what would be considered a victory without actually winning the game (get a shot on goal, score a run, etc.).

Advances are the setup to the game. The stories should be interesting and engaging, and include minimal statistics. Too often sports journalists clutter the advance with scoring averages and statistical mumbo-jumbo. Other than including the teams' records, be selective on which stats to include. Oftentimes the statistics can be placed in a separate box accompanying the story. The box can also include the time, day, and place of the event. That means there will be fewer statistics bogging down the advance story.

Here is an advance of two top college tennis teams that includes some history and a matchup of two top teams:

Losing last year's Valley Athletic Conference women's tennis title to Roseville College was tough to take for Brentwood College coach Jessica King and her squad.

Getting beat head-to-head would have been one thing, but losing because of the total number of sets lost during the weekend tournament was something completely different.

The Broncos had lost 14 sets to Roseville's 12, thus placing second in the VAC tournament.

"We knew it was going to be really close," King said. "They had beaten us in the regular season, 5–4, so I guess they deserved it. But we're ready for them this time."

On Saturday, Brentwood hosts Roseville in a rematch of last year's top teams. The Broncos are 5–1 (5–0 VAC) while Roseville is 6–0 (4–0 VAC).

Notice the advance does not mention "revenge" or payback. It includes a short history that allows the story to flow into the current match.

This advance explains what's on the line between two college football teams, but also includes some history:

> The Shackford College football team has a seven-game winning streak, is atop the Western Conference standings and ranked high enough to draw one of eight playoff bids. And the Lions are not about to share those accomplishments.
>
> Shackford plays Fairview State University on Saturday in its final regular season game. Fairview has a 1–6–1 record with its only win coming via forfeit.
>
> Still, Shackford coach Mike Carter has never beaten the Falcons. He is 0–3–1 against Fairview and the Lions haven't defeated the Falcons since a 3–0 victory in 1999.
>
> If the Lions were to lose Saturday, they'd not only have to share the conference title with Conquer College, but would drop from their No. 7 national ranking and probably miss out on their first playoff berth in five seasons.

Generally speaking, the advance sets the stage for the upcoming event without boring the readers with statistics or by rehashing previously reported information. It provides context as to what is expected to happen or at least creates a setting in which the game events will unfold. The best advances are usually short and concise. They do not have to be drawn-out affairs that drag the reader through needless paragraphs of information. With the advance, get to the story and get out.

The Follow

The follow-up story is the third part of the event trilogy. After the game has been hyped and played, an assessment of the event is in order. The follow is sometimes written like a sidebar story where a slice of the larger game is examined. Other times the follow takes a broader view of the occurrences on the field. The follow-up can be many things, but primarily it should provide some context to the game. In the aftermath, readers want to understand why the action unfolded as it did. It's the sports journalist's job to provide context.

All too often, the follow-up is a regurgitation of the game story. Writers rehash the game's events as if writing it twice changes the outcome. You will want to avoid rehashing the game. Granted, there will be some repetition of material. It's difficult to analyze the game-winning play without describing the play. The point is, minimize the redundancy between the game story and the follow. Readers want to know the "why" more than the "what." They already know the what.

As with all stories, the follow provides several avenues of approach. The follow can be linked to the advance by:

- Evaluating the outcome of key matchups between teams or players.
- Assessing the performance of the player who replaced an injured player.
- Determining if the star rebounded after the bad performance.
- Focusing on the continued winning or losing streak.
- Dissecting the game's redemptive qualities. If the first-game loser wins the second game, what was done to change the outcome?
- Evaluating the team's reaction and if that reaction alters the season.
- Determining how the game might have changed the season momentum for the team—either good or bad.

Some of the advance stories do not make good follows, such as the rivalry game, milestone event or season-ending game. The season-ending game can be a season wrap-up story that does not necessarily emphasize the previous game. That would change, of course, if the final game prevented the losing team from reaching the playoffs. Then the importance of the game would find a more prominent place in the story.

If a team wins the championship, the follow story could be coupled with a playoff advance. Similar to coaches, sports writers want to look ahead and not behind. Spinning the story forward by building on the previous game is one way to do that. In that case, the follow becomes similar to a season preview except this time the story previews the playoffs. So the follow would include some context as to how the championship was won in the final game but then mostly include information about the playoffs.

All follow-up stories should include an element of "What's next?" Once the event is finished, it's history. In that spirit, the follow should actually be looking forward, answering some of the questions: How will the previous win/loss affect the next game? How did the win/loss affect the league standings? How did the win/loss affect playoff chances? What did the win/loss mean for the team as a whole?

As discussed earlier, the advance, gamer, and follow are the sports writer's trilogy. They have minimal redundancies and are loosely connected. Follow-up stories are the final word on the event. They allow the sports writer to add context where he or she wasn't allowed to do so in the game story. They allow the writer to not only fill in the gaps of the previous event but also create a bridge leading to the next event.

This follow takes the approach, "If you think things are bad now, just wait."

> If you think things are tough for the Shackford Lions now just wait about four more weeks.
>
> Shackford's 17–13 loss to Dundedin on Saturday at Memorial Stadium drops the Lions to 2–2 in the Western Conference and 2–5 overall. But that's not the worst of it.
>
> The Lions still have to play North Haven (4–3), Prate State (7–2), Clamor (4–1–1), and South Cascade State (6–1).
>
> "I think it's definitely going to be tough to practice but we have to overcome that," sophomore tailback Frank Wayward said Saturday. "We've got to get mentally focused that we can win."
>
> Before Saturday's loss to Dundedin, the Lions were third in the conference with a respectable 2–1 record. Unfortunately for the Lions, their only two wins were against the worst teams in the conference.

The follow also acts as a mini-advance, not only discussing the implications of Saturday's loss but also what the future holds.

This follow discusses how what appeared to be a problem for the team earlier in the season has become an asset.

> Probably the biggest question mark for Northside's girls' basketball team this season was the forwards. But now, most of those early-season questions have been answered.
>
> The young forwards, consisting of two sophomores and a junior center, have catapulted the Cougars' offense to the top of the league scoring statistics. Following Saturday's 65–42 victory against Southside, the Cougars rank first in average points per game (58.7) as two Northside players rank in the top five.

There is nothing sexy about the follow but it adds perspective—long and short range—to Northside's success and how a perceived weakness has become a strength.

Follows are the nightcap to the event. It's the final word before moving forward to the next event.

Figure 14.1 Graham Watson.

Professional Perspective
By Graham Watson
ESPN.com

When writing a follow for any game story, I try to look at things off the field and sometimes that leads to the sideline.

In 2004, I was covering a University of Missouri football game and I picked up my binoculars to look at the sideline. That year, Missouri had struggled to win games in the second half and it was adversely affecting the team's mentality. In this particular game, Missouri was winning, but there was no one on the sidelines smiling or jumping around or doing any of the things football players do when they're on top.

Missouri ended up losing the game in the final few minutes.

I noted some of the players I had seen on the sideline and found them after the game. I waited until the media horde had cleared and asked them about the mentality of the team while they were winning. One player told me that despite the team's success, there was this sense on the sideline that it was still going to lose. It was a better quote than I could have imagined, but was exactly what I had seen through my binoculars.

The quote spurred on other quotes, which made for a great follow about whether Missouri was too fragile to finish the season on a high note. It made readers question the coaching staff and dedication of the players. It even prompted a team meeting.

That's the thing about follows, you want them to provide perspective on the game. It's a way to delve further than you can in a game story and perhaps provide answers to questions posed during play.

(Graham Watson is a
college football writer for ESPN.com.)

Professional Perspective
By Chad Jennings
Scranton Times-Tribune

For athletes, "off day" is a beautiful phrase. It means no game, no practice, and no worries—except figuring out what time the matinee starts at the local theater. For sports writers, "off day" is a nightmare. It means filling 15 inches by writing about absolutely nothing: no game, no practice, and no chance of convincing an editor to fill the news hole with a wire story about curling.

Figure 14.2 Chad Jennings.

In reality, there's no need to panic.

Off-day stories can be easy and interesting as long as you look ahead, plan accordingly and be specific.

Sports writers work on a schedule, so off-day stories should never be surprising. If an off day is coming up, start thinking early and get interviews out of the way a day or two in advance. Talking to players and coaches early should provide a chance to get in depth with coverage on off days. There's no deadline pressure and no limit on subject manner, so pick a topic and run with it. The worst thing to do is to simply rehash a game that's two days old.

If a third baseman is suddenly crushing the ball, talk to the hitting coach about the mechanics of the player's swing. What changes has he made? Go beyond the fact he's 10-for-24 in the past six games, which is probably all that can fit in a game story.

Is a team's front court being dominated on the boards? Look at rebound statistics and talk to players and coaches to find out why. Is a lineup change in the works? Should that be a consideration?

Remember that on off days, you're writing for the diehards, for the fans who care about more than whether the team won or lost the night before. Fans who read about their teams every day are debating the merits of every little thing, and off-day stories provide an opportunity to dig into those subjects.

Still crushed for a big idea? Take a bunch of little ideas and write a notebook. If all else fails, or the big idea falls apart, a notebook is an easy back-up plan.

Ultimately, off-day stories shouldn't be nightmares. Just plan ahead, write something insightful, and figure out for yourself when the matinee is showing.

(Chad Jennings is the Scranton/
Wilkes-Barre Red Barons beat writer for the
Scranton Times-Tribune.)

15

OTHER TYPES OF STORIES III

Sports Columns

The most coveted position in the sports department at most newspapers is the job of sports columnist. The sports columnist usually can write on any subject he or she wants. Sports columns are typically given good play in the sports section.

The sports columnist position is typically given as a reward to the most talented writer at a newspaper. However, the sports columnist is expected to attract readers. This column should be among the best read articles in the newspaper. In fact, if readers aren't reading the sports columnist, what are they reading? And if readers aren't reading the sports columnist, why is the newspaper paying him big bucks?

Accordingly, sports columnists often become well known in a community. Jim Murray, for example, was an institution at the *Los Angeles Times*. Blackie Sherrod was one of the most highly respected journalists in Dallas. Current columnists also are well known across the country.

While at first blush sports columns appear to be easy to write—what could be easier than writing what you think?—they are, in reality, extremely difficult to write. They demand great effort in both writing and research. The US Supreme Court may have ruled that there is no such thing as a wrong opinion, but sports columnists still need evidence to back up their claims.

Types of Columns

Sports columns are difficult to classify. Every sports column is different in some way from every other column. Fensch (1995) identifies six types of sports columns.

- Editorial. This type of column is most closely aligned with the traditional editorial columns written for the newspaper's op-ed page. The main purpose of the column is to form an opinion about some aspect of the sports world. It could involve a criticism of baseball's steroid policy, or a call for closer scrutiny of an athletic program. The opinions expressed in the column are often supported by the editorial board of the newspaper.

- My view. Slightly different from the editorial, this type of column allows the columnist to talk about his or her personal experiences. A columnist may write about a player having a particularly good (or bad) year, based on the personal observation of the writer.
- Ask the expert. Some newspapers run columns that answer questions sent in directly from readers. A reader may ask about a sports record, or about the status of a player's injury. The columnist will answer the questions through his or her extensive network of sources.
- Reader response. If columnists are doing their job, they should get plenty of mail from readers—either critical or complimentary. Columnists can use these letters as a basis for columns, either pointing out why a criticism is unwarranted (or warranted), or expanding on points raised by the reader.
- Sports trivia. Because sports have so many records—many obscure— a columnist could devote articles to pointing out some of these records. Historical events often make for interesting column topics.
- "Irish stew". This approach can include all of the above. A columnist can take a stand on an issue, mix in his or her own observations, include some expert commentary, include reader responses and throw in some trivia. In other words, this type of column defies definition.

Structure of Columns

As with the types of sports columns, the structure of columns can vary greatly. A typical structure, however, follows the same formula that editorial writers use. This involves three sections:

- Premise. The introduction should address the main point of the article. What is the purpose of the article? It often helps if you can state the premise of the column in one clear and concise sentence, for instance, "Steroid users should not be allowed into the baseball Hall of Fame." By reducing a column into one sentence, a writer can focus more clearly on the topic and avoid wandering off on tangents.
- Evidence. The point of the column needs to be supported with facts, figures, quotes, statistics, etc. A column that merely states an opinion with no factual evidence appears unfair.
- Conclusion. Good columns return to the premise and clearly point out why the original premise is correct.

Some sports columns take a "two-sided" approach, showing both the pros and cons of a premise. This also adds a degree of fairness to the column by noting opposing points of view. Of course, the columnist can refute these opposing points of view with additional evidence.

Problems with Columns I: Being Wimpy

Columnists are supposed to take stands. It doesn't matter if they are right or wrong. What matters is that the columnist makes a cogent point and backs it with solid evidence.

So don't write a column that says: "Yes, this Super Bowl should be a good game. Either team could win..." Don't be afraid of picking a winner, even if it turns out to be a loser. Sometimes it's good to be wrong. Readers will think that you're human.

And they certainly can laugh at you... Remember: If readers write derogatory letters to you, at least you know that they're reading you.

Problems with Columns II: Take my Wife, Please.
Inserting Yourself Too Much Into the Column

Readers typically want to see what you think, but they don't necessarily want to read about you personally. Don't go overboard telling personal tales about your background.

For example, I once read in a column dealing with Billie Jean King that said, "My eight-year-old daughter doesn't know what a lesbian is..." Would readers really care what an eight-year-old girl thinks? Or another column said, "My mother thinks it's embarrassing that we can't beat Oregon State..." Unless your mother is Hillary Clinton or Queen Elizabeth, readers probably aren't interested.

Many of the best sports columnists rarely write in the first person. One important point, though, is if you are going to write a column using the first person, do not abruptly use "I" late in a column. Readers will wonder why you changed the writing style. If a reader is noticing the writing style of the column instead of the content of the column, this is not a good sign.

Problems with Columns III: Keep it Simple, Stupid.
The Egghead Syndrome

Some columnists get too complicated in their columns, pointing out aspects of sporting events that go beyond the comprehension of most readers. Readers expect to learn from a column, but they also expect to be entertained and enlightened in understandable terms.

Don't get overly technical. So instead of writing: "Patellular diseases, chondromalacia, Osgood Schlatter's Disease, swelling and edema of the knee, ligament instability, knee instability, recurrent knee pain, arthritis, degenerative joint..." how about writing "knee problems."

The point is that sports columnists, as well as all writers, should write to express, not to impress. Readers will think you are phony if you try to write over their heads.

Problems with Columns IV: I've Seen This Before: Coming Up With Something Fresh

Some sports columnists tend to repeat themselves. Some sports columnists tend to repeat themselves... It is very easy to slip into a comfort zone by writing similar content over and over. If a journalist writes four columns a week for 50 weeks a year (two weeks off for vacation, of course), that's 200 columns a year. Chances are some of the 200 columns are going to be very similar to one another. How can you stay fresh? It's not easy.

Good columnists experiment with different writing styles. They look for story ideas in unusual places. And they avoid dry, dull issues that can be written practically every day.

Avoid things everyone knows or would expect: "Steve Spurrier was very excited about his 2006 recruiting class..." Has a coach ever been disappointed with his recruits? "Bobby Knight marched angrily into the press room Tuesday night..." That's standard operating procedure. Tell the reader something new.

Problems with Columns V: Don't Insult Our Intelligence

Sports columnists sometimes take themselves too seriously. They can call for a coach's firing, or for a player to be dropped from a team. These are legitimate topics for columns, but you have to remember that you are writing about people's lives.

Problems with Columns VI: Crossing the Line From Clever To Cute

Sometimes, columnists try to be too funny. It's important to always keep in mind, though, that what one person thinks is funny, another will think is stupid. It's a fine line between clever and cute. Some columnists have a difficult time navigating between the two.

Always think about content before presentation. Don't try to make puns on names of people or places. One columnist wrote, "Have

Mercer on me" when Mercer University won a basketball game against a favored opponent. Someone once wrote, "Rod wasn't Lavering" during a tennis match involving Rod Laver. Since "laver" is not a verb (it's a noun referring to a wash basin, or a noun referring to seaweed), the use of the term as a verb is well within the "cute" category.

Problems with Columns VII: What Planet Are You From? Strange Topics

Sports columns, by definition, should deal with sports. Columns that don't deal with sports don't belong on the sports page. At times, however, columnists will go beyond sports to discuss other issues. Often these columns defy logic.

A columnist once wrote a column about Cincinnati chili. Granted, Cincinnati does have professional baseball and football teams, and therefore is technically a "sports city." On the other hand, food from this city is not actually related to sports—unless it somehow plays a role in the success of the Reds and Bengals.

Imagine what an avid sports fan would think if he or she opened up the newspaper expecting to find a thoughtful sports commentary dealing with pertinent topics of the day, like baseball pennant races, or football training camps, only to find a column explaining why chili in Cincinnati tastes different from chili anywhere else.

Problems with Columns VIII: Wandering the Universe. Lack of Focus

Some columnists try to cram too much information on too many topics in a column. These "notes" columns typically lack a common thread and so tend to wander across several topics. Oftentimes, it would be better to concentrate on one main topic and devote the entire column to it. After all, if a topic is newsworthy enough to be mentioned as an item in a notes column, isn't it newsworthy enough to command attention as the lone topic of the column? If not, then the topic isn't very newsworthy.

Problems with Columns IX: Homerism

Because a sports columnist is the top writer for a newspaper, they must spend a great deal of time getting to know the key sports figures in an area. This can sometimes cause reporters to get too cozy with the sports figures, making them lose sight of their objectivity. If a team deserves criticism, don't be afraid to be critical.

I recall reading a column about a football team that went winless one year. The columnist wrote that although the team went 0–11, there was reason for optimism because it had nowhere to go but up. The trouble was that the team played 12 games the following year.

Problems with Columns X: Empty Statements

Sports are full of statements that don't mean anything. Go beyond these statements. Don't state the obvious.

"Turnovers will be the key to the game." Turnovers are a key in 99 percent of football games, so isn't this obvious? "The team that scores first will have the advantage." Can you have an advantage if you fall behind?

Columns

Below is an excellent example of a sports column, written by one of the best sports columnists in the country, Thomas Boswell of the *Washington Post*. Note how his column makes strong points and uses great metaphors.

What, Us Worry?
By Thomas Boswell
Washington Post
August 30, 2006

Let's not jump the gun and say the Redskins are in turmoil after their 41–0 drubbing by the Patriots on Saturday. But consider this: Yesterday punter Eddie Johnson may have had the shortest career in Washington history—less than six hours. Some guys just have a cup of coffee. Johnson didn't even have time to say, "Cream and sugar."

On Monday, the Redskins phoned the unemployed punter in Arizona. Yesterday morning, they auditioned him as a possible replacement for Derrick Frost, the resident shank artist. By lunch, Johnson, who's spent time with four other NFL teams, was signed and running back Jesse Lumsden released to make roster room. "I was going to apply for a sales job at a personal training gym in Scottsdale," Johnson said. "I was still asleep when they called." Suddenly, he thought he was dreaming.

However, after practice yesterday afternoon, Johnson made the mistake of saying, "My leg is kind of tired." So, he went to get iced. These days, that's a bad idea at Redskins Park, where only tough guys need apply. Many a coach has a hair trigger after watching the team be outscored 87–17 in this 0–3 month. By sundown, Johnson himself has been iced—cut, booted out of town. With luck and a red-eye flight he may still get that gym job by today. But how would you like to be Jesse Lumsden?

By nightfall, one question hung in the air: Can Tom Cruise punt?

Almost nothing seems too weird to happen around the Redskins this month. On Monday, owner Daniel Snyder cut a deal with Cruise's production company to pay development costs in exchange for the chance to finance his film projects. Thus was born "First and Goal LLC." Cruise's production partner said, "We are entering into a profitable relationship with unlimited creative and financial potential." Isn't that what Steve Spurrier said?

This Redskin preseason has been so star-crossed or goofy, that the NFL must be tempted to think, "Same old Redskins—champs of the offseason." However, this time may be far different from the years of Deion Sanders and Jeff George. With less than two weeks left before their opener, the Redskins may be doing a wonderful job of fooling the league and hiding their hole cards. Or else they're deluding themselves completely. It's going to turn out to be one or the other.

Only exceptional teams can afford to play with one hand tied behind their backs, even in the exhibition season. Yet that's exactly what the Redskins have tried to do, according to their coaches and players. This organization, whether correct, thinks that it is so loaded for a Super Bowl run that it would rather risk losing by lopsided scores than revealing its strategy.

Al Saunders, who runs the offense, maintains he has only used "two percent" of his 700-page playbook in exhibition games. "I know what the end product is going to look like... I've been in this offense a long time and I know it works," said Saunders, pointing out that "the last [exhibition] team here that went 0–4 was 1982, and their next 32 games after that their record was 28–4."

When you look as bad as the Redskins have so far, that self-evaluation is either incandescent coaching confidence or hubris. What's indisputable is that the Redskins have shown an offense so simple it would make a high school team look exotic. On Saturday, the Redskins put a man in motion or shifted formations only a half-dozen times. "That's by plan," quarterback Mark Brunell said. "That's not just in one game [against New England]. That's in all three games."

"If the same thing happens in the season opener," tackle Chris Samuels said, "then we've got a problem."

Yesterday, assistant head coach-defense Gregg Williams joined this Redskin chorus. "Everybody seems to place so much emphasis on the third exhibition game. Why would we do that? Why wouldn't we wait until they're using real bullets," said Williams, who described the defensive game plan for the Pats as "zero." As for tomorrow's final exhibition, against the Baltimore Ravens, the Redskins show no indications that they will change their game plan. Or, rather, their game non-plan.

Saunders and Williams maintain they want to see their players perform in the simplest circumstances, unaided by deception and left to beat their opponents physically at old-fashioned football. In other words, get some answers about basic talent levels, player by player. Unfortunately, those answers have been extremely ugly. Redskins tackles, including Jon Jansen, had trouble protecting Brunell without chip-blocking assistance. Tom Brady read Williams's defense with ease and shredded the middle of the secondary. And special teams continued to be so bad that Johnson was summoned, and dismissed, perhaps as an object lesson.

Most teams would not risk exposing their personnel so starkly. Is that coaching wisdom or folly? Is the Redskins' staff stripping down egos, Marine-style, to build back a tight-knit, ego-free, championship unit? Or is confidence, which only reappeared in this organization one season ago, being destroyed prematurely? In short, is the Redskins' much-praised and expensive coaching staff acting with supreme self-assurance or with the kind of cockiness it would see as a flaw in a player?

"In the first 10 plays against Cincinnati, we brought the house with blitzes," said Williams. "We said, 'Looks like we're pretty good at that.'" So, since then, he has chosen not to "avalanche it" but simply line up and "let 'em play."

"We never think that [41–0] is going to happen," Williams said. "But we have to have a certain confidence in our systems and in who we are coaching," to take the chance on such minimalist game plans.

The Redskins once lost a world title game 73–0. Presumably no coach found a silver lining in that one. But the Redskins, now that they've had a few days, have found their rose-colored glasses for 41–0. "After a game like that, you have a more receptive group," Williams said. "It's been nice in the meeting room this week. 'Coach, what do you think you can do for me?' That's better than having guys who are already booking tickets to [the Pro Bowl game in] Honolulu.

"They all think they know more than you. They become more of a captive audience when they have been humbled. Saturday night, we got humbled."

The most adult of all the Redskins is, of course, Coach Joe Gibbs. So, he sees both sides. He and his staff took the risk of under-scheming for the sake of analyzing personnel but paid a high, and presumably unnecessary, price in team embarrassment.

"I'd like to say I was smart enough to plan it that way," Gibbs said of the notion that brutal exhibition experiences might prevent overconfidence and ensure an attentive and intense team in the regular season.

"We have not played well, so we're all concerned," said Gibbs, who frequently coaches best when he can play the role of steadying force at the center of a crisis. "We are going to have to work our way out of it."

At the moment, that goal seems far away. Safety Adam Archuleta embodies the Redskins' befuddled state. "At certain times we haven't played the run well. Certain times we haven't played the pass well," he said. "Now we're trying to put it all together." Thanks, Yogi.

16

OTHER TYPES OF STORIES IV
Features and Profiles

Feature stories are difficult to categorize. By definition, feature stories defy definition. Feature stories take creative and unusual approaches in writing styles. The two main types of features are human interest stories and profiles.

Effective Human Interest Stories

This type of story concentrates on human elements: trying to create an emotional reaction, whether it be sadness or horror, joy or excitement, depression or anger. Human interest stories can involve extraordinary experiences, a common problem or a national issue. Broadly speaking, all feature stories could be called human interest stories.

Human interest stories are characterized by several elements. First, the time element tends to be relatively unimportant. Human interest story are timeless—the story could be told at any time. Second, human interest stories tend to focus on people in unusual circumstances. Problems people are forced to overcome, for instance, make excellent human interest stories. Finally, human interest stories tend to be written so that readers can identify and sympathize with the subject of the story.

When the Milwaukee Bucks drafted Yi Jianlian of China in the 2007 NBA draft, Yi's agents were concerned about the lack of Asian-Americans in Milwaukee. The *Milwaukee Journal* wrote a human interest story to address this concern:

By Don Walker
Milwaukee Journal
June 29, 2007

The Milwaukee Bucks hope to convince Yi Jianlian that Milwaukee is a great place on a great lake to start his basketball career.

While that possibility won't be official until Yi signs a contract, the Metropolitan Milwaukee Association of Commerce's China Council has a plan in the works that might make Yi feel more at home.

Ulice Payne, co-chair of the MMAC's China Council, said Friday that the Shougang Group, a large conglomerate that also owns the Beijing Ducks of the Chinese Basketball Association, had asked him to organize a trip of up-and-coming Chinese basketball players to come to Milwaukee in the fall for a six-month visit. Under the plan, Payne said, the players would train with local basketball teams to better learn the American game.

The Chinese refer to the young players, who range in age from 15 to 18, as the Hope Team because they represent the next generation of top Chinese athletes. Payne said he was trying to line up English classes for the athletes, and a place to stay for the lengthy visit.

"They (the Shougang Group) want to do it," Payne said. "It's up to us to get organized."

Payne, whose firm, Addison-Clifton, has extensive ties to China, said every Houston Rockets game is broadcast live in China. Should Yi sign with the Bucks, Payne said he assumed Bucks' games would be beamed back to China.

The MMAC's China Council aims to increase ties between Milwaukee and the world's largest nation and hopes to lure Chinese industrial investment to Milwaukee. Officials in Ningbo, a Chinese port city, have already signed an economic and cultural cooperation pact with Milwaukee Mayor Tom Barrett.

Payne, a member of the 1977 national championship team at Marquette University, said he had not seen Yi play. But Chinese officials who have seen Yi play have told Payne they have high hopes for him in the National Basketball Association.

For the Bucks, Yi represents a huge marketing opportunity. John Steinmiller, the team's vice president for business operations, said the front office was ready to go, assuming Yi signs on the dotted line.

"We don't want to be premature or make any assumptions," Steinmiller said. "Details have to be taken care of. We know there is interest in Yi."

Steinmiller said the team's Web site attracted more than 2,000 hits from readers in China overnight. "We've got a lot of Yi content on our Web site," he said. "We are trying to take advantage of that."

The William Morris Agency represents Yi's marketing efforts. A representative did not return a reporter's phone call.

Effective Profiles

Perhaps the most common feature type is the profile. People like to read about other people. Indeed, that is why we have so many magazines devoted to celebrities. Profiles tell the story behind people in the news.

The sports field is full of interesting people with fascinating backgrounds. Stories showing the personality of a sports figure are very popular with readers.

But because profiles are so common, these types of stories often appear stale. It is difficult to come up with a new approach to a time-worn topic. Would a writer be able to write a fresh profile of Brett Favre or Shaquille O'Neal?

It is important to remember that a profile is not a biography. Biographies include basic information such as the date of birth, marital status, and college degrees. Profiles, on the other hand, concentrate on a person's personality. Thus, anecdotal information is more important than historical data.

Other aspects of profiles that might be included in a story:

- Physical characteristics, such as appearance, dress, and mannerisms. Be careful to show, rather than tell. Don't say a person is "welldressed." Show that the person wears suits from Armani and leather shoes from Milan.
- Unusual tastes and habits. Does the linebacker play the flute? Does the coach drive a Harley-Davidson?
- People who had the largest impact on the subject's life. Was it a teacher, or a family friend?
- Shortcomings. Is the person afraid of spiders? Do they think they have any character flaws?

Writing Tips

Tell a story. The best profiles show something about a subject that has never been shown before. What makes this person unusual?

- Make a point. The best profiles don't just describe a subject, but they make a point about the person.
- Show. As with all good writing, show, don't tell. It's one thing to tell a reader that Brett Favre is helping hurricane victims in Mississippi. It's another thing to show him helping. Give examples.

- Don't get in the way. Underwrite. Let subjects tell their story. Don't interrupt them mid-quote. Let the subjects' quotes carry the story.
- "Not another profile..." Because profiles are so common, writers need to try something uncommon. Go beyond the typical "Meet the Superstar"-type story.
- Be observant. Good angles can come from anywhere. A messy desk can give some insight into a person's personality. An off-the-cuff remark might make for an interesting anecdote. Kimber Williams, a feature writer for the *Eugene Register-Guard*, tells a story about a feature-writing coach who once told her that when interviewing someone for a personality profile "make sure you get the name of their dog."
- Let the subject give you the lead. Writers too often begin with a preconceived idea of what they want to concentrate on in their stories. Sometimes, these pre-writing ideas pan out. More often, the idea needs to be modified. Be flexible enough to change your story angle. Subjects can give clear hints about where they think your story should go. Be sure to pay attention to these cues.

Below is a personality profile that appeared in the *Washington Post*. Notice how the writer begins with an unusual point—that the player has big feet.

By Jason La Canfora
Washington Post Staff Writer
September 9, 2006

The chiseled, 6-foot-4, 265-pound physique—lean and hulking over the other behemoths in burgundy jerseys—is imposing. But the first thing you notice is the feet. They look like two white cinderblocks, size 16 cleats made bulky by layers and layers of athletic tape, as if Frankenstein were corralled in the training room at Redskins Park. Teammates joke that when defensive end Andre Carter walks, the ground rumbles beneath him, and his endless tape sessions have already become legendary.

But should Carter approximate the best season of his pro career—12½ sacks and three forced fumbles in 2002—the unique look might soon catch on. Those massive appendages carried Carter to a substantial free agent contract this offseason as the long-coveted final cog in Gregg Williams's defense—a gifted, versatile pass-rushing end who draws double teams, pressures the passer, and opens up ample space for his teammates. Carter's feet are huge even by NFL standards, in length as well as girth, and would seem to present a formidable impediment to someone expected to charge off the line, make quick, decisive cuts, cross over adroitly, and remain as nimble as possible despite his hefty frame. After years of awkward adaptation, and a youth spent honing his agility through eclectic athletic endeavors, the stumps have become a physical asset, giving Carter superior balance, helping him thrust out of his stance and perhaps even spurring the gargantuan lineman to come up with a sack dance should his season go as well as the coaches hope.

"From a base of support, it really helps sometimes to have big feet when you have to fight guys while being off-balanced and everything," Williams said. "But I'm shocked he can run and be that explosive with those kinds of brogans [work boots]. We've got a younger son at home, 14 years old with a size 14, and you see him kind of go through that awkward stuff. But the fact that Andre just explodes and changes direction so well, that just speaks to his natural ability."

Carter's relatives still tell stories about his feet-induced accidents throughout puberty. The large feet were no surprise—Andre's father, Rubin, a former standout lineman with Denver and now a football coach, wears between a 15 and 15½—but the youngster ended up surpassing the family record. Rather than focus on football, however, Carter was kept out of the pee-wee ranks, and learned to grow into his body through various other pursuits.

"Oh man, I've always had these feet," said Carter, who also boasts long arms and a considerable wingspan. "It was tough for a while as a kid tripping over my own feet, but I just kind of got used to them. When I was young I ran track and played tennis and did tae kwon do and played basketball. So I've always been around sports, and my parents always involved me in something to keep me active."

His parents were careful about what athletic endeavors were allowed at a young age. Rubin did not want Andre to focus solely on one sport, and knew from firsthand experience that certain pursuits would best aid his overall development more than others. Wanting his bones to grow strong, and minimizing the risk of serious injury, Andre was not permitted to play football until he was 15.

"The athleticism and his abilities, some of those things are inherent, and other things he really had to work on," said Rubin Carter, the Redskins' defensive line coach in 1999. "He made a conscious effort to work hard and develop the skills necessary to play his position. With his feet, one of the things that really helped him early with his body balance and eye-hand coordination was martial arts. That's probably the best thing we could have done as a family was placing him in that rather than Pop Warner football. He really developed that explosiveness in martial arts, breaking boards as a young child."

Carter, who also excelled at the shot put at the University of California, was drafted seventh overall in 2001 by San Francisco, where he played until signing with the Redskins in March.

In college he began adopting some of his father's hallmarks. Many linemen wear gloves to get a better grip and hand traction, but Carter is old-school, with his lower forearms and wrists layered with tape like a boxer, and his right index fingers bound to his middle fingers.

"He saw those old pictures of me with my hands all taped up," Rubin said. "It's nice for me to see, and he does it just to get some added support for grabbing and pulling and all of the things you need to do as a defensive lineman."

Andre said: "I tried the gloves and was like, 'This isn't working for me.' So I went with the tape. I guess it runs in the family."

Far more unusual is the elaborate taping of Carter's feet, another homage to his father. Rubin required copious amounts as well, but usually stopped around the middle of his foot, wanting his cleats to feel as snug as possible. Andre, however, often appears mummified from his lower shin to the tip of his cleats.

Carter's explanation is plausible—"Sometimes when I try to turn the corner on the edge, my feet end up sliding, so the tape is mainly for support"—but his teammates joke about him showing up for practice one day with an entire leg taped. (Pretending to trip over Carter's vacant tennis shoes has become a common locker room pratfall as well.)

"I think they use about a roll on each foot, so that'll make them look even bigger," said Bubba Tyer, director of sports medicine who has spent 34 years with the Redskins. "Those feet, I don't know if it's a handicap or good for him, but I'll say this, the rest of his body looks...good, so he can handle those feet."

The coaching staff was enchanted by Carter's size, power, and musculature, too, making him a primary free agent target despite recent lean years. Carter missed most of 2004 because of back surgery, spent 2005 trying to switch to linebacker, and he looked anything but dynamic in this summer's preseason games, albeit without Williams deploying his normally hyper-aggressive scheme.

"He's starting to get accustomed to some of the things we asked him to do," defensive line coach Kirk Olivadotti said. "It's still a transition for him."

Switching back to end—a position he has played his entire football life—should prove elementary enough, though, his father said, and the coaches are not dwelling on the modest exhibition output.

"Character-wise, attitude-wise, and personality-wise, he fits in exactly with the rest of this group," Williams said "He can do things, hopefully, rushing the passer that we've needed."

No player has posted more than eight sacks in either of Williams's two seasons in Washington. Without standout talent on the ends, Williams generally relied on intricate blitzes to cultivate a pass rush, and tackle Cornelius Griffin is the only lineman to register 10 total sacks here in 2004 and 2005 (Griffin, hurt last year, has 10 sacks in that span, a number 16 NFL players equaled or surpassed in 2005 alone).

No Redskin has posted a double-digit sack total since 2002, and no lineman has reached 10 sacks in a season for Washington since 2000. Should Carter become that kind of force, perhaps even his tape-heavy feet will become fashionable. Thus far, there has been just one convert, and that journeyman did not have much of a chance to spread Carter's gospel around.

"I hear all the smart remarks from the players about the tape, I get all of that stuff," Carter said, laughing. "But when [end] Karon Riley was here, he said, 'That's not a bad idea to tape up like that.' I said, 'Hey, it works for me.' He tried it and liked it. Unfortunately, we let him go last week."

Other Types of Features

In his excellent text *Professional Feature Writing*, Bruce Garrison lists several categories of feature stories. Many of the categories fit in well with sports writing.

- Seasonal Features. These types of stories deal with yearly cycles. Certain stories are only stories because they happen at a certain time of year. A story about patriotism is timelier on the Fourth of July. A story about scary costumes is timelier on Halloween. Seasons offer many opportunities for writers. They also offer many opportunities for clichés, such as the most overused, worn out lead "Christmas came early for..."
- Reviews and Criticism. Of course, all sports writing involves some level of criticism. A game report naturally should contain some indication of how well or poorly a team played. Yearly reviews are also common newspaper fare. Here, reporters discuss the strengths and weakness of teams after a season has concluded. Journalists also can write mid-year analyses, pointing to areas that need improvement if a team has hopes for advancing to postseason play.
- Service Articles. Writers can pen stories that explain "how-to" do something. The *Chicago Tribune* several years ago, for example, ran a series dealing with "The Art of Running" and "The Art of Passing" the football. Other service articles could deal with outdoor pursuits or exercise.
- Personal Experience Stories. This type of story is often written in the first person, such as when a reporter personally takes part in some event. Some stories have been written about bad experiences at a sporting event; food served at half-time of a football game might not have been up to standards (would a reader care?). Other stories have been written about exercise programs that reporters undertook.

Common Problems with Features: Leads

- Lack of focus. A feature story should be creatively written, but it also should have a clear purpose. A reader should know why a story is being written from the lead.
- Too long to get to the point. Some writers have a tendency to meander before telling the reader what the story is about. We used to say it's like setting a table. It's great to have a nice-looking table all set before a big meal, but if you take too long to set the table, people will go elsewhere to eat.
- Too newsy. Feature stories are different from hard news stories. The purpose behind the story is different. Feature stories entertain while news stories inform. Get out of the "hard news" syndrome. Some writers who have no problems covering sporting events and writing outstanding reports struggle with feature stories. For them, factual information is much easier to report than personalities or anecdotes. But game reports and other hard news is just one part of the typical menu in the sports section. Looking for

unusual, creative stories beyond game reports separates great writers from average writers.

Common Problems with Features: Bodies

- Too few quotes. Features, especially personality profiles, should have lots of quotes. A subject should be allowed to tell his or her own story. Sources should be allowed to tell stories about the subject. Good quotes should be a main aspect of a feature story.
- Too many quotes. Features writers are reporters, not recorders. Writers need to add perspective and observations. Endless streams of quote after quote make for dull reading, and lazy reporting.
- Not enough description. Describe. Features allow a writer to take full advantage of colorful writing styles. Don't be afraid to use adjectives and adverbs throughout features.
- Too much description (in clumps). Spread description throughout the story. Clumping description together gives the impression that the story isn't smooth or consistent. It also interrupts the rhythm of a story.
- Nut graph comes in too late. As mentioned earlier, sports stories often have a "nut graph"—a paragraph following the lead that summarizes the main purpose of the story. This paragraph should appear early in a story, so the reader understands what the story is about.
- Forgetting about the lead. If properly written, the lead of a feature makes a point. Ideally, the point made in the lead should be the most important point of the story. Otherwise, it doesn't belong in the lead. Sometimes, however, a feature writer will leave the point behind, never to return. Effective feature writers, on the other hand, use the point in the lead as a recurring topic later in the story. At the very least, a writer should make mention of this point at the end of the story.

Common Problems with Features: Overall

- First person/second person. Sports stories, including features, are typically written in the third person. First-person articles can be extremely difficult to handle. Because first-person stories are so rare, writers using this technique often appear to be egotistical—they must be full of themselves or they wouldn't put themselves in their stories. Second-person stories are also tricky. Readers typically want to be informed and entertained. They don't want to be active participants in stories. Thus, when a writer talks directly to the reader through a second-person story, this runs the risk of losing some readers.

- Questions. Asking readers to answer questions is similar to writing in the second person. The writer asks for active participation of the reader, which many readers do not like. It would be best to give readers answers, not ask them questions.
- Choice of topic. Topics of game reports are very simple: one team wins, and another team loses. Sports reporters must explain why. Features, on the other hand, come in all shapes and sizes. What one person thinks is interesting, another person will think is deathly dull. Because of the great range of topics available, writers can miss the boat at times, concentrating on relatively insignificant issues while ignoring more important topics.
- Choice of sources. Not every source is worthy of being quoted. Writers should use news judgment in deciding whom to quote and when.

Final Tips for Feature Writing

- Remember that you are the eyes, ears, and nose of your reader. Be descriptive. Try to create pictures in your readers' minds.
- Don't allow your presence to influence the subject. Let the subject get comfortable with you around. Talk informally. Put the subject at ease.
- Gather an abundance of notes. It is always better to have too many notes and have to discard some, than to have too few notes and have to struggle for things to include in your story.
- A fine line exists between too much description and too little. Too much description can leave a story with flash but no substance. Too little description can make for a dull story. Try to strike a balance.
- Show, don't tell. Look and see. Go beyond the surface. Give examples that show people doing things.
- Be creative, especially in the lead. Try unusual approaches. Experiment.
- Basically, there are two ways of writing features: heavy on description, or heavy on sources. Some great sports features concentrate mainly on descriptions of people or events constructed by the writer. Other great sports features concentrate mainly on quotes for sources. The trick is to identify which type of approach would work best. With great quotes, a writer should let the sources tell the story. With mediocre quotes, a writer should explain the story more from his or her own perspective.
- Watch out for clichés. With the freedom that comes from the feature-story approach comes the danger of using worn out phrases and terminology.

17

OTHER TYPES OF STORIES V
Sports News and Enterprise

Some would call sports journalism an oxymoron. That's not completely true. Most journalists outside of sports would call sports journalism an oxymoron. Your newsroom colleagues generally view you as an over-grown kid who earns a paycheck by "playing" at journalism. There is a reason for that perception among newsies. Oftentimes sports writers are the ultimate sports fans, publicly praising the team in victory and criticizing it following losses. Also, sports writers are often expected to be shills for the sports teams they cover. Sometimes with a wink and a nod, representatives for those teams tell the writer to "give us some good pub." The division between being a supporter of a team and an unbiased reporter is sometimes so narrow that you can hear a sports writer quietly—or not so quietly—cheer between paragraphs while writing a story.

The late legendary sports columnist Jimmy Cannon once wrote, "Sports are the toy department of human life." Cannon probably wasn't the first sports writer to acknowledge the journalistic shortcom-ings of his profession, but he is traditionally regarded as the first sports writer to do so in print.

But there are inherent reasons why sports writers prefer "journalism lite." While growing up, news reporters do not generally "play" city government, business or courthouse like sports writers play baseball, basketball or football. Aspiring news reporters do not stand outside city hall to capture a glimpse of the mayor or collect autographs from city officials. No one has ever uttered the words, "Mr. Sewer Disposal Plant Manager, may I have your autograph?" Young newsies do not gather at huge stadiums and arenas to cheer politicians, police or medical profes-sionals; nor do adolescent news junkies swap trading cards of civic leaders or school board members ("I'll trade you two city councilmen for one mayor").

Even the title "sports writer" has a diminished journalistic quality. Why are we called sports writers and not reporters? In other sections of the newspaper the authors of stories are labeled reporters (cops reporter, city hall reporter, business reporter, education reporter, etc.) While news reporters are labeled "news hounds" sports writers are pegged "fans."

Being the newsroom's "toy department" is a blessing and a curse for many sports writers. Covering ballgames, associating with athletes, and enjoying a bit of their own local celebrity in the way of columns and radio shows have allure. But when the big story, the news story, arises, the "toy department" is perceived as being ill-equipped to handle it. The story is often plucked from sports and given to a news reporter, someone who understands the complexities of the "real" world. This does not happen to other journalists. If a school superintendent is charged with embezzling from the school district, the education reporter writes the story. When a police officer is being investigated for police brutality, the cops reporter keeps the story. So why is sports relieved of the same journalistic responsibilities? Well, they shouldn't be.

Sports writers who are more than happy to abandon the news story have created much of that "toy department" perception. They say, "If I write *that* story the coach/athlete/manager might not talk to me." Well, don't reporters on other beats face the same situation? After writing a news story, will some coaches and athletes stop talking to you? Maybe, but that happens sometimes anyway. Besides, if you accurately report the facts, what can they gripe about? Sure, it creates an uncomfortable situation, but your first obligations are to the truth and to the readers.

Covering a sports beat is not about making friends. It's about journalism. You need to garner the respect of your sources. The best way to do that is by accurately reporting the facts and establishing an understanding that you are a journalist on the beat obligated to cover all the stories—good and bad. If court documents say an athlete was charged with assault, and you write about it, you are only fulfilling your journalistic obligations. Ignoring the assault charge by not writing about it does not make the charge disappear. If athletes only desire "good" stories then they should act as good citizens.

Sports journalists should not treat stories that involve police reports, civic government or financial budgets like airborne diseases. Although you might pursue a sports journalism career for the sports, it's the journalism that requires top priority. By asking the tough questions and writing the difficult stories you will gain respect from your newsroom colleagues and sources. Sometimes athletes and coaches will get in your face and scream, "Why did you write that story?" Instead of screaming back, just say, "I was reporting the news. If it hadn't happened I couldn't have written it." It might not satisfy the screamer but truth makes for a strong counterargument.

Getting the news on the sports page is just as important—or more important—as providing the game scores. When arenas and stadiums are constructed with taxpayer money, you need to understand the innerworkings of state government. After an athlete is arrested and charged with a crime, knowing how to obtain a police report is imperative. And you have to know if it's legal under the Sunshine Law for school board members to kick you out of a public meeting when they want to discuss the employment status of the girls' basketball coach.

Sports are a reflection of life. As a sports journalist you need to report and write about all aspects of sports. Sometimes that includes sports news.

Dealing with "Celebrities"

The sports section is the crossroads of a newspaper. It encapsulates the best and worst of humanity. Although game stories, advances, follows, features, and columns are the meat and potatoes of the sports section, it also includes an array of news typically found in other newspaper sections. Readers turn to the sports section to escape the reality of life, but what they find—or at least should find—are life's successes, failures, joys, heartaches, loves, hates, crimes, and misdemeanors.

When a professional sports team receives state revenues to construct a new stadium, it's as much a business story as a sports story. After an athlete is arrested for sexual assault, his police mug is as important as his media guide mug. When a popular coach dies, it's a life story and not just an obituary. When athletes donate time and money to assist the homeless, it's a social issues story.

We must first recognize that athletes are celebrities. They utilize the media to benefit their own purposes, which include financial rewards such as scholarships, lucrative contracts, and endorsement deals. Sometimes you are considered a tool to provide that "good pub." This seems somewhat cynical, but with hundreds of millions of dollars on the line, image is everything. Portraying a positive image in the media has become as important to athletes as lucky T-shirts and tattoos. Image is so important that college and professional teams actually provide instruction to athletes on how to interact with the media. Some might call it "Media Manipulation 101."

Similar to other celebrities, athletes view the media as an opportunity for self-promotion. Athletes will interact with media as long as the news is good. When things go wrong—Kobe Bryant rape allegations; Duke lacrosse scandal; Barry Bonds steroid accusations, etc.—the conversation well dries up. Lawyers, agents, and other handlers advise the athlete to say little or nothing. Instead, the athlete will stumble through a written statement that usually lacks sincerity. And more often than not the statement is presented as a non-apology apology. It's an overarching statement where the athlete fails to take responsibility while saying, "Sorry to those who might have been offended."

The non-apology apology reads something like a formatted job rejection letter:

"Ladies and gentlemen,
I realize that something regrettable occurred and I apologize to anyone who was offended. Those who know me realize this was out of character. I consider myself a consummate professional.

This has been a difficult time for me and my family, and I appreciate their love and support. I regret the embarrassment I have caused them.

I feel the media have blown this way out of proportion. They have exaggerated the story and made this difficult for everyone.

I just want to thank my fans for supporting me during this difficult time.

Thank you."

After former Texas Rangers pitcher Kenny Rogers tussled with a cameraman in 2005, Rogers read a prepared statement saying, in part, "I feel compelled to come before you and express my deep regret for my actions. An incident that should have never occurred... I've been around this game for over 20 years. I prepare myself every day to control my emotions and act accordingly. In this instance, I failed miserably... I should have acted professionally, and I regret that was not the case. I'm deeply disappointed and embarrassed in myself... This incident was completely out of character, and I think without question you know that it will never happen again." (Sanchez, 2005).

Absent were the words "I'm sorry" or even an acceptance of responsibility for his actions. Rogers was no doubt "compelled" by his agent and lawyers and the prospect of losing endorsement or contract revenue. He regrets the fallout from the incident but hardly displays remorse for roughing up the cameraman.

As journalists, we need to recognize the non-apology apology and ask questions because covering the press conference or statement reading is not enough. What punishment will the team issue the athlete? Will the league take action? How are teammates reacting to the incident? Is the recipient of the non-apology apology satisfied? Could the incident result in a trade or dismissal from the team? In cases of court-related activity, the story could continue for months or possibly years. Staying on the story is the beat writer's obligation as well.

What truly needs to be recognized is that if athletes and teams utilize the media for their own benefit, then they are bound to face the fire during "difficult" times. Journalism is not attached to a spigot that can be turned off when a source desires. The flow of news and information should not be restricted to the whims of celebrity athletes. Your job as a sports journalist is to keep the spigot flowing with news, both good and bad.

As a journalist working in sports, your first obligation is to the truth. Providing truthful, reliable, relevant, and unbiased information to the readers assists in building your credibility. If you choose not to write about a high school football coach's arrest for driving while intoxicated, you have compromised your credibility. If you cannot be trusted to report the crime of a person who works with our young people, how can you be trusted at all. Is a coach's DWI harmless? Some might say "yes," but why is he above the law? Or what if the coach is suffering from alcoholism? Do parents want to place their children in that environment? At the minimum, the coach is a public figure who works with young people. And, coaches at public schools are paid with taxpayer money. Taxpayers have a right to know if the football coach has violated the law. Additionally, any arrest document is public record, so anyone could obtain the information.

Fans, team officials, players, and coaches place a tremendous amount of pressure on sports journalists to report only the "good" news. Nonetheless, news is news. Sports journalists do not create it or instigate it. They report it.

Sources might disagree with some of the stories you write. If you are careful with the facts and provide the athlete/coach/team official the opportunity for fair comment, the sources will have a better understanding of sports journalism. Along the way, you will develop respect and credibility among your colleagues, readers, and even some of those sources.

The Crime Story

Avid sports page readers have a practiced routine. They pick up the newspaper, reach into the center, and gut out the sports section. The remainder of the paper is discarded, destined to become fish wrap or bird-cage lining.

In addition to missing the day's "serious" news, the sports reader has trashed a valuable resource—the police blotter. The police blotter lists all the calls the police responded to during a certain time period. It also lists names and addresses of those arrested. In a newsroom it's not uncommon for a police reporter to approach the sports desk and ask, "Isn't Joe Schmo the starting center for Podunk U's basketball team?" That's great, but what if Joe Schmo is the starting football center? Would the police reporter know that? Probably not. That's why it's prudent for you, the sports writer, to scan the blotter every day. Here is an example of a blotter:

BEAT 00

ASHLAND STREET: Paul James Thomas, 19, was arrested on suspicion of first-degree property damage, possession by a minor and false identification at 12:30 a.m. Aug. 18 at Ashland and Fifth streets.

WALNUT STREET: Joe Schmo, 21, was arrested on suspicion of public intoxication and disorderly conduct at 2:35 a.m. Aug. 22 at Walnut and Sixth streets.

Discovering that Mr. Schmo was arrested for public intoxication at 2:35 a.m. is only the first step. Before asking him about his late-night endeavors, you will want to visit the police department and obtain a copy of the police or incident report. The report includes the essentials such as name, date of birth, and address of the accused (and victim if there is a victim), time and date of the incident, and the offense. It sometimes includes a description of events that led to the arrest. In essence, the incident report is a play-by-play of the crime.

The police report is not the only document that can provide valuable information. The computers in police cruisers where officers record information is public record and can be useful when writing stories. Also, records of 911 calls can be obtained from the police department.

Although each police department has its own police report, Table 17.1 on the next page, is a basic example of what the report might look like.

After tracking down the police/incident report, you must confirm that Joe Schmo is actually the same Joe Schmo who plays for Podunk U. Check date of birth, address, and middle initial against other information you might have—the university's media guide for example or a student directory. Comb the report for unusual details. The DOB indicates that Joe celebrated a birthday just hours before his arrest. In fact, it was his 21st birthday. The arrest occurred at the corner of Walnut and Sixth. The police department is located on Sixth Street. Was Joe creating a ruckus in front of the police department? Also, Joe blew a 0.12 on the breathalyzer. Was that just over the legal limit in your state? A 0.08 is over the limit in some states while others use 0.10 as a guide. Speaking with arresting officer U.B. Arrested can assist in providing additional details, such as how Joe did impede the traffic.

Just as coaches use coachspeak ("We were in Dog 2 when they ran that slant."), police use language that might be unfamiliar. Using a John Facenda-like voice (think NFL Films' *Voice of God*: "The frozen tundra of Lambeau Field"), a report reads: "On June 9, 2006, at approximately 0242 hours, deputy Joe Dowd and deputy Bob Burke of the Podunk Police Department were dispatched to the area of Chesterfield Road and Burbank Avenue, to check the welfare of a man reportedly involved in a

Table 17.1 Example of a basic police report

Podunk Police Department

601 Walnut St., Podunk, IN   Incident Report

Incident

Offense
Public intoxication; disorderly conduct

Date	Day	Time occurred	Date	Day	Time reported
08/22	TU	2:35 a.m.		same/3:15 a.m.	

Victim

Victim's name/Business name		Address City State	
State of Indiana		Corner of Walnut/Sixth streets	

SNN	Race	Sex	DOB	Occupation

Suspects(s)

Name 1. Last/First/MI	Race	Sex	Address	DOB
Schmo, Joe, S	W	M	2415 Monroe St.	08/21/85
Name 2.				
Name 3.				

Witness(es)

Name 1. Last/First/MI	Race	Sex	Address	Phone
Name 2. Last/First/MI	Race	Sex	Address	Phone

Vehicle

Owner	Make	Model	Year	Description/license

Narrative
Suspect was witnessed stumbling down the sidewalk and yelling. At one point, he impeded the flow of traffic at the corner of Walnut and Sixth. A breathalyzer indicated a blood-alcohol content of .12.

Reporting officer	Badge No.	Signature	Date
U.B. Arrested	0001		

domestic disturbance, and stranded alongside the roadway." In English it would say, "On June 9, 2006, at 2:42 a.m., Podunk deputies Joe Dowd and Bob Burke went to Chesterfield Road and Burbank Avenue to check on a man who got into an argument/fight with someone he knows. The man was left at the intersection."

After receiving the police report, and verifying the subject of the report, attempt to get comments from the individual. If Joe Schmo doesn't want to talk, that's his choice, but be certain of two things: 1) That Joe had a fair chance to comment. Providing fair comment allows for balance in a story; 2) In the story, tell the readers that Joe refused to comment. And be specific. If Joe hangs up and does not answer questions, say so. "When contacted by phone, Schmo hung up before commenting." If Joe says, "no comment," then write, "When contacted, Schmo said 'No comment.'" If Joe says, "I'm not going to talk about that," write that. Be specific and provide details as to what transpired.

Also, make a sincere effort to be fair. Do not let the phone ring three times, hang up and say, "Well, he's not home." Instead, leave a message and call every 30 minutes. If you are unable to reach the source but left a message, write, "A message at Schmo's house was not returned." Or, "Six messages left at Schmo's house..."

Media get a bad rap for not allowing for fair comment. Give the story's subject an opportunity to respond and explain how the reporting was conducted. If the subject says nothing, write the story that can be extracted from the police report and other sources (media relations personnel, coaches, teammates, witnesses at the scene of the incident, the reporting officer, etc.). Regardless of the sources, the sports crime story cannot be ignored. And when a newsie attempts to take it from sports, be adamant: "No, I've got it."

The Business Story

Sports have become such an enormous business that in 1998 the weekly trade magazine *Street & Smith's SportsBusiness Journal* began publication. According to its Web site, the *Journal*'s mission is to provide "the critical news and information sports industry leaders need to compete, negotiate, and succeed." It has reporters in 47 offices throughout the United States, publishes 49 times a year and has a circulation of about 17,000.

The *SportsBusiness Journal* publishers had a reason to believe their magazine would draw a crowd. In February 2006, the *Journal* reported that the sports business industry was one of the largest and fastest growing in the United States at $213 billion per year—twice the size of the US automotive industry. In 1989, the sports business industry was a $50 to $60 billion industry (Shaw, 1989; Rambo, 1989).

Even for sports, the bottom line is the bottom line. Sports teams are commodities and owners want a commodity that earns money. When popular players are traded, released or remain unsigned, it's a business move. As reporters, you need to understand the dynamics of the business and why the team you're covering makes certain moves.

Loyalty is for Disney movies involving dogs, and sons who love their mothers. Sports ownership has little to do with loyalty. The same can be said for players. They might say they want to remain with a team, but money does the real talking. Sure, players prattle on about respect and dedication to an organization, but when translated they are really saying, "Put up or shut up." Every player is a mercenary with a price, and every owner is a Goodwill shopper searching for a better deal.

Because most professional sports teams are privately owned (the exception being the Green Bay Packers), access to financial information is limited. In fact, some teams do not even announce the terms of some players' contracts. Sometimes that information can be obtained through the player's agent or the players' association, which serves as the union for the players.

Court documents are another avenue for retrieving business information about a privately owned team. Court documents are public records. If a sports owner or team has been named in a lawsuit, the records can be viewed.

Business trends in sports always provide for interesting reading. For instance, the average baseball salary for 2006 was almost $3 million. That's a dramatic change from when the Minnesota Twins made Kirby Puckett the first $3 million man in 1989. Trends in attendance, television contracts, and ticket prices demonstrate dramatic shifts in sports.

New stadiums are almost always partially funded by state revenues. Teams routinely hold cities and states hostage in an effort to extract publicly funded stadiums. But what is the trade-off? How does the business community benefit from the local professional team? How much local and state tax revenue does the team generate? Also, what's the financial impact for the team between the current stadium and new stadium? Luxury boxes are all the rage but how much money do they actually generate? And stadium naming rights is a cash cow for teams. Reliant Energy pays $10 million a year to have its name pasted to the Houston Texans stadium. The 30-year contract, which is due to expire in 2032, is valued at $300 million. That's a lot of cabbage.

Although your sports editor might not expect or even encourage sports business stories, they are a significant part of sports, even at the high school level. The salaries of high school coaches, and the differences between the coaches of boys and girls sports, can certainly make for an interesting story. The cost of stadium renovations or re-flooring the gymnasium is worthy of a story. What's the cost to have a football team compared to soccer? How much does it cost to host a playoff game? In fact, any project or expenditure that is paid through taxpayer money is sports business. And all public schools are supported by tax dollars.

Where there is money there are business stories. And because so few sports journalists write them, there are dozens of business sports stories to be had. Just follow the money.

Freedom of Information Act

On July 4, 1966, President Lyndon B. Johnson unceremoniously signed the Freedom of Information Act. The FOIA makes documents produced by government agencies public record. The most essential premise of the Act is to prevent the government from operating in secrecy.

Similar to your laptop or notebook, the FOIA is a tool. Although it is primarily utilized by newsies, there's a place for FOIA in sports journalism.

Public high schools, colleges, and universities receive tax revenue and are subject to open records laws. The FOIA permits anyone to request public records. Those records include coaches' salaries, construction costs, and possibly e-mails of athletic administrators. Because athletic directors use the campus e-mail system, depending on the state, correspondence of coaches and administrators could be subject to an open-records request. The firing of a coach usually does not just happen. E-mails to and from the athletic director might provide details as to what transpired.

Not all information is subject to open records laws. Personnel issues, such as the reasons why a coach was fired, do not fall under FOIA. Information about students, such as grades, personal information, and medical records, are not subject to FOIA. But names of those who violated NCAA rules might be. For instance, the Ball State University student newspaper, the *Daily News*, submitted a FOIA request to the athletic department for the names of athletes who violated the book purchasing policy. Student-athletes had bilked the university out of about $10,000. After some fuss, the athletic department provided the names of the 43 athletes who violated the book purchasing policy. The next day's paper featured an impressive display with a picture of every athlete and the length of his or her suspension. To ensure he received a response in an appropriate time, *Daily News* reporter Justin Hesser asked the communication's office to time stamp the request. Under the Indiana FOI statute, a public agency has 24 hours to respond to an electronic FOI request. The actual FOI letter sent to the university is shown overleaf.

Some public bodies, such as school districts, might not require a FOI request and may voluntarily provide the information. Generally, school districts publicize the average cost of educating each student. A good

Heather Shupp
Ball State University
Executive Director of University Communications
AC Building, Room 224
Muncie, IN 47306

Dear Heather Shupp,

Pursuant to the Indiana Access to Public Records Act (IC 5-14-3), I would like to obtain a copy of the following public records:

> The names of all 43 student-athletes that were identified violators of the book loan program. These athletes were identified in the spring, according to a university release.

I understand that if I seek a copy of this record, there may be a copying fee. Could you please inform me of that cost prior to making the copy. I can be reached at 765-730-1831.

According to the statute, you have 24 hours to respond to this request. If you choose to deny the request, then you are required to respond in writing and state the statutory exception authorizing the withholding of all or part of the public record and the name and title or position of the person responsible for the denial.

Thank you for your assistance on this matter.

Respectfully,

Justin Hesser

Figure 17.1 FOI Request Document.

sports journalist will request the district's sports budget. Some simple math could determine if athletic spending per student is higher or lower than academic spending.

The Sunshine Law works in conjunction with FOIA. It allows average citizens to attend meetings held by public officials. On occasion, a sports journalist might want to attend a school board meeting, particularly when the budget is being discussed. How do you know when that happens? Well, read your newspaper or talk with the education reporter. In fact, working in conjunction with the education reporter or any news reporter will benefit you and the newspaper. It never hurts to ask questions.

For more information about FOI requests, contact the Freedom of Information Center at: http://foi.missouri.edu/.

Enterprise Stories

For 25 years, sports editors have been harping about "enterprise stories." "We need more enterprise stories in our section," he or she might say. "That's what the readers want." All too often, the sports editor fails to define what constitutes an enterprise story. So it becomes this mythical entity that is discussed during yearly employee evaluations but then never materializes.

Besides lacking definition, enterprise stories are not prevalent in the sports section because there's so little time dedicated to writing them. Enterprise stories are a combination of news, features, analysis, and perhaps commentary. They generally take time to develop. If a sports writer is working a beat, enterprise is not a priority. The day-to-day grind of covering the team takes precedence. And usually, sports writers are not allotted time to write enterprise stories.

An enterprise story is a unique perspective to an existing story. It provides a deeper meaning to an issue and examines the broader consequences. Enterprise stories are the unusual stories that seldom get told. (Cliché alert, cliché alert.) They are stories that are "off the beaten path" and force you to "think outside the box" without "following the herd." With traditional newspapers facing circulation declines, enterprise stories could be the lifeblood that still attracts readers. Television and the Internet have cornered the market on timeliness. Additionally, the Internet allows for interaction with readers. What can the newspaper offer that radio, TV, and the Internet do not?

Enterprise encapsulates the best reporting and writing a journalist can muster. It's journalism for the thinking person. Ask yourself, "How do social issues relate to sports?" Even at the high school level there are issues that can be addressed. For instance, what has become of the three-sport athlete? What has specialization done to high school athletics?

How do stars deal with "groupies?" What is a college recruiting trip really like? How are athletes pumping up—are they still using Creatine and Andro or have they moved on? What happens at high school football film sessions? How mandatory are voluntary practices? And the list goes on.

Another aspect of the enterprise story is taking a national issue and localizing it. Tons of research on young athletes is conducted each year. Discussing the issue with local coaches, athletes, parents, and athletic administrations can put a human face to the issue. For instance, what is the wrestling coach's policy on cutting weight? Weight cutting can have serious health implications. How does a coach keep his wrestlers safe? Or, at the college level, athletes are routinely suspended for "violating team rules." Well, what are the team rules and the designated punishments? Does the coach have a punishment chart (underage drinking = four laps around the stadium; missing curfew = equipment duty)? And are the athletes issued the rules before the season begins? You don't have to wait for a suspension to occur before writing the story.

The premise of the enterprise story is to take readers to a place they have never been before. The stories not only provide insight but also address some serious cultural and social issues that can include race, gender, religion, and socio-economic factors.

Of course, not all enterprise requires huge amounts of time and investigative reporting. Creativity can turn general, mundane stories into compelling reads. If a new coach is hired, have former players describe his or her coaching style. If a team hires its first minority coach, examine what the groundbreaking move means in a larger context of the school and community.

In the business section of this chapter we discussed trends. Enterprise can also be trend stories. If over the course of five years a college coach has a high number of recruited athletes leave the team, it could be a trend story. Talking with those who have left might show a pattern of abuse or neglect. It's not unusual for coaches to run off players they no longer feel will help the team.

Enterprise stories can be the most rewarding and enjoyable to write. Creating time for them is the biggest obstacle. One approach is to work on the stories in your spare time (insert laughter here). Granted, there isn't much "spare time" in sports journalism, but you can chip away at a story by making a phone call or two before covering a night game or when a game gets rained out. It might take months to complete, but because enterprise usually isn't as timely as daily news, your deadline is flexible.

The traditional sports section consists mostly of game stories and box scores. But the traditional sports section is evolving. Providing sports news gives readers information they might not get on TV or the Internet.

Taking readers beyond the playing field has been a natural progression in sports journalism, one that has met some resistance. Some sports writers prefer not to delve into the headier side of sports, but sports have become an enormous business that is intertwined with the daily lives of millions of Americans. Being a journalist who covers news is one way to fulfill the needs of those readers. Sports journalism is no longer just for those who want to play in the toy department.

Professional Perspective
By Greg Mellen
Long Beach Press-Telegram

If sports game stories, previews, recaps and notebooks are the meat and vegetables of a sports section, sports enterprise is the spice. Unfortunately, the flavor of good enterprise in a sports section is about as rare as seasoning in a bowl of oatmeal. And it's the rare bowl of oatmeal that doesn't benefit from a little cinnamon and brown sugar.

A 2005 study by the Project for Excellence in Journalism and Princeton Survey Research Associates found that on average American newspapers devote only 10 percent of the coverage on the front

Figure 17.2 Greg Mellen.

pages of sports sections to enterprise. Planned events, by contrast, made up 88 percent of the coverage. The survey also found the front pages of A sections and metro sections were twice as likely to contain enterprise reporting.

Clearly, the cliché of sports writers as first in the buffet line and last with an original thought isn't entirely unwarranted. Also clearly, sports enterprise is the place where the forward-thinking reporter can set himself apart from the pack at the chow line.

It's not an easy task for sure. Beat reporters are typically inundated with the aforementioned previews, gamers, notebooks, wraps and follows that often accompany a sports event and are dutifully jammed into sports sections. But the reporter who can look beyond the box score can find a rich and fairly open landscape in which to work.

Describing what enterprise is exactly is an inexact effort. The dictionary describes enterprise as a project requiring boldness or energy. For the survey, enterprise simply meant something generated by the reporter and not an event or a personality in sports. The Associated Press Sports Editors, which sponsors a national contest, gave up having enterprise as a contest category and settled instead for replacing it with two categories: explanatory and project reporting.

Good enterprise, sometimes called expanding the story, is reporting that goes beyond the usual scope. It is reporting that looks for trends and issues. It expands the context of sports to the larger world. It breaks to the perpetuated idea that somehow sports exists in its own world rather than being a part of the larger world and society. Rather than a microcosm, sports is a part of a larger whole. It uses sports as a lens through which to view that larger whole.

Sports enterprise can come from anywhere and often has small beginnings. Go to a high school game, see a new Pepsi logo on a scoreboard and open the door to a myriad of stories about the relationships of businesses, advertising, and sports. Hear a conversation between high school parents in the stands and think about the roles of booster clubs. Want to expand it? Compare a school's football booster program in members and money generated to other sports. Then compare it to the physics club.

Student sports writers I taught at the University of Missouri School of Journalism won a number of awards for enterprise writing in the APSE and other competitions.

One day we received a basketball schedule from a school for at-risk youth that was playing the sport for the first time. This evolved into a series that profiled the team, naturally, but also looked at the sociological and psychological importance of sports programs for these kids and others like them. As a side benefit, we learned the school was located on the premises of an old formerly segregated black high school. The irony of it now being used to segregate at-risk kids from the rest of the student body notwithstanding, this opened the door for yet another series of retrospective historical series about the old sports programs at the school and a segregated world that's often forgotten. We were amazed to find many former athletes who still lived in the area whose exploits were utterly overlooked by the white press back in the day.

Another example was the announcement of a new boys' golf coach at a local high school who was black. That begged the question, how many black golf coaches are there in the state? At about the same time we learned of a woman coaching a boys' sports team. Those two small things eventually led to an award-winning equity series that looked into race and gender in coaching in Missouri.

As sports is not always self-contained, neither is enterprise. Often the best features, gamers, etc., are the best because of the enterprise used in the reporting.

At Missouri, we won our first first-place award in the APSE national contest for a story that was entered as a feature. However, it was much more. A defensive back on the football team was arrested for stalking a former girlfriend, an event initially played off by the coach as a "boy-girl" thing. Because domestic abuse is rarely a one-time occurrence, we dug deeper. Not surprisingly, we found this particular player had a history of such incidents dating back to high school. While that was in itself strong stuff, we also wrote companion pieces about domestic abuse and athletes, the culture, psychology and sociology that lead to it. We talked to victims of abuse and counselors and presented a package that took the story and issue to another level. We found something else from that series. We found readers from a number of demographic groups (in this case women mostly) who said they never read sports, but they read that series.

As a side note, the reporter was contacted years later by a woman who had started dating the ex-player. She said he was starting to act odd and she was concerned. She had heard the writer had written about the player. He sent her a copy of the story. The woman's enterprise met the writer's enterprise and possibly spared her harm.

In a time of declining readership and, some would say, relevance for sports sections, enterprise becomes even more important. It makes a sports section relevant and it's something that is best done in print.

Enterprise is all about looking around the world beyond the yard-markers of the field. It's about thinking and wondering. It's not only about looking outside the box, but examining those things in the box that you might not have thought about before.

(Greg Mellen is a news reporter for the
Long Beach Press-Telegram.
He is a former sports editor and writer.)

18

FINAL POINTS I
Stylistic Errors to Avoid

Noun Agreement

Some of the most common writing mistakes involve the relationship between nouns and either verbs or pronouns.

It sounds very elementary to say that singular nouns need to have singular verbs. But this is not always the case in non-American writing. Those zany Canadians, for example, will often say things like "Montreal are skating well." This is not acceptable in American English writing. Montreal is a city, and thus is a singular noun. We would say "Montreal is skating well." Of course, it would be better to say "The Canadiens are skating well," since the players (the Canadiens) are doing the skating and not the city (Montreal).

Generally, collective nouns, such as cities, would take a singular verb, while team nicknames, at least those that are plural, would take a plural verb. Confusion enters when some nicknames, the Red Sox for instance, look like they are singular but for some reason are treated as plural. Thus, "The Red Sox are playing well" is proper and "The Red Sox is playing well" is not.

A similar error involves agreement between nouns and adjectives. "Green Bay won their third straight division title" is incorrect. "Green Bay won its third straight division title" and "The Packers won their third straight division title" are correct. Care also should be paid when talking about collective nouns such as teams, leagues, etc. A committee may decide it would review a case, or committee members may decide they would review a case.

Possessives

Confusion also enters into the mix when nicknames are used as possessives. Years ago, almost every newspaper in the country simply added an apostrophe to a plural nickname to form a possessive (The Cardinals' victory). Increasingly, some newspapers are now dropping the apostrophe with nicknames (the Cardinals victory) especially in head-lines. Newspapers also often would drop the "s" on nicknames to form a possessive (the Cardinal victory). Dropping the "s" did cause some problems, however. Some editors required writers and editors to do strange things like changing the "x" in Red Sox and White Sox to form the awkward construction of "the Red Sock victory." Thankfully, there is no law that forces awkward wording to take the place of smooth writing—how about "the Boston victory"?

Regardless, writers and editors should always check with colleagues in the newsroom about what the newspapers' policies are for tricky grammar and style guidelines. Some sports editors have pet peeves, such as the Red Sock example above.

The "Wicked" Which, That, and Who

Another common mistake—though the rules on this are much clearer—involves the uses of which, that, and who. "Which" introduces non-restrictive clauses—those clauses that are not necessary for the sentence to make sense—and is always preceded by a comma. "That" introduces restrictive clauses—those clauses that are needed in the sentence—and is not preceded by a comma.

For example: "The Boston victory, which snapped a three-game losing streak, left the Red Sox two games behind New York." Here, the clause "snapped a three-game losing streak" is not necessary in the sentence. The clause could be eliminated and the sentence would make complete sense. The victory left the Red Sox two games behind New York and, by the way, it snapped a three-game losing streak.

On the other hand: "The Boston victory that clinched the champi-onship came last Tuesday night." Here, "clinched the championship" is a necessary description of "victory." Likely, Boston had several victo-ries in its season (especially if it won a championship), but the one that clinched the championship came last Tuesday night. Therefore, the clause is needed for the sentence to make sense.

When the clause is modifying a human noun, however, the clause should be introduced with "who" or "whom." You would not write: "The player that is leading the league in home runs is Albert Pujols." The correct version would be: "The player who is leading the league in home runs is Albert Pujols." Likewise, "The Red Sox, who won for the first time in five games, lead the Yankees by two games" is correct.

And of course, "who" and "whom" can create confusion as well. Generally, if the clause can be rewritten with the nouns "he, she or they," you would introduce the clause with "who." If the clause can be rewritten with nouns "him, her or them," you would introduce the clause with "whom." For example: "Pujols, who struck out three times against Maddux Tuesday night, hit a three-run homer in the ninth inning." ("He" struck out three times.) But: "Pujols, whom Maddux struck out three times Tuesday night, hit a three-run homer in the ninth inning." (Maddux struck "him" out three times.)

Sentence Structure

Two common writing errors dealing with sentence structure involve run-on sentences and misplaced modifiers.

A run-on sentence occurs when a writer tries to merge two complete sentences into one complex sentence. Thus, a sentence such as: "The Colts played poorly last night, Peyton Manning did too" is incorrect. Both the first half and the second half are complete sentences, spliced together with a comma. Obviously, the comma after "night" should be a period.

Sometimes, reporters use comma splices in quotes. In the example above, if the run-on sentence was a quote from an opposing coach, the quote is still a run-on sentence and should be punctuated as two sentences. Sources don't put punctuation into their quotes. Thus, reporters should punctuate the sentences in quotes accordingly.

Misplaced modifiers are more difficult to spot because they often sound correct. The sentence "Because they have the largest payroll in baseball, one would think the Yankees would win championships every year" seems correct. However, the opening clause (Because they have the largest payroll in baseball) refers to the subject of the sentence (one). "One" doesn't have the largest payroll in baseball. Either the opening clause or the subject needs to be revised: "Because the Yankees have the largest payroll in baseball, one would think the Yankees would win championships every year" or "Because they have the largest payroll in baseball, the Yankees should win championships every year."

Simple (Dumb) Errors

Two especially dumb mistakes writers sometimes make especially irk editors. The first is the problem with its and it's. "Its" is the possessive form of "it." For example, a story (an it) can possess something: A story has its problems. "It's" is a contraction of "it is." It's very frustrating to read a story when its contents are full of errors.

Second, writers should be careful they don't miss adding apostrophes on possessives. Too often, people turn possessives into plurals—an embarrassing mistake. "The teams quarterbacks" should be "The team's quarterbacks" if you're writing about one team or "The teams' quarterbacks" if you're writing about two or more teams.

Wordiness

The sports field is full of wordy terms and phrases. Many terms, such as "defensive secondary" (is there an "offensive secondary"), include unnecessary words. Some clutter is obvious: "The referee called time out on the field (would there be a time out in the press box?)." Other clutter is less obvious, for instance, "a player scoring with a minute left in the first half" ("a minute left in the half" is fine; if the player scored with a minute left in the second half, we'd say, "with a minute left in the game").

A player might have "fumbled the ball in the end zone" but what else would a player fumble (how about "fumbled in the end zone"). A team could be "favored to win" but are teams ever favored "to lose"? A team could "set a new record," but do teams ever set old records?

The Appendix to Chapter 18 lists some common wordy phrases. Many come from a paper written by Kenn Finkel, former sports editor of the *Dallas Times Herald*. Others have been gathered through the years.

Clichés

Reference has been made here several times about avoiding the use of clichés. Inexperienced writers fall victim to clichés, perhaps because it is unclear what is and isn't a cliché. Clichés don't become clichés until the terms are worn out from overuse. The first time someone wrote that a player "hit paydirt" by scoring a touchdown, this wasn't a cliché. Now, however, all writers know better than to use the term "paydirt."

Whether a term is a cliché is not always clear. For example, if a basketball player scores on a three-point basket, can you safely write the player scored on a "trey"? Can you write that the player "scored from three-point land"? Did the player "hit the three-spot"?

The best rule of thumb is to find out what is acceptable and what isn't acceptable in your newsroom. What isn't acceptable might surprise you. One newspaper didn't like the term "tip" to describe a close game (Bucks tip Hornets) but did like "nip" (Bucks nip Hornets).

A second rule of thumb: if it looks like a cliché and sounds like a cliché, it probably is a cliché. The Appendix to Chapter 18 contains a list of clichés compiled through the years.

Other Pet Peeves of Editors

Besides clutter and clichés, Kenn Finkel had a problem with something he called a T*A*N synonymania: "The*Adjective*Noun" sentence structure. Peyton Manning, for example, might be referred to as "The 6-foot-3 quarterback." The argument is that if the adjective is important, it should be included after the person's name. Otherwise, it is implied that there is also a 6-foot-2 quarterback, and a 6-foot-4 quarterback, and even perhaps a 3-foot-6 quarterback.

T*A*N synonymania also can be confusing when it is unclear to whom the term is referring, for example, "Manning tossed a third-quarter touchdown pass to Marvin Harrison. The 6-foot-3 quarterback..." The T*A*N construction here refers to the previous noun—Harrison.

Overall, Finkel argued that the T*A*N synonymania technique is lazy and unimaginative.

Another editor hated when reporters used "feel," "hope," or "thought" without using "said." His argument was "Manning thought the Colts played well" is not accurate, because we don't know for certain what Manning thought. Emotions and attitudes are impossible to see first-hand. But we do know whether or not "Manning said he thought the Colts played well."

Still another editor refused to allow writers to include possessives of inanimate objects. Writers couldn't write "Fenway's press box" because a building can't own something. The correct term would be "the press box at Fenway."

These may seem like minor points, but if they drive your editor crazy, you ought to make sure you avoid them. It'll definitely improve your job security.

APPENDIX

COMMON WORDY PHRASES

absolute perfection
35 acres of land
acute crisis
advance planning
a distance of
all-time record
among the delegates expected to
    attend
an authority in his own right
a number of examples
any and all
appear on the scene
appear to be
appointed to the post
appreciated in value
as compared with
as never before in the past
as yet
a team of 12 workmen
at some time to come
attach together
awkward predicament
back home
best ever
blends in
blue colored car
bold and audacious
broad daylight
calm down
circular shape

close proximity
collaborate together
commented to the effect that
complete monopoly
complete overhaul
completely destroy
completely untrue
completely outplay
consensus of opinion
cooperate together
cost the sum of
dates back from/to
depreciated in value
descent down
died suddenly
divided off/up
doctorate degree
downright lie
drink up/down
driver by occupation
during the course of
early hours
eat up
eliminate altogether
enclosed herewith
endorse on the back
end product/result
entirely new departure
entirely spontaneous
equally as well

essential condition
ever since
face up to
favored to win
few in number
included among them
first ever
flatly rejected
follow after
for a period of
for the month of
for the purpose of
fresh beginning
frown on his face
full complement of
future draft choice
future prospect
gainfully employed
gather up/together
general public
good benefit
good speed
grateful thanks
have been engaged in producing
have got
heard various requests
he lost his eyesight
he was seen in the morning on his
    pre-breakfast walk
he went in an effort to determine
hoist up
hour of noon
in abeyance for the time being
if and when
intents and purposes
in the city of
in the course of the operation
in the process of building
in the interim period between
invited guests
involved in a car crash
it is interesting to note that
join together
join up

joint cooperation
just recently
last of all
link together
little sapling
lonely isolation
low ebb
made out of
major breakthrough
matinee performance
may possibly
meet together
men who are unemployed
merge together
more superior
mutual cooperation
necessary requisite
needless to say
never at any time
new creation
new innovation
new recruits
new record
new renovations
new tradition
not at all
generally available everywhere
offensive plays
old adage
old veterans
one of the last remaining
on the occasion when
on the question of
original source
over and done with
overtake a slower-movinq vehicle
pay off the debt
pare down
past history
patently obvious
peculiar freak
penetrate into
period of time
personal friend/friendship

polish up
poor state of disrepair
presence on the scene
pressing for imposition of a law
prominent and leading
protrude out
quite empty
quite perfect
radical transformation
really unique
recalled back
reduce down
revert back
results so far achieved
resigned his position as
root cause
saved from his earnings
seldom ever
settle up
short space of time
sink down
small in size
smile on his face
spent his whole life
still persists/continues
sunny by day
surgeon by occupation
surroundinq circumstances

temporary reprieve
to be named later
to consume drink
topped the 200 mark
total contravention
total extinction
totally destroyed
traded in exchange for
true facts
12 midnight
12 noon
uncommonly strange
unite together
universal panacea
utterly indestructible
usual customs
vandals willfully broke
violent explosion
vitally necessary
watchful eye
ways and means
widow of the late
win out
worst ever
seriously inclined
serious danger
nobody else but

SPORTS CLICHÉS

As long as there have been sports writers there have been sports clichés.
And as long as there have been sports writers writing clichés there have
been sports editors yelling at them to stop. With the assistance of
www.sportscliches.com, here is a list of sports clichés that should not
appear in your writing. Any variations of these phrases should be
avoided as well. For an extensive list of sports clichés (for print and
broadcast), go to www.sportscliches.com.

Player Analysis

He's an impact player.
He's a physical player.

He's an explosive player.
He's a tough, hard-nosed player.
He's a scrappy player.
He's an unselfish player.
He's a finesse player.
He's some kind of player. (*Mind telling us what kind?*)
He can take over a game.
He can flat out play.
He's a proven winner.
He has a passion for the game.
He's a serious student of the game.
He has a great feel for the game.
You can't say enough about him.
He's one of the best in the business.
He's the real deal.
He's legit.
He's in a league of his own.
He's silenced all the critics.
He's silenced all the naysayers.
He's their spark plug.
He's their role player.
He understands his role on this team.
He's the consumate team player.
He's a good guy to have in your locker room.
He's a steady player.
He's a complete player.
He's a real throwback.
They count on him week in and week out.
He's the heart and soul of this team.
He's the unsung hero on this team.
He's a leader on and off the field.
He's their workhorse.
He's their floor general.
He's their field general.
The team looks to him for leadership.
He's their playmaker.
He's as good a player as there is in this league.
He's a warrior.
He can carry the team on his shoulders.
He's their go-to guy when the game's on the line.
He always comes through in the clutch.
He thrives under pressure.
He's got ice-water in his veins.

He has a tireless work ethic.
He plays with a lot of emotion.
He plays with reckless abandon.
He's all heart.
He has great instincts.
He has a killer instinct.
He has elevated his game.
He can take you to school.
He's really been in the zone.
He's really been in the groove.
He's been feeling it.
He's finally playing his natural position.
He's on top of his game.
He knows what it takes to win.
He's really coming into his own.
He's finally getting his due.
This has been his breakout season.
He's having a career year.
He lets the game come to him.
He makes it look easy.
You can't stop him; you can only hope to contain him.
Just watching him is worth the price of admission.
He has a nose for the ball.
He'll have his game-face on.
His ability to do that is just uncanny.
He's got game.
He has great vision.
He has eyes on the back of his head.
He has great lateral mobility.
He moves well for a big man.
He has a great pair of hands.
He has lightning-fast reflexes.
He has cat-quick reflexes.
He has the heart of a champion.
He makes the players around him better.
He's the glue that holds this team together.
He can break the game wide open.
He can make things happen out there.
He gets stronger as the game goes on.
He makes his presence known out there.
He plays bigger than his size.
He's an integral part of their offense.
He adds a new dimension to their offense.
He has a linebacker mentality.

He's the stalwart of their defense.
He has a rifle for an arm.
He's built low to the ground.
He has a low center of gravity.
He's a speed merchant.
He has speed to burn.
He has blazing speed.
He has blinding speed.
He can turn on the jets.
He can turn on the after-burners.
He has both speed and quickness.
He's a cutter and a slasher. (*Fallen out of favor in the wake of the OJ Simpson trial.*)
He's poetry in motion.
He's the best player you've never heard of.
He's the league's most underrated player.
He does things that don't show up in the stat column.
Last week was his coming-out party.
He's a rookie sensation.
He's a highly touted freshman.
He's a talented young freshman. (*Aren't all freshmen young?*)
He's a freshman phenom. (*Note that all "phenoms" are young; there are no senior or veteran phenoms.*)

Pre-Game, Post-Game, Half-time Analysis

A tie is like kissing your sister.
You win as a team, you lose as a team.
It's been a tale of two halves.
Turnovers will be the key.
The intangibles will be the key.
Statistics can be misleading.
Statistics tell the whole story.
That's the key statistic.
That's the key to the game.
You take what the defense gives you.
This is always a tough place to play.
We don't play these games on paper.
Both teams are playing at a high level.
We've got an intriguing matchup. (*Used most often to describe first-round games in the NCAA basketball tournament.*)
We've got the league's best offense against the league's best defense—something's got to give.
These two teams don't like each other.

There's been a lot of trash talking.
There's no love lost between these two teams.
There's bad blood between these two teams.
When these two teams get together you can throw out their records.
It's gonna be a war out there.
It's going to be a battle of the titans.
It's going to be a battle of epic proportions.
This is a game for the ages.
This is a pivotal game for them.
This is their watershed game.
They're coming off a heartbreaking loss.
A win today snaps their four-game losing streak.
This game is for the bragging rights.
They're the sentimental favorites.
They match up well.
He gets the most out of his players.
There are no easy games in this league.
The season is a marathon, not a sprint.
Bad calls even out over the course of a season.
On any given day any team is capable of beating another team.
Good teams get better down the stretch.
They really have to take it to them.
They have to play with their ears pinned back.
They need to turn up the intensity.
They have to step up and make plays.
They have to come out of the locker room fired up.
They're loaded for bear.
They have to go out and take care of business.
They can't let the crowd faze them.
They have to get after it.
They have to rise to the occasion.
They have to leave everything on the field.
They have to stay hungry.
They have to keep the continuity.
They can't look past these guys.
They can't take these guys lightly.
They have to avoid a big letdown.
They have to come together as a team.
They have to believe in themselves.
They have to play within themselves.
They have to play like they're capable of playing.
They have to step up their offensive production.
They have to get the big guy involved in the offense.

They'll have to find a way to contain John Elway.
They'll have to find a way to limit what Elway can do.
They can't expect to shut Elway down completely.
They can't be intimidated.
They must control the tempo of the game.
They have to dictate the tempo.
They have to stick to their bread-and-butter offense.
They should stick to the fundamentals.
They have to eliminate the mental mistakes.
They have to dig deep.
They have to suck it up.
They have to crank it up.
They have to turn it up a notch.
They need to step up to the next level.
They must capitalize on their opportunities.
They have to take advantage of their opportunities.
They have to bend but not break.
They have to stretch their defense.
They have to shore up their defense.
They have to pull out all the stops.
They have to be more aggressive.
They should just go out there and have fun.
They're playing for pride.
They're playing the role of spoilers.
The final score was not a true indication.
The game was a lot closer than the final score indicates.
It's easy to be a Monday morning quarterback.

For a Team on the Rise

He's a good Xs and Os coach.
He runs a squeaky-clean program. (*Said when any college team has not been under NCAA investigation within the last 5 years.*)
They're a blue collar team.
They've gone to a youth movement.
They've got tremendous mental toughness.
They're a dark horse team.
This team is showing flashes of brilliance.
They're finally hitting their stride.
This team is really starting to gel.
This team is starting to make some noise.
This could be a sleeper team.
They're a team to be reckoned with.

Everybody's on the same page.
The players have bought into the system.
This team is not going to sneak up on anybody.
This team has turned the corner.
This team has raised the bar.
They've gotten over the hump.
This team has finally gotten off the schneid.
They're loaded this year.
They have a strong supporting cast.
They've added a new wrinkle to their offense.
This team travels well.
Those players form their nucleus.
He's really whipped them into shape.
He's got them headed in the right direction.
This team takes on the personality of their coach.
He must challenge his players.
These guys have been working their tails off.
These guys have been busting their butts.
They're finally getting the respect they deserve.
They've been playing with confidence.
They've got great team chemistry.
This team is like a family.
They've got die-hard fans.
The city has rallied around this team.
You have to respect their quickness.
You have to respect their athleticism.
They do a great job defensively.
They're a multi-faceted team.
They're an offensive-minded team.
They have a high-octane offense.
They have a potent offense.
They've got a lot of depth.
They pride themselves on their defense.
They have a stingy defense.
They have a swarming defense.
They play tough "D".
They play tenacious defense.
They play punishing defense.
They play tremendous pressure defense.
They play in-your-face defense.
They've been on a roll.
They're over-achievers.
They can go the distance.

They won't be denied.
They strike fear in the hearts of their opponents.
They've come out of nowhere.
They've returned from oblivion.
What an incredible turnaround.
They're a real Cinderella story.
They're having a storybook season.
They're having a dream season.
They're a better team than their record indicates.
They're no pushovers.
They give you so many different looks.
They have a lot of weapons.
They've got a tremendous ballclub.
This franchise has a storied past.
They're the winningest team in league history. (*Winningest?*)
They can put up big numbers.
They're a team of destiny.
They're on a mission.

For a Team in Decline

It's a rebuilding year.
They've been struggling offensively. (*Teams never struggle defensively.*)
Their offense has been sputtering.
They're a bit banged up.
They've got some players who are dinged up.
They've got a few guys who are nicked up.
They're nursing some nagging injuries.
They've had a few players go down with injuries.
They've been riddled with injuries.
They need to get healthy.
A week off will do them some good.
They've got to ignore the off-field distractions.
They need a win to stop their five-game skid.
They're still missing a few pieces to the puzzle.
Their defense has been much maligned.
They're the league doormats.
They're the league cellar dwellers.
This team is searching to find its identity.
The coach has been under fire.
The coach is on the hot seat.
The coach's head is on the chopping block.

Fired Coaches

The press conference held to announce the firing of a coach is a cliché
bonanza. While there is always an atmosphere of high drama, these events
are completely scripted. The athletic director, general manager, or owner
starts and the remarks invariably contain one or more of the following:

Unfortunately there are days like this.
We're in the business of winning.
It's the nature of this business.
It's time to move on.
We have to look forward.
We need a change of direction.
We need a clean slate.
We need someone who can take us to the next level.
Pete is a class act.

Then it's the axed coach's turn. You are certain to hear something like:

Everyone has to be held accountable.
It's all about winning and losing.
I take the blame.
I'm the last one to make excuses.
Obviously I'm disappointed things didn't work out.
I'm looking forward to my future endeavors.
I'm going to spend more time with my family.

A short time later, the new coach is announced. There will be another
   press conference where the new coach faces the media for the first time:

I'm excited about this opportunity.
I'm looking forward to the challenge.
I have high expectations for this team.
This franchise has a great winning tradition.
We've got a good, solid foundation to build on.
We're going to right the ship.
We're going to get things turned around.
These fans deserve a winner.
This is a great sports town.

The Playoffs

The wildcard race is heating up.
They're still in the hunt for that final playoff berth.

They're still very much alive.
They're still in the mix.
They're peaking at the right time.
They're capable of making a deep run in the postseason.
They're on the bubble.
They've got some good, quality wins. (*Used when a college basketball team is on the bubble for the NCAA tournament.*)
They're on the outside looking in.
They have to run the table.
They have to win out.
Their magic number is five.
They managed to back into the playoffs.
They've played a soft schedule.
They have to remember what got them here.
They've been here before.
They have a lot of big game experience.
They control their own destiny.
Anything less than a championship is unacceptable.
They're going for back-to-back championships.
They're going for a three-peat.
This team has a chance to do something special.
They're not just happy to be here.
In the playoffs anything can happen.
Hopefully they can steal one on the road.
They need to get a win in their building.
They're in the driver's seat.
They have to do the things they've been doing all season.
A win tonight will force a decisive game seven.
It doesn't matter who they play in the next round.
They've battled back from the brink of elimination.
It's do or die.
They're behind the eight ball.
They're in a must-win situation.
They need a win to stave off elimination. (*Stave off? Staving? Has any normal human being ever "staved" anything? The only time you hear about 'staving' is in this classic sports cliché.*)
This is for all the marbles.
There's no tomorrow.
If you lose, you go home.
They're down but not out.
They've got their backs against the wall.
They've been mathematically eliminated. (*Teams are never eliminated. They are always "mathematically eliminated," which makes the sportscaster sound like a number genius.*)

The Winners' Locker Room

I'm really proud of the way our guys hung in there.
We were really on our game.
We came to play.
We brought our A-game.
We took them out of their game.
We knew what we had to do and went out and did it.
We proved we're the better team.
We're tickled to death.
We're glad to get out of here with the "W."
They gave us a big scare. (*Said when a team narrowly escapes a major upset.*)
It's tough to win in a hostile environment.
We're happy we could pull this one out at the end.
We feel fortunate.
We knew this would be no cakewalk.
It wasn't pretty but we'll take it.
We managed to eke out a win.
The important thing is that we won.
A win is a win.
This was a good win for us.
This was a confidence booster.
We're going to use this win as a building block.
We'll use this win as a stepping stone to the next level.
We're not going to rest on our laurels.
This win was no fluke.
We finally got the monkey off our backs.
Everyone counted us out before the season started.
It was a hard-fought contest.
It was a total team effort.
I'm happy I could make a contribution.
I was just doing my job.
It was a workman-like effort.
We made our own breaks.
We played our hearts out.
We really took it to 'em.
We snatched victory out of the jaws of defeat.
This team has finally learned how to win.
We weren't going to just lie down.
We weren't going to just roll over.
We knew we had to defend our home turf.
This team always seems to find a way to win.
This team has overcome a lot of adversity.

This team shows a lot of character.
This team shows a lot of poise.
This team shows a lot of pride.
This team shows a lot of resiliency.
This team shows a lot of heart.
We're going to savor this victory.
This team has served notice.
We made a statement here today.
We sent a message here today.
This win is for all the fans.
Our fans were the 12th man today.
We feed off the energy of our fans.
We've got the greatest fans in the world.
I want to thank my Lord and Savior.
It hasn't sunk in yet.
I'm in a state of shock.
I'm speechless.
We shocked the world.
You dream about this as a kid.
It feels great to be world champions. (*It is very common for players to anoint themselves "world champions" even if they compete in a league with only North American or American teams.*)
This is a dream come true.
This is the greatest feeling in the world.
After blowing-out the other team
They're tough competitors.
They're a class act.
Give them a lot of credit.
We beat a very good team today.

The Losers' Locker Room

The final score is the only statistic that matters.
They outplayed us in every phase (facet) of the game.
They wanted it more than we did.
We had our chances but we let them slip away.
We came up a little short.
We don't care about moral victories.
They caught us on an off night.
Turnovers killed us.
They out-hustled us.
They out-muscled us.
They out-coached us.
We got a wake-up call.

We weren't mentally prepared.
We came out flat.
We beat ourselves.
We only have to look in the mirror.
They ate our lunch.
They've had our number all season.
They own us.
This is a bitter pill to swallow.
It's going to be a long plane ride home.
I take full responsibility for this loss.
We didn't get the job done.
Not to take away anything from Denver, but we didn't play like we're
    capable of playing.
My hat's off to them.
I tip my hat to them.
You've got to hand it to them.
Give them all the credit.
The best team won today.
He always has his team ready to play.
We can still hold our heads high.
These guys have nothing to be ashamed of.
They just made the big plays and we didn't.
They stepped up and made the plays.
We didn't match their intensity.
We didn't maintain the intensity for the entire 60 minutes.
We lost our focus.
I don't want to point fingers.
There were too many defensive lapses.
Our defense was a non-factor.
Our defense didn't show up today.
We dug ourselves a deep hole.
We shot ourselves in the foot.
The ball just didn't bounce our way.
We didn't get the big breaks today.
We'll just have to put this loss behind us.
I'm really proud of our guys.
It's been a great ride.

19

FINAL POINTS II

Sports Journalism Ethics

What James Madison was to the authorship of the US Constitution, Hal Bodley was to the first ethical guidelines established by the Associated Press Sports Editors.

Just five years after APSE's formation, its leaders accepted the arduous and contentious task of formulating a standard for ethical behavior. Ethics in sports journalism were unfamiliar territory in 1979. For decades, teams and athletes presented sports writers and editors with gifts and favors. Writers hitched rides on the team's chartered plane, and before that, the passenger cars of trains. They fraternized with the players and even received meal money from the team during roadtrips. And that was only the beginning.

"At Christmastime, many of the larger sports enterprises in the area would give very, very big gifts to their sports editors—television sets, cases of liquor, clothing, and that type of thing," said Bodley, a former baseball editor and columnist for *USA Today*. "I remember back in the early '60s when I started working, I used to get a clothing gift certificate from the Philadelphia Phillies every year. At that time it was like $50 but to me it was a lot of money. Delaware Park, which was a thorough-bred race track, would give me a case of booze of whiskey liquor. I just thought it was wrong."

And while the team was taking care of the writers and editors, the writers and editors were taking care of the team. "We took care of certain people," Bodley said. "The race tracks, University of Delaware football."

According to the APSE, the organization's founding fathers, which included Dave Smith (*Boston Globe*), Joe McGuff (*Kansas City Star and Times*), Wayne Fuson (*Indianapolis News*), Earl Cox (*Louisville Courier-Journal*), Ed Storin (*Miami Herald*) and Bodley (*Wilmington News Journal*), realized some ethical standards were necessary. At the 1980 convention, the first APSE ethical guidelines were unveiled. It's reception was a real, "You can have my 24-inch Magnavox when you pry it from my cold dead hands," kind of moment.

"You wouldn't believe when we started introducing these guidelines the response we got," said Bodley, who was the primary author of the guidelines. "A lot of the papers were really opposed to it. A lot of papers didn't have large enough sports budgets. Some of the major colleges are in small towns and the paper didn't have the budget to travel on long trips to cover football or basketball or whatever the sport might be. The university certainly wanted the coverage, so they (the writers) climbed aboard the charter."

Some sports editors argued and debated with the APSE leadership, while others stormed out of the meeting. "When we presented them, it was a hated day," Bodley said. In the end, the ethics guidelines were adopted while keeping the APSE membership intact. The guidelines were revised in 1991 and remain the cornerstone for sports journalism ethics.

"I worked awfully hard on that and I was very proud of it," Bodley said.

APSE Ethics Guidelines

1   The newspaper pays its staffer's way for travel, accommodations, food, and drink.

   a   If a staffer travels on a chartered team plane, the newspaper should insist on being billed. If the team cannot issue a bill, the amount can be calculated by estimating the cost of a similar flight on a commercial airline.

   b   When services are provided to a newspaper by a pro or college team, those teams should be reimbursed by the newspaper. This includes providing telephone, typewriter or fax service.

2   Editors and reporters should avoid taking part in outside activities or employment that might create conflict of interest or even appearance of a conflict.

   a   They should not serve as an official scorer at baseball games.

   b   They should not write for team or league media guides or other team or league publications. This has the potential of compromising a reporter's disinterested observations.

   c   Staffers who appear on radio or television should understand that their first loyalty is to the paper.

3   Writers and writers' groups should adhere to APME and APSE standards: no deals, discounts or gifts except those of insignificant value or those available to the public.

   a   If a gift is impossible or impractical to return, donate the gift to charity.

b   Do not accept free memberships or reduced fees for memberships. Do not accept gratis use of facilities, such as golf courses or tennis courts, unless it is used as part of doing a story for the newspaper.

c   Sports editors should be aware of standards of conduct of groups and professional associations to which their writers belong and the ethical standards to which those groups adhere, including areas such as corporate sponsorship from news sources it covers.

4   A newspaper should not accept free tickets, although press credentials needed for coverage and coordination are acceptable.

5   A newspaper should carefully consider the implications of voting for all awards and all-star teams and decide if such voting creates a conflict of interest.

6   A newspaper's own ethical guidelines should be followed, and editors and reporters should be aware of standards acceptable for use of unnamed sources and verification of information obtained other than from primary news sources.

a   Sharing and pooling of notes and quotes should be discouraged. If a reporter uses quotes gained secondhand, that should be made known to the readers. A quote could be attributed to a newspaper or to another reporter.

7   Assignments should be made on merit, without regard for race or gender. Guidelines can't cover everything. Use common sense and good judgment in applying these guidelines in adopting local codes.

The APSE guidelines are just that—guidelines. Sports journalists find themselves in all sorts of precarious situations. The following are some examples of ethical dilemmas that can occur in sports journalism and some advice on how to handle them.

Payola

The assigned story was a retrospective of a college football team that played in a major bowl game 50 years earlier. During the month-long project, the young college reporter was diligent in scouring the country to locate and interview several former players. A week after the reporter had conducted an extensive interview with a former player in another state, the player sent the reporter a check for $25. The note read, "I enjoyed our conversation. I know college students are poor so I thought this might help."

A few days later, the reporter contacted the player again to ask a few follow-up questions. Soon after, a $35 check with a note arrived. "This will help pay for your long-distance phone calls," the note read. All the calls had been made from the office so the reporter did not accumulate a phone bill.

After the story was published, the reporter informed his sports editor of the unsolicited financial incentives he received.

Sports editor: What did you do with the $60?
Reporter: I spent it. I'm a poor college kid.
Sports editor: You spent it! You have to return that money.
Reporter: Why? He gave it to me. I didn't ask for it.
Sports editor: That may be true, but accepting money for stories isn't what we do. It's not ethical.
Reporter: I didn't know that. Why isn't it ethical?

The sports editor explained that receiving pay from sources for stories compromises the credibility of the newspaper and the reporter. If people could simply pay for stories, what's the purpose in trying to be unbiased journalists? Besides, there's already a place for that in the newspaper— it's called advertising.

The argument can be made that the historical retrospective of a college football team does not carry the importance of a political story or crime story. The old football player was not making any requests or demands of the reporter. He also didn't initiate the story or attempt to persuade the reporter to alter the facts. The source was simply being generous. But the player's motivations are irrelevant. Accepting the money creates a perception that the reporter was being paid by an independent source to write the story. If there's a perception that you are being paid, how can readers trust what is written? And if a reporter will take $60 to write a harmless history story, how much will it cost to ignore a player's domestic assault charge? What's the cost for writing a "warm-and-fuzzy" story about a player in a contract year?

Payola does not only come in terms of money. Discounted tickets, merchandise, and favors can also be considered payola. If you receive special treatment because of your status as a journalist, then the incentive is off limits.

Most sources understand the ground rules and won't create problems. But there are temptations, and the allure of payola can be great. Just remember that what you receive in terms of goods and services cannot replace what you lose in credibility. Receiving payment can also lead to unemployment. If in doubt about payola, ask yourself, "Would I want the entire world to know about this transaction?" If the answer is "no," then you should probably pass it up.

As for the young reporter, he returned the $60 to the old football player. He also wrote a note explaining journalism ethics and payola.

Freebies

If you want to rile a pack of sports writers, tell them all freebies are off limits. Nothing stirs their emotions quicker than the accusations created by freebies.

Receiving free items from sports teams is akin to payola. Ethically, payola and freebies emerge from the same tainted pool. But there are differences. While payola requires an exchange of favors (money for desired coverage), freebies only allude to that concept. A free T-shirt or press-box hot dog will not necessarily persuade you to write positively about the team. But, once again, there is a perception problem. How does it look to the readers if you are willing to accept "stuff" from a team? Are you expected to wear the T-shirt or baseball cap?

Professional baseball teams routinely have special promotions (bat day, ball day, seat-cushion day, etc.). Once, a sports writer returned to his newsroom with a half-a-dozen helmets from helmet day. He then distributed them to his colleagues in sports. What do you think he looked like walking out of the stadium after the game with an armful of helmets? What did it look like to those in the newsroom when the sports department sat at their desks that night wearing their helmets? Or what did it like look for readers and sources when they came to the newsroom?

Public relations personnel do not sincerely believe they can buy your loyalty with a sandwich or cooler cup. But, they also know that it can create some goodwill at a very low cost.

In terms of freebies, food is probably the most common. First, let's dispel the myth that press-box food is good. For the most part, it's awful. It has enough fat and calories to clog the purest of arteries. As for taste, it falls between high school cafeteria food and what you can scavenge by dumpster diving. So why eat it? A beat writer gets to the event hours before it starts and leaves hours after it ends. During that time, he or she is gathering information and writing a majority of the time. There are notebooks to write, sidebars, features, columns, enterprise, and the list goes on. Having food close at hand is for convenience and not media manipulation by the PR staff.

Many professional teams have an alternative meal (not just hot dogs, popcorn, and soda) that requires a small fee, usually about $5. The other option is the concession stand, but eating from the ballpark for 162 baseball games can be costly to your physical and financial health.

Free food is an acceptable part of sports journalism. And although newsies cringe, they have to realize that the options are limited.

Besides, what do political reporters eat when they are working the campaign? How many business lunches do business reporters attend? Now, that does not give license to pull up a chair at the press-box "buffet" and pig out. Gluttonous behavior is what gives sports journalists a bad reputation.

As for T-shirts and baseball caps, ask yourself, "Do I really need this and when would I wear it?" It hurts no one by not accepting the items. If items are sent to you, donate them to Goodwill or another charity. Also, sometimes newspapers have yearly sales of the freebies that have been collected. The money is then donated to a charity.

Just remember, it's your reputation on the line. Nothing in life is free. What does not cost financially could cost something far more irreplaceable—credibility.

Misrepresentation

The football player's résumé wasn't impressive, but the university wanted to retire his jersey number anyway. He had played a major role on his college team and went on to become a special teams player for a couple NFL seasons before retiring.

The reporter was among those who did not believe the player deserved to have his number retired. In writing a column, the reporter made the case that the player was unworthy of the honor by providing statistics of those who already had their numbers retired. The reporter also spoke with the player. The player, known for his tremendous work ethic and modest disposition, politely answered the reporter's questions.

"When you consider the others who have had their numbers retired, do you think you deserve to have your number retired," the reporter asked pointedly.

"Those guys are great athletes," the player said. "I can hardly carry their jockstraps."

So, the reporter dropped the quote into the story. The set-up paragraph before the quote read, "Not even he believes he deserves to have his number retired."

Early the next day, the player called the sports editor. "I was attempting to be humble. Of course, if they want to retire my number then I think I deserve it."

Because the reporter clearly could not overcome his biased opinion, the story was biased. Therefore, the quote was presented out of context. Journalists are expected to present an accurate picture of events. Portraying facts to suit your opinions is unethical. Although you might disagree with an opinion, it isn't your job to pass judgment. It's true that the reporter accurately quoted the player. The issue isn't the accuracy of the words but how the words were presented.

Misrepresentation can also occur during the fact-gathering process. Falsely telling an athletic director you have two confirmed sources naming the new baseball coach is misrepresenting the truth. They have a word for that kind of misrepresentation: it's called lying and it can be incredibly detrimental to your credibility. Some sports writers will say the ends justify the means. Maybe. But is the payoff worth burning a source?

The best approach is to be honest with the AD: "I understand John Smith will be your new baseball coach. When will you make the announcement?" He or she might respond, "Where did you hear that?" *Do not* reveal your sources. Instead, continue to ask the AD questions. "Hearing it" and "confirmed sources" are completely different. Some might say it's just semantics, and maybe so, but at least you are being honest. At the very least, the AD won't think you're altogether a lying scumbag.

There are other forms of deceit and misrepresentation that also need to be addressed. Some call it ambush journalism. One time a sports writer posed as someone he wasn't to get inside the apartment of a college basketball player accused of assault. "My car broke down. May I use your phone," the sports writer said. The player allowed him into the apartment, and after a short conversation the reporter revealed his true identity. In a similar case, a sports writer sent reading materials to an athlete serving a short jail sentence in an attempt to curry favor. The reporters in both instances used deceitful tactics to get close enough to the source in an effort to get an interview. Those maneuvers might work, but the honesty and sincerity of the reporters have to be questioned. Would you want the world to know how you conduct business? And if the world did know, how would future potential sources react? Would they still want to talk with you?

Another form of ambush journalism is when you tell a source you want to talk about one thing but then ask about something else. Telling a coach you want to talk with him about the upcoming game and then asking him about a player's shoplifting charge might not go over well. Sometimes interviews are conducted with dual purposes. So, gather the information needed to write the preview story and then say, "Coach, do you have a few minutes to discuss another issue regarding one of your players?" That allows the coach some latitude without feeling as if you have duped him. Ambush journalism might seem like a good idea at the time, but more often then not, it does not work well and the reporter damages the relationship with a source.

As for the misrepresented football player, he ended the conversation with the sports editor by saying, "I will never talk to your newspaper ever again." And to this day, he has kept that promise.

Professional Relationships

The sports writer had been working at the newspaper for a few years covering the high school beat. He enjoyed the beat and the camaraderie of the coaches. He occasionally would even meet some coaches at a local drinking establishment after Friday night games and shoot the bull.

During one basketball season, an assistant basketball coach had been arrested for driving while intoxicated. Realizing his name would appear in the newspaper's police blotter (see Chapter 17), he called the sports writer.

Coach: Hey, could you keep that out of the newspaper?

Reporter: No, that wouldn't be ethical. And actually I'm writing a brief about it for the sports section.

Coach: Come on, man, don't do that. You know me. We're buddies, right? And if you do that I'm going to get fired.

Reporter: I don't have a choice. It's public record. And besides it's news.

Coach: If that appears in the newspaper I'm going to kill myself.

At that, the reporter fell silent. Nothing in his journalism training prepared him to deal with a potential suicide. The reporter did not feel the coach would follow through with his threat but didn't want to take any chances. What exacerbated the situation was the casual relationship between reporter and coach. The reporter found it difficult to separate his professional obligations and personal feelings.

Contrary to public perception, journalists are people. They develop relationships with sources. When people work together they naturally become familiar with each other on a personal basis. It isn't always business. But there are boundaries reporters and sources must recognize and respect. As a journalist, you cannot expect a university sports information director to provide information about a coach's firing when the athletic director has instructed him or her to keep it confidential. And the SID cannot expect you not to write about the starting linebacker's bar fight.

As with any relationship, there must be trust. A source has to trust a journalist and vice versa. Once that trust is violated, the relationship is over. If an SID provides information and says, "Don't print anything until Friday," it might be in your best interest to agree. But first you'll want to know why you are being asked to hold the story. Second, negotiate. You don't want to get beat on the story. "What if I write it for Thursday? What difference will it make?" Just be certain that you and the SID can live with the arrangement. And if another outlet is going to break the story before Thursday, insist the SID contacts you immediately.

Now, there are sports editors who will demand that you write the story for Monday's paper. You have to be prepared to explain why you agreed to hold it until Thursday. Remember that news is new, so waiting a few days could impede that premise.

The long-term benefits of holding the story can be tremendous. If you gain the SID's trust, he or she might provide story tips that other reporters don't receive. Also, he or she can assist in confirming stories that are in doubt. "I know you can't tell me if John Smith is the new baseball coach, but if I write that would I be wrong?" The SID does not want wrong information in the newspaper. Good public relations personnel will assist you in those situations. If the SID responds, "Printing that probably would not be wise," you should hold the story. Of course, if the SID is lying, you must confront him or her. Like any relationship, there are good times and bad. Open discussion can assist in getting through the bad times, although rebuilding trust is incredibly difficult.

A relationship with people behind the scenes is always a good idea. Equipment managers, trainers, waterboys, etc. seem to have the scoop on everything. They can be tremendous background sources. You probably won't ever quote them but they take a measure of pride in providing newsworthy information. For instance, a professional team had recently signed a new player who hadn't played in about three years. The reporter asked the equipment manager, "Hey, what's with this guy? Has he been in prison or something?" "Yeah," the equipment manager said. "Three years in upstate for rape. But you didn't hear it from me."

As for the "suicidal" coach, the reporter called one of the other coaches and told him of the exchange. The reporter wanted to be certain someone looked in on the "suicidal" coach. The next day, the brief ran in the paper. The coach did not commit suicide and was not fired. But after that, the reporter was reluctant to meet the coaches for drinks after Friday night games.

Plagiarism

Plagiarism is the scourge of journalism. There's a special place in journalism Hades for those who violate this premise. Plagiarism is the act of passing off someone else's work as your own. In journalism, plagiarism includes, but is not exclusive to:

- Copying verbatim sentences and paragraphs from previously published material and presenting it as your original work.

- Copying and pasting sentences or paragraphs from Internet sites and presenting it as your original work.
- Using quotes that have been previously published without properly identifying the origin of the quotes.
- Copying verbatim sentences, paragraphs or quotes provided by a press release without attributing the source of the information.

There are several reasons for "word theft." For one, the Internet has made plagiarism increasingly easy. A couple of clicks of the mouse and suddenly you're Shakespeare—or at least a thief of Shakespeare's work. Second, time constraints might encourage a journalist to steal someone else's words. Third, someone else's words sometimes sound better. Did you ever notice that when food is prepared for you it tastes so much better? Why? Because you were able to relax while someone else did the work. The same can be said for journalism. Some would rather not work at it because stealing is so much easier.

Several sports writers in the past few years have lost their jobs or been suspended for plagiaristic activities. Ken Powers, a 20-year veteran journalist, was fired from the *Worcester (Mass.) Telegram & Gazette* after the newspaper determined he had plagiarized from several sources, including Peter King of *Sports Illustrated*. At the time, Powers had been the New England Patriots beat writer for five seasons. *Boston Globe* sports writer of 24 years Ron Borges was suspended without pay for two months after it was discovered he plagiarized a portion of a football column taken from another sportswriter in 2007. In 2004, *Winnipeg Free Press* sports columnist Scott Taylor resigned after being accused of plagiarizing parts of his column. The veteran reporter denied any wrongdoing. In 2003, sports writer Michael Kinney was fired from the *Sedalia Democrat* (Missouri) after an internal investigation found instances of plagiarism in some of his sports columns and parts of movie reviews he wrote for the newspaper. You can be certain that if you plagiarize, and get caught, you will be unemployed. And you will get caught.

There have been instances of "accidental" plagiarism. Much of that rises from plagiarism ignorance. Because you are reading this chapter, that ignorance is no longer a defense. But, sometimes it is tempting to "lift" something rather than rewrite it. Here are a few suggestions for rewriting sentences that have the same meaning.

The press release: "Tuesday, Backwoods University named Bubba Johnson to be its new director of intercollegiate athletics."

Your rewrite: "After a three-month national search, Backwoods University named Bubba Johnson its new athletics director Tuesday."

The solution: Include additional material that the press release fails to mention. Be creative in your writing. Press releases simply provide the most elemental information. Also, write in a common vernacular. Administrators say "director of intercollegiate athletics," while the rest of the world uses "athletics director."

The press release: "I am thrilled to be Backwoods University's new athletics director. It's my dream job," Johnson said.

Your re-write: "I am thrilled to be Backwoods University's new athletics director," Johnson said in a press release. "It's my dream job."

The solution: Attribute the information from whence it came. By not including "said in a press release," the writer gives the impression he or she spoke with Johnson. Do not deceive the readers. Or better yet, interview Johnson and garner your own quotes.

Attribution is necessary for any information plucked from another source unless the information is common knowledge. Writing, "George Steinbrenner is the New York Yankees' owner, the *New York Times* reported," would not be necessary. It is a common statement of fact that does not require attribution. But when quotes from other sources are used, such as television or radio interviews, other newspapers, press releases, or Internet sources, credit to the original source must be provided. On occasion, it's wise to include the setting from which the quote came. For instance, "It's my dream job," Bubba Johnson said at a press conference. That shows that the event was "staged" and not an impromptu or one-on-one interview.

Fabrication

Although it isn't a plagiarism issue per se, fabricating material in a story is an ethics issue. Writing fiction and passing it off as fact can also get you fired. You might be surprised to learn there is much more fiction writing happening out there than you can imagine. Once again, much of it is unintended fiction, but nonetheless, the authors must be responsible for their words. Here's one example:

"The dry leaves crunch beneath his shoes like Rice Krispies on a linoleum kitchen floor as he scampers along the winding path. Oak and maple trees line the trail, and the smell of rotting wood and wet soil consume his nostrils. He doesn't hear the tree frogs or migrating geese as he quickens his pace. In fact, he doesn't notice the leaves or the trees or even the dead smell of autumn. Jim Stone is fixated on one thing—the finish line."

223

Sure, it's descriptive, and even some of the descriptions are accurate, but unless the writer was in the woods running with Jim Stone, how would the writer know what was happening? Writing with assumption—assuming what is happening or how someone is feeling or thinking—can only lead to problems. Solving the problem is as easy as going to the woods with Stone. Or, having Stone provide the descriptions. Even in those cases, writing such detail requires an accuracy check. Read the information to the source and let him or her assist in determining its accuracy.

During the 2005 NCAA Men's Basketball Final Four, popular *Detroit Free Press* sports columnist Mitch Albom fabricated portions of a column. Albom, who has been named APSE's No. 1 columnist in the nation 12 times, wrote the column Friday about a Saturday game to run in a special section Sunday. The Friday deadline clearly created problems. Although he was being asked to write about an event before it happened, it did not give Albom the license to fabricate the material. In part he wrote that two NBA players and former Michigan State players, Mateen Cleaves and Jason Richardson, were attending Saturday's game. Writing in past tense, Albom described how the players acted at the game, what they wore and how they arrived. It was all fabricated. Cleaves and Richardson never attended the game. Albom issued an apology a few days later.

There are two basic rules to follow in terms of avoiding plagiarism and fabrication: 1) Do your own work; and 2) Be true to the journalistic principles of truth, accuracy and fairness. Your name is the one that sits atop the story. It should be a badge of honor not disgrace.

Accuracy

When in doubt, check it out. Accurately presenting facts is a sports journalist's lifeblood to credibility and trust among readers and sources. As a sports writer, at some point you will write something someone does not like. Accuracy in reporting and writing eliminates much of the reason someone can be upset with a story. If the story is based on fact, and not opinion, the source's complaints ring hollow. For instance, if a police report says a player was arrested for disorderly conduct, that's a fact. The guilt or innocence of the player might be in question, but the report is not. So when the player gets in your face and asks, "Hey man, why'd you write that?" you can respond by saying it's an accurate story based on the police report.

If some piece of information creates doubt or confusion, contact the source and check for accuracy. Never be too proud to contact a source, perhaps several times, and ask. It's much better to feel a little embarrassed among an audience of one (the source) than to be greatly embarrassed among an audience of thousands (the readers).

This chapter cannot cover every ethical situation sports journalists face. We have attempted to hit some highnotes and at least present a few guidelines to follow when an ethical dilemma arises. Probably the best advice we can offer is to consult your sports editor, news editor, and colleagues early and often. Ethical decisions should not be made in isolation. Your experience and the experience of others are invaluable when making these decisions. Ethics is a gray area caught between two thin lines of black and white. No one is expected to make the correct decision every time, but making a decision that is consistent with newspaper policy and ethical guidelines can help. Also, be true to yourself and the journalist you want to become. Each time your byline appears, you are subjecting yourself to the criticisms of the entire world. Sometimes that criticism is unjust and other times it's well deserved. If you are thorough, fair, and accurate, little room is left for valid criticism. Remember, it's better for sources and readers to hate the game than hate the player.

Professional Perspective

Sports Journalism's Unwritten Rules

Sports writers from a variety of publications were asked to provide the unwritten rules in sports journalism. Although the rules are not usually discussed in an open forum, they are expected to be followed. This is what the sports writers said:

1 Don't cheer in the press box. You're not a fan, you're a reporter.
2 Don't ask for autographs no matter whom you're covering.
3 Dress appropriately. Wear something that shows you're a professional.
4 Don't ask someone whether they're happy or sad about winning or losing. That should be a given.
5 Address coaches as Coach _____ unless you know them.
6 Although you might use a recorder, write things down as well. You never know when your recorder might fail you.
7 Stay off the message boards. It's good to browse, bad to post.
8 Have thick skin. Don't be afraid to write things that are going to piss people off. You're never going to please everyone.
9 The players and coaches are not your friends. No matter your relationship with a player or coach, when it comes to writing a tough story you need to be able to do your job and not worry about offending someone.
10 The other reporters are not your friends. Sure you might go out for a beer after games or on weekends, but when it comes to a story, it's war. Don't spill your secrets in a drunken state.
11 Don't bet on games you're covering.

12 If you're a female, don't wear anything too sexy. You won't be respected.

13 Respect the sports writer hierarchy. Beat writers of home teams have precedent over visiting reporters in terms of press-box seat selection. Also, veterans outrank rookies.

14 Don't ambush an interview. If someone is conducting an interview, it's all right to join the conversation but don't be rude or interrupt. Also, don't just piggyback on the questions the first reporter is asking. In other words, make a contribution to the interview.

15 Be willing to share an interview, particularly on deadline. A player or coach should not have to answer the same questions twice.

16 Don't be a slob in the press-box. Clean up your papers and garbage.

17 If on deadline, ask significant questions. "How does it feel to be .500 in your career?" is not a significant question. It can be answered in a follow up interview. When everyone is on deadline, stick to the purpose at hand and do not waste everyone's time.

18 Don't ask too many favors of the sports information personnel. Check the media guide and gameday notes before asking for assistance.

19 Even if you're a beat-writer brainiac who knows everything about a team, read every note in the game notes provided by media relations. Sometimes there are random nuggets of information you did not know.

20 Don't stick your tape recorder right in a player's face. It doesn't need to be that close to his or her mouth. And all it will do is frustrate them anyway.

21 Never try to interview a player when he or she is eating.

22 Never go into the training room to do an interview unless you are given permission.

23 When you have a multi-city road trip, rest is imperative. It's easy to get excited about being on the road and go out boozin' that first night. But by the fourth day and the third city, you can't keep your eyes open at courtside. Pace yourself. It's a long season.

24 Always check to see if you can get online as soon as you get to a venue. Don't wait until deadline.

25 Before the game, ask where the postgame interviews will be held. Don't wait until the chaos of the final minute to get directions from the press box down to the visitor's locker room.

26 Be respectful to professional writers, but also pick their brains as much as you can during pre-game meals, down-time before interviews, etc. Learn from the veterans. But don't be that smug 20-year-old who thinks because you wrote some big feature in the student paper that you're a better journalist than the writer who has been working a lifetime.

27 Always give a firm handshake.
28 Don't interview pitchers on days they're starting...well, before the game, that is.
29 Always take it easier on high school kids and college players than you would pros.
30 Don't be a "peeker" in the locker room. Eye-to-eye contact is the best policy, or use your notebook to strategically block certain body parts. Once a writer gets the label of "peeker" by the players, he or she will never live it down.

Professional Perspective
By Chad Jennings
Scranton Times-Tribune

The biggest mistake of my career could have been avoided by simply taking 30 seconds to actually think about what I was writing.

Here's the scenario: I was covering a Division I men's basketball team that seemed to be on the verge of losing its head coach. His record was so-so and fans had been openly jeering him, but he was a young, up-and-comer so other job opportunities would be easy to find.

It had been an ongoing subplot for weeks. When the head coaching job at a major university in his home state became available, I wrote a column about the likelihood the coach would be leaving to take the new job.

I had some good information from the new university, including some of the other candidates and some of the reasons the coach I covered wasn't likely to take the position. That part of the story was solid.

My mistake came in a simple recap of all that had come before. In retelling the story of fans turning on the coach, I said that he received "death threats," which simply wasn't true.

How did I come up with something so outrageous? I heard it somewhere along the line and lost track of what was real and what wasn't. After reading story after story on the topic and after discussing it over and over with friends and other writers—some discussing facts and others discussing theories—I lost track of reality.

When I wrote that ill-fated column, I confused fact with theory.

At some point in covering a beat, you become so immersed in the day-to-day activities of the team that you become an expert. You can crank out a 15-inch story without so much as looking at a note-book or checking a page of statistics. You know things about that team, its players and its coaching staff like the back of your hand.

That's the way I felt about the coach and his not-so-kind fans. There were death threats, I was sure of it, and so I wrote it.

And I was wrong. Dead wrong, if you will.

In the days after my column, fan message boards went berserk, sports radio shows quoted and discredited me, and my newspaper had to run a correction. All because I wrote a story quickly and didn't take the time to really think about what I was writing. I knew there weren't death threats, at least none that were documented, but I got cocky and wrote quickly without reviewing the facts. I was positive I knew everything off the top of my head.

The lesson? Slow down. Don't get ahead of yourself, don't forget to do the most basic reporting and don't let your fingers hit the keyboard without being absolutely certain you know what you're writing.

(Chad Jennings is a sports writer for the
Scranton Times-Tribune.)

Professional Perspective
By Wright Thompson
ESPN.com

My daddy, an old country lawyer, had a good definition of ethics. He used to say, "If it feels wrong, it probably is." Underneath all the journalistic navel gazing about what we should and shouldn't do, that's the only thing to remember. If something makes you feel sleazy, it probably is sleazy.

Covering sports, we live in a world populated by men and women used to being used. Everyone's wanted something from him or her for as long as they can remember. So treating people with honesty, with straight-forwardness, in addition to being the right thing to do, is also good business. Honesty will set you apart. Being fair will make you different. The thing I'm most proud of is that, during my career, I've had zero corrections. It's because I'm a tad OCD about the facts. I check and re-check and

Figure 19.1 Wright Thompson.

go over again and again. I think being as right as you can be is a big part of ethics. People deserve to have the things they say and do presented, at the very least, correctly to the massive audiences you will command.

The big ethical problems are no brainers: Don't make things up. Don't misrepresent yourself or your story. Don't plagiarize. But beyond the obvious idiotic things that can derail your career, the real ethical quandaries lie in the gray spaces. Should you tell a lie of omission to get someone to talk to you? Should you stretch the truth to sources? Should you run with a story that could damage someone even if you're not sure the information is solid?

Sports journalists, like political reporters, live in this shadow world of in-betweens. You will make many tough decisions in your career, decisions they can't prepare you for in college. I've interviewed people who had never spoken to a reporter before. They didn't know what on-the-record or off-the-record meant. It was up to me not to take advantage of them. It was up to me to be able to look in a mirror at night. They should be treated differently than a sharkish flak who is shamelessly selling something.

In moments like these—and there will be many, many moments like these—remember what Walter Thompson said: "If it feels wrong, it probably is." There will be countless other stories. You have but one reputation.

(Wright Thompson is a senior writer for
ESPN.com and a contributing writer
for *ESPN The Magazine*.)

20

FINAL POINTS III
Writing for Online and Blogging

Writing for online continues to be a challenge for journalists, particularly in sports. There is no definite online writing style. Professionals and academics are unable to agree on what online writing should entail. Changing technology is partly to blame. Resistance to embrace online writing is another. And while we're trying to figure out the best use of the World Wide Web, sports fans have taken it upon themselves to play "sports writers."

Newspapers have been reluctant to invest in online reporter staff for a variety of reasons, mostly financial. The old days were relatively simple: reporters wrote stories, advertising representatives sold ads and the stories and ads were placed in a paper package and sold for a moderate price to consumers. Now, newspapers struggle to garner advertising revenue from their Web pages. Most stories are "shovelware"—the print story moved to the Web—and only a few papers charge for the viewing rights to their Web page. So, if you're keeping score, almost no revenue is generated from the Web page, and the product (the stories) is a rehash of old news. No wonder newspapers have been so reticent to embrace the news platform of the future.

While newspapers have not fully committed to their Web product, one thing is certain: newspaper sales having been drastically declining for more than a decade. In 2006, the Newspaper Association of America reported that daily circulation dropped 1.2 million compared to a year earlier. The good news: viewership on Web sites increased 5 million in that same year, up to 56 million. (Whoever thought "viewership" would be used to describe newspapers?) It's difficult to determine what people are "viewing," but it's clearly a sign that they are turning to newspapers for something.

No one can debate that newspapers in their traditional fashion—ink on paper—are headed for a slow, reluctant death. But while newspaper owners have been apathetic in their efforts to invest in an online product, newsrooms are making attempts to incorporate the new platform. Although few newspaper reporters are writing exclusively for the

Web, reporters have taken it upon themselves to integrate more interactive methods of journalism, such as blogs.

Because the future of newspapers is destined for the Web, this chapter will discuss some online writing approaches that you might find useful.

The Audience

Where newspapers are a passive form of transmitting information to the audience, the Web is an interactive form. Newspaper readers purchase a newspaper, thumb through the pages scanning headlines and choose what to read. The readers are restricted to limitations of what the paper can offer.

The Web, on the other hand, allows readers to make far more liberal choices. Remembering that the first two "Ws" in "WWW" stand for "World Wide," readers can travel to any online newspaper. Once there, he or she can click the stories of his or her choosing. That's where the comparison between traditional newspapers and online newspapers end. Instead of a pre-selected menu, online readers choose news à la carte.

Because news has become a selective process with unlimited choices, capturing the reader's attention is more important than ever. Sure, some readers will always read about their favorite team no matter how interesting the material. The issue isn't if the Yankees fan will read the material but where he or she is going to retrieve the information. A Google search for "New York Yankees" renders nearly 15.5 million sites as of June 2008. The first 10 sites include the Yankees official site, ESPN.com and SI.com (*Sports Illustrated*). Wikipedia's Yankees reference, and a handful of ticket outlines are posted before stumbling upon a newspaper Web site. The *New York Post* is listed 13th. Even Wiki gets better play on Google than the newspapers. In the scope of coverage or quality information, Google is hardly a reliable measure. Nonetheless, it demonstrates the magnitude of competition newspapers face.

Online readers want more than the straight 15-inch game story that leads with the score. They want insight and interaction. They want to be linked to related sites that can provide depth to the coverage. They want to read what other fans are saying. They want to see and hear the sights and sounds that traditional newspapers cannot provide.

The Web is a living, breathing venue that allows readers to use more of their senses. The news isn't just read but it can be heard and seen as well. Suddenly, readers can participate in the journalistic process either as proactive news consumers or interactive news contributors. The challenge for those writing for online is keeping the readers involved.

Writing Style

Although there is no one form for writing online, shovelware is not the answer. Initially posting a story online shortly after a game is understandable. Readers want the basic information quickly and the Web is far more efficient than a 12-year-old on a bike delivering the newspaper. But the Web reader will not be satisfied by only getting tomorrow's newspaper story. So here are a few tips:

Use a high-octane inverted pyramid style. Some have argued that the inverted pyramid style is dying. Some said that with so many media outlets cramming the who, what, where, why, when, and how in the first couple of paragraphs was outdated. They argued that a more literary style captivates an audience that had already been exposed to the basic information. The Web has changed that. Readers do not like to scroll down their computer screens. What they see on the screen is all they will read. Providing the essentials early in the story caters to that need. So, the straight lead again is fashionable. That does not mean you forego good writing. Boring the reader is still a fatal mistake. You can write lively, entertaining stories *and* include the essentials before running out of screen space. *Sports Illustrated*'s Andrew Lawrence wrote this US Open story for SI.com in 2006:

> NEW YORK – Andy Roddick stood at center court Wednesday night under the full moon, scratching his sweaty head in disbelief, a star seemingly on the rise again. It had taken him fewer than two hours and only three sets to do away with Lleyton Hewitt, 6–3, 7–5, 6–4, in his first triumph over the Aussie in a Slam in three tries.
>
> "I just appreciate playing good tennis again," said Roddick, through to the US Open semis for the first time since he won it all in 2003.
>
> And he has Jimmy Connors to thank for making this breakthrough possible. Since Connors signed on as Roddick's coach earlier this summer, the two have been on a tear. Wednesday night's hewing of Hewitt extended an 11-match win streak for Roddick and improved Connors' coaching record to 17–1. It has also raised their modest expectations for the Open.

The three paragraphs provided the who (Andy Roddick), what (US Open semis win), when (Wednesday night), where (New York), why (the coaching of Jimmy Connors), and how (6–3, 7–5, 6–4). He also used descriptive writing ("under the full moon, scratching his sweaty head in disbelief"), an insightful quote and context (11-match win streak; Connors coaching record to 17–1). Although the story shared the screen with a picture of Roddick raising his arms in victory, and an ad running down the right side, the reader did not have to scroll down to read the story. It was no trick. Andrew understands the time/space continuum facing online journalists. He knew he had to get to the story quickly while still making it interesting. Andrew's training also helped. He worked for a period of time for the Associated Press where every word and every syllable is valuable. Interestingly, this story was not filed until 11:36 a.m. Clearly, it wasn't a deadline story yet Andrew wrote it as if immediacy was important, which of course it was for the reader.

Write in chunks. Web pages, like life, come at you fast. With all the flashing lights and ads streaming across the screen sensory overload seems inevitable. Readers are used to sorting through the clutter to find the prize. One way to eliminate clutter is by presenting your story in chunks.

Stories can be divided into segments. One segment can be the essentials of the story. Another can discuss the historical implications of the game. Another can provide a breakdown of the key play. The chunks can all relate to the main story but provide different perspectives, similar to sidebars. Of course you're probably thinking, "That sounds like I'm writing several different stories." Well, yes and no. Making one chunk a question and answer session with a coach or player doesn't take any more time than transcribing your notes, which you would have done for a full newspaper story. Breaking out the key play in four or five paragraphs is not more difficult than including those paragraphs in the newspaper's game story.

Chunks make the Web page "reader friendly" and convenient. If a reader already watched the game, he or she might skip the gamer but want to read the quotes. Chunks also allow the sports writer to put different aspects of an event into perspective. Each chunk adds a layer of context to the larger story. The more media-saturated sports fans are, the more important layers have become. Also, newspaper space limitations prevent expansive coverage of some events. There is no space limitation on the Web, so chunk it up.

Link to other information. One of the beauties of the Web is that it's an unlimited resource of information. Even after the story has been broken into chunks it can be divided further. Attaching links to key words in a story allows readers to venture deeper into the story. It enables readers to pick and choose what they want to read. For instance, a game story might provide the essentials but linking to team history, game statistics, player profiles, fan blogs, the definition of fumbleroosky, etc., enriches the story. You have now provided the reader a smorgasbord of information to choose from. Of course, as with any smorgasbord, some readers will venture to the dessert table and never return to the entrée. That's all the more reason to write interesting stories. The alternative is to not provide the links and allow the reader to fish for the information. Once that happens, you risk losing the reader altogether. Why should he or she read your online story if another site better suits his or her needs?

Utilize multimedia storytelling methods. Although you are a "sports journalist," nothing says you are limited to words. Visually, how can your story be told? Audibly, how can it be told? Too often, we assume readers only like to read. The fact is, even calling Web consumers "readers" is a misnomer. They not only read, but watch, listen, write, and someday soon, taste and smell online material. Do not handicap yourself by ignoring the sensory astute Web user. Why not download the interview of the coach onto the Web page? How about including a slide show of the newspaper photographer's work? Imagine a game story linked to a slide show of the game's big plays. Or, a link to a series of photos that show a controversial play, accompanied by an audio description of the play from a player or a coach? The options are limitless.

At many newspapers, the technology might not be available to provide some of these multimedia methods. But work within your technology to develop creative ways that will benefit readers. If you host a weekly radio sports talk show, download the show to the newspaper's Web page. Streaming video is always another option. Now that might be outside the realm of your abilities, but find someone who is equipped to do it. It's just one more way to keep the audience coming back to your newspaper's page.

The idea of using multimedia storytelling methods is to take the best of all media to inform your online readers. Take the best from radio and TV and make it work for you.

Write like broadcast. Writing for online is not exactly similar to writing for newspapers. Because the event occurred hours before the newspaper is delivered, newspapers are traditionally written in past tense. "Southside scored three fourth-quarter touchdowns to beat Northside 28–7 Friday night." Because online is immediate, similar to TV or radio broadcasts, adopting a more immediate style is prudent. "Southside scores three fourth-quarter touchdowns to beat Northside 28–7 tonight."

Web readers oftentimes read for immediacy. Providing present tense allows them to read in real time—or almost real time. If the story is posted 20 minutes after a game, use present tense. The same can be said for sports news. "Early in today's practice, Jack Henry fractures his leg and expects to the miss the rest of the season." The story can be updated several times as information becomes available. As the story get old (as in a few hours old), it can be converted to past tense.

Make information palatable. Sometimes sports readers want information in a "just the facts, ma'am" format. Before TV started displaying the scoreline during games, millions of Americans spent Sunday afternoons screaming at the screen, "WHAT'S THE SCORE?" Before sports fans delve into the why and how of a story, they want the basics.

For online writing, providing lists and small nuggets of easily digestible information is essential. Newspapers do this as well but space restrictions limit its utility. With an effort to place four or five stories on a newspaper sports front, lists of a team's top 10 all-time leading scorers might not be practical. But online can do much more than that. An online writer could actually summarize the story in a bulleted list of highlights. Sports business stories can list costs of a project or salaries of coaches. Those lists can link to other similar lists so readers can dig deeper into the story.

Providing a list of sources, like a scorecard, can be useful for the readers, particularly with complicated stories. Alternatively, include a timeline on how a story was reported:

10 a.m.: Received press release saying starting wide receiver Cameron Jones was being suspended by the team for violating team rules.

10:15 a.m.: Telephone coach Bill Yalek. No answer. Leave a message.

10:20 a.m.: Telephone Jones. He says, "No comment," and hangs up.

11 a.m.: Telephone coach Yalek again and leave a message.

11:30 a.m.: Go to the sports information office in an attempt to extract more details. Ask for and receive a list of team rules. Ask for punishments for violating the rules, but sports information director Greg Hamill did not know.

1 p.m.: Telephone coach Yalek. No answer. Leave a third message.

3 p.m.: Attend practice. Yalek said he'll talk after practice.

5:30 p.m.: Yalek talks with reporters about Jones' suspension. When asked about the punishment for violating team rules, Yalek said each infraction is dealt with on an individual basis.

During the past two years, four football players have been suspended for violating team rules.

Transparency assists in developing credibility with readers. This timeline demonstrates that the reporter didn't just call the coach once and give up. Or, that he or she provided Jones fair comment and he refused. Of course, that would be included in the story as well.

Provide readers a voice. Allowing readers to chime in is what makes the Web incredibly appealing to millions of viewers. Sports fans have something to say and desire a platform to say it. While sports talk radio is fine, it does not have the same appeal as message boards, chat rooms, and blogs. Sports talk is restricted by time. Only a limited number of callers can express their opinions before the program ends. Online interaction is not restricted by time or space. The conversation may seem never-ending but that's not completely true. Many times the conversation dwindles to a trickle and then ends.

For your stories, provide a forum for people to weigh in about a game or event. Ask unscientific survey questions, such as, "Do you think the Packers will beat the Vikings on Sunday?" or establish a weekly topic and invite readers to contribute. Online is interactive, so allow the readers to interact with you and the other fans.

A word of caution: If you are a beat writer, be conservative in your online opinions. It's not your place to start a campaign to get a coach fired or question the play calling. Your first priority is to non-partisan reporting. As a journalist, provide information without tainting its meaning. You can still have an opinion, but sometimes it's best kept to yourself.

The main objective of an online forum is to allow the readers to interact. It also can possibly lead to story tips. On the other hand, rumors can run rampant on a discussion boards. And no sports writer has the time or inclination to chase down every rumor.

Blogs

Blogs have been stereotyped as superficial personal journals people feel compelled to share with the world. That's not always so. While some blogs are primarily filled with personal information, other types of blogs are incredibly informative.

Before the 2005 football season, former *St. Louis Post-Dispatch* sports writer Graham Watson convinced her Web page designers to add a blog. As the University of Missouri beat writer, Watson thought blogging from fall football camp would be an additional service to the readers.

"I wanted to do something different to set us apart from some of the other papers and the other coverage," she said.

Because the *Post-Dispatch* had never posted a blog on its Web page, it did not have the software to properly provide it. So, Watson e-mailed her blog to the Web designers and they would post it as a document. They would then continue to add to the document. Although it was primitive and didn't allow for much interaction, the blog was a hit— literally. It received 5,000 hits the first day, the second-most hits behind the St. Louis Cardinals coverage.

"People loved the extra coverage," Watson said. "We were breaking news; not big news but depth-chart moves and stuff like that. It ended up being a big resource for people who wanted to know exactly what was going on with the football team. A lot of people said it was like being in practice because it was so in-depth."

The "Tiger Tracker" has come along way from those first few days. Watson continued to develop the blog into a need-to-know place for Missouri football information. It was no longer just a "postcards from camp" type of site. She provided "staples" five days a week, including an overview of Monday's press conference, a practice report from Tuesday's practice, the teams' position-by-position preview for Wednesday, a player-by-player matchup for Friday, which includes who has the advantage, and a look back at the game on Sunday. She would not post Thursday or Saturday.

For the paper version of the *Post-Dispatch*, Watson was expected to provide two stories during the week, a notebook and complete gameday coverage. Although time consuming ("It takes me about three hours to research the position-by-position matchups") the blog allowed her to more than double the coverage. Watson also logged between 60 and 70 hours a week with no days off during football season. She was compensated with extensive time off after the season.

"I do in-depth analysis of matchups for the games and stuff we can't get into the paper because of the space," she said. "It's a lot of opponents' stuff and analysis...I keep trying to add new things to it and diversify it. It's a lot more of my time now than it was the first year because you're trying to maintain that edge over someone else."

Besides the additional coverage, the benefit to fans is the blog's immediacy. During spring scrimmages, Watson provided play-by-play as it occurs. If something important happened at practice, for instance, the starting linebacker breaks his leg, she got it posted within minutes instead of waiting for the next day's paper.

It isn't just the Missouri fans who tapped into the blog. Coaches and players also checked what Watson had to say.

"One of the coaches actually said he reads it and he likes reading the opponents' stuff because it makes his job easier," she said. "One of the players asked me if I was the girl who writes the blog. That makes it even more important to me to get the stuff that I write correct. I don't know how much stock they put into it, but I don't want there to be false information."

Watson also said the blog made her a more-informed reporter. Because she read everything she can about the opposing team, she was well-prepared to do her job on gamedays.

"I do a lot of reporting for the blog, but it carries over into my stories. It makes my stories easier to write. And I would say a majority of my stories are Missouri-based than they are opponent-based. This actually gives me another outlet to learn about the opponent and write about the opponent. It's the sort thing we've been trying to do at the paper."

In its first year, Watson was more inclined to include her opinion on the blog. At times that created problems with fans, coaches, players, and even her bosses.

"I've had fans get on me and say, 'You're not a columnist. You're a beat writer so be a beat writer. Write the news and don't write your opinion.'

"You have to find that medium in a blog because you're putting yourself out there...The most important thing is to be credible. Anybody can write a blog, but you have to be credible and have something to say and be able to provide analysis of things that maybe somebody else can't."

Blogging, similar to a tape recorder or laptop, is a tool. It can provide readers with not only large amounts of information and perspective, but an opportunity to share their views as well. It can be used as a gauge to see what fans are thinking and talking about. And with a vast network of people chiming in, it can provide tips that lead to good stories. But remember to blog with a purpose. Your random thoughts and opinions are not enough to satisfy the blogosphere.

Writing for online is still in its developmental stages. The newspaper industry is still trying to determine the best approach to present material in an economically savvy fashion. Meanwhile, some reporters and editors are forging ahead with the understanding that the future lies with news consumers who take an interactive role in their information gathering. Sports journalists have been challenged to adhere to those needs. Those who are meeting that challenge head-on will be more equipped to do their jobs.

However, there can be pitfalls. During the 2007 NCAA super-regional baseball game between the University of Louisville and Oklahoma State, *Louisville Courier-Journal* sports writer Brian Bennett's credentials were revoked because he was blogging from the press box. The NCAA prohibits reporters from live blogging because it claims that live reporting is an infringement on its product and could interfere with broadcast television contract rights.

That should not discourage you from venturing out into this great world of online journalism. Perhaps next time Bennett could sit in the stands and blog. Can the NCAA control what happens in the stands? Who knows? But confiscating cell phone cameras and recording devices at the gate could prove problematic. So, blog away.

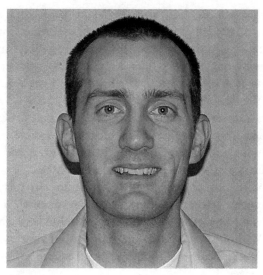

Figure 20.1 Rob Hurtt.

Professional Perspective
Proffesional Perspective
By Rob Hurtt
Formerly of *Sporting News*

Increasingly, writers in news organizations have been asked to blog. Sports blogs particularly have grown in number as newspapers and magazines settle on them as a way to better engage the audience. Blogs provide direct interaction between readers and the writer, and when done well, they invite readers into the writing process and create a dialogue.

Before you get started, you must realize the key differences between writing for a print publication and writing a blog.

Bloggers can write much longer. Because bloggers are not limited by space, in-depth analysis that wouldn't fit in print can be published online. It becomes the perfect haven for insider-type information that doesn't interest the average reader but does appeal to a hardcore fan.

Bloggers can write much shorter. There is no set space to fill and usually no set deadlines. At times, bloggers are not writers as much as they are collectors of information. In these cases, a blogger strings together research from elsewhere on the Web. The result is a compilation of sources for readers to use to learn more about the topic.

Bloggers can write less formally. Make your work scannable. Bulleted lists, bolded type, frequent subject headers and lots of links create a piece that is easier for readers to digest in a glance. Having numerous entry points isn't a trick unique to online writing, but it is more critical. If readers can't get a quick feel of the topic, they'll surf off elsewhere.

Bloggers can write subjectively. Remember that a blog is more journal than it is journalism. The blog format allows writers to share opinions and personal stories. Even better, it allows readers to share theirs and become part of the conversation.

OK, you're not scared of blogs anymore. In fact, blogging sounds much less restraining than traditional journalism. However, bloggers can't just toss the basic fundamentals out the window. Without that journalistic foundation, your work will be indistinguishable from the thousands of amateurs who have their own Web page.

Reporting is still important. Although blogs can be written with little legwork, the best ones are those that include fresh reporting, not just fresh analysis. A good weblog should not become merely a compilation of thoughts with assorted links tossed in as garnish.

Factual reporting is even more crucial. The common blogger can get away with occasionally overlooking an important detail or missing the whole story. That's not going to work when you're blogging for an employer. You still need to get the facts right. That's not to say that blogs can't pass along rumors as long as they are clearly labeled as such. As always, use good news judgment.

Correct style and grammar remain important. A great part about online publishing is that those minor mistakes that writers and editors read over aren't set in unalterable ink. Bloggers can fix their mistakes or clarify confusing points.

Needed: one thick skin. Not everyone will agree with the opinions you express, and sometimes, they won't respond kindly. Be ready to withstand the attacks. They can get ugly.

(Rob Hurtt is a former Associate Editor for
Sporting News.)

Figure 20.2 Andrew Lawrence.

Professional Perspective
By Andrew Lawrence
Sports Illustrated

Ten years ago, being a sports writer on the Web was a lot like being an Ol' West prospector at the dawn of the Gold Rush: space abounded, the rules were few and the competition was sparse. But as more readers have settled into the medium—many to satisfy their insatiable appetites for sports news—sports writers took to their laptops like cowboys to covered wagons and gave chase, hauling with them every two-bit cliché and rote opinion they'd ever co-opted. Area beat writers and columnists aren't the only ones hacking it up online. Fans are blogging day and night, teams report their goings-on from within, and players soft-serve personal scoops on their own tricked out portals. Is there any room left for the diligent cub reporter in a 24-hour news cycle where breaking news is as easy as breaking the bank on a pricey camera phone? In a word: yes. Congested as the medium might seem, there remains plenty of good nuggets to be panned, provided you're willing to roll up your pant cuffs and dig. The following three tools are essential to any reporter looking to carve out a niche on the 'net: a lot of substance, a little style and a different spin. Call it The Three Ss:

Substance

Popular as it has become online to trade in opinion, information remains the more valued currency. And your notebook should be the first place you look to make a withdrawal. Rather than relying on your ranting to carry you from start to finish, take the time to do a little legwork. Pick up the phone. Pay a visit to the team's facility. To an athlete's house. To his momma's house. To Lexis-Nexis or Google News if you lack the wherewithal to do the sourcing yourself. Any of these things is likely to enrich your copy more than whatever thought you might have had while half asleep on the La-Z-Boy during the fourth quarter of the big game. Once you've got your facts, make sure you've got 'em straight as the fast pace of cyberspace makes mistakes easier to publish. The good news is you can correct them just as quickly (though you should aim to get them right on the first go).

Style

Think of the Internet as a place to stretch the limits of your voice. It should be a place where you can let down your guard a little bit more than traditional mediums when you're trying to pass yourself off as an unbiased conduit of the news. If you're funny, be funny. Introspective? Then tell us what's on your mind. Whatever you are, just don't be long winded. Tempting as the Internet's endless column space makes it to rhapsodize, consider what your prose might be up against: a box with links to more popular stories, banner ads bearing down from all sides, an e-mail or instant message alert just off the corner of the screen. Suffice it to say, the Internet has a lot going on, and readers are never left wanting for ways to be distracted. So if you've got a point to make, make it snappy...

Spin

...and make it different. Often the best takes are the ones furthest afield from the mainstream—not that you shouldn't take your cues from a USA Today or ESPN. There's nothing wrong with stabbing at a hot topic, but realize the topic might be tired by the time the reader gets around to you. A different writing approach can go along way toward freshening a stale subject. Terrell Owens grabs headlines for sleeping through a practice? Try a running diary of how he spent the night before. Another athlete proffers a lame excuse for testing positive for steroids? Try it on for size; get tested yourself. Also, take advantage of the 'Net's other dimensions: There's audio, there's video, there's pictures, and they're all aching for the words to help them come alive. Those words could be yours. Above all, don't be afraid to trade in the quirky to experiment in the unknown and let your personality come through. The best part about writing on the Internet is there's no right or wrong way to do it.

Well, maybe just one wrong way: boring.

(Andrew Lawrence is a sports writer for *Sports Illustrated*.)

GLOSSARY

NEWSPAPER AND MAGAZINE TERMS

Advance   A sports story about an event, written prior to the event.

Angle   The point-of-view, focus or emphasis in an article.

Annual   Yearly special or extra issue devoted to seasonal subject, such as a Christmas annual (issue).

Art   Illustrations, drawings, diagrams, or other nonprint material that accompanies an article; common name for all nontextual material.

Assignment   Any specific task given to an individual; for example, a commissioned article assignment to a freelancer by a magazine.

ATT   The *As Told To* story. An athlete's autobiography that is prepared for publication by a writer; the writer shares the byline credit, such as, "My Life in Football" by Joe Jock, As Told To Writer Charley Someone.

Author's Alterations (AAs)   Changes or corrections made by the writer in textual material (usually in galley proof form) before the material is printed.

Back Issue   Any issue of a magazine or newspaper printed prior to the current-date (newsstand) issue.

Back-of-the-Book   Secondary articles, columns, and other material literally or figuratively printed behind the primary articles.

Back Shop   Composing room area of a newspaper.

Bingo Card   Postage-paid insert in a magazine, that readers can complete and return to begin a magazine subscription. So called because they are often the size of bingo playing cards.

Bleed   To run an illustration past the margins to the edges of a page.

Blue-Pencil   Slang for editing corrections. So-named because blue pencil or ink can't be photographed by photo-offset cameras.

Blurb   Short description of an article or subject.

Body (of the article)   The core of an article; that is, material following the lead segment.

Book   Industry slang for *magazine*. So named (perhaps) because some monthly dummies are the sizes of books.

Byline   A line of type printed before or after an article, identifying the author.

Camera-Ready   Material that has been corrected and is ready to be photographed for photo-offset printing.

Caption   Material that explains the contents of a photograph or illustration. Sometimes called *art lines* or *cut lines.*

Center Spread   The two facing pages at the exact center of a magazine.

Circulation   The number of copies of a magazine or newspaper printed, distributed, or sold during a specific period.

Clean Copy   Pristine text, unmarred by many editing symbols. Opposite of *dirty copy.*

Close (Closing date)   The deadline for all material for a newspaper or magazine to be on the press.

Cold Type   Material prepared for printing without old-fashioned hot metal; that is, without Linotype machines.

Commission   Same as *to assign an article.*

Contents Page   Page usually near the front of a magazine that lists the contents of the issue.

Copy   All written material in manuscript form that will eventually be considered for publication.

Copy editor   Person who reads and corrects all copy prior to publication.

Copyright   The legal ownership of a manuscript.

Cover (noun)   The outside front page, inside front page, inside rear page, and outside rear page of a magazine or *to cover* (verb): To gather all the facts necessary for an article.

Crop   To mark unwanted sections of a photograph or illustration.

Cut (noun)   A metal engraving of an illustration. Or *to cut* (verb): To edit material.

Cutlines   Same as *caption* or *art lines.*

Dateline   Line on an article, giving the location and date that the article originated; such as, Washington, Feb. 23.

Dead   Material that has been *killed*; that is, material that will not be printed.

Deadline   Time when all material to be published must be written, copyedited, and ready for the press.

Department   Specific section of a magazine or newspaper, involving special features or area of interest.

Dirty copy   Material that has been heavily copy edited, such that it is illegible. Opposite of *clean copy.*

Double-Spread   Two facing pages treated as one unit.

Dummy   Planning or proof pages for an issue that has not yet been printed; a checking copy to make sure changes and corrections have been made to a particular issue.

Edition   Same as *issue.*

Editor   Person who reads, changes, or verifies all material and makes it ready for publication, in a newspaper or magazine.

Editorial Content All nonadvertising material in a newspaper or magazine; the literary contents of a publication.

Editorialize To express a position or opinion on behalf of the publication, as in an editorial or publisher's or editor's column.

Editor's Note Material that helps explain an article or author or a position that a publication has taken on an issue.

Engraving Same as *cut*.

Feature (noun) A human-interest article, or *to*.

Feature (verb) To emphasize or give permanence to.

Filler Incidental (usually short) material that is used to complete columns or pages.

Flag The name of a newspaper or magazine recognizable not only by name, but also by design; for example, the Gothic flag of *The New York Times*.

Format The size, design, and appearance of a magazine.

Four-Color Pages that are printed in the colors of red, yellow, blue, and black inks.

Free Lance Person who contributes articles, photographs, or any other material without the security of a staff salary.

Front-of-the-Book Articles of primary importance literally or figuratively printed at the front of the magazine.

Galley Proof Vertical column of material typeset for checking purposes.

Gatefold A page in a magazine, that is larger than the normal page and that must be folded to fit inside the magazine; for example, the *Playboy* Playmate-of-the-Month pages.

General Magazine Any magazine edited and published for a wide reading audience, all ages, interests, religions, and so on. *Life* and *The Saturday Evening Post* are examples. Opposite of special-interest magazine.

Ghost Writer Person who writes material that will eventually be published under the name of another person.

Graf (or Graph) Short for *paragraph*.

Gutter The inside margins of pages.

Handout Publicity release.

Head Headline.

Horizontal Magazine Same as *general magazine*.

Hot Type Material prepared with hot metal; that is, Linotype machines. Opposite of *cold type* or photo-offset composition.

House Ad Advertisement that promotes the same newspaper or magazine that published it.

House Organ Publication issued by a commercial firm to promote interest in the firm by employees, stockholders, or the public.

HTK *Head to Come*; headline not yet ready.

Human Interest Feature article with emotional appeal to the reader; different than straight news, which is presumably toneless in content.

Insert   Material that has to be added to the inside of a previously completed article, or a specially prepared advertising supplement to a newspaper or magazine.

Inventory   Material on hand in a magazine or newspaper office, that may be used at any time.

Issue   Same as *edition.*

Italic   Script type that slants to the right, like handwriting. Italic type is often used to emphasize or highlight material.

Jump   To continue a story from one page to another or from one section to another.

Jump Head   Headline over the second or continued part of a story.

Keep Standing   Material that is held in a newspaper or magazine's inventory. Opposite of *kill.*

Kill   To delete material set for publication.

Kill Fee (Kill Rate)   Payment made to a writer after an article is assigned, completed, then killed by a magazine. The kill rate or kill fee is usually a percentage of the fee paid for a published article. The writer usually retains legal rights to material killed by a publication.

Layout   The design of a page including textual material, or art that will later be published.

Lead or Lede   Beginning segment of an article.

Libel   A defamatory statement or representation published without just cause, expressed in print or by pictures, that exposes the subject to public hatred, contempt, or ridicule.

Linotype   Trade name for a keyboard-operated typesetting machine that produces a line of type in the form of a metal slug.

Little Magazine   Small circulation magazines, often less than 8½ "× 11", that contain poetry, fiction, or avant garde material. Because of lack of advertising or subscription base, little magazines often die quickly. They are the publishing equivalent of the Mayfly.

Localize   To stress the local angle of a story.

Logo   Same as flag or masthead.

Magazine   Regularly issued publication that contains fiction, nonfiction, and art, and that is aimed at a specific reading public. Carries the original definition of powder magazine, that is, storehouse.

Makeup   The consistent design of a total publication.

Mark up   To edit copy and make corrections on galley proofs.

Market   The audience for a magazine or publication.

Masthead   Material usually printed toward the front of a magazine, that lists title, editors and staff members, address, and subscription rates.

More   Used at the bottom of a page, often in parentheses, to indicate that there are additional pages to the article.

Morgue   Newspaper or magazine library, archives or files.

Ms.   Manuscript.

Must Material so marked has a high priority and should be printed.

Nameplate Same as *flag* or *logo*.

Nonfiction Material based on facts; not fiction.

Obit Obituary; biography of recently deceased person.

Offset Printing process in which an inked impression is made on a rubber "blanket" and then transferred or "offset" to paper.

OK for Press Notation meaning "Can now be printed."

Op-Ed Page The right-hand page opposite, or facing, the editorial page. Many metropolitan newspapers use the Op-Ed page as a continuation of editorials, essays, letters-to-the-editor, and other allied material.

On-Sale Date Date on which a particular issue is available for sale throughout the publication's circulation area.

One-Shot Book Magazine that has only one planned issue. One-shot books are often published after the death of a president, the Pope, or other famous or notorious people. There were a variety of one-shot books published after the death of Elvis Presley.

On Spec (On speculation) Any material written and submitted for publication without prior financial agreements with a magazine.

Outline Topic-by-topic skeleton of an article.

Overset Material that has been set in type but not used by a newspaper or magazine.

Over-the-Transom Unsolicited material that is submitted to a magazine, that must be sorted, read, bought, or returned. (Some magazines will not read over-the-transom material because of the costs of staff member's time to read and reply to it.) Over-the-transom material becomes part of the magazine's *slush pile*.

Pack Journalism The tendency of journalists to deliberately or accidentally write like each other. The press that covers Washington, D.C., has been accused of pack journalism, as have many sports writers.

Pad To lengthen with additional materials.

Periodical Publication issued at regular intervals longer than one day; that is, for example, magazines, not newspapers.

Personality Piece Biography on a person in magazine form.

Pics or **Pix** Pictures.

Piece Slang for *article*.

Play up To emphasize.

Policy Official viewpoint of a magazine as stated in editorial columns or other features; such as "The Playboy Philosophy," a series in *Playboy* written by publisher Hugh Hefner.

Profile Personality article.

Promotion Active campaign to enhance the acceptance and sale of a newspaper or magazine.

Proof Copy of material used for checking and correction purposes.

Proofread To check such material prior to publication.

Pulp   Magazines printed on cheap newsprint; often carries the connotation of sensational material.

Put to Bed   To put on press; to close an issue.

Query Letter   Letter from a freelance writer outlining an article idea and asking for an acceptance from a publication on the idea.

Quote   Quotation.

Readability   The ease with which a story can be read; visually, pertains to legibility and design of article or layout.

Readership   Surveyed or estimated audience of a magazine; not the same as circulation.

Regional Advertisements   Advertisements that appear in issues of a magazine for a particular region.

Rejection Slip   Small letter sent to freelancers with articles that a publication has decided not to buy.

Reprint   Article printed separately and sent to readers or advertisers after the article has first appeared in print. Scholarly magazines often sell reprints to authors for their own distribution. Or, an article that had appeared previously in another publication.

Researcher   Editorial staff member who supplies facts necessary for an article or who verifies facts in an article. Slang term for researcher is *checker*, in news magazines.

Résumé   Summary of education and experience, sent by individual to prospective employers.

Rewrite   To write manuscript again.

Rim   Edge of copy desk, where editors check material.

Rough   Full-size sketch of layout.

Roundup   Article that is largely summary in nature.

Running Head   Headline that gives magazine title, date, volume, and page, printed at the top of magazine pages.

Running Story   Story that is continuing and that may demand follow-up articles on a day-to-day or week-to-week basis.

SASE   *Self-addressed stamped envelope.* Many magazines require a writer to enclose a SASE to receive an answer to a query. The writer pays the return postage.

Scoop (noun)   Exclusive material, or to *scoop* (verb): To beat the competition.

Seasonal Story   An article emphasizing a season, holiday, or celebration. Must be prepared well in advance, sometimes as much as a half-year in advance for monthly magazines.

Shelter Books   Magazines related to the home.

SID   Sports Information Director. The promotion-and-publicity arm of a college or university's athletic department.

Sidebar   A short feature that accompanies a longer article. The sidebar usually focuses on one aspect of the larger article; an aspect that the larger article may have only touched on.

Sister Publications   Magazines that are published by the same firm: *Time, Life, Fortune, Money, People,* and *Sports Illustrated* are all sister publications, published by Time, Inc.

Slant   To emphasize a particular aspect of a story.

Slick   A magazine printed on high-gloss heavy paper. Common industry term for mass circulation consumer magazines.

Slug   Abbreviated headline used to identify each story. In hot metal composition, a line of type.

Slush Pile   Unsolicited manuscripts that arrive at magazine editorial offices and that must be sorted, read, and accepted or returned.

Solicit   To commission an article, photographs, or other material from contributors.

Special-Interest Books   Magazines that are edited for a special subsection of the population; those interested in a hobby, craft, or other particular subject.

Split Run   A press run that is stopped to change an advertisement.

Staffer   Magazine staff member, writer, researcher, editor, and so on.

Style   A writer's individual expression through the special use of grammar, spelling, punctuation, and point of view.

Summary Lead   A lead that generally covers most of the "5 W's and the H:" Who, What, When, Where, Why, and How.

Syndicate   Organization that sells photographs or textual material to a variety of publications. A journalism wholesaler.

Taboo   Words, phrases, or subjects that cannot be published for moral or legal reasons.

Take   One page of copy. As more and more publications are written and edited on computers, *take* is likely to fade from writers' vocabularies. Originated (perhaps) in earlier years when a fast-breaking story was *taken* page by page from the writer to the backshop.

Tear Sheet   Articles or advertisements torn from a published newspaper or magazine and sent to writers or advertisers to verify that the material (article, ad) was published.

Teaser   Headline or blurb printed on the front cover of a magazine to interest readers in the magazine's content.

Think Piece   Interpretative article or essay slanted to make a reader think about the subject. Sometimes condescending term referring to such issues as oil production, taxes, and other hard-to-explain subjects.

Thirty (30)   Used on the last page of an article to indicate *the end*.

Tight   Issue that has little room for any additional material.

Title   Same as headline.

TK   Indicates material *to come*; not yet ready.

Typo   Typesetting mistake.

VDT   *Video Display Terminal.* Typewriter keyboard and television-type screen that allows a writer to compose his story on the keyboard, view it on the screen, edit it, and enter it into a computer for storage and retrieval.

250

Electronic storage and publication is said to constitute the third stage of communications, from mechanical to electric to electronic.

Vertical Magazine   Same as *special interest magazine*; not necessarily a magazine that is vertically designed.

White Space   Blank spaces on a page, left blank for design purposes.

Work-For-Hire   Writing that is assumed by a magazine to be done as staff work. Freelancers who sell material on a "work-for-hire" basis generally lose all other further legal rights to the work.

XXX   Used in copy to indicate *facts to come* (or needed); "There are XXX automobiles in Russia this year." Newsmagazine usage.

SPORTS TERMS

Archery

American Round   30 arrows from 60 yards, 50 yards, and 40 yards each.

Anchor Point   Point on the archer's face to which the bowstring or arrow nock is brought for each shot.

Archery Golf   Game similar to golf in which archers shoot for the target—that is, a small ball—and count the number of arrows required.

Arm Guard   Protective cover made of leather or other material that protects the forearm from the bowstring as the arrow is released.

Arrow Plate   Material set in a small ledge in the bow to protect the bow as the arrow slides across it.

Arrow Rest   The ledge on the bow that the arrow sits on prior to release. The arrow slides across it upon release.

Back   Side of the bow away from the string.

Backed Bow   Bow in which the back and belly are made of different material.

Belly   Side of the bow nearest the string.

Brace   To string the bow.

Broadhead   Arrow with large, flat point used in hunting.

Butt   Target backing, usually made of a bale of straw.

Cast   The distance a bow can shoot.

Cock Feather   Feather of a different color than the rest, which is set at right angles to the arrow head.

Columbia Round   For women   24 arrows shot at 50, 40, and 30 yards each.

Composite Bow   Bow that has pulleys at the top and bottom ends, which *lessen* the pull as the string is drawn back. State-of-the-art in archery.

Creeping   Letting the hand slowly inch forward momentarily before the arrow is shot. Will likely ruin the accuracy of the shot.

Double Round   Round shot twice.

Drift   Inaccurate shot because of crosswinds between the archer and the target.

Fletching Jig   Small mechanical machine to attach feathers to arrow.

Fletchings   Feathers attached to arrow to help it "fly" smoothly and accurately through the air.

Flight Arrow   Used for long-distance accuracy shooting; has small feathers.

Flight Shooting   Competition to shoot flight arrows the farthest.

Follow   Tendency of some bows to "warp" to their strung shape.

Form   The archer's stance and technique.

Full Draw   A bow is said to be at full draw when the archer pulls the arrow back completely, just before releasing.

Handle   Midsection of the bow, which the archer grips.

Hen Feathers   Feathers other than the cock feather.

Holding   Keeping the arrow at full bowdraw momentarily before shooting.

Limbs   Upper and lower parts of the bow, with the handle in between.

Loose   To release tension on the bow; to shoot the arrow.

National Round   For women   48 arrows shot at 60 yards, 24 at 50 yards.

Nock   Groove in the end of the arrow opposite the point; the bow string is inserted in the nock.

Nocking Point   Point on the bow string where the nock is placed. Usually marked by archer.

Overbowed   Using a bow that has a pull too strong for the archer.

Point Blank   Target distance so short that there is no allowance for trajectory of the arrow.

Quiver   Receptacle for holding arrows, usually leather, often decorated.

Range Finder   Mechanical device used to determine distance to target.

Reflex Box   Bow whose tips curve toward bow back when unstrung.

Round   Shooting a determined number of arrows at a target at a specific distance.

Shaft   Main part of the arrow.

Shooting Glove   Glove that protects the two fingers that hold the arrow nock on the bowstring.

Spine   The relative stiffness of an arrow.

Tackle   Archery equipment. Similar in usage to fishing tackle.

Target Face   Front of a target.

Trajectory   Path of an arrow in flight toward the target.

Underbowed   When a bow is too weak for the archer.

Vane   The feather of an arrow.

Weight   The pull of a bow in pounds or the weight of an arrow in grams.

Wide   Arrow that misses the target on either side.

Windage   Effect of wind on the arrow in flight.

BADMINTON

Backhand   Stroke made with the back of the hand toward the opponent's end of the court. Usually cross-body stroke.

Bird   See shuttlecock.

Clear   High shot that falls near the back line.

Cross-Body Stroke   A shot, in which the player's arm crosses in front of the torso.

Cross-Court Shot   Any shot that crosses the net on a diagonal path.

Drive   Hard shot that crosses the net horizontally.

Driven Clear   Any drive that goes to the back court, but not high enough for the opponent to kill.

Drop   A shot that falls close to the net.

Fault   A violation of the rules that involves the loss of a point or the loss of a serve.

Forehand   A shot made with the palm of the hand facing the opponent; a shot that is not a cross-body shot.

Hand-Out   The loss of a serve.

Let   A shot that hits the top of the net, but falls on the opponent's side of the court.

Over-Head Stroke   Shot made over the player's head.

Rally   To return the shuttlecock several times without scoring a point.

Receiver   Player who receives a serve.

Server   Player who puts the shuttlecock in play.

Setting the Game   Deciding how many further points will win the game, when it is tied.

Short Serve   Serve that barely clears the net, but lands in the opponent's court.

Shuttlecock   Feathered object—now usually plastic—that is batted back and forth across a net in the game.

Smash   Powerful overhead stroke that sends the shuttlecock over the net and in a downward arc.

Toss Serve   To throw the shuttlecock into the air so it comes down to be served across the net. Similar to a tennis serve.

Ballooning

Aeronaut   Person who pilots or acts as crew-member in an aerostat.

Aerostat   A flying machine using a container filled with hot air or gas that is supported by its bouyancy relative to the air surrounding it.

Airspeed   Speed in flight relative to the air surrounding the vehicle. Airplanes and powered dirigibles have air speed. Hot air balloons, which drift with the wind, have only ground speed.

Airway   An air corridor designated by the Federal Aviation Administration (FAA), controlled by Air Traffic Control (ATC) and marked by radio navigation beacons.

Airworthy   The state of being ready to fly.

Altimeter   A barometer that measures height above sea level.

Altitude   Generally cited as height above sea level, but may be given as height above ground level, abbreviated A.G.L.

Annual   Inspection that must be conducted every 12 months to certify airworthiness. Also applies to airplanes.

Apex   The top of a balloon.

Approach   The act of losing altitude to come to rest on the ground. Also applies to airplanes.

ATC   *Air Traffic Control.* The federal-government-sponsored agency that regulates air traffic, especially in and around large airports.

Attitude   A position relative to the horizon.

Ballast   Weights used to maintain a flight altitude. Now seldom found in hot air balloons.

Balloon   Lighter-than-air vehicle that obtains its "lift" from hot air or a gas such as hydrogen, helium, or methane. Also refers to the envelope itself, which contains the air or gas.

Barograph   A barometer that shows variations in air pressure as altitude or height above a specific point, on a paper graph.

Basket   Same as *gondola.*

Blast Off   Quick ascent.

Blast Valve   A valve control that sends full pressure through the balloon's burner system, to provide maximum hot air for lift.

Blimp   A nonrigid or semirigid airship.

Burner   Heating device that mixes air and butane or propane to produce a hot flame as a heat source for lifting hot air balloons.

Burner Mount   Frame that supports the burner unit in the gondola.

Ceiling   The height above ground level of a cloud base.

Champagne   Sometimes carried in a gondola to celebrate a first flight, or a solo flight, or sometimes given to a farmer to placate him for a forced landing in a farm field.

Checklist   A list of safety items to check before ascent, to make sure the balloon is airworthy. Also applies to airplane safety.

Cross-Country Flight   Flight between two points.

Crown   Same as *apex.*

Dirigible   An aerostat that can be steered.

Downwind   Flying in the same direction as the wind is blowing.

Drag Line   Line formerly used with dirigibles and blimps. The line was held by crew members on the ground to prevent premature ascent.

Drift   A flight away from a specific target designation, caused by crosswinds along the flight path.

Envelope   The fabric part of the balloon, that holds the hot air or gas.

Federal Aviation Administration (FAA)   The federal government agency that regulates air traffic.

Forced Landing   Landing accomplished in an emergency situation.

Gondola   The lightweight basket that contains the crew and instruments for a flight. Formerly wicker, now usually aluminum.

Ground Speed   The speed of a craft in flight, as measured in relation to miles-per-hour on the ground.

Inflator   Gas or electric blower that forces hot air into the balloon envelope on the ground, to inflate the envelope.

Loft A balloon repair shop.

Lofting The act of landing in which the gondola hits the ground, bounces into the air, then hits the ground again.

Logbook A pilot's book of all flights taken. Also applies to flying, sky diving, and boating.

North Pole Same as *apex*.

Preflight Inspection before ascent to check that all parts of the envelope and gondola are airworthy. Also applies to airplanes.

Pyrometer Device that measures the temperature of air or gas inside the top of the envelope. The pyrometer will warn if the inside temperature is getting too high—above 250° to 300° (Fahrenheit). Excessive heat will damage the envelope fabric.

Red Line Warning line on a pyrometer that shows when the inside temperatures of the envelope are too hot.

Regulator Valve Adjustable valve that controls the fuel flow through the burner system.

Rip Cord A cord that is attached to the balloon envelope, that allows a slit to open to vent hot air or gas, to allow the balloon to deflate.

Skirt Fabric around the bottom edge of the balloon.

Solo Single flight; flight without passengers.

Suspension Lines Lines that connect the balloon envelope to the gondola.

Temperature Differential Difference between temperature inside the envelope and outside.

Tether Line used to hold a balloon near the ground.

Touch-and-Go Series of landings and takeoffs without a complete stop on the ground.

Variometer Device that measures that rate of rise and descent of a ballon.

Weigh Off Slow ascent of a balloon.

Baseball

Aboard On base.

Advance To move to the next base.

All-Pro Player elected to a team of exceptional players. (Also appropriate in basketball, football, and other sports.)

All-Star Same as *All-Pro*.

All-Time The best who ever played a game at that particular position. (Appropriate for almost all team sports.)

Alley Imaginary line or lane between out-fielders playing in their normal positions.

American League One of two major professional major leagues, now split into three divisions. In the East Division are   Baltimore, Boston, New York (Yankees), Tampa Bay, and Toronto. In the Central Division are   Chicago (White Sox), Cleveland, Detroit, Kansas City, and Minnesota. In the West Division are   Los Angeles (Angels), Oakland, Seattle, and Texas. Abbreviated AL.

Artificial Turf   Synthetic grass substitute, sold under a variety of brand names. Also called *carpet*.

Assist   Credited to a player who throws to a base to aid in an out.

Babe Ruth Baseball   Non profit organization that sponsors summer baseball for youth aged 9–18.

Backstop   A screen that protects spectators behind the plate from pitches that might get away from the catcher.

Bad Hop   Awkward bounce that allows a ball to get away from a fielder.

Balk   Illegal act by the pitcher that allows all runners on base to advance one base. A balk is technically a pause during the normal pitching motion.

Baseball Annie   Woman attracted to baseball players. Also known as a groupie.

Basket Catch   Catch made with the glove held at waist level with the palm up.

Battery   The pitcher and catcher as a team.

Battery-Mates   Same as *battery*.

Batting Average   Number of hits divided by the number of times at bat.

Batting helmet   Protective hatlike helmet now required of all professional teams, to prevent injury to the head by a pitched ball. Protective helmets were first used in 1941 by the Brooklyn Dodgers.

Bean Ball   Ball thrown to deliberately hit (or just barely miss) a batter's head. In 1920, a ball thrown by Carl Mayes of the Yankees hit and killed Ray Chapman, of the Cleveland Indians, which has been baseball's only fatality. Also called *brushback* and *knockdown pitch*.

Bench Jockey   A player who seldom plays. He "rides the bench."

Big League   Either or both professional leagues.

Bleachers   Seats in the outfield area, usually cheap seats, in an area of a stadium without a roof.

Bottom of an Inning   The last half of an inning.

Box Score   A condensed report of a game that shows the lineups for both teams, runs batted in, score, and so on. The baseball equivalent of shorthand reporting.

Breaking Ball   A ball that curves in or out as it crosses the plate area.

Bronx Cheer   A "razzberry" sound made by a spectator. Usually made in contempt.

Bullpen   Area behind the outer fences of a baseball field where relief pitchers warm up and wait for their possible entry into the game.

Bunt   A ball that is not swung at. The batter holds the bat horizontally and taps the ball into the infield.

Bush League   Minor leagues. Carries the connotation of amateurish, unprofessional, not yet top-flight.

Cactus League   Spring training league that plays in the Southwest.

Cellar   The lowest team statistically in a league's standings is said to be "in the cellar."

Charley Horse   A slight muscle pull or strain, usually in the leg muscles. Also appropriate in football, track and field, and other sports.

(To) Choke Up   To be unable to play to the best of a player's ability because of fear or tension.

To choke up on a bat   To hold it higher than the normal grip position.

Clean-Up   The fourth position in the batting order.

Clothesline   Baseball hit in such a straight line that clothes could be hung on the level.

Contact Hitter   A player known for an ability to hit the ball regularly for base hits, although probably unspectacular ones.

Count   The number of balls and strikes a player has when he is batting.

Cup of Coffee   A brief visit to the major leagues by a minor league player. He is said to have visited the majors just "long enough for a cup of coffee."

Curve   A ball thrown in such a way that it curves in flight toward the batter's box.

Cy Young Award   An award made annually to the pitcher who has made an outstanding record that year. Voted by the Baseball Writer's Association.

Designated Hitter   A player who comes to bat for a team, but who does not field. Allowed in the American league, but not in the National League. Allowed during AL home games in the World Series. Abbreviated DH.

Diamond   The infield part of a baseball field.

Disabled List   A player who is injured and can not play is placed on the disabled list. Also appropriate in football.

Doctor   To secretly treat a baseball to gain an advantage.

Doctored Bat   To treat a bat so it is not of regulation weight, for an advantage to the batter. A doctored bat is usually made lighter by drilling a hole in the bat and covering the hole so the doctored area cannot be seen.

Double-Dip   Two games played in one day, a doubleheader.

Double Play   Two consecutive outs during the same play.

Downtown   A home-run ball that clears the outfield fences and flies into the seats is said to have gone downtown.

Dugout   An area where team benches are located, usually slightly lower than the spectator's seats so as not to block the view of the field. One is located on the first base side of the field, the other on the third base side.

Earned Run   Run that scores as a result of base hits, stolen bases, sacrifice hits, walks, hit batter, wild pitches, or balks and before fielders have had a chance to retire the side.

Error   Is charged against a player when a misplay (ball that is dropped, etc.) causes the play to continue, when without the error, the play would have been over.

Extra Innings   A game that goes beyond the normal nine innings to break a tie.

Fair Ball   A hit ball that remains inside the playing area of the field.

Farm Team   A minor league team associated with a major league team is said to be a farm team because that's where major league players are "grown" or developed.

Fast Ball   A baseball thrown at 100 mph or more.

Fielder's Choice   When a defensive player chooses to retire a base runner previously on base, rather than the batter who hit the ball. It is considered an at-bat and works against the hitter's batting average.

Fielding Average   Put-outs, assists, and errors, divided into put-outs and assists.

Fireman   A relief pitcher who wins games in the late innings by putting out the opposition's "fire."

Flake   A psychologically unreliable ball player.

Foul Ball   Ball that rolls off the field of play before reaching first base or third base, or lands off the field of play past first or third base.

Foul Tip   A batted ball that fields directly into the catcher's mit and is caught by the catcher. This is a fair ball.

Frame   An inning.

Free Agent   A player not under contract to any club and who can negotiate a contract with any club in the league.

Fungo Bat   Lightweight bat used by coaches or managers to hit infield practice.

Gamer   A player who plays with an injury.

Goat   Nickname for a player who loses a crucial game.

Go Down Looking   To take a called third strike for an out without swinging.

Go Down Swinging   To swing and miss at a third strike and be called out.

Golden Glove Award   An award made every year to the fielders with the best performance at each position.

Grand Slam   A home run hit with the bases loaded, thus scoring four runs.

Grapefruit League   Spring training league, played largely in Florida.

Ground-rule double   A hit that bounces over the outfield fence, allowing a batter to automatically go to second base.

Hit   Ball hit in such a way that the batter may reach base safely or preceding base runners may reach an additional base or bases safely.

Hook Slide   To slide into second or third base or home plate while avoiding a player's tag, but while keeping one foot pointed toward the base.

Hot Corner   Third base.

Iceman   A relief pitcher who can "ice" an opponent's "hot streak." Same as *fireman*.

Iron Mike   Pitching machine that is used during batting practice.

Infield Fly   Fly ball with runners on first and second, or on first, second, and third, that is hit into the infield and that can be handled by the infielders for an out.

In the Hole   Unfavorable position for the batter. If the batter has two strikes against him and no balls called, he is said to be in the hole. Also, the batter positioned behind the on-deck batter.

Junk Pitch   An unorthodox pitch or slower than normal pitch.

Juiced   Slang for on steroids or human growth hormone.

Junk Man   Pitcher who relies on junk pitches for effectiveness.

Knockdown Pitch   A pitch deliberately thrown at the batter's head or thrown so close to the batter that he must fall to the ground to avoid being hit by the pitch. Same as *bean ball.*

K   Indicates a strikeout in a baseball box score. A backward K indicates a watched third strike.

Lead   A few steps away from a base taken by a runner toward the next base.

Line Drive   A ball hit in a straight line.

Lineup Card   Card given by the manager to the umpire that lists all the players to be used during a game by their position in the batting order.

Little League   A minor league for youngsters that plays on a field that is one third smaller than normal. Now headquartered in Williamsport, Pa., the Little League plays a World Series every year.

Load the Bases   To have runners on first, second, and third base at the same time.

Long Reliever   Relief pitcher who can pitch five innings or more.

Magic Number   The number of games that a particular team must win to win a divisional race and thus qualify for playoffs leading to the World Series.

Major League   Refers to either or both the National League or the American League.

Minor League   Any league other than the two major leagues.

MVP   Most Valuable Player. Award given to the outstanding player in each league each year. Awarded by the Baseball Writers Association.

National League   One of two professional major leagues, now divided into three divisions. In the East Division are   Atlanta, Florida, New York (Mets), Philadelphia, and Washington. In the Central Division are   Chicago (Cubs), Cincinnati, Houston, Milwaukee, Pittsburgh, and St. Louis. In the West Division are   Arizona, Colorado, Los Angeles (Dodgers), San Diego, and San Francisco. Abbreviated NL.

Nightcap   Second game of a doubleheader, often played at night.

No-hitter   A game in which a pitcher does not allow any base hits by the opposing team.

Off-Speed Pitch   Slower than normal pitch.

On Deck   Player waiting to bat next.

Outfield   That part of a baseball field beyond the base paths that connect first, second, and third bases.

Out In Front Of   To swing too early at a pitch.

Passed Ball   Is charged against the catcher when he drops the ball or loses possession of it and that loss causes a runner to advance a base or bases. Called an error if the catcher drops a called third strike; the player is allowed to advance to first base.

Pennant   A league divisional champion team. So called because the team is allowed to fly the league flag or pennant during the next season.

Perfect Game   A game in which a pitcher allows no opposing players to safely reach base.

Pick Off   To throw a runner out with a quick throw to a fielder who tags the runner out, off base.

Pinch Hit   To hit in place of another player; to substitute for.

Pinch Run   To run in place of another player.

Pitcher of Record   The pitcher who is officially charged with winning or losing a game.

Pitcher's Duel   A close game in which opposing pitchers have both performed well.

Pitcher's Mound   A slightly elevated part of a playing field that the pitcher throws from. Generally elevated 10 inches higher than normal ground level.

Pitch Out   A pitch that is thrown wide of the plate so a catcher can throw to put out a runner who is off base.

Play-by-Play   A running account of a game in progress.

Playoff   Games conducted at the end of a season to determine a league championship.

Pop Fly   A high fly ball.

Portsider   Same as *southpaw*.

Put-Out   Credited to fielder who handles a ball in a play that results in an out for a baserunner.

Rabbit Ball   A ball that bounces or hops in a lively manner.

Rain Check   A ticket stub that can be used again if a game is rained out and replayed later.

Rain Out   To rain hard enough to cause a game to be postponed.

Ribbie   Abbreviation for *Runs Batted In*. Important offensive statistic for ball players.

Relief Pitcher   A pitcher who does not start a game, but who comes in to relieve the starting pitcher in late innings.

Retire the Side   To put out three batters to end an opposing team's turn at bat.

Rhubarb   A noisy argument.

Rookie   An inexperienced player, a novice.

Rookie of the Year   An award made by the Baseball Writers of America to the outstanding first-year players in the American and National Leagues.

Rosin Bag   A bag that contains powdered rosin. This is handled by the pitcher between pitches to allow him to keep a firm grip on the ball.

Rotation   The regular order in which pitchers are used by a team.

Run Batted In   A run that scores because of a hit by another player. Also known as an RBI or ribbie.

Run Down   To chase a runner between bases and tag him for an out.

Running Squeeze   Runner on third base begins running toward home plate, as the ball is pitched, hoping that the batter will bunt safely and allow him to score.

Sack   The first, second, and third bases.

Sacrifice Bunt   Batter bunts the ball to advance a baserunner and is called out while the baserunner advances safely.

Sacrifice Fly   Ball hit to the outfield that results in an out for the batter, but a successful advance for a runner on base.

Safety Squeeze   Runner on third heads for home plate when the ball is bunted. Slightly different than running squeeze.

Sandlot Ball   School yard baseball, or any other informally organized game.

Save   When a relief pitcher wins a game begun by a starting pitcher, he is said to have saved the game.

Set Down   Same as *retire the side*.

Seventh-Inning Stretch   Spectators' tradition of standing and stretching before the home team comes to bat in the seventh inning. Spectators usually go to the restrooms, get a beer, or otherwise take a break.

Shake Off a Sign   Occurs when a pitcher refuses to pitch a specific type of ball that the catcher signals him to pitch.

Shoestring Catch   Catch of a ball made at the shoe level. Also appropriate in football.

Short Reliever   Relief pitcher used for only a few innings, or a relief pitcher who is effective for only a few innings.

Shut Out   To prevent an opposing team from scoring through an entire game.

Sign   Signal shown to the pitcher by the catchers to indicate what kind of ball to throw next. First base and third base coaches may also signal to runners and batters, and the manager may signal to his team from the dugout.

Sinker   Pitch that drops vertically as it crosses the plate.

Slugger   Hitter known for many hits and runs.

Southpaw   Left-handed player. Usually refers to left-handed pitcher.

Speed Gun   Portable radar unit used to determine the speed of a pitched ball.

Spitball   Illegal pitch caused by the pitcher adding some foreign material, such as spit or vaseline, to the ball.

Spring Training   Time before the start of major league season in which players regain playing abilities lost during the off season. Major leagues also test minor league players during this time. Generally starts in March and ends just prior to the season.

Stand-Up Double   A hit that allows the runner to reach second base without sliding.

Stand-Up Triple   A hit that allows the runner to reach third base without sliding.

Stolen base   Runner advances successfully without the aid of a base hit, put-out, walk, force-out, fielder's choice, passed ball, wild pitch, or balk.

Strike Zone   The area that the pitcher must throw in to successfully throw strikes. Generally from the hitter's armpits to his knees, when he is in a normal batting position.

Stuff   A pitcher's effectiveness; either he has good stuff or not.

Switch Hitter   Player who bats both right- and left-handed.

Tape-Measure Homer   Long home run that might be measured for a record.

Texas Leaguer   Fly ball hit just over the head of the shortstop or second baseman, just barely into the outfield.

Three and One   Three balls and one strike on the batter.

Tools of Ignorance   Mask, glove, and pads used by a catcher.

Top of the Inning   The first half of an inning.

Top of the Order   The first batter in the batting order.

Triple   A hit that allows the batter to reach third base successfully.

Triple Play   A play in which three baserunners are put out on one batted ball.

Twin Bill   Same as *doubleheader*.

Twilight Doubleheader   A doubleheader with the first game scheduled about twilight.

Unearned Run   Any run that scores on the basis of an error by an opposing player.

Walk   To be awarded first base because of four balls pitched by the pitcher.

Wild Pitch   Pitch thrown so that the catcher cannot control it.

Wind-Up   The motion of a pitcher prior to releasing the ball.

Winter Ball   Organized baseball played during the off season.

World Series   A best-of-seven game series played by the champion teams of the American and National Leagues.

Basketball

Air Ball   Shot that misses the basket and the backboard and hits "only air."

All-Court Press   To closely guard the offense all over the court.

Alley-Oop Shot   Pass made by one player to another player on the same team who is waiting under the basket to instantly tip the ball in for a score.

Assist   A pass from one player to another, which results in a quick score.

Backboard   Flat 4- × 6-foot surface, suspended above and perpendicular to the floor, to which the basket rim is attached. In some cases, the backboard may be fan shaped and approximately 35 × 54 inches, with a 29-inch radius. Players may bank the ball off the backboard to score.

Back Court   The half of the court that a team defends.

Ball Control   The ability to maintain possession of the ball through dribbling or passing.

Bank Shot   A shot that bounces off the backboard into the basket.

Basket   An 18-inch metal ring with a suspended cord net. Players attempt to shoot the ball through the ring to score.

Blocking   To impede an opponent. (Blocking is a foul.)

Boxing Out   The position of a defensive player under the basket that does not allow an offensive player a favorable position for a shot or rebound.

Buzzer Shot   Shot that is made as the buzzer goes off, signaling the end of the first half or the end of the game.

Center   The player responsible for the center jump and for playing the "pivot position" near the basket. Usually the tallest player on the team.

Charging   Contact against an opponent by a player with the ball. (Charging is a foul.)

Charity Line   Free-throw line. Cliché that should be avoided.

Charity Shot   Free throw. Cliché that should be avoided.

Clutch Player   Player who can be depended on to score in a crucial moment.

Cold   A player or team temporarily unable to score.

Collapse   When two defensive players converge on an offensive player the moment he receives the ball.

Conversion   A successful free throw.

Corner Men   Forwards who are key rebounding players.

Defensive Boards   The backboard of a defending team's basket.

Double Dribble   A dribble that is resumed after having once been stopped; this is a rules violation. The ball goes to the opposite team.

Double Figures   To score 10 points or more during a game.

Double Foul   When two players on opposite teams foul each other at the same time.

Double Team   To guard one offensive player with two defensive players at the same time.

Down Court   The end of the court that a team is defending.

Draw a Foul   To behave so as to deliberately be fouled by an opponent.

Dribble   To control the ball by bouncing it repeatedly on the floor.

Drive   Powerful effort toward the basket.

Dunk   To jump up and push the ball through the basket from above.

Fade-Away Shot   To shoot while moving away from the basket.

Fast Break   To drive toward the basket before the defensive team has a chance to set up in position to block the drive or the shot.

Follow-in   To follow the progress of the ball to be position for a rebound.

Forward   Player who operates to the side of the offensive back and who is usually a good rebounder.

Foul   Violation of a rule, which results in a free throw by the opposing team. Fouls generally include   blocking, charging, pushing, holding, tripping, illegal substitution, and delaying the game.

Free Throw   Opportunity to score one point unhindered from the foul line as a result of a foul by the opposing team.

Freeze   An attempt to keep possession of the ball by one team, to maintain a lead in the score, or to dribble to kill time on the clock.

Front Court   The half of the court that contains the team's own basket. Opposite of *back court*.

Full-Court Press   Same as *all-court press*.

Garbage Shot   Any easy or uncontested shot.

Give and Go   To pass to a teammate and drive to the basket to await a return pass, which would set up a scoring opportunity.

Goaltending   Any interference with the ball when it is in its downward arc above the rim of the basket, or trapping the ball against the backboard.

Guard   Usually a small player who brings the ball into the forecourt and passes to the forwards or the center for a shot.

Gunner   Player who shoots obsessively at the basket.

Hardship Case   A college basketball player who enters the professional basketball draft before his college eligibility is used up, pleading that family poverty necessitates an early entry into professional basketball. Also called *poverty case*.

Held Ball   When two opposing players each hold the ball and neither can gain complete possession.

Holding   To prevent an opponent from moving freely. Usually a foul, if caught by the officials.

Hook Shot   High arcing shot made by swinging the arm from behind the back, up over the shoulder.

Hot Hand   Player who temporarily has a high shooting average.

Inside Man   The center of the team, usually the tallest player, who plays with his back to the basket, then jumps for a rebound.

In Your Face   Player who is guarding his opponent in a close and intimidating manner. Often refers to schoolyard tactics.

Inside Game   Refers to maneuvers close to the basket.

Jump Ball   To put the ball in play by tossing it in the air between two opposing players; the one who can jump up highest for it takes possession.

Lay-Up Shot   A shot made close to the basket that bounces off the backboard into the basket.

Loose Ball   A ball that is in play but not in possession of either team.

Man-to-Man   Defensive play in which each defensive man has a special offensive player to guard.

Mid-majors   Term used to describe conferences that are not part of the six BCS confferences in college football. The 31 mid-major conferences include the Missouri Valley, the Mid-American, and the Atlantic 10.

Multiple Foul   Two or more fouls committed at the same time.

NBA   National Basketball Association.

Net   The mesh sleeve that is attached to the basket rim.

Offensive Boards   The backboard rebounding area of a team's offensive basket.

One-and-One   A rule in college basketball in which a player receives the right to a second foul shot if the first foul shot is successful. This rule is also used in women's and high school basketball.

One-on-One   A situation in which a specific offensive player is guarded by a specific defensive player, or when a specific offensive player challenges a specific defensive player.

Open   A player who is not guarded by an opponent or who has an unguarded path to the basket.

Outlet Pass   Player who grabs a rebound and passes to a teammate to establish a fast break.

Outside Shooter   A player who has the ability to make long shots.

Overhead Shot   A two-handed shot in which the ball is released over the player's head.

Overtime   A 5-minute period of play to decide a game that is tied at the end of regulation time. Abbreviated OT.

Pass   To move to the ball to a player on the same team by throwing it across the court.

Personal Foul   Rules violation when a player contacts an opponent when the ball is in play.

Pivot   To take one or more than one step with one foot, while in possession of the ball. The other foot must remain stationary.

Play for One   To possess the ball and to shoot when there is time for only one shot.

Post   Same as *post man*.

Post Man   Player who stands in a particular position on the court. The high post is near the free-throw line; the low post is close to the basket. He coordinates offensive plays from that position. Also called pivot man, because his play is crucial to the play.

Pressing Defense   Defense that attempts to break an offensive drive by closely guarding the ball.

Rebound   To attempt to gain possession of the ball when it has bounced off the basket or the backboard without going through the net.

Rim   Metal hoop, 18 inches wide, through which the ball must fall to score. The net is attached to the rim.

Run-and-Gun   Aggressive type of play in which a team frequently runs the length of the court for a fast break. Also called *run-and-shoot*.

Screen   To protect a teammate in the act of shooting by standing between him and an opponent.

Set Play   A play in which offensive positions are deliberately taken; opposite of run-and-gun play.

Shave Points   To illegally limit the number of points scored, to affect a bet on a basketball game.

Shot Clock   Clock that indicates that the team with the ball has a time limit to take a shot.

Sky Hook   High hook shot that is impossible to block.

Slam Dunk   Hard dunk shot.

Stall   To keep possession of the ball to maintain a lead or to keep the opposing team from gaining control of the ball. Usually occurs when a team is trying to run out the clock.

Technical Foul   Foul committed by a player not in possession of the ball, or a foul committed by a coach, or an unsportsmanlike call while the ball is dead. Often abbreviated T.

Thirty Second Clock   Same as *shot clock*.

Three Point Play   Foul committed during the act of successfully scoring; the player then gets one foul shot after the basket.

Three-point shot   A basket made from behind the three-point line.

Throw In Act of beginning play by throwing the ball into the court from an out-of-bounds position.

Tip-Off The jump ball used to begin play.

Toss-Up A jump ball.

Tower See tree.

Traveling To take more than the maximum steps allowed while in possession of the ball at the end of a dribble.

Tree A center who is so tall and powerful that he cannot be moved or outrebounded.

Trailer Player who follows behind a player with the ball.

Turnover To lose the ball to the opposition because of a mistake, a foul, or a stolen ball.

Two Against One Two offensive players playing against one defensive player, or vice versa.

Two-Time Same as *double dribble*.

Upcourt The end of the court that one team is attacking.

Zone Particular area of the court.

Zone Defense Type of play in which each player is responsible for a particular part of the court and responsible for the play when the action enters that zone.

Zone Press Type of play in which a player is responsible for close man-to-man coverage when the action is in his zone.

Boating and Fishing

Aft Towards, near, or at the stern of a boat.

Back Cast Drawing the rod back, the first movement in the cast.

Backlash Line that becomes tangled by rolling over itself in the reel during the cast, because there is too much play in the reel. (Note Some modern reels have an anti-backlash mechanism built in.)

Bait Natural or artificial lures to attract fish.

Bait-Casting Placing a natural or artificial lure in the area of fish by using a rod and reel.

Ballast Weight, usually metal, placed low in the boat, or externally, on the keel, to provide stability.

Batten A light wooden or plastic strip inserted into a pocket in a sail to help shape it.

Beam The width of a boat at its widest.

Berth A bunk or sleeping place in the cabin of a boat.

Boom A spar that is used to extend the foot of a sail.

Bow The forward part of a boat.

Bucktail A fly used in bass fishing.

Clew The lower aft corner of a fore-and-aft sail or either corner of a spinnaker.

Cork Arbor The part of the reel to which the line is attached.

Cowling   A cover over the engine of a boat.

Dry Fly Fishing   Casting a fly so it resembles an insect on the water.

Ferrules   Metal connections between sections of a take-apart rod.

Flies   Artificial lures that resemble insects.

Fly-Casting   Placing a fly in the area of fish by using a rod and reel.

Fore   Toward or at the bow of a boat.

Fore-and-Aft   In line from bow to stern; on, or parallel to, the centerline.

Forward Cast   Forward movement of a rod that places the lure into the water. Final step in back cast-forward cast movement.

Furl   To roll a sail and secure it to its yard or boom.

Gaff   Small hook used to bring fish on board a boat.

Genoa   A larger jib used in light breezes.

Gimbal   A device consisting of a pair of rings pivoted on axes at right angles to each other so that one is free to swing within the other   A ship's compass will keep a horizontal position when suspended in gimbals.

Guides   Small loops on the rod. The line runs through these guides.

Halyard   A rope, wire, or chain by which a sail, flag, or yard is hoisted.

Head   Toilet on board a ship.

Helm   The steering apparatus.

Hooking the Fish   Setting the hook in the fish after it takes the bait or lure.

Hull   The frame or body of a ship, excluding the spars, sails, and rigging.

Inboard   Motor mounted inside the boat or ship.

Jib   A fore-and-aft triangular sail, set forward of the mast.

Keel   The fixed underwater part of a sailing boat used to prevent sideways drift and to provide stability.

Knot   A measure of speed   one nautical mile (6060.2 feet) per hour.

Lanyard   A short line or rope used to attach one object or item to another.

Leader   Material that connects the lure or hook to the line.

Leech   The aftermost edge of a fore-and-aft sail; both side edges of a square sail.

Lures   Artificial or natural bait used to attract fish.

Mast   A pole or system of attached poles, placed vertically on a vessel, used to support the sails.

Net   Mesh device on a metal frame to pull fish out of the water.

Outboard   Motor attached to the stern of a vessel.

Plane   To gain hydrodynamic lift as the boat lifts up on its bow wave.

Port   Left side of a ship when looking forward.

Reel   Mechanical device that winds or unwinds line for fishing.

Reel Set   Part of the rod handle to which the reel is attached.

Rig   The form in which a vessel's mast, spars, and sails are arranged.

Rudder   Movable underwater part of a vessel used for steering and to prevent side-slipping.

Sheet   The line attached to the clew of a sail, used to trim it. When the sheets are brought in and made fast they are said to be sheeted together.

Ship   Vessel large enough to carry its own life-boat or lifeboats.

Shrouds Wires that support the mast on either side; part of the standing or permanent rigging.

Spar Long wooden beam, generally rounded and used for supporting or extending the sails of a ship.

Spinnaker A lightweight three-cornered sail, set flying from the masthead and controlled by sheets from each clew.

Spinner Artificial lure that spins as it is drawn through the water.

Spoons Artificial bait that generally resemble kitchen spoons.

Starboard The right side of a vessel when looking forward.

Stern The aftermost part of a vessel.

Still Fishing Fishing with bait held motionless in the water.

Strike When a fish grabs the bait or hook.

Tack (noun) The forward lower corner of a fore-and-aft sail. Or *to tack* (verb): To turn the bow of a boat through the wind so that it blows across the opposite side.

Tackle Fishing gear—rod and reel.

Tip Smallest end of the rod.

Torque A force that produces a twisting, rotating, or spinning motion.

Trapeze A support used by the crew of a racing boat to enable them to move their weight outboard.

Trim The adjustment of the sails of a vessel.

Trolling To fish with a moving line.

Winch A crank with a handle.

Windlass A device used for hauling or hoisting, usually for sails.

Yacht Vessel used for private cruising, racing, or other noncommercial purposes.

Bowling

Alley Same as *lane*.

Anchor Last bowler on a team.

Approach The act of taking 3, 4, or 5 steps, swinging the arm and releasing the ball toward the pins.

Beer Frame Frame during a bowling game in which the player with the lowest score buys beer for the team.

Box See *frame*.

Brooklyn Ball that crosses the lane and hits the 1–2 pins first, instead of the 1–3 pins.

Creeper A ball that rolls slower than normal.

Double Two strikes in succession.

Foul To go beyond the foul line during the approach.

Foul Line Line that marks the end of the approach and the beginning of the lane. To step over the line during the approach results in a foul.

Frame Box in which the scores are marked 10 frames make a game.

Gutter   Channel on each side of a bowling lane in which balls can drop and roll into the pit without touching any pins.

Gutter Ball   Ball that drops into side gutter without hitting any pins.

Handicap   Bonus score or adjustment to an individual's score or team score, based on averages.

Head Pin   No. 1 pin.

Hook   Ball that breaks to the left for a right-handed bowler.

Kegler   German for bowler.

Lane   Bowling alley   41 inches wide and 60 feet long from the foul line to the head pin, usually made of wood. An additional 16 feet, consisting of the bowler's approach to the foul line and from the head pin to the end of the lane, is made of maple, the lane of pine. Formerly called *alley.*

Line   Complete game scored on a scoring sheet.

Loft   To loft a ball means the bowler releases it too late; the ball arcs into the air and hits the lane heavily, instead of sliding onto the lane from the bowler's grip.

Mark   A strike or spare in a particular frame.

Pit   Area behind the lane where all pins are scooped for resetting.

Open Frame   Frame in which the bowler has made no strike or spare.

Pocket   Space between the 1 pin and the 2–3 pins.

Sleeper   A standing pin hidden from the bowler's view.

Spare   All pins knocked down on two balls.

Spot   Aiming point on the alley.

Strike   All pins knocked down on the first ball.

Three Hundred (300)   Perfect game.

Boxing

Ali Shuffle   Rapid series of front-and-back foot movements made famous by Muhammad Ali. The advantage was said to be tactical—to show his opponent he was in control of the fight and could still move quickly.

Answer the Bell   To get up from a corner to begin fighting when the bell sounds. If a fighter fails to answer the bell, he is declared the loser in that round.

Apron   The floor outside the boxing ring. It is approximately 2 feet wide.

Arm Puncher   A boxer whose strength is only in his arms; lacks the power of his body behind his punches.

Arm Weary   Tired of throwing punches.

Backpedal   To retreat across the ring.

Bang   To punch hard, without finesse.

Beat the Count   To get up before the count is over.

Bell   A bell that is rung to indicate the beginning and the end of a round.

Below the Belt   A punch that lands below the top of the hipbones, generally in the crotch. If a *low blow* is deliberate, a fighter may be disqualified.

Bleeder A fighter who cuts easily.

Bob and Weave To move side to side and up and down to evade an opponent.

Body Punch Blow delivered to the body of an opponent; that is, the abdomen or ribs.

Bolo Punch Punch that begins in a wide arc from below the hips swinging upward. Popularized in the early 1940s by middleweight champion Ceferino Garcia, who described the punch as comparable to the swing of a bolo knife cutting through the jungles. Now thought of as any wildly exaggerated punch that begins low.

Break To withdraw from a clinch when ordered to do so by the referee.

Bum Unskilled fighter, often thought of as being *punch-drunk*.

Can't Lay a Glove On A boxer so clever defensively that his opponent can't hit him.

Canvas The floor of a boxing ring.

Carry (To Carry a Fight) To hold back from ending a fight to make a weak opponent look better than he is.

Cauliflower Ear A deformed ear; caused by too many blows to the ear.

Challenger A fighter who fights a reigning champion.

Class Same as *division*.

Clean Break To separate from a clinch.

Clinch To hold an opponent with both arms so neither fighter can score cleanly.

Club Fighter A small-time boxer with mediocre skills; a fighter who fights mainly in local clubs.

Coldcock To knock out an opponent with one blow.

Combination Two or more punches in rapid succession.

Contender A fighter good enough to be a challenger. Popularized in a speech by Marlon Brando in the film *On The Waterfront*, "I cudda been a con-tenda …"

Corner Any of the four corners of a boxing ring, or, the particular corner assigned to each fighter.

Cornerman One of the assistants allowed to be in a fighter's corner between rounds.

Count Counting 10 seconds after a fighter has been knocked down. If a fighter does not arise after the 10 count, the opponent wins the fight by a knockout.

Counter To respond to an opponent's punch by returning a punch.

Counterpuncher A boxer who prefers to wait for an opponent's punch to deliver a punch.

Cover Up To protect the body and head from an opponent's punches, with the arms.

Cross A punch delivered over and above an opponent's lead, such as a right cross.

Cut Man Assistant in a fighter's corner who is responsible for stopping cuts or bleeding.

Cut Off The Ring   To move sideways across the ring to reduce the room an opponent can maneuver in.

Dance   To use rapid footwork.

Decision   To win a fight based on the number of points scored by judges witnessing a fight, in which there is no *knockdown or technical knockdown*.

Distance   The maximum number of rounds in a fight. (*To go the distance*, to fight 12 rounds in a 12-round fight.)

Division   A category of fighters based on weight. In general, these are the professional divisions:

Flyweight	112 pounds
Bantamweight	118 pounds
Featherweight	126 pounds
Junior Lightweight	130 pounds
Lightweight	135 pounds
Junior Welterweight	140 pounds
Welterweight	147 pounds
Junior Middleweight	154 pounds
Middleweight	160 pounds
Light Heavyweight	175 pounds
Heavyweight	Unlimited

Down and Out   To be knocked down and be unable to rise.

Down for the Count   Same as *down and out*.

Draw   Same as tie.

Drop a Guard   To lower the gloves; to leave face or body unprotected.

Elimination Bout   One of a series of matches to determine an eventual champion.

Fight Card   Series of bouts on the same program.

Five-Point Must System   A method of scoring in which the winner of a round is given five points, the loser, less than five. In the case of a tie round, both fighters are given five points.

Five-Point System   A method of scoring in which the winner of a round is given one to five points and the loser is given fewer, usually less than one point difference. In the case of a tie, neither fighter is awarded any points for the round.

Footwork   The movement of the feet during a fight.

Foul   Any illegal action or blow during a prizefight, usually a blow to the back of the head or neck, a blow below the belt, wrestling or head butting, or punching after the bell.

Go Into the Tank   To intentionally lose a fight.

Golden Gloves   A program of locally sponsored amateur fights that lead to the National Golden Gloves Tournament.

(To) Guard   To hold the gloves close to the face or body to protect from an opponent's punches.

271

Gym Fighter   A fighter who looks good in the gym, but bad during a bout.

Handler   Someone who helps train a fighter or acts as a cornerman during a fight.

Haymaker   A knockout punch.

Headgear   Padded headpiece that is used during training to protect the head.

Heavy Bag   Large stuffed canvas bag, approximately 1–1½ feet in diameter and at least 3 feet long, hung from the ceiling of a gym, that a fighter punches to help strength, power, and technique.

(To) Hit on the Break   To punch during the break period, as required by a referee.

Hungry   A fighter who financially or professionally desperately needs a win.

Infighter (Infighting)   Fighting close to an opponent.

In the Bag   Fight that has been decided before it has begun.

In the Tank   Fighter who deliberately loses a fight.

Jab   Direct punch used to bother an opponent or keep him off balance. Usually not a knockout punch.

Kayo   To *K*nock *O*ut.

Knockdown   To punch an opponent and cause him to fall onto the canvas. Once a fighter has been knocked down, the referee begins the 10-count.

Lead   The first in a series of punches.

Left   A punch thrown with the left hand.

Long Count   Any count that takes longer than a strict 10 seconds. Usually is a controversial count.

Low Blow   A blow below the hip-line, usually to the crotch and usually a foul.

Main Event   The most important and the last bout during a boxing program.

Majority Decision   A decision made by two of three boxing judges.

Make the Weight   To gain or lose pounds to enter a specific weight class, for a fight in that class.

Mandatory Eight Count   A rule that indicated that when a fighter has been knocked down, the referee must count to eight before the fight can proceed, to protect the downed fighter.

Measure   To hold a gloved hand against a stunned fighter to guide a knockout blow.

Mouse   A swelling around the eye.

Mouthpiece   Protective rubber guard worn inside the mouth to protect the teeth and lips of a fighter.

Neutral Corner   Either of the two corners of a ring *not assigned* to a particular fighter and his cornermen.

No Contest   An act of ending a fight by a referee because of problems not directly connected to the two fighters, such as a power blackout.

No Knockdown   A rule by a referee during a fight that a fighter who was on the canvas was not there because of a knockdown, but rather a slip or a push.

On the Ropes   Leaning helplessly on the ring ropes; usually means the fighter cannot defend himself.

Out Knocked out.

(To) Outpoint To win a fight with the highest number of points awarded by the judges.

Palooka An unskilled fighter.

Preliminary Bout One bout on a boxing program before the main event.

Pugilism The art of boxing, from the Latin *pugunus*, fist, and *pugil*, boxer.

(To) Pull a Punch To land a punch without full force.

Punch-Drunk To suffer the effects of taking too many punches to the head. A punch-drunk fighter is said to slur his speech and generally give the impression of being drunk on alcohol.

Punched Out Tired from throwing too many punches.

(To) Put Away To knock out an opponent.

Quick Count A count that takes *less* than 10 seconds.

Rabbit Punch An illegal punch to the back of the opponent's head.

Reach A measure of arm length. Generally speaking, a boxer with a longer reach than his opponent will have an advantage in the ring.

Referee The official in the ring who controls the action during a fight, watches for fouls, and separates fighters in a clinch. Sometimes called *the third man*.

Rematch A bout in which two fighters who have fought each other previously fight again.

Ring An elevated 18- to 20-foot square area surrounded by three ropes attached to vertical posts at each corner. Sometimes called *the squared circle*.

Ring Savvy Knowledge of the tricks and techniques of boxing.

Roadwork Running that is part of a boxer's training and conditioning.

Rope Ropes that are strung at 2-foot, 3-foot, and 4-foot heights around a boxing ring.

Round Any 3-minute period during a boxing match.

Saved By the Bell A boxer who is about to be counted out is said to be saved by the bell when the bell to signal the end of a round is rung before the count is up. No fighter can be saved by the bell during the final round of a bout.

Scorecard A card on which an official keeps score of rounds won or lost by each fighter.

Second One man who is allowed in a boxer's corner between rounds to advise him.

Slip To dodge a punch.

Slug To punch hard.

Slugger A fighter with little finesse.

Spar To box in practice.

Sparring Partner An opponent during a sparring match.

Speed Bag Lightweight punching bag used for coordination.

Split Decision Decision of the judges in which two judges vote for one fighter, and the third judge votes for the opponent.

Standing Eight Count A count of eight given by the referee when a boxer has been hurt. In professional boxing, this is a knockdown.

Step Back   To separate from a clinch.

Stop a Fight   The act of a referee to end a bout, when one fighter cannot continue.

Straight-Up Fighter   A boxer who does not bob or weave.

The Sweet Science   A famous book on boxing by the late boxing critic A. J. Liebling.

(To) Take a Dive   To deliberately lose a fight.

Take the Count   When a boxer allows himself to be counted out.

Tale of the Tape   A boxer's measurements   reach, chest, weight, and so on.

Technical Draw   Termination of a bout because of an accidental injury to one fighter.

Technical Knockout   The end of the fight as ruled by the referee when one fighter is unable to continue. Abbreviated on fight cards as *TKO*.

Ten Point Must System   A method of scoring a bout in which the winner of a round is given 10 points and the loser of the round about 2 points less. In the case of a tie, both fighters receive 10 points.

Three Knockdown Rule   If a fighter is knocked down three times in one round, the fight is over and he loses. Not a universal rule.

(To) Throw in the Towel   A fighter's cornermen concede defeat by throwing a towel into the center of the ring from the corner.

Timekeeper   Official at ringside who keeps track of the time of the rounds and the time between rounds.

Title   Highest level of any weight class.

Twenty Point Must System   A method of scoring in which the winner of each round is awarded 20 points and the loser a lesser number. In the case of a tie, both fighters are awarded 20 points.

Unanimous Decision   A decision in which all judges vote for one boxer.

Undercard   Any bout on a program prior to the main event.

Warning   A statement by the referee that a boxer has fouled his opponent and points will be subtracted from his score.

WBA   World Boxing Association.

WBC   World Boxing Council.

Weigh-in   Ceremony before a bout to ensure that boxers' weight is within the class designations.

Weight Division   See *division*.

White Hope   A White boxer who is a contender for a title held by a Black boxer.

Win on Points   To win by a decision.

Fencing

Advance   To move toward the opponent.

Attack   To attempt to hit the opponent by moving the body or the weapon forward.

Attack of Second Intention   An attack that is meant to be defended, so the attacked may score on a counterattack.

Balestra   See *jump advance.*

Benefit of the Doubt   If two side judges disagree and if the meet director has no opinion, no point is scored.

Blade   Strong   near the guard.

Middle   center section.

Weak   tip end.

Bout   Contest between two fencers.

Button   Small pad on the tip of a weapon to prevent injury to an opponent.

Competition   Contest with one type of weapon.

Epee (Dueling sword)   Weapon generally similar to the foil, but with a heavier handle and heavier guard.

Fleche   Running attack. Illegal in college fencing, women's fencing, and public school fencing.

Foil (French Foil)   Weapon approximately 35 inches long, with a flexible four-sided blade, and cup guard for the hand, weighing about 17.5 ounces. The tip has a small guard or button to prevent injury to the opponent during a bout.

Guard   The standing position when two fencers face each other momentarily prior to the bout.

Invitation   To invite an attack by moving toward an opponent.

Jump Advance   A lunge in which both feet leave the ground at the same time and meet the floor at the same time.

Jury   Usually four judges and a meet director.

Lunge   Key offensive movement in fencing; a long reach with one leg, pre-ceeded by a thrust with the foil. In a successful lunge, the fencer's whole body follows the arm and leg thrust instantly.

Mask   Mesh protector for the competitor's face.

Match   Contests between two teams with one type of weapon.

Meet   Contests between two or more teams in which more than one type of weapon is used.

Pass   A touch that would not inflict a puncture or wound.

Phase   Continuous action during a bout. Similar to a tennis volley.

Pool   Fencers or teams in a round-robin tournament.

Redoubled Attack   A lunge, followed by a second lunge.

Remise   A delayed riposte.

Retreat   To move away from an opponent.

Return (Riposte)   To advance after a successful defense.

Sabre   Weapon similar to the foil in size and weight, but with a two-sided blade, instead of the four-sided blade of the foil.

Touch   A hit on the opponent that would inflict a puncture or wound if the tip of the blade was not padded.

Tournament   Series of competitions with one or more types of weapons, organized on an individual or team basis.

GLOSSARY

Field Hockey

Advancing   Foul committed when the ball rebounds from a player's body.

Backing Up   Defensive play behind or outside the bully.

Bully   Action to start or restart a game. Two opposing players alternately strike the ground and each other's stick three times before touching the ball.

Circular Tackle   An attempt to take the ball from an opponent on the player's right side.

Covering   To guard the goal—usually refers to a player away from the action on the field.

Defensive Hit   A free hit toward the goal from 15 yards away.

Dodge   To elude an opponent while controlling the ball.

Dribble   Series of strokes used to control the ball while moving it down the field.

Drive   Hard stroke with a backswing to propel the ball downfield.

Fielding   To control an approaching ball before passing it or moving it downfield.

Flick   Stroke with no backswing.

Foul   Violation of the rules.

Free Hit   A play following a violation of the rules. Taken by the team that was fouled.

Goal   Score made when the ball crosses the goal line after being touched by a player inside the striking circle.

Holding the Whistle   When a play continues after a whistle by an official, when, in the opinion of the official, it is better to allow the play to continue than to stop it and award a penalty.

Lunge   Play used to take the ball from an opponent on the opponent's left.

Marking   Defensive position close to an opponent. Similar to guarding in basketball.

Obstruction   To interfere with an opponent by placing any part of the body between the opponent and the ball. A foul results.

Offside   A foul when a player receives the ball while in an illegal position.

Push-Pass   Quick pass without any backswing on the stroke.

Roll-In   Method of putting the ball in play after it has gone out of bounds.

Scoop   Short pass in which the ball is lifted with the front end, or toe, of the stick.

Stick Side   The player's right side.

Sticks   Foul committed when the player raises the stick shoulder high or higher at the beginning or end of a stroke.

Striking Circle   Inside the curved line that is the goal-shooting area.

Football

Activate   To move a player from a reserve or injured list to a list of eligible players.

All the Way   To score a touchdown.

Audible   When a quarterback changes the play by the use of a code, at the line of scrimmage, just before the ball is snapped. By calling an audible, the quarterback hopes to fool the defense, which may be ready for a different play.

Backfield (Defense)   Consists of four players, two defensive cornerbacks, and two safeties or three defensive backs, and one safety.

Backfield (Offense)   Usually consists of a quarterback, a fullback, a halfback, and a flanker back.

Backfield in Motion   On the offensive team, one player is allowed to run parallel to the line of scrimmage or back away from the line of scrimmage before the ball is snapped. If the back runs toward the line of scrimmage, it is a penalty for backfield in motion or illegal procedure.

Balanced Line   Offensive line in which there are an equal number of linemen on each side of the center.

Ball Control   To keep possession of the ball by gaining yards until a score is made. To keep gaining yards (and first downs) prevents the opposing team from gaining possession.

Blitz   When a defensive back moves toward the quarterback before the ball is snapped, he is said to be blitzing.

Block   Offensive maneuver in which a player uses his body to keep a defensive player from the ball carrier.

Blue-Chip   Quality college player to be selected by a professional team.

Bomb   Long arcing pass that may be caught for a touchdown. Also sometimes called a *rainbow*.

Bootleg   A running play in which the quarterback hides the ball from the defense by holding it against his thigh, away from the defensive line. He may or may not run in the direction of the rest of his backfield.

Bowls   Postseason games college teams are invited to play.

Bowl Championship Series   A selection system used to determine which top two teams will play for the NCAA national championship.

Breakaway Back   Offensive backfield player with enough speed and agility to elude the defense.

Bring in the Chains   To call time out to allow the sideline crew to bring in the 10-yard chain to determine if the team on offense has made 10 yards and thus a first down.

Broken-Field Runner   Runner with the ability to dodge defense players in the open.

Broken Play   Play that was not executed. The defense may have guessed the play, the offense may have not heard the quarterback's count, the offense backfield players may have run into each other—any number of reasons (excuses) may account for a broken play.

Bump and Run   Occurs when an offense player bumps a defensive player to slow him down, then runs past him.

Buttonhook   A pass play in which the receiver runs downfield 10 or 15 yards, then turns back in a semicircle toward the quarterback, to catch a pass.

277

Because many football fans don't know what a buttonhook looks like, this play also resembles a fishhook (without the barb).

Cadence The rhythm that a quarterback has when he shouts the codes for the play and the ball snap.

Chalk Talk Teaching session, usually at half-time, in the locker room, by a coach, often illustrating what the team is doing wrong, by the use of X's and O's on a chalkboard or blackboard. Sometimes an assistant coach will briefly conduct a chalk talk on the sidelines for a small group of players, the defensive line, for instance, when the offense has the ball.

Chain Crew Team of officials who stand along one sideline and measure whether a team has gained 10 yards in four plays, from the first down. The chain crew will move onto the field to measure, if they are not certain from the sidelines that a team has gained 10 yards. A time out is called during the measure.

Circus Catch A catch made by a receiver that shows great ability and dexterity—usually made one-handed.

Cleats Small knobs or stubs on the bottoms of the players shoes to help them gain traction. Sometimes a cleat will catch in the turf and a player may break or sprain an ankle.

Clipping To illegally block an opponent by hitting the backs of the legs and knees. Very risky and potentially injurious.

Clothesline Tackle To tackle an opponent by thrusting a stiff arm out to catch the opponent by the neck.

Coach The equivalent of a teacher or professor, the coach teaches the team fundamentals, his methods, and playing philosophy. It is said that a football coach "has to be smart enough to teach the game, but dumb enough to think that it's important."

Coffin Corner(s) To kick into either corner of the defensive end of the field so the ball goes out of bounds and leaves the defense to begin an offensive series of plays within their own 10-yard line.

Color Man (Color Commentator) TV announcer who adds feature material to the commentary of a game.

Conversion The opportunity that a team has, after scoring a touchdown, of gaining additional points by running or passing the ball over the goal line again, or by kicking it over the goalposts.

Cornerback Defensive backfield player who has the responsibility of stopping an offensive play once the ball-carrier reaches the "corners" (sides) of the defensive backfield.

Crackback Block Run by an offensive player that ends with a block at the back by a defensive player. Like a clip, it too, is potentially very dangerous to the defensive player, who may not be watching or know the offensive player is about to block.

Crawling To gain added yardage when the play is over by crawling with the ball at the bottom of a pile of tacklers.

Cut Back   Offensive play by a receiver who runs down the side of the field and cuts back toward the center of the field.

Cup   Same as *in the pocket.*

Dead Ball   After a play is over and when the referee blows his whistle to indicate that the play is over. Any foul after that is a *dead ball foul.*

Delay   To hold a position at the line of scrimmage momentarily to confuse an opposing lineman.

Delay of Game   The offensive team has 30 seconds to begin a play. If the play has not begun in 30 seconds, the referee may call a delay of game penalty.

Depth Chart   A coaching chart showing the No. 1 player at each position, then No. 2, then No. 3, and perhaps even No. 4 at some positions.

Diamond Defense   Defensive formation with seven men on the line, then one back (fullback) then two backs behind him (halfbacks), then one back (safety) behind them. Called a diamond because from above, the backfield formation would have the shape of a diamond.

Dime Defense   Six defensive players (one more than the *nickel*, or five-man defense).

Dive Play   Offensive play in which the ball carrier literally dives over the line of scrimmage.

Double Team   Occurs when two offensive players block one defensive player.

Down and In   An offensive play in which a receiver runs down the field and in toward the center of the field.

Down and Out   An offensive play in which a receiver runs down the field then out, toward the sideline.

Downing the Ball   On a kickoff, a player on the receiving team may catch the ball in the end zone. He may elect not to run the ball out of the end zone. In that case, he downs the ball, by touching one knee to the ground. The next play begins on the offensive team's 20-yard line.

Draft   The act of choosing eligible college players, on a team-by-team basis. The worst team in the professional league has the first chance at eligible college players, to (in theory) equalize the teams in terms of player-by-player ability.

Draw Play   An offensive play in which the quarterback drops back from the line of scrimmage as if he is going to pass, then hands the ball to a runner, who may gain substantial yardage through the defense, which was expecting a pass.

Drop Back   Occurs when a quarterback receives the ball from the center and moves away from the line of scrimmage to pass, or to hand the ball to a runner.

Dump Pass   To quickly throw the ball to the closest eligible player to avoid a loss in yardage (or an embarrassingly inept play).

(To) Eat the Ball   To down the ball with a loss of yardage, to prevent a more substantial loss of yardage. Usually involves embarrassment to the ball carrier.

End Around Offensive play in which an end runs in an arc through his own backfield, receives the ball and carries it into the defense at the other end of the field. The end must have superior speed to make much yardage on an end around play.

End Zone Teams score points by running, passing, or kicking the ball into the end zone. It is 10 yards deep; there is one at each end of the playing field.

Extra Points Awarded after a touchdown; on a play from scrimmage, two points are awarded if the ball is run or passed successfully over the goal line; one point if the ball is kicked between the goal posts.

Face Mask Metal cage that prevents injury to the player's face. May be grabbed by an opponent and still cause injury to the player's neck. A penalty results if an official catches a player grabbing or holding another player's face mask.

Fade Back Occurs when the quarterback takes the ball from the center and retreats from the line of scrimmage to pass the ball or hand it off to another back.

Fake Any movement or motion intended to fool the opposing team.

Fair Catch A player may make a fair catch on a kickoff, return kick, or kick from scrimmage by raising his hand clearly above his head. If he is tackled after a fair catch signal, a penalty results. He may not take more than two steps after catching the ball. The ball is put in play at the point of the catch. If the player drops or fumbles the catch, it is a fair ball and may be recovered by the defense.

Field Goal A kick over the crossbar and between the goal posts that results in three points for the kicking team.

Films Films of an opponent's previous games are studied by a coaching staff to prepare a team for an upcoming game.

Fire Out To move from the line of scrimmage offensively when the ball is snapped.

First Down An offensive team has four tries to gain 10 yards. If they gain 10 yards within the four tries, they have a first down and are then eligible to gain 10 more yards in another four tries.

Flag Penalty marker used by officials.

Flag Football A nontackle form of football in which players wear (usually) two streamers of cloth. The play is stopped when a defensive player grabs one or both flags from an offensive player's waist.

Flak Jacket Padded protective vest worn under their uniforms by quarterbacks (and occasionally by others) to prevent rib, abdomen, or kidney injury. Named after the similar jackets worn by World War II airmen to prevent injury by anti-aircraft fire.

Flanker A backfield player who is positioned away from the rest of the linemen.

Flat Pass A pass thrown parallel to the line of scrimmage and with a flat trajectory.

Flea Flicker Play An offensive play in which the quarterback fakes a pass, then laterals to an offensive back, who then passes to a third offensive player; a risky play because the ball may be fumbled or the pass intercepted.

Flex Defense   In this defense, as the ball is snapped, the ends drop away from the line and become additional linebackers.

Fly Pattern or Fly Pass   Play in which an end runs ("flies") past the defense and hopes to score by simply outrunning the defense and catching a pass for a touchdown.

Football Championship Subdivision   Formerly known as Division I-AA. This division has a playoff to determine its national champion. Teams competing are in conferences such as the Big South, the Ivy League, the Ohio Valley Conference, and the Southern Conference.

Foul   Any violation of the rules.

"Four Yards and a Cloud of Dust"   Famous Ohio State techniques, used by coach Woody Hayes, of using a fullback down after down to gain "four yards" (and a cloud of dust) into the line, without passing each down.

Franchise Player   A single player so valuable to a team he is said to be able to "save a franchise," financially, by himself.

Free Ball   A ball that is not in possession of either team.

Free Safety   Defensive backfield player who plays in the deep defensive and has no specific man-to-man responsibilities.

Front Four   The two tackles and two guards on the offensive line.

Fullback   Offensive player who lines up behind the quarterback and who usually has the job of gaining short yardage in tough situations.

Fumble   To lose control or possession of the ball.

Fundamentals   Basic skills that any football player should know. Also applies in other sports.

Game Plan   Strategy devised by the coaches to cover general offensive plans and general defensive plans.

Gang Tackle   To tackle the ball carrier by two or more players at the same time.

Gap   Real or imaginary hole between two players in correct position.

Giveaways/Takeaways   The relationship between fumbles lost by Team A and recovered by Team B to fumbles lost by Team B and recovered by Team A; a relatively new NFL statistic.

Goal-Line Defense   Special defense when the offensive is within the 10-yard line and is close to a touchdown. Generally, defensive players will be closer together, as they have less field to cover.

Go Against the Grain   To run away from the traffic flow; for example, if all the offensive backfield is running to the right, the ball carrier runs to the left.

Gridiron   Common name for the football field.

Grind it Out   To make yardage in short gains, as in Woody Hayes' "Four Yards and a Cloud of Dust" system.

Grounding the Ball   If a passer cannot find an eligible receiver, he may throw the ball over the heads of all receivers. This is called *grounding the ball* or *intentional grounding*. The passing equivalent of *eating the ball*.

Gut Check   A crucial situation; team members pause to check their courage. Do they have enough to win the game? Variations: *gutting it up*, and so on.

Halftime A 30-minute pause between the second and third quarters of a football game. Allows teams to rest and regroup and allows TV networks a chance for commercials.

"Hail Mary" Pass Long bomb, usually thrown in a desperate situation. When the pass is in the air, the quarterback (and coach) pray that some offensive player will be under it and catch it for a touchdown. Doug Flutie of Boston College threw a Hail Mary and defeated The University of Miami 47–45 in the last second of the game during the 1984 collegiate season.

Hand-off An offensive play in which one player (usually the quarterback) hands the ball to a second player.

Hang Time The seconds of time a kick stays in the air. A longer hang time will allow the kicking team a chance to get downfield and stop the receiving team from advancing the caught ball.

Head Hunter Player who willfully looks for an opportunity to injure an opponent.

(To) Hear Footsteps To hear (but not see) an opponent moments before a tackle.

Heisman Trophy Award given annually to the best collegiate player in the country.

Holding To illegally impede an opponent by grabbing the uniform, arm, leg, or any other available part of the opponent.

Honey Shot Shot of cheerleader or other pretty girl during a televised game.

Hot Dog Player who deliberately shows off for the opposition, audience or TV cameras.

Huddle Brief meeting before a play. The quarterback announces the play and the count to the rest of the team.

I Formation Offensive backfield formation in which the halfback is behind the quarterback and the fullback is behind the halfback. So called because the backfield formation looks like the letter I.

Impact Player A player whose presence can make a significant difference to a team's winloss record. Similar to *franchise player*.

Ineligible Receiver Player (usually a lineman) who may not catch the ball.

Interception Occurs when a defensive player catches a ball intended for an offensive player.

In the Trenches Offensive and defensive linemen at work doing their jobs at the line of scrimmage when the ball is snapped.

Intentional Grounding When the quarterback passes the ball during an offensive play, the officials may call intentional grounding if they decide that there was not a receiver near the play and that the quarterback simply threw the ball away to avoid a loss. A penalty results.

Interception Pass caught by a defensive player, that was intended for an offensive player.

Interference Penalty for illegally blocking the action of a player or a play.

Jammed A running play that is stopped at the line of scrimmage is said to have been jammed.

Keys   Movements by certain players, or team formations that signal how a play will develop. Coaches watch previous game films in order to discover keys.

Kicking Tee   Small plastic device that holds the ball in correct position for a kick.

Kicking Unit   Special team used in kicking situations.

Line of Scrimmage   An imaginary line or vertical plane passing through the ball and parallel to the goal lines, marked by the nearest yard number (line of scrimmage, 35-yard line). There is a line of scrimmage for each team and the area between the two is the *neutral zone.* Any player who enters the neutral zone before the ball is snapped is guilty of being offside.

Look In   A pass play in which a receiver runs diagonally down the field and "looks in" (looks back toward the quarterback) for the pass.

Man-to-Man   Defense in which each player is responsible for one specific offensive player.

Messenger   Player who enters the game with a specific play from a coach.

Mid-Field   The 50-yard line.

Misdirection   Play in which the "flow" of the backfield misdirects the defense away from the path of the actual ball carrier.

Momentum   Enthusiasm working for a particular team. Momentum can "flow" from one team to another depending on the game, score, or players.

Mousetrap   Offensive play in which a defensive player is allowed past the line of scrimmage after the ball is snapped, then blocked (mousetrapped) so he may not reach the ball carrier.

Multiple Set   Offensive plays that can't be predicted. A variety of possible plays.

NFL   National Football League.

Nickel Defense   A pass defense in which the coaches insert an extra defensive backfield player—the fifth back; thus the name.

Nose Tackle   Defensive player whose position is in the center—the nose—of the line.

Numbering System   In the NFL, numbers from 1–99 are assigned to particular positions, in this system:

1–9:	Quarterbacks and kickers
10–19:	Quarterbacks, receivers, tight ends, and kickers
20–49:	Running backs and defensive backs
50–59:	Centers and linebackers
60–79:	Defensive and offensive linemen
80–89:	Receivers and tight ends (or 40–49 if those numbers are taken
90–99:	Defensive linemen and linebackers

Nutcrackers   Drills or exercises during training camp in which coaches hope to find the toughest players.

Offside   A penalty when one player—offensive or defensive—moves across the line of scrimmage before the ball is snapped.

Off the Ball   How quickly a lineman can react when the ball is snapped.

On the Same Page Everyone knowing what to do and going out on the field and doing it; being in sync with the playbook.

One-Back Offense Formations that involve only one offensive backfield player, other than the quarterback. This back, usually the biggest and the most powerful, is used in running situations.

On-Side Kick A kick that is deliberately short—10–15 yards, so that the kicking team can recover it immediately if the receiving team fumbles it.

Option A play in which the quarterback has the choice, depending on the offense and the defense, of keeping the ball or passing it.

(To) Pay the Price To play while injured as a condition of keeping the job; to receive an injury while playing; a masochistic macho image of a football player who will play while hurt without complaining or without leaving the game. Considered a complimentary term by most players. Also applied to other contact sports.

Penalty A loss of yards as a result of a foul.

Penetration Moving into the opponent's part of the field, either defensively or offensively.

Period A 15-minute segment of a 60-minute football game. Also known as quarter.

Piling On Jumping on or tackling the ball carrier after the play is officially ruled ended.

Pit Offensive and defensive linemen "in the trenches," at or near the line of scrimmage, are said to be "in the pit."

Pitchout An underhanded toss of the ball from the quarterback to another player.

Place Kick To kick a football when it is held motionless by a player or when it rests on a kicking tee.

Playbook A team book of possible plays, offensive and defensive, that team members usually memorize during summer camp. Highly guarded by team coaches, even though most plays are no longer secret.

Plug a Hole To fill a gap in the line, during a play.

Pocket Protective screen of players around a quarterback, who is getting ready to pass. A quarterback who is "out of the pocket" has inadvertently outrun or been chased away from his protective cover of players.

Pooch Kick Short- or medium-range kick, usually soft and high. Similar to an approach shot to the green in golf. A finesse kick. The pooch kicker may not be the same as a field goal kicker or a kick-off specialist.

Post Pattern A pass pattern in which the receiver runs toward the goalpost.

Power Back (power runner) Offensive back who can gain yardage because of his superior size or speed.

Power Sweep An offensive play in which the ball carrier runs around the end of the line of scrimmage and has at least two players ahead of him blocking.

Prevent Defense Defense that will give up small yardage but that will not give up extensive yardage. Often, if time is running out, the defense will go into a prevent defense, willingly giving up small gains by the offense, but not yielding a touchdown.

Pulling Guard   An offensive guard who "pulls" away from the line of scrimmage when the ball is snapped, to help protect the quarterback or ball carrier.

Punt   A kick on fourth down by the offensive team when it cannot get a first down on the next play.

Quarter   Same as *period.*

Quarterback   Offensive team leader who calls the plays in the huddle, then takes the ball from the center to begin the play. He either runs with it, passes it, or hands it off to another.

Quarterback Sneak   Short yardage play in which the quarterback takes the ball from the center and follows the forward motion of the center, into the line of scrimmage.

Racehorse   Pass receiver with exceptional speed through the defensive backfield.

Read The Defense   To know what defensive men will do in a play because of their positions (or keys) at the line of scrimmage.

Read The Offense   To know what offensive men will do in a play because of their positions (or keys) at the line of scrimmage.

Red Dog   Same as *blitz.*

Red Shirt   To hold a player out for a season, usually to allow an injury to heal.

Referee   Senior official during a football game. He stands behind the offensive backfield before each play.

Reverse   A running play in which the ball carrier hands the ball to another back, running in the opposite direction.

Retire a Number   To honor a player by holding a ceremony and officially declaring that the number he wore during his playing days will never again be used by the team.

Rookie   Novice member of a football team. A player recently out of college on a professional team.

Roughing the Quarterback (Roughing the Catcher, Roughing the Kicker, etc.)   Hitting the player unnecessarily hard, or after the play is over, perhaps with an intent to injure. Calls for a penalty if the officials see the incident.

Run to Daylight   Run to an open part of the field.

Running Back   Offensive ball carrier other than the quarterback.

Rushing   To gain yardage by running with the ball.

Sack   To tackle the quarterback for a loss.

Safety   Is scored when a ball carrier is tackled behind his own goal. A safety scores two points for the defense.

Sarah   Coaching code for a strongside formation or play.

Screen Pass   A pass that is thrown parallel to the line of scrimmage or a pass that is completed behind the line of scrimmage. Or, a pass that is thrown to a receiver who is screened (blocked) from the defensive by another offensive player.

Scrimmage   The line on which a play takes place.

Secondary   Defensive positions behind the line of scrimmage.

Shank a Kick   To miskick a ball so that it travels only a few yards (football equivalent of hooking a golf ball).

Shoestring Catch   To catch a football at the ankle (shoestring) level.

Shoestring Tackle   To tackle a ball carrier below the knees.

Shotgun   Offensive formation in which the quarterback stands to receive the snap a few (5–10) yards behind the center. This gives the quarterback slightly more time to find his receivers for a pass.

Shovel Pass   Pass that is thrown underhanded to a receiver.

Skirt the End   To run offensively around the defensive end.

Smurf   In the NFL, a "midget," that is, a player under 6 feet tall and under 180 pounds.

Snap   To start a play, the center throws the ball upwards between his legs to the waiting hands of the quarterback.

Soccer Kicker   To kick the ball with the instep of the foot, instead of with the point of the toe. Soccer kickers are said to have more accuracy than regular kickers. Soccer kickers are often Europeans who learned their technique by playing soccer first, then football.

Spear   To hit an opponent using the top of the helmet as a weapon. It is illegal and calls for a penalty when caught by the officials.

Special Teams   Players assigned to a kickoff team, for instance, or a prevent defense team or a nickel back team.

Spike   To energetically throw the ball down after a touchdown. Many players make a real show of spiking the ball. Too much spiking (or dancing) in the end zone after a touchdown is now a penalty.

Split the Uprights   To accurately kick an extra point or field goal straight through the goalposts.

Squib Kick   A kick that is hard to catch because it is wobbly or bouncing.

Straightarm   A defensive play in which the player uses a locked arm to thrust an opponent away from a tackle.

Strongside   The side of an offensive line having more players than the opposite side of the same line.

Student Body Right or (Student Body Left)   A running play in which the entire team, plus coaches, cheerleaders, and trainers seem to be running in the same direction to protect the ball carrier. Established at the University of Southern California.

Stuffed   Same as *jammed*.

Stunting   Defensive formation in which players are out of their usual place, to fool the offense.

Submarine   To hit a ball carrier low.

Substitute   A player who is not a starter, sent in to play because another player has to leave the game. Also appropriate in other team sports.

Sudden Death   A period after the normal four quarters of play. If the game is tied at the end of regulation play, the game goes into sudden death and the first team to score wins. There is no additional play after a score in sudden death.

Suicide Squads   Kickoff and kickoff return teams in which individual players are assumed to sacrifice themselves for the team. Usually a thankless job, but a position in which a rookie can prove himself worthy of a permanent job on the team.

Super Bowl   The championship game of the National Football League. Played at various locations at the end of the regular season.

Sweep   Running play in which the offensive line swings toward a sideline and the ball carrier follows that protective wall.

Swing Pass   Short pass thrown by the quarterback toward the sideline.

Tackle   To stop a ball carrier and throw him to the ground.

Tailback   Running back in the offensive backfield farthest from the line of scrimmage.

Taxi Squad   Players good enough to keep on the team but not exceptional enough to use regularly. So named because an early professional team owner used them to man his fleet of taxi cabs to give them work and also keep them available for the team. Now used for any group of nonregular players.

T Formation   Offensive formation in which members of the offensive backfield are lined up parallel to the line of scrimmage and behind the quarterback. So called because the backfield formation looks like the letter T.

Three-Point Stance   Stance that the linemen assume before the ball is snapped. They have both feet on the ground, are crouched low to the ground, and have one hand touching the ground. ground.

Throw Into a Crowd   To throw toward more than one receiver. Usually a Hail Mary pass will be thrown toward a crowd.

Throw It Away   When a quarterback deliberately throws a pass over or past a receiver so that he will not risk having the pass intercepted.

Time Out   To stop the clock that marks the 60 minutes of the game.

Touchback   Occurs when a ball is dead off the field behind the goal line in possession of the offense, when the ball was downed or the ball carrier was downed by the defense. Different than a safety   A safety occurs on the field of play behind the goal lines; a touchback occurs *off* the field of play behind the goal line. The ball is put into play at the nearest 20-yard line.

Touchdown   Scores 6 points for the offensive team when the ball is carried or passed over the goal line.

Touch Football   Informal game in which the play is stopped when the ball carrier is touched with two hands of an opponent.

Trap   To allow a defensive player to cross the offensive line, then block him from the ball carrier once he has crossed into offensive territory.

Triple-Threat Player   Player who has the ability to run, pass, and kick the ball well. Because college and professional football is so complex, there are few triple-threat players. Most are happy to specialize in just one aspect of the game.

Turk Nickname for assistant coach or other member of the coaching staff who has the job of telling players in training camp that they have been cut from the team. So named because of the image of a Turkish fighter with a broad sword.

Turn In Pass pattern in which the receiver runs downfield then turns toward the middle of the field to catch a pass.

Two-Minute Drill Special exercises to take advantage of the last 2 minutes before the end of the first half or before the end of the game.

Two-Minute Warning Special warning given to each coach by the officials that there is 2 minutes left before the end of the first half or before the end of the game.

Two-Way Player Player who can play offense and defense. Because of the specialization of football, there are as few two-way players as there are triple-threat players.

Umpire Another key official during a football game.

Unbalanced Line Offensive line that has an unequal number of players on one side of the center than on the other side.

Uprights Vertical poles on the goal posts. Place kickers must kick extra points and field goals between the uprights to score.

Veer Offense Complicated offense in which the quarterback can either (a) run with the ball; (b) give it to the fullback; (c) run toward the sidelines and pitch to a running back; or (d) pass. The veer takes advantage of the fact that the defense may react quickly to one of these options, thus allowing the quarterback to quickly execute another of these four options. How to prevent the success of the veer? Down the quarterback behind the line of scrimmage before he gets a chance to execute the veer.

Wanda Coaching code for a weakside formation or play.

Weakside Opposite of strongside. The side of the offensive line with the fewest players from the center.

Wide Receiver Formerly known as the split end, a lineman eligible to catch passes, whose position on the line of scrimmage separates him from the rest of the line.

Wild Card Team eligible for playoffs in the National Football League that did not outright win its division race toward the Super Bowl.

Wishbone Offensive formation in which the quarterback lines up behind the center and the three other backs are behind him; seen from well behind the line and from above, the formation looks like a Y or like a chicken wishbone. The quarterback may keep the ball with two of the backs blocking ahead for him, or he may pitch out to one of them; similar in general respects to the option-style play of the veer offense.

X's and O's Chalkboard symbols for offensive and defensive players and strategy. It's a compliment to a coach if it is said, "He really knows his X's and O's."

Zebras   Because of their black-and-white striped jackets, officials are sometimes called zebras (also true in basketball).

Frisbee

Acceleration   Any technique used to add spin to a disc.

Aid   Any device such as a stick or thimble used to add spin to a disc.

Air Bounce   A throwing style in which the disc bounces off a cushion of air that builds up underneath it.

Backhand   A cross-body throw of the disc with the thumb on top of the disc and the fingers underneath.

Belly   The underside of a disc.

Blind   Any throw or catch performed while looking away from the disc or target.

Bobble   To mishandle or juggle a catch.

Body Roll   Any technique in which any part of the body is used for the disc to skip or bounce off of.

Bottom   Same as belly.

Break Tip   Any contact made with a disc in flight to alter its flight pattern or speed.

Brush   To accelerate the spinning action of a disc by slapping it on the side edge.

BTB   Behind the back.

BTH   Behind the head.

BTL   Between the legs.

Burbled Air   Turbulent, unpredictable air.

Catapult   To throw a disc with the fingers.

Cheek   Inside rim of a disc.

Co-oping   Two or more players sharing the same disc; usage similar to team play in other sports.

Cross-Body Throw   Any throw on the left for a right-handed player and vice versa.

Crown   Top of the disc.

Delivery   A player's complete throwing motion.

Dip   Any sudden drop in the flight of a disc.

Discwork   Any movement or motion to control a disc.

Drop   A missed disc catch that hits the ground.

Edge   Bottom surface of the disc rim.

Facing Stance   Any stance taken to the disc in which the thrower faces the target.

Flamingo   Any catch a player makes close to the ground, on one leg.

Floater   A throw that hovers in the air.

Frisbee   Trade name for a specific plastic flying saucer, now a generic term for all plastic flying saucers.

Frisbee Golf   A game played with discs similar to golf. In frisbee golf, players aim toward a large basket, instead of a small golf hole.

Gyre   A wobbling motion in a disc in flight caused by a bad throw, turbulent air, or a warped disc.

Hover   A throw in which the disc drops to the ground slowly, with little or no forward glide.

Lead   To throw ahead of another player who is running so that that player can catch the throw without breaking stride.

Lip   Outside rim of a disc.

Move   Any motion used to throw or catch a disc.

Nose   The leading edge of a disc in flight.

Siamese Catch   Any catch made by two (or more) players at the same time.

Slider   A throw that makes the disc skid across the ground.

Stability   The "flying properties" of a plastic disc.

Stall   Occurs during the flight of a disc when forward motion dies.

Tacking   When a disc holds its course without deviations across a wind.

Terminations   Any movement on the part of a player that stops the flight of a disc.

Tipping   To control the disc by repeatedly touching the underside of the disc.

Top   The upper side of a disc.

Trail   Any movement to catch a disc by grabbing the back edge as it passes the player.

Trap   To catch a disc with two parts of the body   both hands, hand and a leg, and so on.

Tricking   Performing disc routines.

Z's   The spin that a disc has in flight.

GOLF

Ace   Hole in one.

Action   To put spin on the ball.

Address   Correct body position before hitting the ball.

Approach   To hit a short- or medium-length shot to the green, with an iron.

Apron   Area immediately surrounding the green.

Away   Refers to the ball that is furthest from the cup, when more than one golfer is playing a particular hole.

Best Ball Tournament   Tournament in which the better score between members of a two-person team on each hole is used as the team score.

Birdie   One under par on a particular hole.

Bogey   One over par on a hole.

Bunker   Common name for a sand trap.

Caddy   Person who carries the golfer's clubs.

Can   To sink a putt.

Casual Water   Water on a course after a rain-storm; not part of a permanent hazard such as a pond or lake.

Course Rating   The difficulty of a particular course.

Divot   Ground cut up by the clubhead during a swing.

Dog-Leg   Hole that has a sharp bend to the left or the right from tee to green.

Double Eagle   Three strokes under par for any particular hole.

Driver   No. 1 wood, usually only off the tee.

Eagle   Two under par for a particular hole.

Fairway   Ground between the tee area and the putting green, excluding any hazards.

Flag   Banner on top of a metal pole inserted in the cup, to indicate the hole, to golfers at a distance from the green.

Fore   Signal shouted to indicate to those on the course that a golfer is about to take a stroke.

Foresome   Match in which two players play against two other players, or all four play against each other.

Green   Manicured grass area where each hole is located.

Handicap   A number that represents a golfer's playing ability based upon previous performance. A lower number (2 handicap) is better than a larger number (10).

Hazard   In golf, any bunker, water (except casual water), trees, brush, or other natural obstacles.

Head   The part of the club that strikes the ball.

Hole   In golf, the hole is 4¼ inches deep and 4 inches in diameter. The hole may be anywhere on any particular green, and may be moved from time to time.

Hole High   An approach shot that is on the green as far as the hole, but to the right or the left.

Hole in One   A drive shot from the tee that hits the hole.

Hole Out   To sink a putt.

Home   The green.

Honor   The first person or the first team to drive from the tee is said to have the honor. Generally, those who have the honor are those who won the previous hole.

Hook   A shot that curves in flight from the right to the left, for a right-handed golfer.

Iron   A golf club with a metal lead, used for medium shots toward the green.

Leader Board   A billboard-size chart, generally located near the clubhouse, that shows the leader of a tournament. Lowest scores (below par) are at the top of the board, followed by par, then above par.

Lie   The position of the ball on the fairway or green.

Match Play   Competition in which the winner is decided by the total number of strokes taken for each *hole*. A team may win a *hole*, lose a *hole*, or halve a *hole* (take the same number as the opposition).

Medal Play   Competition in which the total number of strokes by a player is used in determining the winner.

Nassau   Another alternate method of scoring   one point for the first 9 holes, one point for the second 9, and one point for the entire 18 holes.

Open A tournament that allows both amateurs and professional golfers to play.

Par Average shot for a particular hole.

Penalty Stroke One stroke added to the total for a violation of the rules.

Pigeon Easy mark. Victim.

Provisional Ball Ball played when a previous ball was hit out of bounds or lost.

Pulled Shot A shot that is straight, but to the right of the green (or hole) for a right-handed golfer.

Push-Shot A shot that is straight, but to the left of the green (or hole) for a right-handed golfer.

Putt A delicate stroke on the green to roll the ball toward the hole.

Rough Weeds or other natural hazards at either side of the fairway.

Shank To hit the ball with the heel of the club.

Slice A shot that curves from left to right for a right-handed golfer.

Storke Play Same as *medal play*.

Summer Rules Playing the ball as it lies anywhere on the course.

Tee Small wooden peg that a ball is placed on before being driven.

Topping To hit the top of the ball, thus causing it to roll along the ground without any loft.

Trap A bunker, a sand trap.

Waggle To wiggle the body, arms, or legs, when the golfer addresses the ball.

Wedge Heavy club used for hitting out of sand.

Whiff To miss the ball completely during a swing.

Winter Rules To drop the ball for an advantage if it is in the rough during play.

Wood A golf club with a wood head, used to hit distance shots from the tee.

Gymnastics

All-Around Competition in which the gymnast must perform in the floor exercise, side horse, long horse, horizontal bar, parallel bars, still rings, and long horse.

Approach To walk to the equipment, prior to the gymnastic routine. Similar to the approach in golf.

Balance To maintain equilibrium during a routine.

Break To stop to dampen the bounce of a trampoline.

Check To slow or stop body revolutions during a trampoline routine.

Gainer A backflip in which the performer lands ahead of the take-off spot.

Perfect Ten Redundant phrase. Ten is the top score that any gymnast can receive.

Pommels The curved iron handles of a side horse.

Spotter Guard who stands beside a trampoline to catch the gymnast if he or she bounces or falls off the trampoline bed.

Vault A leap or jump aided by the gymnast's hands.

GLOSSARY

Handball and Racquetball

Ace   Serve that is untouched by an opponent; scores a point. Same usage in table tennis, tennis, badminton, and other sports.

Anticipation   The ability that a player has to guess where the opponent's shot will rebound so the player can be in a position to return it.

Avoidable Hinder   Intentional interference of one player by another. Penalty is the loss of a score or the addition of a score by the player who was hindered.

Back Court   The area behind the short line to the rear wall.

Backswing   Beginning motion to hit the ball. Similar usage as in a golf backswing.

Back-Wall Shot   A ball that is hit after it rebounds from the back wall.

Ball   In handball, the ball is 1⅞ inches in diameter and weighs between ²/₁₀ and ³/₁₀ of an ounce.

Blocking   To hinder an opponent's shot by placing all or part of the body between the opponent and the ball.

Bolo Shot   A shot hit with the fist, underhanded (handball).

Bone Bruise   Deep bruise of the palm of the hand (handball).

Bottom Board   Lowest part of the front wall.

Bye   Tournament in which some favored players are allowed to progress without playing the first rounds.

Ceiling Serve   A serve that strikes the ceiling after it bounces off the front wall.

Ceiling Shot   A shot that is hit directly to the ceiling, then the front wall, then the floor, and then rebounds to the back wall.

Center Court Position   The middle of the court about 3 to 5 feet in front of the short line. Ideal position for offensive and defensive play.

Change of Pace Shot   Any shot that changes the tempo of the game, either faster than normal or slower than normal.

Consolation   Round of a tournament in which first-time losers face each other.

Control   The ability to hit a ball to any specific spot.

Court   A standard handball court is 40' by 20' by 20'.

Crosscourt Shot   A shot that is hit diagonally across the court.

Crotch   Any place where two surfaces meet   wall-wall, wall-ceiling, or wall-floor.

Crowding   Playing too close to the opponent.

Cutthroat   A game for three players in which two play against the server.

Dead Ball   Ball that is not in play.

Die   A ball that hits the front wall without much bounce.

Dig   To return a low shot before it reaches the floor.

Doubles   A game in which two players oppose two other players.

Error   The inability to return a playable ball.

Fault   Illegally served ball. Generally similar usage as in tennis.

Floater   A ball that travels so slowly that the opponent has time to set up a return shot.

Fly Shot   A shot that is returned before it hits the floor.

Forehand   Shot made from the same side of the body as the playing hand.

Front-and-Back Doubles play in which one partner covers the front court and the other partner covers the back court.

Game When 21 points are scored by one player or team.

Game Point Point that will win the game for a player or team, if it is won.

Half-and-Half Same as *side-by-side* play.

Hinder To accidentally interfere with an opponent.

Hop To put spin on the ball by snapping the wrist (handball).

IRA International Racquetball Association.

Inning One complete round of play in which each player or each team has the opportunity to gain or lose the serve.

Kill Shot A shot that strikes the front wall so low that it is unreturnable.

Lob Ball that hits the front wall high then rebounds in a high arc toward the back wall.

Masters In singles competition, players must be over 40 years of age; in doubles, one must be at least 40 and the partner at least 45 (racquetball).

Match Two out of three games.

Off-Hand The left hand if the player is right-handed, and vice versa.

Pass Shot A shot that is hit out of reach of the opponent.

Place To hit the ball accurately to a particular part of the court.

Power Serve A ball that is hit low off the front wall and bounces toward a rear corner (hand-ball).

Ready Position The stance taken by a player to receive a serve.

Receiving Line A line 5 feet in back of the short line. Players waiting for the serve must stand behind this line until the ball is served.

Roadrunner Player whose specialty is retrieving (racquetball).

Run-Around Shot A shot that hits one side wall, the back wall, and a second side wall.

Screen Ball that passes too close to a player's body for it to be seen clearly by the opponent.

Seamless 558 Ball used for racquetball. Ball is 2½ inches in diameter and weighs approximately 1.4 ounces.

(To) Serve To put the ball in play.

Service Box 18"-wide boxes at each end of the serving line. Nonserving partners must stand in one of these boxes while the other partner serves the ball.

Service Court Area in which the ball must land after hitting the front wall.

Service Line Line 5 feet in front of and parallel to the short line.

Service Zone Where the server must stand when serving the ball.

Sharp Angle Serve A shot that hits the front wall close to the floor and bounces at an angle to the right side wall and back toward the server.

Shooters Players who rely on kill shots (racquetball).

Short Line Line in the middle of the floor from side to side halfway between the front and back walls. The serve must carry over this line from the front wall.

Side-by-Side Doubles play in which partners stand side-by-side, as opposed to front-and-back.

Straddle Ball Ball that moves between the legs of a player.

Straight Kill Shot Ball that hits the front wall and returns on the same line.

Volley Same as *fly shot.*

Wallpaper Ball Ball that hugs the wall so closely that it is hard or impossible to return (racquetball).

Winners *Kill shots* (racquetball).

Hang Gliding

Aileron Hinged panel at the rear of a wing that can be adjusted to tip up or down to control maneuvers in flight.

Airfoil Wing or other surface shaped to obtain lift from the air through which it moves.

Airframe The structural skeleton of a hang glider or aircraft.

Airspeed Speed measured in miles per hour of a hang glider relative to the air that surrounds it.

Altitude Height above mean sea level or above ground level, abbreviated as A.G.L.

Angle of Attack The angle at which the air meets the forward tip of a wing.

Axis Line of a plane. May be *longitudinal* (nose-to-tail); *lateral* (wingtip-to-wingtip); or *vertical* (bottom-to-top) of the aircraft.

Bank To tip to one side.

Biplane Aircraft with two wings.

Center of Gravity Center point of the weight of a hang glider.

Chord Length of a wing, measured from tip to back, or trailing edge.

Crab To move through the air sideways to the wind.

Control Bar The bottom end of a metal triangle suspended beneath the wing of a hand glider. The pilot holds this bottom end and uses it to control the flight of the flighter.

Dive To descend steeply through the air.

Drag Resistance through the air created by the hang glider.

Drift To move sideways through the air.

Elevator Hinged, horizontal tail surface of a hang glider that will force the nose up or down.

Empennage All tail parts of a hang glider or airplane.

Fin Vertical section of tail assembly.

Foot Launch Take off accomplished by the pilot without mechanical aids.

Fuselage Body of a hang glider.

G Force The total force on the surface of a hang glider, measured in terms of the force of gravity.

Glide To coast along the wind, in flight.

Glider Motorless aircraft that depends on gravity and winds for flight.

Glide Ratio   Ratio of glide distance to height lost because of weight.

Ground Effect   A cushion of air under the wing when the glider is in flight close to the ground.

Ground Loop   To roll a hang glider end-over-end on the ground.

Ground Speed   The speed of a glider rated in miles per hour.

Hang Glider   An unpowered single- or dual-seated vehicle whose take off and landing capability is dependent on the pilot and whose flight characteristics are generated by air currents only.

Landing Speed   The rate in miles per hour of the landing.

Leading Edge   The front edge of a wing.

Lift   The upward or "carrying" capability of wing surface.

Mushy   Inadequate hang glider response to pilot control.

Logbook   Record of all flights.

Pancake   To fall to the earth flatly is "to pancake in."

Pitch   Nose-up or nose-down flying characteristics.

Porposing   A series of nose-up and nose-down maneuvers, resembling a swimming porpoise.

Prone Harness   Harness used to enable the pilot to lie flat in a hang glider.

Rogallo Wing   Triangular or V-shaped wing developed by Francis Rogallo.

Rudder   Hinged panel attached to the rear edge of the tail fin. Controls yaw in flight.

Soar   To fly without power and without loss of altitude.

Sink   To lose altitude in the air.

Sink Rate   The rate of descent.

Sock   Wind indicator used to indicate direction of winds on the ground.

Span   Length of wing, tip-to-tip.

Spin   Downward corkscrewing action.

Stability   Ability of an airworthy hang glider to fly in a controlled position if the pilot lets controls loose.

Stabilizer   Fixed horizontal tail panel.

Stall   Loss of air flow caused by an excessive angle of attack (excessive wing up or wing down).

Strut   Wing brace.

Stick   Control bar used to move ailerons and elevator.

Swing Seat   Suspension system that allows the pilot to sit upright to pilot a hang glider.

Tactile Flight   Flight control through the use of the senses. Opposite of instrument control in aircraft flight.

Trailing Edge   Rear edge of a wing.

Trim   The balance of a hang glider in flight.

Turbulence   Unpredictable and "bumpy" air currents.

Updrafts   Air currents moving up.

U.S.H.G.A.   United States Hang Gliding Association, official representative of the sport of hang gliding.

Wind Sheer   A sudden and dangerous "waterfall of wind" that often accompanies thunder-storms and that can knock small or large aircraft from the sky.

Wing Loading   The total weight of the hang glider and pilot divided by the total wing footage.

Yaw   To turn flatly on the vertical axis.

Horse Racing

Allowance   A race in which horses are matched by age, sex, or money won and in which poorer horses are allowed to carry less weight.

Bug Boy   An apprentice jockey, one who has not won 40 races.

Chalk   The odds-on favorite to win—as in "the chalk horse."

Claiming   A race requiring owners to state their horses' values before the race. The horses then can be bought, or "claimed," for that price before the race.

Colors   Also called "silks" these are the distinguishing jackets and caps worn by jockeys.

Daily Double   A wager in which the player attempts to pick the winners of two races on the day's card.

Exacta (also called Perfecta)   A wager in which the player attempts to pick the winner and second-place finisher in order.

Field Horses   Two or more horses grouped together for betting purposes. A bet for one field horse is a bet for all in that group.

Furlong   Either 220 yards or ⅛ mile.

Futurity Race   A race for 2-year-olds scheduled far in advance, sometimes before the horse is born.

Handicap   Weight added to superior horses to make a race more even.

Handicapper   The person who assigns the amount of weight to be added to a horse. More commonly, the term refers to someone who rates horses and their chances of winning.

In the Money   Gamblers can win on three positions   win, place, and show. The horse owners, however, take a portion of the purse for running fourth, or "in the money."

Irons   The stirrups. A jockey is said to be "in the irons" when he races.

Inquiry   A review of a race by track officials, who look for violations of racing rules.

Maiden   A horse that has not won a race.

Morning Line   Odds set by a handicapper on the morning of race day before bets are taken. Generally not considered a good basis on which to place a bet, because ratings are based on past performance only.

Objection   A complaint filed by a jockey as soon as a race ends; leads to an inquiry.

Player   Anyone who bets on horses.

Paddock   The enclosure where horses are saddled immediately prior to a race.

Pari-Mutuel A system of odds-making determined by the bettors, based on the amount of money wagered on each horse. Means "between ourselves" in French.

Photo Finish A race so close at the finish that a final decision is withheld until a photograph taken at the wire can be developed.

Post time All horses are in the gates and ready to race. Signals the end of betting.

Purse The prize money awarded in a race.

Quinella Similar to the Exacta, but bettor wins no matter which of his two chosen horses finishes first and second.

Rail The fence around the infield. A horse running the shortest route is said to be "on the rail."

Slow Track Refers to a wet track, which slows down the horses.

Scratch A horse that has been withdrawn from a race.

Sprint A short race designed for fast horses with less endurance.

Stakes Race A race for superior horses that have owners who must nominate them far in advance and must pay an assortment of high fees, assuring a big purse.

Steward A race official, usually on horse-back, who monitors the race, horses, jockeys, and trainers for any improprieties.

Super Six A wagering opportunity in which the player is asked to pick the winners of six consecutive races.

Tarmac The paved outdoor viewing area near the finish line.

Thoroughbred A specific breed of horse developed in England from the Arab, Turkish, and other breeds.

Tip Sheet Any number of supposedly authoritative printed sheets bearing the names of horses given the best chances of winning.

Totalizator (or Tote Board) Big computer board that "totes" the odds on each horse and figures payoffs.

Trifecta Wagering requiring player to pick first-, second-, and third-place finishers.

Win, Place, and Show First, second, and third placers.

Wire The finish line.

Wire-to-Wire Refers to a horse that leads a race from start to finish. Reprinted by permission of *The Dallas Times Herald*.

Ice Hockey

Advance To move the puck toward the goal.

Attacking Zone Area of the opponent's goal.

Back Diagonal Pass To pass to a teammate across the ice on a diagonal line and behind the passing player.

Blind Pass To pass to a teammate without looking at that player.

Blue Line Line that shows each team's defensive zone. Similar to the 25-yard line to the end zone in football.

Bodycheck   To use a player's body to stop an opponent. Generally the same usage as "block" in football.

Breakaway   To skate toward the opponent's goal with only the goalkeeper to beat for a score.

Center Zone   Area between offensive and defensive zones.

Check Back   To skate toward the player's goal to help the goalkeeper.

Clearing the Puck   Moving the puck away from the team's own goal.

Cover Up   To guard an opponent near a team's own goal to prevent a score or attempted score.

Defensive Zone   Area of the team's own goal.

Deke   To fake a defender or goalie.

Dig   To fight for the puck; to take it away from an opponent.

Drop Pass   To stop the puck and allow a teammate to pick it up.

Face off   When the puck is dropped between two opposing players to start or restart play.

Feeding   To pass the puck to a teammate.

Forechecking   To check an opponent in his zone of the ice.

Goal   In hockey, the goal is 4 feet high and 6 feet wide and made of net. When the puck enters the net, one point is scored.

Hat Trick   Three goals in one game by the same player.

Hooking   A penalty when a player uses his stick to prevent another player from moving.

Icing   When a player shoots the puck down the ice from his zone across the opping team's goal line. The result is a stoppage in play and a faceoff in the defending zone of the team that committed the icing.

Major Penalty   Five minutes (or more) in the penalty box.

Minor Penalty   Two minutes in the penalty box.

Neutral Zone   Center area of the ice from one blue line across the red line to the other blue line. Roughly similar to the area from the 25-yard line across the 50-yard line to the opposite 25-yard line in football.

Offside   When a player precedes the puck into the attacking zone.

Offside Lines   Same as blue lines.

Penalty Box   Seat off the ice that a player must sit in to serve time for a foul.

Penalty Time   Specified time that a player must spend in the penalty box.

Poke Check   To stab at the puck with the stick.

Red Line   Line that separates the ice into two halves. Similar to the 50-yard linee in football.

Save   Defensive play by the goalie that prevents a score.

Slapshot   A shot on goal in which the players winds up and violently slaps the puck.

Short-handed goal   when a player scores a goal while his team has fewer players on the ice than the opposing team due to penalty

Uncovered   Offensive player left in front of opponent's goal without a defensive player blocking the goal.

Zamboni   Machine that rebuilds and smoothes the ice. To suggest that a player skates "like a Zamboni" would hardly be a compliment.

Motor Sports

Altered   Automobile or motorcycle that has been modified after it leaves the factory.

Apex   The point during a turn in which the car comes closest to inside edge of the corner. A tight apex usually means a good turn.

Back Off   To reduce speed.

Banking, Banked Turn   Turn that has a raised outer side to help driving control during the turn.

BHP   (Brake Horse Power)   Net power available at the output end of the engine. Brake refers to a dynamometer, a measuring mechanism, not the brakes of the car.

Bite   Tire traction on the road.

Block   Cylinder-containing unit of the engine.

Blower   Supercharged engine.

Blown   Two meanings   a blown engine may mean (a) an engine equipped with a supercharger, or (b) an engine that has a massive failure during a race.

Brick Yard   Common name for the Indianapolis 500.

Bucket Seat   Single seat contoured to body shape.

CC   Cubic centimeters. Engine displacement is usually referred to in CCs.

Camber   The angle at which the tires sit on the road.

Can-Am   The Canadian-American Championship for race car drivers.

Charger   Aggressive driver.

Chassis   Underside part of the car, usually consisting of frame and axles, brakes, wheels, engine, transmission, driveline, and exhaust components.

Chicane   Barriers added to an existing road to make the turns tighter or to add a turn or series of turns to an existing straight road.

Christmas Tree   Series of vertical lights that act as a "countdown" to the start of a drag race. There is a green "Go" light; a yellow "Warning" light, and a red "Foul" light, which means the driver jumped the start. The Christmas trees is positioned so that the driver can see it at the start of a drage race.

Circuit   Course used for racing in which drivers repeat the same route.

Closed Event   Race in which spectators or unauthorized drivers are not admitted.

Club Race   Race for members of a particular sports car club; usually refers to an amateur race.

Cool-Off Lap   Extra lap after a course that is driven at a slower speed than the race, to ensure that the engine parts cool slowly.

Cut-Off Point   A location before a turn at which point the driver takes his foot off the throttle and brakes the car for the turn.

Detroit Iron   Uncomplimentary term used by sports car elitists to describe most Detroit-made vehicles.

DNF   Did Not Finish. Started the race, but did not complete it.

DNS   Did Not Start. Entered the race, but did not start.

DOHC   Double Over-Head Camshaft cylinder head.

Dial In   To make adjustments to an engine. To "fine tune" it.

Differential   Gear-drive mechanism that transfers power from drive shaft to wheel. Differential refers to different speed of each wheel in a turn.

Displacement   Volume in cubic measure of a cylinder or engine.

Drafting   Same as *slipstreaming*.

Drift   Controlled slide, using engine power to keep the car on the road.

Driver's School   Special school for race drivers, using a closed race course to teach time trials, racing, and so on.

Esses   Winding curves on a race course.

ET   Elapsed Time. Drag racing term for a timed ¼-mile straight run.

Fire Suit   Protective fire-resistant suit worn by drivers.

Flags   Flags used in motor racing carry the following meanings:

- **Black**   Return to pits.
- **Blue (motionless)**   Another car is following you closely.
- **Blue (waved)**   Another driver is trying to pass you—make room.
- **Checkered (black and white)**   Driver has completed the race.
- **Green**   Starts the race.
- **Red**   Stop—clear the course.
- **White**   Emergency vehicle on the course.
- **Yellow (motionless)**   No passing, caution.
- **Yellow with red stripes**   Caution—oil on the course.

Flagman   Official responsible for displaying various flags to drivers.

Flat Four   Horizontally opposed four-cylinder engine (old VWs had flat four engines).

Flat Out   Racing at maximum speed.

Flat Six   Horizontally opposed six-cylinder engine (the Corvair had a flat six engine).

Flip   To turn over or to roll over.

Flying Start   A "running start," passing the starting line at race speed, or nearly race speed.

FoMoCo   Parts made by Ford Motor Company.

Formula   Regulations governing a race car that involve engine displacement, length and width, weight, size of fuel tank, and type of fuel used. In general, these are common formulas for race cars:

- **Formula I**   Race car powered by a non-supercharged V-8 or V-12 engine from 1,600 to 3,000 cc (up to 450 horsepower). Generally has a wedge shape, wide treadless tires, and 13-inch wheels. Has a self-starter and a transmission with four or five forward gears, plus reverse.
- **Formula II**   Slightly smaller version of Formula I car, has supercharged four-cylinder production engine of 1,300 to 1,600 cc. Generally more popular in Europe.

- **Formula III** Racing car powered with a production engine up to 1,600 cc. Has specific limitations on air intake to the engine.
- **Formula A** Similar to Formula 5000.
- **Formula Atlantic** British car similar to American Formula B.
- **Formula B** Formula car powered by a nonsupercharged production engine of 1,100 to 1,600 cc, powered by gasoline. Formula B is smaller and lighter than Formula 5000.
- **Formula C** Formula car powered by an engine up to 1,100 cc.
- **Formula F (Formula Ford)** Formula car powered by a nonsupercharged 1,600 cc English Ford or Ford Pinto engine.
- **Formula 5000** Formula car powered by an engine of 1,600 to 3,000 cc or a production V-8 engine of up to 5000 cc. No supercharging allowed. Must run on gasoline. Generally similar to the Formula I automobile.
- **Formula V** Formula car that is powered by a Volkswagon 1,200 cc engine, gearbox, transmission, and wheels.
- **Formula Super V** Formula car that is powered by a Volkswagon 1,600 cc engine and gearbox, and runs on gasoline.

Four Wheel Drive Mechanism that allows power to be distributed to all four wheels.

Fuel Cell Special rubber-like container for gasoline, built so that it will not be split open during a crash. Might be called a "safety gas tank."

Full Bore Driving at maximum throttle.

Funny Car Drag race car that has had unorthodox modifications. Generally, a funny car has a one-piece body, is powered by a supercharged engine and has a driver's compartment behind the engine. The engine is completely exposed, rear wheels are wide, and front wheels are bicycle-type. Often contains a parachute-stopping device.

FWD Four Wheel Drive.

Getting a Tow Same as *slipstreaming*.

Grid Position for cars at beginning of race. Also refers to markings on a track.

Gymkhana Competition for best time on a Chicane-type course.

Hairpin Ultratight turn on a race course.

Hairy Frightening occurrence.

Hemi Car with hemispherical combustion chambers.

Hill Climb Race for the best clock time up a prescribed hill course.

History Same as *totalled*.

IFS Independent Front Suspension.

IRS Independent Rear Suspension.

Impound Area Area where cars may be required to be taken after a race so that officials can inspect them to make sure they have satisfied entrance requirements.

Jet Dragster Drag racer powered by a jet engine.

Lap One complete circuit of a race course.

La Mans Start   A start in which drivers run from a starting line, get into their cars and drive away.

Line   The best path through a race course.

MPG   Miles per gallon.

Mags   Wheel rims made of magnesium; used because magnesium is very light.

MoPar   Parts made by Chrysler Corporation.

Mule   Unattractive prototype automobile, made for testing or demonstration purposes only, usually without finishing touches, such as chrome.

NASCAR   National Association for Stock Car Racing.

OHV   Over Head Valve.

Oval   Oval-shaped track.

Pace Car   Vehicle used to pace racers at the start of a race.

Paddock   Area near the track where cars are worked on. Usually similar to *pits*.

Pit   An off-the-track area where a driver can get gas, minor repairs during the race, tire changes, and advice from crew members.

Pit Lane   Lane that drivers use to enter and exit the pit area to and from a race course.

Pit Stop   Stop made during race for fuel, minor repairs, and so on.

Prototype   Test model of a new car.

Pump Fuel   Fuel that is "consumer quality," that is, that can be obtained at any gas station.

Qualifying Times   Trials used to determine race position based on best time during trials.

Rally   Race organized to test navigational skills of driver and navigator. Contestants are given a route map and must check in at various predetermined points to obtain their time from point to point. Best time wins.

Roll Bar   Safety bar that protects the driver in the case of a roll-over accident. Sometimes called headache bar for obvious reasons.

SCCA   Sports Car Club of America.

SOHC   Single Over Head Cam engine.

Shut the Gate   To block a driver's path during a race.

Slipstreaming   To drive slightly behind another driver during a race to take advantage of reduced air resistance.

Slingshotting   To drive around the lead car after slipstreaming.

Sports Car   Racing automobile with high performance characteristics.

Sporty Car   Car that is promoted as a sports car but because of mediocre characteristics, is really not a sports car.

Stand On It   To hold the throttle pedal completely on the floor.

Standing Start   Race start with all cars motionless, with drivers ready and engines idling.

Starter   Official who controls the start of a race.

Stock   Automobile that has not been modified since being delivered from the factory.

Street Legal   Automobile that has been modified for race use, but has to be remodified for safety (street) purposes.

Supercharger   Engine that has been modified by a mechanism that blows exhaust air back into engine at a higher rate than air entering the engine from the outside. Gives a power boost to the engine.

Tach (Tachometer)   Meter that measures engine speed in revolutions per minute.

Time Trials   Laps on a specific course for the fastest speed.

Totalled   Completely wrecked.

Torsion Bar   Rod in a suspension system attached to prevent side slipping of the automobile.

Transaxle   Transmission and rear axle mounted as a single unit.

Pocket Billiards (Pool)

Action   Betting on games. *Fast action* is heavy betting.

A "G"   One thousand dollars.

Angled   When the lip of a pocket prevents a straight shot from the cue to an object ball.

Army   Betting money   "I've got my Army with me."

Backer   Banker for a gambler. A nonplayer usually, who supplies betting money. The backer will usually cover all losses, but will take a percentage of the hustler's winnings.

Bank Shot   A shot against a cushion and then into a pocket.

Billiards (or three-cushion billiards)   A game played on a table without pockets. Billiards is played with three balls, two white and one red. Each player (only two can play at one time) uses a white ball as a cue, and shoots to strike the other two. The cue ball must touch the cushions at least three times before striking the second of the two object balls. Billiards is a very difficult game that demands a thorough knowledge of table angles and English. Billiards is played for money much less frequently than pocket pool.

Break   The shot that opens the rack; the first shot of a game.

Bridge   The act of holding the table end of the cue stick between the index finger and the thumb. There are two kinds of bridges   the closed bridge, with the index finger circling the cue, or the open bridge, with the cue sliding down the fleshy part of the hand, between the thumb and index finger. The closed bridge is more accurate and preferred. Bridge also refers to the mechanical bridge, a device used to aid the player in making shots he couldn't normally make.

"C" Note   One hundred dollar bill.

Call Shot   A shot that requires the player to tell others which ball he or she intends to shoot into that pocket.

Carom   A rebounding shot of one or more balls.

Chalk   Dry lubricant for the cue tip. Without frequent chalking, scratches (missed shots) are likely.

Combination Shot A shot in which the cue ball strikes one or more balls. The object ball finally is hit by one of the other balls. A "chain reaction" type of shot.

Con The art of making a bet, that is, "to con." From the criminal's lexicon—"the con game."

Cue Ball The plain white ball that is hit into the numbered balls.

Cue Stick The instrument of the game. Sticks usually weigh between 15 and 21 ounces and average 55 inches long. Pros and hustlers prefer a heavier cue, usually 20–21 ounces.

Cue Tip The leather end-piece of the stick that is chalked.

Cushion The cloth-edge of the table rails.

Cut To hit an object ball so that it will angle.

Draw or Reverse English Stroking the cue ball below its center will cause it to "draw" (spin) back toward the player.

Dumping A game that a hustler deliberately loses to fool spectators who have bets on the match. Not a common practice. No hustler wants a reputation as a "dumper."

English The art of adding spin to the cue ball to make it swing to the left or right after hitting the object ball. An essential part of a position game.

Eight-Ball Mostly an amateur's game. Players pocket either the low balls (numbered 1–7) or the high balls (numbered 9–15), then call the shot on the eight ball to win.

Follow Shot Stroking the ball above its center will cause it to follow the object ball. Follow shots are also used in position games.

Fun Players Lambs. Tournament winners. Amateurs.

Heart Courage. "That player has real heart."

High Run The number of balls consecutively pocketed before missing, in one game or tournament.

Hugging the Rail Stroking action that will cause the cue ball or the object ball to roll down the rail along the edge of the table.

Hustler A lion. A money player. Not an amateur.

Jaw When the object ball hits the sides of the pocket and bounces back and forth without dropping, it is said to have "jawed."

Knife and Fork Hustlers' eating and sleeping money. That is, "I have to remember my knife and fork" (remember not to bet it on a game and thereby risk going broke without money to eat with).

Kiss See Carom.

Lamb An innocent; an amateur.

Lemoning Winning in an amateurish fashion or deliberately losing a game.

Lion A hustler.

Lock-Up A game that can't be lost, because of inferior opponents. A cinch.

Locksmiths Hustlers who specialize in playing lock-up games.

Making a Game Setting up some action or betting.

Massé Extreme English on the cue ball. Perhaps the most difficult shot in the game. The cue stick must be held almost straight up and down.

Miscue The scratch or miss shot, caused by inaccurately stroking the cue ball.

Natural A simple shot; a lock-up shot.

Nine-Ball A hustler's game, because it is fast and because bets can be made on individual balls, usually the five ball and the nine ball. Only the first nine balls are racked. They are pocketed in rotation (1–9) and the game is won by pocketing the nine. The nine can be pocketed on a good break shot or by shooting it from another ball, such as, cue ball to three ball to nine ball to pocket.

One-Pocket Another hustler's game. Each player shoots into one corner pocket of the table.

O.P.M. Other People's Money, which hustlers prefer to play with.

Position The arrangement of the balls on the table. A good player can keep all balls on one-half of the table, thereby enabling him or her to shoot short shots and stay alive in the game.

Rack The triangular arrangement of balls on the table before the game begins. Also refers to the wooden triangle used to form the balls into this shape prior to the game.

Rotation Shooting the balls according to numerical sequence.

Run Consecutively pocketing as many balls as possible (see *high run*).

Safe To shoot so as not to leave your opponent room to shoot. "Playing it safe."

Scratch A playing error in which the cue ball falls into a pocket. Some hustlers scratch deliberately to fake incompetence.

Setup An easy shot. Same as "natural."

Shortstop A player who can be beaten only by the top players.

Snookered A bad position, that is, one in which the player can not shoot a straight shot.

Speed or True Speed The player's ability.

Spot To give away points or balls to one's opponent; that is, to handicap.

Stalling Occasionally losing a game to keep an opponent betting.

Stroke The act of hitting the cue ball. "To find my stroke," is to develop a good swing. The stroke is as important as the golfer's swing.

Sucker The object of the hustler's attention; a loser.

Takedown The amount of money won on the tables.

Weight Points of ability. To "give away weight," is to give away points in a handicap game. "A heavyweight," is a top-flight player.

Rugby

Advantage Play may be allowed to continue after a rules violation if the fouled team gains territory or a technical advantage.

Cross-Kick An attacking kick across the field of play.

Dead Ball Play is dead when the referee blows the whistle.

Defending Team   Team on defense in its own half of the field.

Drawing Your Man   To make an opponent commit himself to attack the ball carrier, rather than to attack a player about to receive a pass.

Dribbling   To control the ball with short kicks, often with the shins or with the instep of the foot.

Drop Kick   The ball is dropped to the ground and kicked on the rebound. Similar to old usage in American football.

Drop-Out   Method of starting play from behind the 25-yard line, when an attacking team kicks, passes, or knocks the ball into the in-goal without a score. A drop kick is also used to begin play again from the center of the field after an unsuccessful conversion attempt.

Dummy   To pretend to pass the ball.

Falling on the Ball   A player may fall on the ball usually by turning his back to the opposing team. The player may not hinder the play by doing so and may not handle the ball in falling on it.

Field   A rugby field is 110 yards long from ingoal line to in-goal line; 75 yards wide.

Five-Yard Scrum   If a defending player kicks, passes, or knocks the ball out of the field of play or over his own goal line, the referee may call a scrum on the 5 yard line on the opposite side of the field from where the ball went into the in-goal area. The ball is given to the attacking team.

Fly Kick   A wild kick.

Foot-Up   Any member of the front row of either team in a scrum who advances either foot before the ball goes into play. A penalty results.

Foul   A foul results in rugby when a player strikes an opponent, tackles early or late, kicks or trips another player, or holds or pushes an opponent without the ball.

Free Kick   A kick for a score that may be made after a fair catch.

Game   Consists of two halves of 35 minutes each (40 minutes in an international game). There is a 5-minute period at halftime, but no player is allowed off the field.

Goal   A successful kick that results in 3 points.

Grounding the Ball   A player grounds the ball by falling on it or holding it on the ground to score a *try*, which is somewhat similar to a touchdown in American football.

Grubber Kick   A kick that bounces along the ground.

Hacking   To fly kick the ball.

Halfway Line   Similar to the 50-yard line in American football.

In-Goal Area   Equivalent to the area behind the goal line in American football.

Knock-On   This occurs when a player propels the ball toward the opponents dead-ball line. (Beyond the end zone in American football).

Line-out   A line formed by two teams parallel to the touch line waiting for the ball to be thrown in between them.

Locks   The second line of players in a scrum.

Lying Deep   In attack, the backs adopt a deep formation to allow themselves running room. Somewhat similar to the backfield formation in a kick return in American football.

Lying on the Ball   There is a penalty for stopping play by lying on the ball.

Lying Shallow   In defense, the backs adapt a formation closer to their opponents.

Mark   A fair catch from a kick or an intentional throw forward. The player must shout "mark." Similar to a fair catch in American football.

Maul   Action surrounding a player with the ball.

No-Side   The end of the game.

Number of Players   There are 15 on each side in amateur rugby, 13 in professional play.

Numbering System   There is no set numbering system for players as there is in American football.

Offside   This occurs when a player is ahead of the ball, when it was last touched by a member of his team. No penalty except if the player obstructs an opponent, plays the ball himself, or is within 10 yards of an opponent who is waiting to play the ball.

Penalty Kick   This is awarded to a team after a rules violation by the opposing team.

Penalty Try   If a try would have scored (in the opinion of the referee) without a foul, a team that has been fouled may attempt a try.

Place Kick   A kick made from a ball on the ground.

Player Ordered Off   Player has been thrown out of the rest of the game for a rules violation.

Punt   A kick made before it touches the ground. Similar usage to American football. This is a tactical movement in rugby, but does not score.

Push Over Try   When the ball is in a scrum and the defending team is pushed into its own in-goal area, a push over try is scored when a member of the attacking team falls on the ball.

Referee   Sole rules judge on the field during play.

Ruck   A loose scrum.

Rugby league/rugby union   The two main branches of organized rugby. The main difference between the two involves contesting for possession of the ball. Rugby union allows players to contest the ball after tackles in scrums, line-outs, etc.

Scrummage   A scrum is formed by players from each team prior to the begin of play. The front row of each team in a scrum is composed of three players. The ball is thrown into the scrum and the players fight to control the ball with their feet. When one team controls the ball, the scrum is wheeled and opened and field play begins.

Substitutions   Players may not be substituted in rugby except when they are injured so badly that they are unable to continue. In special matches or international matches, now more than two players may be substituted for medical reasons and the injured player may not return to the game.

Tackle A player holding the ball may be tackled so the ball is on the ground or so that he is not free to continue play.

The Pack The forwards.

Touch-Lines Similar to sidelines in American football.

Touch-Down Not a score. This occurs when a player downs the ball in his own in-goal area.

Try A score in the goal area. Counts 4 points in rugby league and five points in rugby union.

Up and Under A kick within the field of play timed so that the kicking team is under the ball when it comes down.

Wheel When the ball is in a scrum, the scrum turns and breaks open and the team possessing the ball advances.

Scuba Diving and Skin Diving

Air Embolism Illness caused when a diver holds his or her breath during an ascent to the surface.

Anoxia Insufficient supply of oxygen.

Aqualung Trade name now synonymous with scuba.

Atmospheric pressure Air pressure at sea level.

Ballast Weights used to allow the diver to sink or maintain a specific depth.

Bends (Caisson Disease) Excess nitrogen in the body, that expands as the body ascends.

Buddy Line Safety technique in scuba diving in which two divers are linked by a safety line.

Buoyancy The upward force exerted by water or other fluids on a submerged or floating body.

Compressor Machine that is used to fill air tanks for scuba diving.

Cousteau Jacques Cousteau, famous explorer, co-inventor (with Emile Gagnan) of the Aqualung, in 1942.

Cylinder Same as *tank*.

Decompression To lessen the pressure underwater; to ascend to the surface.

Dry Suit Waterproof rubber suit worn by scuba divers.

Embolism Presence of air bubbles in the diver's circulation system.

Face Mask Mask used by scuba divers and skin divers that allows a clear view under water.

Fathom Approximately 6 feet.

Fins Rubber froglike "feet" that aid in scuba diving and skin diving.

Flotation Gear Life vests and other bouyant material that allow the diver or swimmer to float.

Frogmen Scuba divers trained for underwater demolition, exploration, and so on.

Hyperoxia Excess oxygen in body tissues.

Hyperventilation Breathing rate higher than normal.

Mae West Life jacket for use on the surface of the water.

Narcosis (Nitrogen narcosis)   Illness that results when the diver dives too deep and nitrogen in the diver's air supply has a narcotic effect. Divers have been known to spit out their scuba mouthpiece and drown.

One Atmosphere   Air pressure at sea level; 14.7 pounds per square inch.

Recompression   Treatment for decompression illness by the use of a compression chamber that reduces compression levels at a safe rate.

Regulator   Mechanical device that governs the flow of air from the scuba tanks to the scuba diver.

Scuba   Stands for Self-Contained Underwater Breathing Apparatus.

Skin Diving   Diving, generally on the surface of the water without scuba tanks, and usually with a snorkel.

Snorkel   J-shaped breathing tube that allows the skin diver to view under water (face down) while breathing surface air, without inhaling water.

Spear Guns   Pressure power guns used underwater to stun or kill marine life.

Tanks   Metal containers used to contain the scuba diver's air supply.

Tidal Volume   The volume of air that enters and leaves the lungs during normal breathing.

Toxic   Poisonous.

Shuffleboard

Court   A shuffleboard court is 6 feet wide and 52 feet long, with a concrete or terrazo surface.

Cue   A stick no longer than 6 feet, 3 inches, used to propel discs toward the target.

Dead Disc   Disc that remains on (or returns to) the court after striking an object other than a live disc.

Disc   Shuffleboard discs are made of wood and are 6 inches in diameter and ¾ to 1 inch thick. Four are red and four are black.

Foot of Court   The end opposite the Head.

Game   Based on 50, 75, or 100 points. Match play is best 2 out of 3 games.

Head of Court   The end where play begins to start a match.

Heistation Shot   A shot in which the player pauses momentarily during the shot. Illegal.

Round   Playing all discs from one end of the court is a round.

Scoring   One 10-point area, two 8-point areas, two 7-point areas, and one 10-off area.

Sky Diving (Parachuting)

"A" License   Beginning license issued by the U.S. Parachute Association.

A.O.D.   Automatic Opening Device. A barometric- and speed-oriented mechanism that will automatically open the jumper's main parachute after a predetermined number of seconds (CAP-3) or will automatically open the jumper's reserve parachute at a minimum safe altitude (Sentinel). Basic Safety Rules (BSRs) suggest outfitting all novice jumpers with Sentinels on their reserves.

A.S.O. Area Safety Officer, in charge of safety requirements and minimum safety standards for several area drop zones or clubs.

Accuracy The art of free-fall jumping in which competitors aim for a target disc. Expert accuracy jumpers can hit the disc time after time; misses are usually measured in cents in competition. *Style* and *accuracy* are slowly fading in popularity in favor of *R W* and *Sequential R W.*

Altimeter Mechanical device that automatically gives the jumper a readout of actual height above ground. Altimeters are getting smaller and smaller. They are now sold to fit on the wrist, strapped to the chest strap of most parachute harnesses, or worn on the top of a chest-mount reserve. Altimeters measure in thousands of feet or in meters.

Apex The top of a parachute.

Arch and Count Basic student learning technique and position. The arch prepares the student for free-fall and the count prepares him for a delay before opening his parachute.

Assist Pocket A pocket built into the top of a *sleeve* that catches air during deployment and aids in proper deployment of the sleeve.

"B" License Second license issued by the U.S.P.A.

B.S.R.s. Basic Safety Rules (Regulations). Rules, laws, and guidelines issued by the F.A.A., U.S.P.A., and local officials governing jumping.

B 4, B 12 Surplus parachutes, modified for sport use.

Backloop Back flip done in free-fall. Completion of backloops, front loops, and barrelrolls are requirement for the U.S.P.A. "C" license and are highly recommended for good RW jumping.

Backpack The main parachute, worn on the back and the reserve on the chest, as opposed to the *piggyback* or *pigrig*, a tandem combination of the main and reserve, both worn on the back.

Bag Deployment Deployment of the main parachute from a bag, similar in size and shape to a knapsack, as opposed to a sleeve deployment. A bag will usually, although not always, allow a parachute to be packed smaller and tighter than a sleeve.

Barrelroll Side roll, to the left or right, done in free-fall. Also a requirement for the class "C" license and good RW techniques.

Base The "anchor" position in any relative work formation. The base is caught in free-fall (*pinned*) by the second, or pin jumper. A good base-and-pin combination is necessary to good fast stars. Without a stable base-and-pin the rest of the formation may be sacrificed.

Base Jumping Skydiving from an altitude high enough to be reasonably safe, but without an airplane or helicopter (*without any aircraft*). The sky diver may jump from a skyscraper (*Building*), TV Antenna, a bridge (*Span*), or a natural height such as a cliff (*Earth*). Not for the inexperienced. Jumpers usually face arrest if they jump from office buildings or other such "non-jumpable" facilities. Has nothing to do with "base-and-pin" RW jumping.

Baton Pass   In the earliest days of RW jumping, a baton pass between two jumpers in freefall was considered the ultimate achievement. Now no one bothers with this; everyone goes to four- or eight-man or larger stars.

Batwings   Rigid or semirigid extensions on the jumpsuit arms and legs. Because rigid batwings made it impossible for the jumper to bend his or her arm and pull the ripcord, batwings were judged suicidal and outlawed years ago. Not to be confused with underarm additions to the jumpsuit that are cloth and flexible.

Beech   Twin Beech aircraft. Beeches and other aircraft capable of carrying 8, 10, or 12 jumpers (or more, in the case of aircraft like the SkyVan and the DC-3) made RW jumping possible.

Beer Run   In many parachute clubs, the achievement of some individual goal— first free-fall, first two-man, SCR jump, first ride under a high performance canopy, or other achievement—means that the participant buys beer for everyone; sometimes beer to drink, sometimes beer to be showered over the jumper in question. Requirements vary with each parachute club. It's a rare jumper who hasn't had to buy beer for everyone sooner or later.

Bells   Jumpsuits with bell-bottomed sleeves and legs. The bells flare out in free-fall like the skin of a flying squirrel and allow the jumper greater capability for falling faster or slower and approaching a star with greater accuracy.

Blown Star   Free-fall star formation broken by a jumper who approaches the star too fast or too hard.

"Bomb Out"   Unpoised exit out the door of a jump plane. Mass exits during RW jumps are usually bomb outs.

Breakaway   See *cutaway*.

Break-Off Altitude   The altitude at which jumpers abandon RW jumping and get clear of each other for opening. With large stars (say 40 or 50 jumpers), break-off for some may well be as high as 5,000 feet.

Bungee   Heavy elastic bands that surround the container. When the sky diver pulls his or her ripcord, the pins and cones separate, the bungees pull the sides of the container apart, and the pilot chute emerges to begin the deployment sequence. Spring-loaded pilot chutes would probably emerge without the aid of bungees, but most old-style backpacks employ two or three bungees to ensure that the pilot chute emerges.

Butterfly Snap   Wide, butterfly-shaped flange used to connect the chest reserve parachute to the main harness.

Butt Strike   A classic fall in which the jumper hits the ground tailbone first rather than feet first. May cause temporary injury to tailbone, but is usually not serious. Jumpers who land with a butt strike in front of *whuffos* usually injure their pride most of all.

"C" License   Third license issued by the U.S.P.A.

C.S.O. Club Safety Officer, who ensures safe jumping at a particular sport parachute club or drop zone.

Calendering A process of treating fabric so that threads in the fabric are compressed and thus, less air gets through the fabric. A tighter weave results.

Canopy The fabric. The umbrella. The parachute. Does not usually include lines, risers, or capewells.

Canopy Assembly The parachute, sleeve, pilot chute, lines, sleeve retainer line, and sleeve. Everything ready to be packed into a container and harness.

Canopy RW Relative work in which parachutists "fly" two or more canopies. The upper parachute of a two-man *canopy stack* may fly with his feet entwined in the top of the canopy below him. Usually, although not always, attempted with square parachutes.

Canopy Release Mechanism that will release a main parachute so that a parachutist may deploy a reserve. Formerly all metallic, although modern state-of-the-art releases may be velcroed fabric.

Capewell Canopy release made by the Capewell Manufacturing Company. Generic term for all canopy releases is "capewell."

Caterpillar Club Club for all pilots who had to make a parachute jump to save their own lives in early aircraft. Charles Lindbergh was a member. Presumably named because of the lowly caterpillar that produced the silk used for early (pre-World War II) parachutes.

Center A commercial parachute business that rents gear, sells supplies, offers the first jump course, and offers aircraft for RW jumps. Comparable to a ski center.

Center Pull Reserve parachute harness with the ripcord centered, neither on the jumper's left nor right.

"Cents" Centimeters away from dead center, a nearly perfect score in accuracy jumping, as in "I had a three-cent jump last time."

Cessna Principal aircraft for jumping. Cessna aircraft make up 85% of the jump aircraft used for beginning and novice parachutists.

Chuting Up The act of putting on and checking one's parachute gear prior to boarding the aircraft.

Clear-and-Pull Five second (or less) free-fall delayed opening. Same as *hop-and-pop*.

Clock Before general use of the altimeter, parachutists used a stopwatch to gauge time and height in free-fall. A jump from 12,500 feet to an opening point of 2,500 feet was a *60-second-jump:* Because of the clocklike face, altimeters are now often called *clocks.* Sky divers who formerly used both an altimeter and a stopwatch now generally use only the altimeter. timeter.

Cloverleaf Ripcord handle with general shape of three-leaf clover.

Cone Cone-shaped piece of hardware, pierced to allow a pin to be inserted. The *pin-and-cone* lock the parachute pack closed. When the ripcord is pulled, the pins pull out of the cones, allowing the container to open and the sleeve or bag to emerge, thus beginning the development sequence.

Conference Multistate subdivision of the United States for administrative purposes, by the U.S. Parachute Association.

Conical One type of reserve parachute, usually 26 feet in diameter.

Connector Links Metal hardware that connects the risers and the suspension lines.

Container The part of the parachute pack that holds the parachute. The container is joined to the harness, which is fitted to the parachutist.

Controlled Air Space The sky above Air Force bases, cities, and other areas where parachuting is generally not allowed.

Control Lines Same as *steering lines*.

Conventional Rig Parachute system with an old-style, chest-mounted rig is considered conventional. New rigs are pigrigs.

Crabbing Steering a parachute sideways to the wind for accuracy in landing. If the wind is north-to-south, the parachutist will crab by facing east or west.

Cross Connector Links A set of lines connecting the risers on some reserve parachutes.

Cross Pull A ripcord that is across the body from the hand and arm used to pull; that is a cross pull for a right-handed parachutist would be a ripcord on his left side.

Crown Lines Lines across the apex of the ParaCommander or other similar parachute. Used to create tension during packing and help straighten the apex.

Cutaway The act of activating the capewells to jettison a malfunctioning main parachute so a reserve may be deployed without opening into the main. The parachutists' first cutaway is usually an awesome and memorable occasion.

"D" License An advanced parachuting license.

D Rings Metal rings, shaped like the letter "D" to which the chest-mounted reserve is attached.

DC-3 The Douglas workhorse of World War II, still in operation on some drop zones.

DL-7 Specific modification in which the steering modifications look like the letter "L" (there are two) and are seven panels apart.

D.O. Jump Delayed Opening. Free-fall of 10 seconds or more.

DZ Drop Zone. Where parachuting and skydiving is permitted.

Data Card Card carried inside the reserve container providing the name of the owner, type of canopy, and particularly, when the reserve was last packed and by which rigger.

Dead in the Air A jumper without horizontal speed; one who is simply moving down. Can be compared to a stalled ship that is "dead in the water."

Delay Any free-fall skydive in which the jumper opens his own parachute after leaving the jump plane. Delays are usually 10 seconds, 20 seconds, 30 seconds, 45 seconds, 60 seconds, and over 60 seconds.

Delta A free-fall body position in which the jumper's head and torso are lower than the legs. This allows the jumper to move diagonally downward and forward through the sky. RW jumpers who wish to become expert in their sport must master the *Delta* and *Track*.

Demo Jump   Any jump made off the usual drop zone, for spectators; usually at a county fair, circus, or other similar event. Only qualified jumpers can make Demo jumpers because of the added hazard of roads, power lines, buildings, spectators, and other obstacles.

Deployment   The act of the canopy opening after the jumper pulls his or her ripcord.

Deployment Bag   An alternative to the sleeve.

Dirt Dive   Rehearsal by all jumpers of a planned RW jump on the ground at the DZ.

Disc   Target for accuracy jumpers.

Dive   A head-down position used to catch a star or other formation. Also refers to the *jump*.

Docking   The art of approaching a star and entering by breaking the grip of two jumpers previously in the star, and thus widening the circle, or completing the formation, if not a round star.

Door Exit   Exiting the aircraft at the door, rather than on the strut.

Dope Rope   See *static line*. Uncomplimentary term.

Downwind Landing   Landing the parachute in the same direction as the wind is blowing increases the parachutist's landing speed. Not usually recommended.

Dummy Ripcord   Handle with a colored "flag" attached. Novice jumpers must make several good, precise dummy ripcord pulls before they can graduate to free-fall jumping. The dummy ripcord pull occurs when the parachutist is still on the static line.

Dump   To pull the ripcord and begin the development sequence, as in "I forgot where I was and dumped at 5,000 feet."

Exhibition Jump   Same as *demo jump*.

Exit   To leave the aircraft; may be either a *poised exit* or *bomb out*.

Expert   Sky diver with a "C" or "D" license.

F.A.I.   *Federal Aeronautique Internationale; international* governing body that controls international sky diving, hang gliding, soaring, and other sky sports. The U. S. Parachute Association licenses sky divers in this country on behalf of the F.A.I.

F.P.S.   Feet-per-second.

Field Packing   Immediate rolling or stowing the canopy in the pack for the trip back to the DZ, in the case of a missed spot or for packing later, if the parachutist wishes to repack at home.

Flake(verb)   To *flake a parachute* is to fold the panels for packing into the container, prior to jumping. A flake (noun) is a psychologically unreliable person to jump with. Most every DZ has its own local flakes.

Flare/Flarepoint   Point at which the jumper ends a dive and raises his head to approach the formation.

Flat Circular   Particular type of reserve canopy.

Flat Spin An uncontrolled spin, caused by inadequate body position and worsened by centrifugal force. Usually encountered by novice free-fall jumpers. If not stopped in time, can lead to blackouts and possible death.

Flat Turn Controlled turn. Jumpers in free-fall can turn left or right by using their shoulders, arms, and legs like rudders.

Flight Line Where the jump planes and other aircraft are fueled. No place to pack or dirt dive.

Floater An RW jumper who, because of weight or jumping ability, exits *before* the base and pin (often by hanging on the edge or outside of the aircraft door) and *floats* (waits) for the base and pin to establish the beginning of the formation.

Flotation Gear Used when a DZ is dangerously close to a body of water deep enough to drown in. Flotation gear comes in a variety of sizes and shapes, but is usually kidney-shaped or basketball-size inflatable balloons. Some jumpers believe that water gear that size is unreliable in keeping an adult afloat for any length of time.

Flyer RW jumper who exits the aircraft last (or nearly last) and has to dive considerable distances to reach the base and pin, substantially lower than he was on exit.

Frappe To *go in*, a fatality.

Frappe Hat Lightweight leather hat worn by RW jumpers. Nonrigid. Officially not recommended for novice jumpers.

Free-Fall Jump A delay of 10 seconds or less. More than 10 seconds is a *delayed opening* jump.

Frog Basic body position in free-fall. The body is relaxed and this is modified stable position. The frog is an accepted position for jumpers past the novice class. The head is slightly raised, chest slightly raised, arms bent at 45 degree angles. May be tightened into more compact position for greater vertical descent. So called because the basic position looks slightly like a frog at rest.

Front Loop Front flip in free-fall. Must be mastered for a class "C" license.

Funneled Star Star that breaks apart and falls into its own center.

Glide Angle The angle in which the parachute moves forward or the angle in which the parachutist approaches the target in accuracy jumping.

Golden Knights Nickname for the U.S. Army parachute exhibition team, headquartered at Fort Bragg, NC.

Grip Hold that the jumper has on another jumper to cement a formation. A *double grip* is a tandem grip by two jumpers on each others' arms, legs, or torsos.

Hand Track A method of moving forward in the air by vectoring air with the arms and hands. Usually an ineffective way to build or sustain horizontal speed toward the objective.

Hard Pull Ripcord pull that takes more than normal effort (more than about 22 pounds pressure). Packing problems usually account for hard pulls. A claim of a hard pull by a novice free-fall jumper is often attributable to unfamiliarity with the gear.

Harness   The part of the parachute system that the jumper tightens to form a cradle for his body. Usually the harness attaches at the chest, legs, and lower belly. The F.A.A. issues regulations regarding the strength of webbing used in the harness. A tight but comfortable harness lessens opening shock; a loose harness distorts opening shock and may cause injury to the jumper, especially in the groin.

Hazards   Anything that can cause injury or death to the jumper. Notably, large and deep bodies of water, electrical wires and power lines, buildings and other obstructions, manmade and natural.

Helmet   Required by all jumpers. Many RW jumpers are using hockey helmets and frappe hats instead of the usual rigid motorcycle helmet. Old cliché and rule of thumb   "If you have a $5 brain, use a $5 helmet."

Hesitation   Deployment sequence slower than the usual 1½ to 3 seconds. Hesitations are usually caused by the failure of the pilot chute to clear the jumper's back quickly enough.

High Performance   Usually defined as a ramair or wing-type parachute. Rates of forward speed for the three basic chute types are   rag chute or cheapo, up to 7 miles per hour forward; ParaCommander or PC-type, up to 17 mph; wing-type chute, 23 mph and faster.

Hockey Helmet   Used by RW jumpers, who think they get a better "feel of the air" with a lightweight helmet. Officially not recommended for novice jumpers.

Holding   Facing the wind, under canopy. If the prevailing wind is coming from the north at 10 mph and if the jumper is using a canopy with a "built-in" forward speed of 10 mph, facing into the wind will give him a speed of zero, thus he is holding. Turning with the wind or *running*, would, in this case, give him a forward speed of 20 mph (wind speed plus built-in speed of the parachute).

Hop-and-Pop   Same as *clear-and-pull*. An exit and free-fall of less than 10 seconds. Usually 5 seconds or under. The jumper *hops* off the step or door of the aircraft and *pops* open his parachute.

Hypoxia   Lightheadedness, giddiness, lack of motor control and reasoning ability caused by lack of oxygen to the brain. Jumpers above 12,000 feet (mean sea level) should be aware of the problems and potential dangers of hypoxia. The F.A.A. has set guidelines regarding use of oxygen at high altitudes.

Inboard Pull   Ripcord handle that is inside the left or right shoulder, rather than on the outside of the harness.

Instructor   Person who has passed all qualifying tests offered by the U. S. Parachute Association and is thus qualified to teach the first jump course and to instruct novice jumpers.

Intermediate Canopy   Paracommander or PC-type parachute.

I/E   Instructor/Examiner. Qualified by the U.S.P.A. to certify instructors.

Jumper Informal slang for all sky divers.

Jumpmaster Qualified leader in an aircraft full of static line or novice parachutists. The jumpmaster will decide the jump run, coordinate it with the pilot, decide on the exit point and generally take command of the aircraft, subject to the flying decisions of the pilot. A *jumpleader* acts as leader in an aircraft full of expert jumpers.

Jump Run Straight and level flight at the correct altitude toward the exit point. The jumpmaster may, during the jump run, offer course corrections to the pilot.

Keel Turn A turn in free-fall using a leg as a fulcrum.

Kicker Plate An inexpensive aluminum "pie dish" that is used to seat the reserve pilot chute. The kicker plate is jettisoned when the reserve is opened. Some jumpers with quick reflexes and even quicker presence of mind are said to be able to catch the kicker plate in mid-air as the reserve opens.

L/D (Lift to Drag) Ratio The relationship between the lifting characteristics of the parachute as opposed to the resistance by air on the forward speed of the canopy and the drag of gravity. Applied in generally the same way to airplanes.

Legal Age Usually 18 to parachute, but may vary by locality. Check with your local DZ.

Lift An airplane load of parachutists. As in, "I've signed up for the next Beech lift."

Line-Over A malfunction in which one (or more) suspension lines has looped over the canopy.

Load Generally same as *lift*.

Lobster Tail Color combination seen on many ParaCommanders and other similar canopies. Front and side panels are one color, back panels a contrasting color, thus making the canopy appear like a lobster tail.

Logbook Record book kept by all serious jumpers. The log will usually list all jumps in sequence, and has space for date of jump, location of the jump, aircraft type, jump type (static line, free-fall, or delayed opening), altitude, delay in seconds, total free-fall time, distance from target, wind speed, parachute type, reserve type, maneuvers during jump (four-man RW, eight-man RW, etc.), comments, and a space for a signature by a licensed parachutist, a jumpmaster, or instructor who witnessed the jump, or the jump pilot. New RW logbooks have space to diagram each jump. Logbooks must be kept for licenses, qualification of 12-and 24-hour free-fall awards, 1,000 jump awards, and other qualified and earned ratings.

Loft Rigger's shop, where parachute repairs and sales are made. Lofts must maintain certain standards as required by the F.A.A.

MA-1 A 36" spring-loaded pilot chute. Used on ParaCommander and other similar parachutes and on many standard backpacks. The new "throw-away pilot chutes" are rapidly replacing the spring-loaded pilot chute.

Mae West Malfunction caused by a suspension line over the canopy. So called because the parachute looks like a large bra, instead of like a round canopy.

Main Principal canopy, as opposed to the reserve.

Malfunction Any problem with the main canopy that may require a cutaway and deployment of the reserve. Malfunctions come in two types: A *total* malfunction occurs when the main parachute does not come off the jumper's back. Often called a *pack closure*. A *partial* malfunction may be either a *streamer*, which occurs when the sleeve deploys but the parachute does not emerge from the sleeve, or a *Mae West*. If the jumper has a total, he activates his reserve; if he has a partial, he does a cutaway, using his capewells and then activates his reserve. Failure to cutaway may mean that the reserve tangles with the partially open main above him, thus offering the jumper a nearly zero chance of safe recovery and descent.

Manifest To sign up a complete load or lift of jumpers. Many jump centers require a complete manifest and tickets before jumpers can board the aircraft.

Mass Exit In large-star RW, a nearly simultaneous exit, in which all the jumpers fall out the door like a line of dominos. Mass exits are an art; the best stars are put together when the mass exit is tight.

Modification Any change in the basic characteristics of a parachute made by the factory or by a qualified rigger. Modifications may be a removal or change in a parachute panel, or change in the suspension or steering lines. Only qualified riggers and parachute factories are allowed to make major modifications. The F.A.A. has issued guidelines about which types of modifications may or may not be made outside the factory.

NB-6, NB-8 Surplus parachutes, Navy issue.

Night Jump Officially described as a parachute jump made from at least 5,500 feet, 1 hour after official dark until 1 hour before official dawn.

Novice Jumper One who has made one or more parachute jumps but not yet qualified by a class "A" license.

O.D. Olive drab. The color of most surplus parachutes (no one in his or her right mind would buy a new parachute in olive drab).

"On the Step" Novice static line or novice free-fall student poised on the step of a Cessna or other similar jump plane, ready for the "Go" from his jumpmaster.

"On the Wrists" In a star and flying with other "skygods."

Opening Altitude Altitude when the jumper should have a good canopy over his head. Usually this is 2,500 to 2,800 feet above ground level. Could be higher for mass jumps—large star attempts.

Open Modifications Modification not covered by mesh. Open modifications are potentially hazardous because a pilot chute may entangle through the modification and cause a partial malfunction.

Opening Shock The quick stop that the jumper comes to when the parachute deploys fully. The velocity goes from 120 mph at terminal to 10 mph within 2 or 3 seconds as the parachute opens. Opening shock used to be a major problem in military jumping, but since the advent of new generations of gear since the late 1940s and early 1950s, opening shock is no longer a real problem, although some jumpers are prone to complain about it. Faulty body position (head down) may lead to a hard opening shock when the harness flips the jumper into an upright position.

Outboard Pull The ripcord handle under the left or right shoulder blade, but outside the edges of the webbing, rather than inside, over the jumper's chest.

Out-of-Date Reserve that needs to be repacked because it is past the deadline for legal use. U.S. Parachute Association members now need to repack every 120 days.

Oxygen Needed for high altitude jumps. Consult your A.S.O. or drop zone operator for specifics in your locality. The F.A.A. sets guidelines for oxygen use by high altitude sky divers.

PC ParaCommander. Since 1964, when it was first introduced, the ParaCommander has been the most popular and generally best received parachute in sport parachuting.

P.L.F. Parachute Landing Fall. The best way to encounter the ground. The P.L.F. is taken with the legs together, knees bent, arms and hands in. The jumper is prepared to roll sideways (never straight forward onto his face or straight back, which may cause a whiplash). The jumper takes the ground shock on the side of his legs, side, shoulders, and does a complete roll, if necessary. The P.L.F. is elementary and necessary; the *stand-up* is a landing in which the jumper takes all the ground shock in his legs. It sometimes feels as if the jumper's knees are going through his spine and skull. The P.L.F. and stand-up are generally approved methods, the alternative is a *crash-and-burn*, in which the jumper encounters the ground with other parts of his or her anatomy, not at all gracefully and often painfully.

P.O.D. Pack Opening Device. Similar to a *bag* system of packing and deployment.

Pack (Noun) *The pack* is the jumper's complete parachute system; to pack (verb) is to flake and stow the parachute to make ready for jumping.

Packing The act of flaking the parachute, stowing the lines and closing the container, to make the equipment jump-ready.

Packing Card See *data card*.

Packing Mat Protective canvas, plastic, or other material used to protect the parachute from dirt, oil, or anything else while packing on the ground.

Packing Table Protective table used when conditions are not suitable for packing on the ground. Some DZ's make packing tables from old diving boards, which are the right width; Several dovetailed together will make a packing table the right length.

Panel One portion of a parachute. Parachutes have different shaped panels for different portions of the parachute.

Pap Short for Papillon, a Fench-designed parachute similar to the ParaCommander.

Parachute From the French words *para* (to guard against) and *chute* (to fall): Thus parachute means literally "to guard against a fall."

Parachutist A jumper who has achieved a Class "A" license. A free-fall jumper. In the eyes of the public, *parachutist* and *daredevil* are still synonymous.

Pass Straight and level flight at the right altitude toward the exit point. One aircraft may have multiple passes at various altitudes "Give me one pass at 2,500, one at 4,500, and one at 7,500 on this lift," the jumpmaster may say to the pilot.

"Peas" Target for accuracy jumpers usually made of *pea gravel*, plastic fiber, sawdust, or other similar material.

"Pencil-Packing" To repack a reserve parachute illegally by simply changing or adding a new "date of repack" to the data card.

Pigrig Tandem main-reserve parachutes worn on the jumper's back. The Wonderhog and other similar systems are the latest "state-of-the-art" in pigrigs. The front reserve is quickly becoming passé in sport parachuting because of increased bulk and inferior flying characteristics.

Pilot Chute Small parachute that leaves the parachutist's container first. The jumper's weight pulling against the fully deployed pilot chute pulls the rest of the assembly out of the container and off the jumper's back. In England, the pilot chute is sometimes called the *Extractor* chute.

Pilot Error In aviation, any crash, injury, or fatality caused by mental lapses or mistakes on the part of the pilot. Many jumping injuries or fatalities are similarly caused by "pilot error" on the part of the jumper.

Pin (noun) *The pin* is a metallic prong that slips into the *cone*, to lock the parachute container closed until the parachutist pulls the ripcord. *To pin* (verb) is the act of catching the *base* jumper in free-fall to establish the *base-pin* section of a free-fall formation.

Pin-Check A last-minute safety check performed before the parachutist boards the aircraft. Another jumper, a jumpmaster, or instructor checks the complete main and reserve to see that the pins and cones are set properly; that the reserve is *in date*; that all latches are properly snapped and; in general, that the main and reserve parachutes are properly set for the jump. A pin-check also includes calibrating a Sentinel, if the parachutist wears one.

Poised Exit An exit from the aircraft step or door in which the parachutist is ready seconds or minutes prior to the actual exit. Poised exits are required of novice jumpers, to learn correct positions and reactions. Later they graduate to *bomb outs* (unpoised exits).

POPS Organization for "senior citizen" parachutists. Stands for *Parachutists Over Phorty*. Its insignia shows a worried Father Time, jumping in a rocking chair, pulling his ripcord with a walking cane, his fingers crossed for good luck. Membership is open to parachutists over phorty—or, forty.

Porosity How much air can get through what kinds of material. Parachute fabric is classified either low porosity or high porosity. *LoPo* parachutes generally drop slower and let the jumper down softer.

Prop Blast Turbulence caused by the aircraft propellor. Jumpers often become unstable on exit when they hit the prop blast, or, as it is sometimes called, *prop wash*.

R2's, R3's Generic name for any surplus round parachute. Same as *cheapo*.

Railroad To strike a free-fall jumper hard enough to cause possible injury, to destroy a formation, or to knock a sky diver out of position. At the least, to railroad a fellow jumper is discourteous; it can cause a possible fatality if the jumper is knocked out and does not wear an automatic opener, such as a Sentinel.

Ram-Air New square type parachute. So called because the air flows into the front of the parachute cells and out the back; similar in concept to the intake and exhaust of a jet engine. Ram-air parachutes have the advantage of increased forward speed in the air (25–30 mph), but are also more difficult to handle and are generally regarded as the "sports cars" of the parachute world. Common ram-air parachutes are the StratoStar, StratoCloud, Cobra 10, ParaFoil, and others.

Relative Wind An aviation concept, introduced to the world of sky diving by Pat Works in his book *The Art of Freefall R W*. Relative wind is the wind that always comes at the jumper from the direction toward which he is moving.

Relative Work See *R W*.

Repack Cycle The dates on which the reserve parachute must be opened, checked and repacked. Repacking now is due every 120 days for U.S. P.A. members. For years, the repack cycle was 60 days.

Reserve The parachutist's second parachute.

Rig The parachutist's complete outfit, ready to jump. Same as *gear*.

Rigger F.A.A. licensed parachute repairman and repacker (in the case of reserves). Only riggers may repack reserves, and the rigger must sign the data card, giving his name, F.A.A. license number, and the dates. *Junkyard riggers* are those who make repairs, or equipment with spare parts or cheap equipment. A good rigger is your best friend when you need to use a reserve in the air. Many jumpers have been known to give their rigger a bottle of his or her favorite liquor when the reserve opens promptly as needed during a malfunction or cutaway. Needless to say, an inept rigger is nobody's friend.

Ripcord Housing Steel conduit that protects the ripcord.

Ripstop Nylon that resists tearing. Ripstop nylon is also used for sailboat sails, as well as parachute fabric.

Risers Webbing that begins at the capewells and extends over the jumper's head, where *suspension lines* are connected to the risers with *connector links*. Risers and most webbing on the parachute harness should withstand 5,000 pounds of pressure before splitting or breaking.

Running The act of facing a parachute in the same direction the wind is blowing, for maximum advantage and speed. To run is to add the wind speed and the built-in forward speed of the parachute for maximum velocity. Opposite of *holding*.

RW Relative work. To make a free-fall sky dive with others; to jump relative to someone else. The act of completing (or attempting) a multiperson formation using hand-holding or other physical connections to establish a formation in free-fall. Most jumpers believe that RW is the best part of sky diving. RW techniques have changed the face of sport parachuting. Only a few years ago, a baton pass between two jumpers in free-fall was considered expert jumping. Now RW techniques involve 50 (or more) jumpers connected in various "megaformations." See Pat Works' *The Art of Freefall RW*.

S.C.R.   Star Crest Recipient. The most respected and generally most sought-after earned award in sky diving. The S.C.R. is awarded to any member of an eight-man (or larger) free-fall formation held together for five seconds or 1,000 feet. Formerly awarded by the Bob Buquor Memorial Star Crest Association.

S.C.S.   Like the S.C.R., but awarded to the eighth, or following jumpers in a free-fall formation. Stands for Star Crest Soloist.

Saddle   The portion of the harness on which the parachutist sits. A split-saddle harness is one with separate leg straps individually connected.

Sentinel   Automatic barometric- and speed-computer that will fire the para-chutist's reserve open if the parachutist falls through the last 1,000 feet without having a good canopy over his head. The most popular automatic opening device in sport parachuting. Manufactured by S.S.E. Inc., Pennsauken, NJ.

Sequential RW   Relative work jump in which several different free-fall forma-tions are completed. A four-man RW team might go from a Skirmish line to a four-man star to a Murphy star during one jump, for instance.

Short-lining   In static line jumping, a jump-master will *short-line* a static-line jumper by pulling in the static line to prevent the jumper from being entan-gled in the line or to begin the deployment sequence faster than normal. To *short-line a canopy* is to trim (shorten) the suspension lines to alter the flying characteristics of the parachute.

Shot Bag   Weighted pouch used to hold down a parachute during packing.

Silk   What parachutes were made of before rip-stop nylon, pre-World War II. The phrase still remains, "Hit the silk," a reference to early military para-troop jumping. Modern jumpers have never even seen a silk parachute, much less jumped with one.

Sitting Up   The jumper sits up in free-fall to stop. He literally raises his torso, arms, and head.

Skirt   The bottom edge of a parachute canopy.

Skygod   Expert free-fall jumper, usually with an SCR, SCS, or other RW experience and achievements. The skygod is sometimes a less-than-compli-mentary term, meaning a jumper who demands an ideal position on the load, or first lift, to the exclusion of others. An inconsiderate RW jumper, obsessed with his or her own perceived importance and abilities.

Sleeve   Long cloth protection for the canopy; the sleeve holds the canopy in the container and acts to slow the deployment sequence during opening. The sleeve also has room on the outside for stowing bands—rubber bands used to keep the suspension lines. In some containers and some systems, the sleeve has been replaced by the bag or P.O.D. (Pack Opening Device). The sleeve is one of the new innovations that make sport parachuting comfortable at opening shock time.

SL Jump Static Line jump, in which the parachutist's canopy is pulled open by a static line, an unbreakable line that runs from the backpack to an anchor in the airframe of the aircraft. The novice graduates from an automatic static line to a self-actuated free-fall parachute rig.

Slots Positions in an RW formation. *Near-side slots* are positions on the side of the formation nearest the aircraft; *far-side slots* are on the side of the formation opposite the aircraft. Far-side slots presume more *flying* ability on the part of RW jumpers to reach the other side.

Smoke (noun) Smoke, in the sense of a smoke grenade, worn on the boot, helps spectators locate a sky diver during a free-fall exhibition, such as a county fair. A smoke grenade will also be dropped on the peas by a competition director to indicate to an aircraft approaching jumprun that winds on the ground have become too hazardous for safe landings. Jumpers will also watch for smoke from "natural" situations such as chimneys and fires, to gauge wind direction during canopy control toward the DZ. "To smoke it in" (verb) means to drop in free-fall below the generally accepted altitudes of 2,500 to 2,000 feet. Smoking it in during competition such as a conference meet or a turkey meet may be cause for grounding.

Split Saddle Harness with separate leg straps.

Spot The art of determining the opening point, to get parachutists back to the general area of the DZ. Inept spotters often receive a chilly reception when the load of jumpers ends up "in the boondocks"—acres or miles away from the DZ, especially on a hot day. Spotters who jump square parachutes are also occasionally received badly because their parachutes can get them back to the DZ when round jumpers may be stuck off where the weeds are high and uncut. Spotters who take separate passes are stuck with their own spot, of course.

Stability The art of achieveing a poised position in free-fall, usually face-to-earth. A stable position is a necessary achievement for all free-fall formations.

Stabilizer Panel Panels at the bottom of the sides of parachutes such as the ParaCommander and at the bottom edge of squares.

Stalling Pulling down steering lines or risers to alter the forward drive of the parachute.

Stand-Up Landing A landing done skillfully, with the shock taken by the knees; as opposed to a P.L.F.

Star Formation achieved by linked free-fall jumpers. Because later formations have involved diamonds, triangles, lines, and other geometric symbols, the star is now sometimes called a *round*.

Static Line Unbreakable line that opens the parachutist's container automatically. Static lines are usually 15 feet long—long enough to clear the tail of the aircraft. Military paratroop jumps are almost always static line jumps; most novice jumpers learn on the static line and most of their gear is military surplus.

Steering Lines Lines that end in *toggles* on the jumper's risers. The parachute can be steered to the left or right by pulling down on the left or right toggle, which alters the flying configuration of the parachute. *Sawing*, or rapid alternate pulling of the toggles, usually does little good and only scares the novice when not much happens to the parachute.

Stick Military slang. A partial or complete load of static-line paratroops dropped on the same DZ.

Stiffener Metallic plate at the top of the ripcord housing used to prevent a pack closure by a stuck ripcord. Used on old-style containers. Containers that employ the throw-away pilot chute have no need for a stiffener because the ripcord (the bridle line for the pilot chute) is velcroed to the harness.

Stirrup Elastic band holding the leg of the jumpsuit tight to the foot of the jumper.

Stowing Band Rubber band used to tuck away the suspension lines neatly and to aid in a neat, clean deployment of the lines during the opening sequence.

Streamer Malfunction in which the sleeve elongates, or the bag clears the jumper, but the parachute does not emerge (or emerge fast enough). Usually means a cutaway.

Strut Diagonal brace between the wing of a Cessna or other similar aircraft and the bottom of the fuselage. Novice jumpers are told to hold the strut until the jumpmaster gives the command "Go!" All jumpmasters have stories about novice jumpers who fail to let go of the strut on command and are either pushed or thrown off the step.

Student Jumper Person who has gone through the ground school but hasn't yet made his or her first jump.

Style The art of acrobatics (front loop, back loop, barrelroll) in free-fall done as quickly and as smoothly as possible in competition. Slowly falling out of favor; most jumpers with experience are working toward RW competition.

Style Tuck Compressed position roughly similar to a "cannonball" position in diving, with the face down. The style tuck allows the sky diver to complete the *style series* in minimum time.

Surplus Army, Navy, or Air Force equipment used largely for novice jumping.

Suspension Line The lines connecting the *canopy* to the *harness*, at the *risers*, with *connector links*.

T.S.O. Technical standard Order. Government authorized gear. Equipment must be T.S.O.'d for use in national competition.

T-10 A surplus main parachute. Originally non-steerable.

Target Center disc used in competition. Generally 3–15/16 inches (10 centimeters) in diameter. ameter.

Temporary Locking Pins Used during the packing of a reserve; must be removed before use.

Terminal The ultimate and faster drop rate in free-fall. A trade-off between the pull of gravity and the drag of the jumper's gear and body position. Usually around 120 mph. A reserve opening at terminal is an awesome experience because the reserve opens faster than a main (usually) and thus exposes the jumper to a harder opening shock. Most RW formations are attempted at terminal because of the momentum that the jumper can use to change positions, and to move across the sky. Nonterminal RW offers the sky diver little leverage with which to work.

Throw-Away Pilot Chute Pilot chute designed without coil spring. Made to be folded up like a pocket handkerchief and stowed in a pocket along the harness. In free-fall, to deploy the main, the jumper pulls the throw-away air-stream; the pilot chute is attached to a *bridle cord*, which pulls the bag or pod out of the container. The advantages of the throw-away pilot chute are (a) without a coil spring it packs smaller, and (b) because the sky diver throws the pilot chute to his side, it enters clear air beside him and thus offers little chance for a hesitation in the turbulent air over the jumper's back. New, state-of-the-art design (introduced about 1976–1977).

Tie-Down Straps Straps that connect the reserve with the jumper's harness to prevent the reserve from bounding around in free-fall, which can be annoying, if not dangerous.

Toggles Wooden pegs used to aid the jumper's hold on the steering lines.

Total Pack closure. No parachute comes off the sky diver's back after a ripcord pull.

Track Body position with the head and torso lower than the legs; allows the sky diver to pick up extensive distance. The sky diver makes his body into a wing and extends his "forward glide."

Tri-Conical Type of reserve canopy design.

Two-Five Common abbreviation for altitude (2,500 feet). Jumpers will abbreviate all altitudes; as in, "I'm booked for a 7,5 (7,500 feet) jump, then a 12,5 (12,500 feet) jump in the Beech."

U.S P.A. United States Parachute Association, headquartered in Washington, D.C.; the governing body for all sport jumping in the United States. Offers liability insurance, a monthly magazine *Parachutist*, and other benefits to members.

Waiver Legal release that most parachute clubs ask jumpers to sign relieving the club of responsibility in case of injury. Note   In many states, the waiver is of little good (to the club) except to warn the prospective parachutist that he or she may be engaging in a risky participatory sport. Some states do not allow anyone to sign away responsibility for injury or death.

Water Jump Deliberate jump into a body of water (lake or river) for a demo jump or for U.S.P.A. license purposes.

Wave-Off A safety measure, especially when other jumpers are in free-fall in the immediate area. Before pulling his or her ripcord, the sky diver waves his or her arms energetically horizontally across the chest to warn other sky divers that he or she will very soon pull the ripcord. A wave-off is done to avoid sky diver–canopy collisions.

Whuffo Any spectator not acquainted with the pomp and glories of skydiving. So named after an apocryphal farmer who watched sky divers and then asked, "Wha' fo' you jump outta them airplanes, fo' "?

Wind Sometimes a hazard to jumpers.

Wind Line A direct line from the opening point to the target. Because of their forward drive capabilities, square parachutists are seldom worried about the wind line.

Wing Square or ram-air parachute, called a wing because of its appearance and flying capabilities.

Wonderhog One type of tandem system sold under that name.

Wrist Mount Velcro band used to attach an altimeter on the jumper's wrist where it is visible.

W.S.C.R. Women's Star Crest Recipient.

W.S.C.S. Women's Star Crest Soloist.

XX-rated Jumper who has been in a 20-man formation.

Zapped Out A jumper who became unstable out the door (or) who broke up a formation.

Snow Skiing

Airplane Turn A turn in midair, as when a skier is jumping a mogul.

Alpine Events Skiing events that were said to develop in the Alpine countries of Europe. Alpine events are the downhill, slalom, and giant slalom. See *Nordic events.*

Camber (Bottom) The built-in arch of the ski as seen from the side. The camber is designed to distribute the skier's weight over the complete length of the ski.

Camber (Side) The built-in arch on the sides of the ski. The cut is designed to allow the ski to turn.

Christi A ski turn in which both of the skis are parallel.

Corn Snow Granular, rough snow, usually develops in the spring.

Edge Set Steel edges of the ski that "bite" into the snow.

Fall Line Shortest distance down a hill.

Flex The bending properties of a ski.

Forebody The part of the ski ahead of the bindings.

Groove The indentation that runs along the bottom of the ski to improve stability. Similar in nature to the tread on a tire.

Herringbone A method of climbing up a hill with skis.

Hip The widest part of the rear end of the ski.

Inside Edge The right side of a left ski and the left side of a right ski.

Inside Ski The ski that is inside a turn. The right ski on a right turn; the left ski on a left turn.

Linked Turns Series of turns in opposite directions; that is, left-right-left or right-left-right.

Mogul   Small mound of snow created by skiers turning in the same place on a hill.

Nordic Events   Ski jumping and cross-country skiing.

Outside Edge   The left side of a left ski and the right side of a right ski.

Outside Ski   The ski that is outside on a turn. The left ski on a right turn; the right ski on a left turn.

Rotation   To turn the skier's body in the direction of a turn.

Safety Binding   Locking device that releases the skis from the skier's boots in the case of a fall, to prevent injury to the skier's ankle or leg.

Schuss   To ski down the fall line, usually too fast to be in complete control.

Sideslip   To ski diagonally down a hill.

Sitzmark   A hole or mark left in the snow by a skier who has fallen.

Snowplow   To form the point of a V with the tips of the skis to slow down.

Spring Snow   Same as *corn snow*.

Sweep   A check of the complete skiing area of a mountain by members of the ski patrol to make sure all skiers are down the mountain for the night.

Tail   The rear end of the ski.

Tip   The front end of a ski.

Torsion   The amount that a ski can twist.

Track   A warning to a skier in front that a second skier may not avoid a collision.

Traverse   To ski across a hill.

Soccer

Bicycle kick   a maneuver in which players throw their body up in the air and flip their legs overhead to kick the ball. The players' legs twirl as if riding a bicyle. Also called a scissor kick.

Caution   Warning by the referee for unsportsmanlike conduct. Because of possible language differences between teams, the referee shows this caution by waving a yellow card.

Charging   Attempting to unbalance a player in possession of the ball.

Chip   A kick that rises above a player.

Clearance   Kicking or heading the ball away from the goal area. The goalkeeper may throw the ball to clear it.

Corner Kick   Kick made by the attacking team from a corner arc; this is awarded when the ball goes across the goal line without resulting in a score, and when the ball was last touched by a defensive player.

Direct Free Kick   Awarded after a severe personal foul. Similar to a free throw in basketball.

Dribbling   To control the ball with the player's feet.

Drop Ball   To put the ball in play by the referee by dropping it between two opponents. The ball is in play when it touches the ground.

Drop Kick   A ball that is put in play by being dropped on the ground; it is kicked on the bounce.

Goal   Is scored when the ball passes over the goal line, between the uprights and under the crossbar.

Goalkeeper   Player who guards the goal. In soccer, the goal keeper may carry the ball in the penalty area, or may throw it or kick it.

Goal Kick   Kick-in by a member of the defending team from the goal box. A goal kick results when the ball crosses the goal line without a score and when it was last touched by an offensive player.

Halfway Line   A line that runs across the field at mid-field. Similar to the 50-yard line in American football.

Hat Trick   Three goals in one game by one player. Same usage as ice hockey.

Heading   Method of directing the ball with the head. A skill that highly rated players have.

Indirect Free Kick   A free kick in which a score can result only after the ball has struck another player.

Instep Kick   Kick made with the instep or inside of the foot. Instep soccer kickers are now highly prized in American football because of their accuracy.

Kick-Off   A kick from the center circle at the beginning of each quarter and after each score.

Live Ball   A ball in play after a free kick or throw-in or after it has been touched by a player, or has touched the ground after a drop.

Match   A game.

Offside   Refers to the position of a player in relation to the opponents when a ball is put in play. A player may not kick a ball to a teammate if the teammate is positioned behind all of the defenders (except for the goaltender).

Off The Ball   Players who do not have possession of the ball.

Overhead Kick   A player who kicks the ball over his own head.

Penalty Kick   Direct free kick made from the penalty mark; this kick is awarded to the offensive team for a foul committed by the defense within its own penalty area.

Save   Play made by the goalkeeper to prevent a score.

Striker   An offensive player.

Tackling   An attempt to *kick* the ball away from an opponent. Players may not be held in tackling.

Touchlines   Side boundary lines in soccer.

Volley   To kick the ball while it is in the air.

Surfing

Angling   Riding across a wave.

Backing Out   Pulling out of a wave that could have been ridden.

Back Wash   Water from a wave that is returning to sea.

Bailing Out   Jumping off and getting safely away from the surfboard.

Barge   A huge, cumbersome surfboard.

Beach Break   A wave that breaks on the beach.

Belly Board   A small surfboard used for body surfing.

Blown Out   Choppy surf, poor for surfing.

Body Surfing   Surfing while lying prone on a belly board, or prone surfing without a board of any kind.

Break   When a wave crests and collapses.

Catching a Rail   When the tip of the surfboard cuts into the water.

Choppy   Rough water.

Crest   The top of a wave.

Crossover   When a surfer moves one leg ahead and in front of the other.

Dig   Paddle actively.

Ding   Blemish in a surfboard.

Double-Ended   Surf board that has similar shape on both ends.

Face of the Wave   The concave shape of a wave as it faces the shore.

Feather   Splashes of water from the top of a wave.

Fiberglass   Composition of most surfboards.

Fin   Keel of a surfboard.

Flat   Water with no waves for surfing.

Glassy   Smooth water.

Goofy Foot   Position on a surf board with the right foot forward.

Gremmies   Rude group of surfers.

Hairy   Big wave, difficult to surf successfully.

Hang Five   To dip five toes over the front edge of a surf board.

Hang Ten   To dip ten toes over the front edge of a surf board.

Head Dip   When a surfer dips his or her head into a wave.

Highway Surfer   Surfer who spends all his or her time out of the water, "talking big waves."

Hot Dogging   "Jus' showing off."

Hump   A large wave.

Inside   The side of a wave toward the shore.

Kick Out   To turn away from the shore to end a ride.

Log   A heavy surf board.

Nose   The front of a surf board.

Outside   The side of a wave toward the open sea.

Over the Falls   Over the top edge of a breaking wave.

(To) Pearl   To nose the board over, in the water.

Pick Up a Wave   To catch a wave for a ride toward shore.

Prone Out   To end a ride by lying down on the board.

Psyched Out   Afraid.

Pushing Out   Paddling out through the breaking waves to get in position to surf in toward the shore.

Rails   Side edges of a surf board.

Shoot the Tube   To ride under the crest of a wave.

Showboating   Same as *hot dogging*.

Soup   The foam a wave makes.

Stall   To slow down to attempt to stop.

Stoked   Excited.

Surfing Knots   Bumps and abrasions that a surfer receives during surfing. Usually on the knees, usually from repeated contact with the board.

Swell   A wave that has not yet crested or broken.

Trimming (or) **Trimming the Board**   Settling into the correct position so the board rides smoothly in the water.

Tube   The hollow or semihollow part of a wave.

Wax   Paraffin used to make the board less slippery.

Wet Suit   Like a scuba diver's suit, this suit protects the surfer from water that is too cold.

Wipe-out   To fall from the board.

Swimming and Diving

Approach   The steps taken toward the end of the board (Diving).

Backstroke   To swim with alternate arm strokes while on the back.

Back Jackknife   Common name for the inward pike dive (diving).

Breaststroke   To swim by stroking under the water, with outward strokes beginning at the chest.

Butterfly Stroke   A stroke in which the arm motion begins with each arm stretched out sideways. The swimmer then brings both arms out of the water, swinging them together and into the water past the head; the arms are then brought sideways underwater.

Cast   Imperfect entry into the water (diving).

Crawl Stroke   Commonly known as *freestyle*. The swimmer's arms are brought forward one at a time over the shoulder and into the water; as one arm is pulling through the water, the other arm is entering the water, after being thrown over the swimmer's shoulder.

Cutaway   Common term for an inward dive.

Degree of Difficulty   Rate for a dive. Each dive has a rating from 1.2 to 2.9 depending on its difficulty.

Entry   How the diver enters the water.

Flutter Kick   Quick up-and-down kick of the feet, to accompany a swimming stroke.

Freestyle   Usually refers to the crawl stroke, but may be any stroke the swimmer wishes to use, during a freestyle (choice) event.

Groups   Categories for all various dives. Forward, backward, reverse, inward, twist, and arm stand groups.

High Board   The 3-meter board.

Hurdle   The jump at the end of the diver's approach to the end of the board.

Individual Medley   A four-course swimming competition in which a butterfly stroke is used in the first quarter; a backstroke used in the second quarter; a breaststroke in the third quarter; and freestyle in the last quarter.

Jackknife Common name for the forward pike dive.

Kickboard Board used to support a swimmer as he or she practices kicking style.

Lap From one end of a swimming pool to the other end.

Layout Diving position in which the body is extended without any flexing.

Low Board The 1-meter board.

Medley A swimming event in which the swimmer must use the butterfly, back-stroke, breast-stroke, and freestyle.

Pike Diving position in which the body is bent at the hips and the legs are kept straight.

Pull The part of a swimming stroke in which the arm motion is exerting the most power.

Push The final part of a swimming stroke.

Reach The lift of the arms and the legs during the take-off from the board.

Riding the Board The act of riding the spring of the diving board for maximum upward thrust.

Scissors Kick A kick used in swimming side-stroke. The cycle is begun with the legs together; one leg is then thrust forward and one backward, on a plane parallel with the surface of the water. The knees are bent during the return portion of the cycle. The scissors kick is somewhat like the opening and closing of a pair of scissors.

Six-Beat Crawl A version of the crawl in which there are six beats of the legs in a flutter-style kick to one full arm cycle. Most common version of the crawl.

Stroke The arm action during swimming.

Tuck Position in which a diver is curled into a ball.

Table Tennis

Note Many of the terms in Table Tennis and Outdoor Tennis are similar.

Ace A serve that is not returned by the opponent.

Ad Abbreviation for Advantage.

Advantage First score after deuce (tie at 20-all).

All Same as tie, that is, 20-all.

Backhand Stroke used with the back of the hand facing the opponent.

Backspin Stroke in which the ball spins toward the server.

Ball Made of celluloid, approximately 4¼ inches in diameter, hollow, and weighing 37–41 grams.

Chop Stroke hit with a downward stroke of the paddle, giving the ball backspin.

Dead Ball Called when the ball bounces twice on the table, or after a point.

Deuce When the score is tied 20-all. Winner must score two consecutive points.

Drop Shot Shot played so that it dies before the opponent can return it.

Finger Spin Spin imparted by the server's fingers during the serve. Illegal technique.

Forehand   Opposite of backhand. Stroke with the palm of the hand facing the opponent.

Game   The winner in table tennis is the player who first scores 21 points, or two consecutive points after deuce.

Let   Means "play the point over" and occurs if the ball touches the top of the net and falls into the opponent's court after a serve.

Mixed Doubles   Male and female player as a team.

Net   Table tennis net is mesh. The top of the net is 6 inches above the table.

Push Shot   Ball is stuck with a pushing motion of the paddle so there is no spin on the ball.

Slice   Stroke with the paddle so that the ball spins away from the server.

Slice   A late stroke so the ball spins away from the paddle.

Volley   Illegal stroke of the ball while it is in the air, and before it has touched the table.

Tennis

Ace   Serve that is not returned by the opponent. Scores a point.

Ad   Abbreviation for Advantage.

Advantage   The point scored immediately after deuce. If the same player scores the next point, that player wins. If the opponent scores the next point, the score returns to deuce.

Advantage Court   The left-hand service court.

Alley   The area between the singles and doubles sideline on each side of the court. The singles court is made 4½ feet wider for doubles play with the addition of the alley.

All-Court Game   Style of play that includes both net play and baseline play.

Approach Shot   Made when a player makes a shot and approaches the net.

Backcourt   The area of the court near the base lines, as opposed to the area near the net.

Backhand   Shot made with the back of the hand facing the net or opponent.

Backspin   A stroke that imparts spin on the ball in the direction of the server.

Baseline   End boundaries of the court, 39 feet from the net.

Break   To win a game served by the opponent.

Break Point   When the score is love–40, 15–40, or 30–40, the next point will win the game.

Bye   A term used to refer to a player who does not have to play in qualifying rounds of a tournament.

Center Mark   Mark in the center of the baseline, indicating the server's possible location. The server may stand to either side of the center mark.

Changeover   A pause in a match when the players change sides of the court after odd-numbered games. They also have a chance to rest, cool off, and have something to drink.

Choke   To hold the racket toward the face (strings); to shorten the grip.

Chop   A ground stroke that applies downspin to the ball.

Clay Court   Tennis court with a service of clay or that resembles clay.

Club Player   Tennis player who plays regularly at a tennis club, rather than a tournament professional.

Consolation   Rounds of a tournament in which first-time losers continue to play other losers.

Cross-Court   A shot made from one side of the court diagonally into the opposite court.

Cut Stroke   A shot in which the racket hits the ball at an angle to apply spin to the ball.

Deuce   When each player has won three points or when the score is tied after three points.

Dink   Soft shot that barely clears the net.

Double Elimination   Tournament in which no player is eliminated until he or she has lost twice.

Drop Shot   A shot that barely clears the net and that has more vertical bounce than bounce across the court.

Fault   An error, usually during the serve.

Fifteen   The first point won by a player.

Five   A scoring term used to indicate the number of games won or the number of the set. Used unofficially as an abbreviation for fifteen.

Flat Serve   A serve that has no spin.

Foot Fault   A serve declared illegal because of the placement of the feet during the serve.

Forecourt   Usually refers to the area of the court near the net.

Forty   The third point won by a player.

Game   A player has won a game in tennis when he or she has four points and is two points ahead of the opponent.

Groundstroke   A stroke that is made after the ball has bounced off the ground, as opposed to a volley, which is a stroke when the ball is in the air.

Gut   The stringing in a racket.

Handicap   A system of equalizing competition between players of unequal ability.

Kill   A powerful stroke, a ball hit so hard or placed so well that the opponent cannot possibly return it.

Let   Play in which the ball touches the top of the net and falls into the correct court. The point is replayed, as in table tennis.

Linesman   An official in tennis who observes the game and decides if the balls are in the court or not.

Lob   To hit a ball in a high arc.

Love   No score.

Love Game   Game in which a player or team fails to score a point.

Love Set   Set in which a player or team fails to score a point.

Match   Two out of three sets or three out of five.

Match Point   A point which, if won by the player, will make him or her the winner of the match.

Net Game   An individual's style of play near the net.

Out   A ball that lands out of bounds.

Overhead   Shot to return a lob, usually with an arm motion over the head. Also called "smash shot."

Poaching   To play in a partner's side of a doubles court.

Rally   Prolonged exchange of shots by both players or by members of a doubles play.

Ranking   Listing of players by their ability and records of past play.

Round Robin   Type of tournament in which all players play all other players.

Seeding   Placing top tournament players in a tournament in such a way that they will not compete against each other until the final rounds.

Service Line   The line drawn across the court 21 feet from the net and parallel to the net.

Set   The first player to win six games provided that the player is at least two games ahead of the opponent (6–3, 6–4, 7–5, etc).

Set Point   A point that, if won by the player, gives him or her the set.

Smash   A stroke used to return a lob, usually powerfully.

Slow Court   A court with a rough surface on which the ball bounces slowly or clumsily.

Stroke   The movement of hitting the ball with the racket.

Thirty   A scoring term; the second point scored by a player.

Topspin   To hit the ball to impart spin away from the server.

Unseeded   Player whose ability does not qualify him or her for special placement in a tournament.

Volley   To return a ball to the opponent by hitting it before it bounces on the ground.

Wightman Cup   Trophy awarded to the winner of the annual tournament between the top women's team from the U.S. and the top women's team from England. Held alternately in the U.S. and England.

Wimbledon   The All England Lawn Tennis Championship played annually in the summer at the All England Tennis and Croquet, Wimbledon, London. Begun in 1877, it became an open event in 1968. The tennis equivalent of the Super Bowl in professional football.

Track and Field

Anchor   Last runner in a relay team.

Baton   Metal, cardboard, wood, or plastic cylinder that is passed from runner to runner in a relay race.

Crossbar   Metal or wood bar about 16 feet long that serves as an obstacle that the high jumper or pole vaulter must cross without knocking down.

Dead Heat   Tie finish between two or more runners.

Exchange Zone Area of race track approximately 20–22 yards long where a baton pass must be made.

Flight One lane of hurdles.

Get Set To hold the starting position in a running race; the command just before "Go."

Go The command to begin a running race.

Heat Preliminary set of races in which the winners qualify for semifinal or final races.

Hurdle Wooden or metal obstacle that a runner must leap over in a steeplechase or hurdles competition.

Lane Path marked on a track. A runner must stay in his own lane during a specified part of a race or a complete race.

L-type hurdle Hurdle and base that resemble the letter L.

Mark The spot where the broad jumper, discus, hammer, javelin, or shot lands.

On the Mark Command to take a starting position behind the scratch line, prior to a running race.

Pace A runner's speed, as in slow pace, fast pace.

Planting Box Slot at the immediate front of the pole vaulting pit, where the vaulter places or plants the pole for a vault.

Pole The inside lane of a running track; or the vaulting pole used in pole vaulting.

Preliminaries Same as *heats*.

Qualify To survive the heats and enter final races.

Rabbit Runner who may lead the field during the early stages of a long race, but who may set a pace too fast to continue the lead to the finish.

Relay Leg One runner's part of a relay race.

Scratch Line A line that runners or jumpers must not cross before the race begins. Similar to the *line of scrimmage* in football.

Seeded To place the fastest runners in separate heats so they do not meet until the final races.

Slipstreaming To run slightly behind another runner so the second runner does not have to fight the wind. Also appropriate in motor sports, where one car will slipstream another.

Starting Blocks Objects that a runner uses to keep correct foot position before a race begins.

Stride One step in a running race.

Take-Off Board Board that a broad jumper uses to begin his jump from.

Throwing Section Area in which a thrown object (javelin, discus, etc.) must land.

Toeboard Board that a shot-putter must not step on or across during the act of putting the shot.

Trail One attempt in field events; one javelin throw, and so on.

Trial Heat Same as *heat*.

GLOSSARY

Volleyball

Antenna 2½- to 3-foot high vertical rod attached to each side of the net. If a ball hits the antenna, it is out of play.

Attack Block An attempt to block the ball before it crosses the net.

Block A defensive move to intercept the ball near the net.

Bump Pass An underhand pass using the forearms to strike the ball.

Contacted Ball A ball that has been touched by any part of a player's body.

Court Playing court should be 59 feet by 29 feet, 6 inches, with a center line under the net.

Dig Underhand pass made near the floor level.

Dive A low attempt to block a ball from hitting the floor.

Double Block A block at the net by two team members.

Floater Serve A serve that travels erratically.

Foul Illegal play.

Game Volleyball games are won when a team first reaches 15 points with a 2-point advantage.

Net Top of net should be 7 feet, 11¾ inches for men; 7 feet, 4½ inches for women.

Netting Making contact with the net while the ball is in play. Offending team loses possession of the ball or the loss of one point.

Off-Speed Spike A slow spike.

Out of Bounds Ball is out of bounds if it strikes any object out of the court, or if it strikes the antenna.

Overhand Pass Pass made with both hands held head-high.

Scoring One point is awarded for each score. Only a serving team may score a point.

Serving The act of putting the ball into play by propelling it over the net and into the opponent's court.

Set An overhead pass designed to allow a teammate to spike the ball.

Spike A ball hit hard into the opponent's court.

Spiker Player who performs a spike.

Spin Serve Serve that has spin imparted by wrist action.

Side Out Exchange of serve after a previous serving team fails to score.

Thrown Ball Judgment by an official that the ball was momentarily caught or came to rest. Penalty results.

Underhand Serve Basic serve in which the ball is struck with the heel of the server's hand.

Water Skiing

Aquameter Device used to measure miles per hour in a speedboat. Now a generic term for all such gauges.

Banana Peel   Trick or slalom ski with rounded tips, which vaguely resembles a banana peel.

Barefoot   Skiing barefoot, which can be accomplished by kicking the skis off while skiing 34 mph or faster.

Barrel Roll   A tumble off a water ski ramp during a ramp jump.

Board   To climb into a boat.

Boarding Ladder   Small ladder to make boarding a boat easier.

Bobble   To lose balance but recover during skiing.

Buoy   Water marker.

Cat   Common abbreviation for catamaran, or twin-hulled boat.

Deep Water Start   A ski tow that begins in water too deep for the ski ends to touch bottom.

Dock Start   Ski tow that begins with the skiier sitting on the edge of a dock.

Double Handles   Twin handles on the end of a ski rope, so two skiiers can be towed behind one boat.

Doubles   Two skiers behind the same boat.

Gate   Entrance to a slalom course.

Heel Hold   To hold the ski tow bar with one heel.

Helicopter Spin   Complete 360° spin in the skis after jumping from a ski ramp. The skis resemble the blades of a helicopter in flight.

Hit It   Command from skier to boat to accelerate to begin a ski tow.

Hot Dog   Showing off. Similar to Surf usage.

In Gear   Command from skier to boat to shift from neutral just prior to "Hit it" command.

Kite   Wing-apparatus used to become airborne while being towed behind a boat.

Pass   Straight run over a ski course.

Plane   The action of skis riding on the surface of the water.

Ramp   Incline plane used for water ski jumping.

Run   Two passes over the same course in competition.

Single Handle   One towing handle at the end of a tow rope.

Slalom   Zig-zag course between obstacles, similar in nature to a slalom run on snow skis.

Three-Sixty   Complete 360° turn while being towed by a ski boat.

Toe Hold   Holding the two line with a toe.

Tow Line   Line used to pull water skiers. Usually made of polyethylene or nylon.

Trick Riding   Any fancy maneuver that can be accomplished while water skiing.

Wake   Turbulance caused by the boat propellor.

Water Skis   Invented and patented October, 1925 in the U.S. by Fred Waller, motion picture inventor (who later invented "Cinerama").

Weightlifting

Barbell   A steel bar approximately 5–6 feet long, with wheel-shaped or disc-shaped weights attached to each end for weightlifting.

Cheating   To lift weights by using muscle groups not appropriate to that event, or to use a body position not appropriate to that event.

Class   Group of contestants as determined by weight. In U.S. powerlifting, the classes are:

Bantam Weight	123 pounds
Featherweight	132 pounds
Lightweight	148 pounds
Middleweight	165 pounds
Light Heavyweight	181 pounds
Middle Heavyweight	198 pounds
Heavyweight	220 pounds
Light Super Heavyweight	242 pounds
Super Heavyweight	Unlimited

These divisions are the same for International Powerlifting, except that there is no Light Super Heavyweight division. These are also the same for Olympic weightlifting, except that there is no Light Super Heavyweight division. *Clean*: First action in a Clean & Jerk competition. To lift the barbell to shoulder height before it is jerked overhead.

Disqualification   To void a lift or other action because of a rules violation.

Dumbbell   Short barbell, 10–20 inches long, used for hand and arm lifts.

Repetition   To repeat a lift or action.

Reverse Grip   A grip in which the knuckles of one hand are under the bar and the knuckles of the other hand are over the bar.

Set   A predetermined number of repetitions.

Steroids   Drugs used by some weightlifters, football players, and other athletes to build muscle bulk. The use of steroids is certainly controversial and potentially harmful.

Supine position   Lifting position lying down.

Sports Gambling Terms

Action   The money wagered on a sporting event.

Bookie   A person who accepts wagers on sporting events.

Buck $100 bet. Also known as a Dollar.

Dime $1,000 bet.

Exotics   A bet other than a straight bet or parlay.

Hedge   To bet opposite original wager to reduce the action on a game.

Juice   A bookmaker's commission.

Laying off   When a bookie gets too much "action" or wagering, he will pass some of the action off to another bookie to reduce the financial risk.

Nickel $500 bet.

Off the board   A game where no bets are being accepted.

Over/under   A figure representing the total points scored in a contest. The bettor can bet on the actual total being greater or less than the predicted total.

Parlay   The coupling of two or more bets as one larger bet. For example, a bettor would pick the winners of three games on a wager. He wins if all three teams win (often against the spread).

Pick (or Pick'em)   A game where neither team is favored.

Player   Someone who places bets, legally or with a bookie.

Press   To bet a larger amount than usual, often when trying to make up for previous losses.

Points spread   The predicted difference in score between the favored team and opponent. Also called the Line or Spread.

Sports book   Wagering specifically on the outcome of sports games. Can be professional leagues or college teams. Sports books are illegal in most areas, but is the main source of betting for bookies.

Squares   Illegal but rarely enforced by the police, football squares allow participants to pick a square off a grid of 100 squares, each corresponding to a possible quarter, half or final score from a football game.

Tout service   A business that sells opinions on sporting events.

REFERENCES

Associated Press Sports Editors (n.d.). APSE ethics guidelines. Retrieved July 2008 from: http://apse.dallasnews.com/main/codeofethics.html.

Beck, D. and Bosshart, L. (2003, December). Sports and the Press, Communication Research Trends, *Centre for the Study of Communication and Culture*, 22: 4.

Berra, Y. (n.d.). Things people said: Yogi Berra quotes. Retrieved July 2008 from: http://rinkworks.com/said/yogiberra.shtml.

Betts, J. R. (1974). *America's Sporting Heritage: 1850–1950*. Reading, Massachusetts: Addison-Wesley Publishing Company.

Boswell, T. (2006). What us worry?, *Washington Post*, Aug. 30, E1.

Cannon, J. (1951). *Nobody Asked Me*. New York: Dial Press.

Carter, A. (2005). San Antonio Express-News deputy sports editor, e-mail correspondence with author, October 18.

Carvalho, J. (1998, August). *World Series Coverage Before and After the Depression*. Paper presented at the annual convention for the Association for Education in Journalism and Mass Communication, Baltimore, Maryland.

Climer, D. (2006). Michigan defeats Vanderbilt, *The Tennessean*, Sept. 3, C1.

College Football Championship, *The New York Tribune*, November 26, 1880.

Cozens, F. W. and Stumpf, F. S. (1953). *Sports in American Life*. Chicago: The University of Chicago Press.

Donaldson, A. and Cook, J. T. (2006). New controversy facing Utah Hall of Fame coach, *Deseret Morning News*, Aug. 19, B1.

Eisenberg, J. (2006). Ravens need lift to avoid an extreme makeover, *Baltimore Sun*, Sept. 9, 1C.

Emery, E. (1972). *The Press and America*. Englewood Cliffs, New Jersey: Prentice-Hall.

Fensch, T. (1995). *The Sports Writing Handbook, second edn.* Hillsdale, New Jersey: Lawrence Erlbaum Associates.

Finley, P. (2001). Missed tackle turned game, *The Columbia Missourian*, Sept. 29, 1B.

Finley, P. (2005). Back on course: Cyclist's first race since amputation is at today's El Tour, *The Arizona Daily Star*, Nov. 19, A1.

Fulton, M. (2005). Delasin is back in the swing of things, *The (Toledo) Blade*, July 9, C6.

Fulton, M. (2006). Ludwick homer pivotal for Mud Hens, *The (Toledo) Blade*, July 2, C1.

Fulton, M. (2006). Phelps connects for Hens in sweet 16th, *The (Toledo) Blade*, June 17, C1.

Fulton, M. (2006). Contestants offer up plenty of souvenirs, *The (Toledo) Blade*, July 11, C7.

Gaddis, C. (2006). Blue Jays defeat Toronto, *Tampa Tribune*, Aug. 16, C1.

Garrison, B. (1985). *Sports Reporting*. Ames, Iowa: Iowa State University Press.

Garrison, B. (2003). *Professional Feature Writing, fourth edn.*, Mahwah, New Jersey: Lawrence Erlbaum Associates.

Gelston, D. (2006). Phillies shut out Mets, *Associated Press*, Aug. 17. Retrieved Aug. 2006 from: http://proxy.mul.missouri.edu:2228/us/lnacademic/ results/ docview/docview.do?docLinkInd=true&risb=21_T4121503956&format=GNB FI&sort=RELEVANCE&startDocNo=1&resultsUrlKey=29_T4121503960&ci sb=22_T4121503959&treeMax=true&treeWidth=0&csi=304478&docNo=1.

Gems, G.R. (1996). *Sports in North America: A Documentary History*. Volume 5, Sports organized 1880–1900, Gulf Breeze, Florida: Academic International Press.

Harper, W. A. (1999). *How You Played the Game: The Life of Grantland Rice*. Columbia, Missouri: University of Missouri Press.

Hasselbeck, M. (1999). The sports cliché list. Retrieved July 2008 from: http://SportsCliche.com/index.html.

Haudricourt, T. (2006). Streak of futility is over: First victory of '06 at PNC, *Milwaukee Journal Sentinel*, Aug. 15, C1.

Hochman, B. (2001). Crouch's 191 rushing yards lead Huskers, *The Columbia Missourian*, Sept. 29, 1B.

Hochman, B. (2006). To ensure your city's future, you have to have a program for your youth. If you want a viable city, you have to get an insurance policy called a recreation department..., *New Orleans Times-Picayune*, June 16, 1.

Hopp, J. (2005). Bumbalough, Stewart receive national honors, *The (Nashville) Tennessean*, July 28, 2C.

Hoynes, P. (2003). Tribe taken to shed: Homers pile up as Texas sweeps, *Cleveland Plain Dealer*, Aug. 4, C1.

Hyde, D. (2008). Marion's elation to join Heat begs question: Why?, *South Florida Sun-Sentinel*, Feb. 11, C1.

Jennings, C. (2006). Life over boxing: The champ's choice, *The Scranton Times-Tribune*, Jan. 13, D1.

Jones, T. (2003). Two former exiles ensure record July for the Rays, *St. Petersburg Times*, July 31, C1.

Kern, M. (2006). Tiger is lurking just behind the leaders, *Philadelphia Daily News*, Aug. 19, 34.

Killion, A. (2006). A's are OK with flying below the national radar, *San Jose Mercury News*, Aug. 17, C1.

Kubatko, R. (2003). O's let Rays off hook in 4–3 loss: Makeshift lineup allows 2-out runs in 8th, 9th as .500 stays out of O's reach, *Baltimore Sun*, Aug. 12, 1C.

La Canfora, J. (2006). For Carter, no small feet: Redskins' defensive end has big shoes to fill – his own, *Washington Post*, Sept. 9, E1.

Lawrence, A. (2006). Got his mojo workin': Roddick's new-and-improved game about confidence. Retrieved July 2008 from: http://sportsillustrated.cnn.com/2006/writers/andrew_lawrence/09/07/roddick/index.html, Sept. 7.

Lippmann, W. (1922). *Public Opinion.* New York: Harcourt, Brace and Company, Inc.

Mott, F. (1962). *American Journalism.* New York: Macmillan

Mount, T. (Producer), and Shelton, R. (Director). (1988). *Bull Durham* [motion picture]. USA: MGM.

Nagel, K. (2004). Betts' time has come to lead Redhawks – life lessons help new QB fill big shoes in Miami, *Dayton Daily News*, Aug. 26, 1C.

New York Morning News, Base Ball Match, October 22, 1845, retrieved from http://books.google.com/books?id=AtRnBVRk9ewC&pg=PA11&lpg=PA11&dq=new+york+morning+news+and+October+22,+1845&source=web&ots=N7kvT0nFNk&sig=_gTIxuzgyWPO0E6XV-YwVHlWjPQ&hl=en&sa=X&oi=book_result&resnum=1&ct=result.

Nugent, W.H. (1929). The sports section. *The American Mercury*, XVI, 334–336.

Posnanski, J. (2006). Huddle up, it's time for a reality check, *Kansas City Star*, Aug. 17, D1.

Rambo, C. D. (1989). Sports coverage plays more vital role, *Presstime*, October, 21.

Reinardy, S. (1995). Slap-happy Noonan, 80, firing away, *The Scranton Times-Tribune*, May 20, D1.

Rice, G. (1924). Notre Dame's cyclone beats Army, 13 to 7, *New York Herald Tribune*, Oct. 18.

Twain, M. (n.d.). Finest quotes: Mark Twain quotes. Retrieved July 2008 from: http://www.finestquotes.com/author_quotes-author-Mark%20Twain-page-6.htm.

Sanchez, J. (2005). Rogers apologizes for altercation: Lefty says he 'failed miserably' in controlling his emotions, July 6. Retrieved September 2008 from: http://mlb.mlb.com/news/article.jsp?ymd=20050706&content_id=1118221&vkey=news_mlb&fext=.jsp&c_id=mlb.

Shaw, D. (1989). Taking sports seriously: It's over the fence, *Los Angeles Times*, June 23, 1.

Spencer, C. (2003). Tomko, Cardinals blank Marlins, *Miami Herald*, Aug. 9, 3D.

Thompson, W. (2005). Federer too much for Agassi, *The Kansas City Star*, Sept. 12, C1.

Unknown author. (1896). Centrals lose at basketball: An interesting match with the New Britain team, *Brooklyn Eagle*, Dec. 27, 8.

Walker, D. (2007). Bucks hope city beckons Yi: Tem wants pick to feel at home, *Milwaukee Journal Sentinel*, June 30, C1.

Williams, J. (2006). Sox strong-armed Bonser, bullpen give Twins reason to celebrate, *St. Paul Pioneer Press*, Aug. 19, D1.

Wolseley, R. E. and Campbell, L. (1949). *Exploring Journalism, second edn.* New York: Prentice-Hall and Co.

INDEX

Lightning Source UK Ltd.
Milton Keynes UK
UKOW05f0629021013

218350UK00009B/462/P